Praise for *See a Little Light*

"Bob Mould. Those two words are synonymous with integrity. From Hüsker Dü in the last century to right at this moment, Bob is the real deal, writing and playing music for music's sake. He's a great songwriter and performer. I have been a fan of Bob's for thirty years now with no end in sight."

—Henry Rollins

"Bob Mould's incredible journey is an inspiring one. I hope to one day be able to write a book like this, to live like this, to rock like this, but in the meantime, I can read this. A poetic and devastating memoir from one of the greatest artists of all time. I love Bob Mould."

—Margaret Cho

"Defiant, courageous, and funny: a disarmingly intimate look into the life-thus-far of someone who is without a doubt one of the most influential voices in all of rock and roll."

—Colin Meloy, The Decemberists

"*See a Little Light* is an honest, from the heart, roller-coaster ride of an autobiography from one of America's great songwriters. Whether with Hüsker Dü, Sugar or as a solo artist, Bob inspired so many to start a band or write a song."

—Matt Pinfield, host of "120 Minutes"

"Any number of veterans of the punk and post-punk campaigns of the 1980s could pack a memoir with endless drives in the van, bad food and bad contracts, shoestring recording sessions, hell-hole nightclubs, sleeping on floors and all the other genre touchstones. A select few could also explore the conflicts, rewards and drawbacks of wider popularity, and the challenges of sustaining a musical life into advanced adulthood. But there's only one who could do all that and also describe dealing with his unresolved homosexuality and, why not, going to work plotting the storylines in professional wrestling. Those last two elements definitely distinguish Bob Mould's autobiography from the predictable pack, and should keep readers from feeling they're on an endless van ride themselves....Thorny, earnest and intense."

—Richard Cromelin, *Los Angeles Times*

"Urgently personal...brisk and enjoyable.... Mould captures something of his terrific will, which is a great gift."

—Matt Morello, NPR

"[A] brutally honest autobiography tour de force..."

—*The Village Voice*

"A blunt, bracing and astonishingly confessional look back at a man who's produced some of the best rock music of the last twenty years."

—Patrick Beach, *Austin American-Statesman*

"As satisfying as [Mould's] best work...compulsively readable."
—Ben Westhoff, *Washington City Paper*

"After all, if you take my word for it, *See a Little Light* is a treat, an absolutely first-tier rock autobiography."
—LAWeekly.com

"*See a Little Light* tells of Mould's struggles with homosexuality, personal relationships and various addictions, but this is not just another titillating rock 'n' roll memoir.... It's a clear, plain account of one troubled musician's life, with a lively and happy ending."
—*Chicago Sun-Times*

"Offers an emotional depth and level of insight absent from most musical biographies."
—Biblioklept

SEE A
LITTLE
LIGHT

SEE A LITTLE LIGHT

THE TRAIL OF RAGE AND MELODY

BOB MOULD

WITH MICHAEL AZERRAD

CLEiS
PRESS

Published in the United States by Cleis Press, Inc., 2246 Sixth Street, Berkeley, California 94710.

Printed in the United States.
Cover design: Scott Idleman/Blink
Cover photograph: Josh Sanseri

First Paperback Edition.
10 9 8 7 6 5 4 3 2 1

Originally published as a Little, Brown and Company hardcover.

Trade paper ISBN: 978-1-57344-970-0

Listen, there's music in the air
I heard your voice coming from somewhere
But look how much we've grown
Well, I guess I should have known

As the years go by, they take their toll on you
Think of all the things we wanted to do

And all the words we said yesterday
That's a long time ago
You didn't think I'd really go now

Are you waiting? I know why
You're already saying goodbye
Are you ready? I know why

I see a little light, I know you will
I can see it in your eyes, I know you still care
But if you want me to go, you should just say so

— Bob Mould, 1988

Preface

"You see this button? If I push this button, you'll be blacklisted from every clothing-optional resort in Palm Springs!"

*　　*　　*

I'm not one for vacations. The idea of setting up camp in an idyllic but remote parcel of land—think western Costa Rica or a bay-view motel in central Florida—doesn't do it for me. I'm a people watcher. Most days I sit alone or with a companion, the parade of humanity tumbling and unraveling in front of me. I love pedestrian cities with mass transit, town squares for shopping and dining, and coffee shops with free Wi-Fi. I love the measured and gently oscillating pace of socially progressive, medium-scale world cities—Amsterdam, San Francisco, Berlin.

Give me a leisurely late morning walk to the Bloemenmarkt for an apple pancake washed down with a double espresso, tempered by a few hits of weed, and I'm on vacation. Give me a seat in the Castro plaza watching the late afternoon fog roll eastward from the Pacific Ocean, over Twin Peaks and into Eureka Valley, and I'm on vacation. Give me a crisp evening stroll down Motzstraße for a takeaway schnitzel, a scoop of ice cream, and an hour of fun at a neighborhood bar, and I'm on vacation.

Since 2005, the Coachella music festival has become one of my annual vacations. Sure, it's a busman's holiday, but over the course of thirty years in the music business, I've earned not only my keep, but the perennial all-access wristband and Lot A artist parking that make everything a whole lot easier. The three-day festival takes place in mid-April at the polo grounds in Indio, a town twenty-five miles southeast of Palm Springs, California. In 2009 I was finally playing at Coachella—Saturday, 2:30 PM, Gobi stage. It's not the main stage, or even the second stage, but the time slot was good—early enough to make a strong impression before people began suffering from sun and/or alcohol poisoning.

Friday morning, Micheal and I flew from Dulles to LAX, rented a car, and drove east on I-10 to Highway 111, which cuts south to the desert valley. Once in Palm Springs, we stopped at Koffi, a midcentury-style coffee shop, then at a drugstore for sunscreen, snacks, and a case of bottled water, before finally arriving at our accommodations—a clothing-optional resort strictly for men. I'd stayed here many times over the years, the most memorable being in 2007 when the local police were called to apprehend a whacked-out guest who'd destroyed one of the suites. After an evening of hearing this guy yelling and throwing furniture, I woke on Saturday morning to the sight of two Palm Springs Police officers in the courtyard interrogating the guest, who stood naked except for a pair of mirrored aviator sunglasses and a poolside chaise recliner cushion he'd fashioned around his torso like a sarong. The police seemed equally perplexed by the fourteen-inch-high by twelve-inch-round black rubber dildo sitting in the middle of his decimated room like a forlorn fire hydrant.

But I digress. After checking into the resort, we grabbed some fast food and drove to the festival site. Friday's highlights included Morrissey (cutting his set short due to the smell of grilled sausage wafting from the food tent to the main stage), Leonard Cohen, and the master of the big stage, Paul McCartney. We left before the end of Macca's set, avoiding the crush of outbound traffic.

From years of loud noise at work, I have tinnitus. In order to sleep, I need a low-level masking sound—typically the television. Our suite had two televisions, each with a unique remote that required a four-digit security code in order to work. The bedroom remote wasn't functioning, so we went to the front desk for assistance. None of the codes they gave us worked, so the TV couldn't be adjusted by remote. We asked a second time, and nothing they told us helped. It was becoming a hassle.

The next morning we woke up at eight—too early for the free continental buffet staged in the porn library room overlooking the main pool area. We headed to Koffi for a quick jolt, then to Sherman's Delicatessen for breakfast. Around ten we returned to the resort, where people were beginning to stir—the usual assortment of nude sunbathers, early-bird day-pass sex cruisers from LA, and older gentlemen with their (much) younger weekend escorts. I wanted to catch a nap before heading to the festival, but I still couldn't adjust the volume of the TV from the bed. Micheal went to ask for help at the front desk one more time, at which point I quickly dozed off.

Minutes later I was woken by the sound of Micheal slamming the door to the room and then locking it with both deadbolt and chain. Visibly shaken, he said, "That man out there is crazy. He's threatening me!" I opened the door to find a wild-eyed troll yelling, "I'm the manager, and your friend called me an asshole. You're both out of here in ten minutes or I'm calling the police to have you escorted off my property." My instinct was to grab him in a front face lock until he was unconscious, but the fact that I had to be onstage in four hours saved his scrawny ass. Rather than argue or reason, we began packing up our stuff. The walk of shame took us from our poolside room, case of water and luggage in tow, past the smirking sunbathers and bagel-nuzzling septuagenarians, and to the front desk. The young employee who handled the cancellation of the remaining two nights' room charges had a puzzled and somewhat sad look on his face, as if to say: Yes, he's out of his mind. But he's my boss and I need this depressing job, so I can't help you either.

Once the charges had been removed, I looked at the manager and said, "You know, you're out of your fucking mind. You see this wristband? This wristband says I'm standing in front of tens of thousands of people today, and you're stuck here with your drugs and delusions and dog shit by the pool." The manager rushed to a hockey puck–size object on the desk, raised his hand, and replied, "You see this button? If I push this button, you'll be blacklisted from every clothing-optional resort in Palm Springs!" I chortled and spat, "Save it for someone who cares," then sauntered away with my partner, my dignity, and our case of bottled water.

We checked into a nearby "clothing required" hotel before heading to the festival. Within a few hours of being thrown out of the clothing-optional resort, I was, in fact, onstage in front of tens of thousands of music fans, blazing through a thirteen-song, forty-five-minute set that encompassed stories from my thirty years of adult life. Not only was I was having a great time entertaining the crowd, but I was also having a hearty internal howl over what had just happened—and the thought of how people would have reacted had I told this particular story onstage.

It was a moment, one of several in the last few years, that showed me how integrated my personal and professional lives had finally become. Clearly, that sunny afternoon on the Coachella stage wasn't the right time or place to tell that anecdote. But the journey that led me to that place—and to self-acceptance, wholeness, and freedom—was ripe for the telling. New Day Rising indeed.

* * *

As a child, music was my escape. It was my fantasy world. Once I understood the value and meaning of music, I began composing. When I'm creating a new piece of music, I float unconsciously for hours, days, weeks at a time. The words and melodies flow through my brain, body, and soul. Imagine standing under the most beautiful waterfall, or in a wonderfully appointed shower, the perfect-temperature water pouring down over you. The infinite loops of history and harmony blend seamlessly into each other and wash my pain away.

But unlike the escapism of composing music, writing this book was an emotionally taxing process. Even though my life and work have been on public display for many years, I have always been a very private person. My desire for privacy has often bordered on secrecy. The thought of revealing certain aspects of my personal life was hard to reconcile. As time progressed, I found myself losing track of certain memories. It felt like it was time to assemble the key pieces into a narrative. Instead of telling individual anecdotes (the typical memoir), I'm telling my story in order—and by doing so, I can see the patterns. In a way, I'm finally making sense of my life.

When I signed on for this project, I had no idea what I'd gotten myself into. Once the rush from the flattery and vanity of the book deal subsided, I was left with three years of gathering, recounting, examining, reexamining, questioning, and, ultimately, letting go of the past. It wasn't a jovial journey through my musical history. It's not a book filled with self-congratulation, glowing reviews, or tales of high and mighty triumph. It's my life story, as best I can remember.

Trying to pull memories from the infinite void has not been an easy feat. In looking back at the first fifty years of my life, I was sometimes appalled by my faults. Be it my uncanny ability to cut off friendships and relationships without explanation, my inability to properly process criticism, or my love/hate relationship with blind rage—in writing this book, my flaws became all too clear.

I've lost chunks of my life floating in limbo, riddled with anxieties and guilt. On my good days, I am a well-meaning person. I am generous, supportive, and a good listener. On my bad days, I exhibit the symptoms of someone afflicted with compensatory narcissistic personality disorder. To use a musical metaphor, I don't understand how I can have perfect pitch but sometimes be so out of tune with my emotions and the world around me.

I tried not to upset or bring shame upon anyone else in writing this book, but there's no way of telling my story—or of anyone telling their story, for that matter—without running that risk. I would like to apologize in advance to anyone who feels hurt by any part of what I'm about to tell. It is not my intent to make anyone look or feel bad.

There's no way I can take back the things I've done, the life I've led. All I can do is take ownership of my failings, ask forgiveness from those I may have hurt through the years, and hope for understanding.

SEE A LITTLE LIGHT

THE TRAIL OF RAGE AND MELODY

CHAPTER 1

When I was born on October 16, 1960, Malone, New York, was a town of roughly four thousand at the very northernmost end of the state, in a thin strip of land between the vast Adirondacks and the Canadian border. That's one thing in my life that hasn't much changed. A working-class town with some light industry and a lot of potato and dairy farms surrounding it, Malone is the seat of what used to be the second-most impoverished county in the state. Main Street's eight blocks are lined with two- and three-story buildings. Winters in Malone are long, cold, and snowy—sometimes the snow would be so deep that my father would have to tunnel from the doorway, through the yard, and all the way to the street.

The rural setting was idyllic—clean air, swimming holes, and a wide-open sky that revealed tons of stars and even the northern lights. But you could say I was raised in a dysfunctional home.

My father, Willis F. Mould III—everyone called him Bill— was once regarded as the best TV repairman in town. He eventually took a job at the post office, but after he left that job he found it difficult to find work again. So it fell to my mother, Sheila Murphy, to be the breadwinner, and for years she worked as an evening switchboard operator for Bell Telephone. My mother was a religious woman, a Catholic, and she'd spent part of her childhood in a convent. She never learned to drive and had little freedom.

My sister, Susan, was seven when I was born, and my brother, Brian, came two years after her. But we weren't the only children my parents had had—their first son, Stephen, died of nephroblastoma, a tumor of the kidney, right after I was born. He was only nine years old, so my parents were under a big black cloud of grief when I came around. Then, a year or so after I was born, my mother miscarried.

Somewhere along the line my father picked up some pretty monstrous behavior. He probably got it from *his* father. That's the way these things tend to work, so I don't blame him, but I do hold him responsible. Over the course of my childhood, weekends settled into a predictable rhythm. Friday afternoons, something would trigger my father's alter ego, and after rising from a midafternoon nap, he would leave for downtown to "run errands." One of the chief errands was an hour or more of steady drinking at Seven's Bar and Grill, a main gathering place for men in Malone.

Before leaving for the bar, my father would press "record" on a portable cassette recorder and hide it behind his living room chair. He didn't realize that everyone in the family knew he did this. How many tapes of whirring vacuum cleaners or shushed silence did he listen to? And, more importantly, when did he find the time or the privacy to listen to them? To put it mildly, my father was not a trusting man. He hammered it into us that everybody is lying to you all the time, everybody is trying to steal from you all the time. It left an impression I'm still trying to shake to this day.

My father would come home around seven in the evening, and that's when the game would begin. Inevitably, something, just about anything, would set him off: it could be a pot boiling over, a chore left undone, something of little significance that happened days before. The whole family would walk on eggshells before the coming shit-storm. I'd wait in dread for the first venomous line, the first accusation, the first degrading comment. Where would it start tonight?

My mother was the usual recipient and Brian took the lion's share of the rest. Sometimes it was only verbal. When it got violent, my mother and brother typically took the brunt of that too. It was frequently just hitting with his hands. And then there were the rare weekends when the violence went beyond mere punching and slapping, and he invoked the threat of, or involved the use of, murderous weapons. My mom would get pretty banged up, sometimes a black eye, and she'd have to put on makeup to cover it. Things would typically wind down late Sunday night, just in time for us kids to get ready for another week of school.

Instead of physical abuse, my father would play psychological games with Susan. He berated her, mostly for her weight, and after reducing her to rubble, he'd build her back up by offering to make her a meal and then bully her into eating more than she wanted. It became a vicious cycle as my sister ballooned. Today, even after gastric bypass surgery, Susan battles with near-morbid obesity.

Somehow I managed to escape the abuse. But why? Because I was the golden child, the one who survived while Stephen died? Was I the constant reminder? I was the only one who could break up the violence. Even when I was as young as four or five, my brother and sister would beg me to go in and get my parents to stop fighting. So I'd go and cry and beg everyone to get along, and things would simmer down for a while.

My parents struggled not only with each other but also for my affection. My father tried hard to sway me, calling my mother all kinds of names. She always remained stoic, martyr-like, taking the blow. But these personalities, this routine, started before I was born and continued through my college years.

We didn't have a lot of money, but that didn't quite explain why Brian and Susan would often get stale week-old pastries instead of birthday cakes. Sometimes they'd get nothing for

Christmas even though my father would give me a jar with silver dollars in it. I'd offer to give some to my brother and sister, but they had to refuse—if my father found out, he'd go nuts. Then he would come back to me and ask for the silver dollars. One winter, when I was nine, Christmas wasn't going to happen at all, so I dragged a tree from my school back home. At the beginning of my journey, the tree was full of paper ornaments made by my classmates and me. By the time I'd gotten the tree the half mile to home, the needles had all worn off of one side and most of the ornaments were gone.

Nonetheless, I was a bright kid. When I was three, my mother would take me to the grocery store and stand me on the counter. As the cashier called out the price of each item she rang up, I would add them in my head without paper, and every time I'd get it right. People would gather around the cash register when this happened; it was an event. There she is, she's bringing the golden kid with the curly hair who can add things up. I am drawing a crowd, I am always right, and it is causing a scene.

I was an early reader as well. One day I surprised my family by reading the headline of the paper out loud—and it was hard to forget: "President Kennedy Assassinated." So when I was four, my mother took me to the convent for an IQ test. Supposedly, I had the intellect of a seven-year-old, with an IQ of 175. In those years, I went to school only three or four days a week and still got near-perfect grades. I don't know why the school made this special dispensation, but I guess they figured, What can we do?

Perhaps this was the beginning of my creative, independent spirit, my self-possession—or maybe I was just bratty—but on my days off, I just sat around at home and listened to music. My earliest recollection of anything musical is the cover of the soundtrack album for *Around the World in 80 Days:* a hot-air balloon soaring off to some faraway place.

I really started to get into music when I was six. It's funny:

although my father had been a saxophonist in the army during World War II, stationed at Lackland Air Force Base in San Antonio, I don't ever remember him playing a musical instrument, and yet he was the person who brought music into my life. A local company stocked the jukeboxes of the two truck-stop restaurants in Malone, one on each end of Main Street, and when songs ran their course, they'd pull the singles out and replace them with new ones. My father somehow realized music was important to me and would buy the old singles from the vendor for a penny each. "Happy Jack" by the Who, "Strawberry Fields Forever" by the Beatles, "Good Vibrations" by the Beach Boys, "There's a Kind of Hush" by Herman's Hermits. In 1967, those were my toys. They were also my refuge, a way of blocking everything else out. And I studied those singles more closely than anything I was taught in school.

I had a little record player, and I'd put a stack of singles on its spindle. The turntable would start up, the arm would lift, the two rabbit ears on the spindle would retract and drop the first record, and then the tone arm would pull over and drop into the groove. Once the needle wound down all the way to the catch groove, the tone arm lifted, pulled back, and another single would fall—then the arm would swing back over to play the next song. I would sit for hours with stacks of records, putting them in different sequences, fascinated by the endless combinations.

I'd study everything, right down to the design of each label and how they looked when they were spinning: Capitol with the yellow and orange yin-yang design; MGM had the rainbow letters and roaring lion; Motown had the map of Detroit; Roulette had the gambling wheel pattern, the o in *Roulette* as the ball. I'd read the precious few notes on each label: the songwriters, the publishing companies, and the length of each song. The writers were usually faceless names like Goffin-King, Boyce-Hart, and Jimmy Webb. I had no idea what these people looked like or how they created these miniature masterpieces, but

I knew some of the performers from seeing them on television or in the newspapers. Their clothes, hairstyles, and all the other visuals added to the sum total of their musical work and the impressions they left on me.

On special occasions, I would go to Newberry's department store with my mother or grandmother and buy a long-playing album by either the Beatles or the Monkees—I didn't know or care that the Monkees had started as a prefab version of the Beatles. In my young mind, the two bands were equally cool.

I knew I could make music too. Around this time, I would occasionally accompany my grandmother to her work caring for a woman who had been struck by lightning. The woman was essentially paralyzed in situ, fingers gnarled like animal claws and a facial expression that was apparently frozen at the moment she was hit. I wasn't afraid of her though. There was a piano in her house, and when I heard a song on the AM radio, I'd walk over to it and within seconds would be able to figure out the melody and even the rudimentary chord structure.

I started writing full songs when I was nine. My parents bought me a small plastic Emenee organ with two octaves of keys and six sets of chord buttons. I'd type out the lyric sheets in stanza form on a mechanical typewriter and carbon paper, notated with "© 1970 ABC-Easytime Music"—my first "publishing company." There were songs like "Let Me Live Today," which was about my dog, Tipper, and there were songs about flowers, songs about being a kid. I taught myself how to record these simple tunes, including overdubbing, using two small reel-to-reel tape machines. I got two of my friends to help me play my compositions, with me on my chord organ. One of them had a toy drum kit and the other had a toy guitar—they just sort of held the instruments and pretended to play along.

My teachers knew I had an aptitude for music since I sang in the school choir, and in fifth grade, they wanted me to play the tuba. I was a larger than normal kid, big boned and growing fast. Even so, I looked at the size of the case and said to myself,

There's no way I am dragging that thing back and forth in the snow. Besides, I thought the kids in band were a little nerdy. They would do the one rock song and let the drummer have the one solo, really letting their hair down.

*   *   *

In 1970 my mother developed rheumatoid arthritis. Her joints swelled to dangerous proportions, and when she had to give up her job at Bell Telephone and go on disability, my parents bought a mom-and-pop grocery store at 23 Elbow Street for roughly $10,000. It was attached to a big two-story house on a large parcel of land not far from the center of town—not a desirable neighborhood, but it was right near the Glazier meat-packing plant, the Tru-Stitch moccasin factory, and the Royal Crown Cola bottling and distribution plant, which provided many of the store's regular clientele.

The grocery store was off the kitchen. In the back of the house, a small door led to a large storage structure that was on a separate heating system so the inventory (mainly beer and soda) wouldn't freeze in winter. In the front yard, there was a large illuminated sign adorned with the Royal Crown Cola logo and the name of the store: B&S Grocery, named after my parents. My father stacked cases of beer throughout the garage, which also had two large green garbage bins for returnable cans and bottles. By watching the recycling, I could tell if my father was accelerating his drinking, which would be an indicator of the level of madness that would build over the course of the week.

But I spent most of my time in the driveway, playing street hockey in winter and basketball in summer. Later, my father got a large plot of land cleared behind the house so we kids would have a larger play area. But the yard was riddled with craters, so we'd often turn an ankle or stumble face-first into the dirt. I suppose that's as good a metaphor as any for the way we lived in that house. Because of the unpredictable psychological control my father wielded over the rest of the family, we were never certain if we stood on firm, level ground.

Separate out my father's behavior, and my childhood was like the old sitcom *The Many Loves of Dobie Gillis,* which was also set in a small-town mom-and-pop store. There was a little mechanical flipper on top of the entrance to the store that was wired to a buzzer that went off in our kitchen. Whenever the door opened, the buzzer sounded and my father would immediately let out an exasperated "God damn" or "Jesus H. Christ"; he'd say it like a hissing teapot. Then he'd rise from his battered recliner, its armrests held together with packing tape, leave the living room, and go out through the kitchen, around the stove, past the telephone on the wall, through the narrow passageway to the store, and one step down to serve the customers—the very customers he would curse because they dared to come and give us the business that kept a roof over our heads.

My father could be brutally mocking once the customers were beyond earshot, muttering things like "You no-good son of a bitch, don't bring those fucking food stamps in here." As he grew older, my father's habit of ridiculing others became a comical flaw; he'd use the same phrases over and over, and the refrains became so familiar that I could sing along to them in my head, to the point that they became kind of hilarious. But still I felt ashamed because of his behavior. I rarely brought friends to my house—I just didn't want them to see my father on a rampage. The Thompson kids were the only neighbors with whom we were close, and they knew the whole deal. My father had alienated most everyone else on the block. Anyone who thought my father viewed them favorably was just plain mistaken.

We all worked the store when we lived there. I was ringing people up at ten years old. There was an old-fashioned cash register and an adding machine, but I simply added the items in my head, the same way I added those items at the grocery store years before. I was a numbers kid. I could look at a sheet of numbers and make something out of it.

When we weren't working at the store or getting chewed out at home, you might have found us at church. I was raised vaguely Catholic. My father's side of the family was English Protestant, but not practicing; I don't think my grandfather, who worked his entire life at the local bank in Malone, was religious at all. My mother, on the other hand, wanted me to have religion, but I always went to public school because that's what my dad wanted. Flanders Elementary School was a large three-story stone building with big, heavy doors and marble floors—utilitarian, built to last. On Wednesdays we would do an exchange program with the Catholic school Notre Dame, farther down Main Street. The Catholic school was much nicer, as if it had money, the building was newer, the desks weren't as beat up, everything smelled fresh and clean, and the students were quiet and deferential. I eventually went through confirmation to fulfill my mother's wishes, and I still remember the Catholic teachings—all the moralistic stories, the guilt-inducing melodrama and self-flagellation.

Still, even with my religious grounding, by junior high I was starting to drift to the bad side of things. I suppose it was inevitable. After all, I watched my dad drink constantly. And I worked in a grocery store, so there was no problem walking off with a six-pack. I could drink as much as I wanted anytime. My brother had finished high school and left home, so I had the upstairs to myself, and most days after school I'd go up there and have a few beers. I'd easily camouflage the empties by drinking whichever brand my father was having at the time: Ballantine, Schaefer, Utica Club. On weekends I'd get together with friends, go into the woods with a twelve-pack of cans—I was a big kid by now and could drink a lot—and chug them down as quickly as possible. Bottles tasted better than cans, but they were more difficult to smuggle out because they rattled and pinged.

Once we'd gotten tipsy, my friends and I would go to the seedy downtown pool hall, where kids with homemade prison-style tattoos sold pot, or to the pizza parlor to play foosball.

Sometimes we'd go to other friends' houses, usually the nicer homes in the hills that had finished basements with wood paneling, and sit around and listen to Foghat. I think their parents knew we were drinking but decided it was better to keep us inside under light supervision, as opposed to letting us race around in cars on unlit country roads.

I don't think my drinking was a direct manifestation of misery. Despite the turbulent home life, I wasn't a particularly unhappy kid. I wasn't the sullen kid in black. I was fairly well-adjusted, somewhat popular, a middle-of-the-pack type of kid. Part of the reason for my drinking was the fact that Malone was terribly dull and seemed more tolerable when I was inebriated. Part of it was peer pressure; my friends were doing it, and in order to be with them, I drank as well. And part of it was emulating my father, with the major difference being that my drinking almost never made me violent.

I started drinking beer at thirteen, and I went for many years without stopping. I can't remember a day when I didn't drink during that time. After putting away at least a couple of beers and smoking a little bit of pot every day, I'd turn it up a fair amount on the weekends. My parents expected me home on time each night, and I was able to follow that rule, even though I was coming home trashed, trying to get upstairs as quickly as I could so they wouldn't smell the booze or pot on me. The fact was, I was staying out of trouble with the law, I was making good grades, I wasn't wrecking the car, and I wasn't stealing. So, as they say, I was functional, and that gave me the latitude to do what I wanted.

* * *

By the beginning of high school, I knew I needed to get out of Malone as soon as possible. There are some college towns relatively close to Malone, like Potsdam, Plattsburgh, and Burlington, but otherwise it's a very isolated place. And I really wanted to get away from my family.

And there was the other big reason I had to get out of Malone: I knew I was different. The actual word for it—homosexuality— I didn't know, but there was never any question as to my sexual orientation. I knew by the age of five. I'd experimented with other boys my age—nothing serious, and probably nothing out of the ordinary. But at the edge of puberty, eleven or twelve, I started doing things of a certain...weight. There are boys who grow out of it, and there are those of us who know, the second we start doing it, that that's what we're going to do. It's our sexual preference. I never questioned it.

All my other friends were starting to get girlfriends and I wasn't. I tried to have physical relationships with girls, once at an end-of-year high school dance and another time during a group camping trip. Nothing happened. Nothing clicked. I just wasn't interested in girls. So I accepted the fact that I would be attracted to the male form for the rest of my life and began to make the adjustments and provisions to my behavior that would both facilitate those desires and disguise my orientation.

There are archetypes that emerged with my initial feelings: Batman, athletes, even my childhood barber. I can look back and say, "Yeah, the barber was sexy, his crotch used to touch my forearm while he was cutting my hair," and I still remember the smell of the shop. That's something a twelve-year-old boy doesn't forget. I know where a lot of my preferences got stuck in. To this day, moments like this still dictate a fair amount of my desires as a sexual being. I think most gay men, like just about everyone else, remember those markers, and those early experiences inform our fetishes and desires, how we lead our lives, sometimes even our professions.

I certainly don't hold the barber responsible for my homosexuality; I'd been engaging in and acting on my sexual feelings for some time. But that kind of experience did, however, heighten and validate those feelings. I've learned the ritual of trying to complete yourself, the events that get you there—events from your childhood that you keep re-creating over and over. We all reenact and try to find completion. Whether it was intentional or accidental, what I thought was happening was occurring with an adult, a figure I was entrusted to. And as a teen, every time I went to get my hair cut, those feelings came back. Every time.

Maybe my blossoming sexuality was why I dropped away from music for a few years. From 1972 to 1975, I was more into wrestling and hockey and playing basketball in the Catholic Youth Organization league. I didn't play high school ball, but instead used my gift for numbers to work as the team statistician. I'd travel with the team to all the games, run drills, and play scrimmage games. This was an interesting time for me, being in the constant company of other boys who were also going through puberty and all the emotional confusion that comes with that physical rite of passage.

If the smell of the barbershop had been my primary olfactory association with male sexuality, it was quickly replaced by the smell of locker rooms filled with young men. Most boys were in the gym once or twice a week, but being part of the team, even if not an active player, I was always around the gym. The team would run drills in the mornings, do "shootarounds" during lunch, and play full scrimmages after class.

With all this physical activity came the need for showers throughout the day. I mentioned the adjustments and provisions, and here I had to come up with an elaborate set. There's a lot of confusion in a boys' high school locker room, and for a homosexual kid such as myself, the stakes were raised. Walking into a group shower with ten or more boys, I was bound to find one of them attractive. At thirteen, it's awfully difficult to suppress the natural reactions. All boys that age have problems keeping their hard-ons to themselves, and the environment opens one up to all kinds of mixed signals. How to handle it? There's no place to hide in a group shower. You can turn your back to the center of the group, face the wall, and think about dead kittens, but chances are, the hard-on is not going to go away by itself.

The smell of the locker room: a heady mix of chlorine from the swimming pool, cleaning agents, and dozens of boys ripening into men—it's an odor you never forget. The visual stimulation is a lot to contend with as well. We're all passing through puberty, all wondering why we're going through these changes, and it's human nature to observe those changes in others. I was an early bloomer and grew a decent amount of hair across my chest. Younger boys would look. And some boys are better endowed than others, and they become the focus of attention in certain settings.

Having already experienced the touch of other boys, I found it all a lot to handle. I was a cool hand, for the most part, but sometimes I would be drawn to certain boys, and then the complications would begin. I was compelled to befriend them, in whatever ways I could devise. They like tennis? I like tennis. They like turkey? I like turkey. I imagine it is the same for boys who are attracted to girls; kids will shape-shift in an attempt to get closer to the objects of their affection. For a gay kid, the dialogue of courtship was tightly yet invisibly twined around the normal camaraderie that young boys need.

It was a confusing time. I often had trouble parsing my feelings for other males. Am I drawn to this boy because we have a shared interest in hockey or because I'm drawn to his smell, his physical being, and his features? This distinction can still be stormy for me; as with all dynamic forces of nature, that cloudiness usually rolls in when I least expect it.

I concocted ways to be close without being overt, disguised my desires for fear of being ostracized or rejected, and built the ability to store vast amounts of personal data and unnecessary knowledge in my young head. Those types of maneuvers began to create mental loops, which manifested into a type of obsessive-compulsive disorder—not the hand-washing kind, but one based around routine, ritual, and numbers. To this day, I still count my steps in sets of ten. Once I establish a pattern, even for the simplest tasks, I have to constantly repeat the pattern in the exact order I did it the first time or else I tend to come unraveled. It's as if I count my steps so I can retrace them and become accountable for a sliver of time in history.

*　*　*

Even while I was immersing myself in the wide world of sports, I was listening to music, but not with passion. Maybe that's because I was listening to mainstream stuff: Elton John, the Bay City Rollers, and especially Kiss. I was a card-carrying member of the Kiss Army. One winter, a bunch of my friends and I dressed up in homemade Kiss costumes, with full makeup and seven-inch platform boots made from work boots and chunks of plywood. On a large flatbed trailer, we built our winter carnival float, which resembled the stage from the *Destroyer* tour. We lip-synced to the blaring music in a fog of dry ice, dragged down Main Street by a pickup truck. I was Gene Simmons. I didn't have a bass, so I used my first guitar, which was a burgundy Gibson SG copy that my father bought me for eighty dollars from the Sears catalog. My friend Steve Bessette, occasionally his brother Chris, and my friend Tom Browning, one of the star athletes in town—we were "the band." (Tom went on to become a top pitcher for the Cincinnati Reds.) We were into it, but basically, we were just killing time.

I got that SG copy guitar as much for lip-syncing on the Kiss float as I did for actually playing it. But I picked it up pretty quickly, just like I had with the piano. I mostly learned by ear— I checked out the famous Mel Bay chord book for a little bit, but soon discovered how to move my fingers around and make chords on my own. It happened fast. I taught myself some Kiss and Ted Nugent songs, but I hadn't figured out how to play leads yet so I stuck with rhythm guitar. Steve Bessette and I eventually wrote songs, mostly rudimentary copies of heavy-metal anthems, nothing of any great note. By now I had graduated to recording and overdubbing those song ideas with two eight-track tape machines.

Female-fronted mainstream '70s rock albums like Fleet-wood Mac's *Rumours* and Heart's *Dreamboat Annie* were big with my friends around this time, but they didn't speak to me. Being into a band was like being in a gang, and I didn't know if I wanted to be in a gang with women. Stuff like that was the soundtrack to my high school social life, but only by default. Nothing had the same impact as my treasured '60s singles collection. Kiss and all that stuff was just spectacle, not an epiphany.

My musical transformation came from *Rock Scene* magazine. It was out of New York City, published by now legendary downtown New York rock scene insiders Richard and Lisa Robinson, Danny Fields, and photographer Bob Gruen. Looking back on it, I think they conspired to make that scene look bigger and better than it really was. Originally, I bought that magazine to follow the star bands they featured on the cover each month: big-time hard rockers like Aerosmith, Kiss, and Ted Nugent. But *Rock Scene* would also do photo features on arty underground bands like Television, Patti Smith, the Ramones, New York Dolls, and Suicide, and they started catching my eye.

Each issue of *Rock Scene* would also focus on local scenes such as Cleveland, which had bands like Rocket from the Tombs and outrageous characters like Crocus Behemoth, Peter Laughner, and Stiv Bators. One issue of *Rock Scene* featured photographs of a handful of acts from Minneapolis–St. Paul, another frigid place 1,200 miles from Malone, and a world removed from my perception of bohemian New York City. I recall a picture of a band called the Suicide Commandos. There was nothing particularly remarkable about the photo, but the band's name stuck with me.

The Ramones, however, really snared my attention—they looked street-smart but innocent. Finally, a gang I'd want to join. Something about them resonated. Was it that they all looked like they had something to prove? They weren't flamboyant and theatrical like Kiss. With their leather jackets and ripped blue jeans, the Ramones were the complete opposite. I had no idea what they sounded like, but they piqued my curiosity and I got their first album for my sixteenth birthday. My father and I did the hour-plus drive out to Record Town in Plattsburgh just to buy it. On the ride back, I studied that twelve-inch-square album jacket with intensity, as if searching for DNA at a crime scene. As soon as we got home, I raced out of the car, past my mother, and upstairs to my bedroom, where I laid the needle down on the record. That was what did it. That was when the light went on.

CHAPTER 2

The cover of the Ramones' first album showed these four thugs in leather motorcycle jackets and jeans standing against a brick wall, looking like nothing I had ever seen before in music. And while everyone else's album covers were colorful and flamboyant—Boston had its spaceships, Aerosmith had its wings, Kiss had its lightning bolts—the cover of the Ramones' album was in black and white, simple and stark.

And the second I put the needle on the record, the sound came so quick and distorted; it was really electric, this fast, frantic energy. It gave me a rush. Everything before was now slow and plodding. Metal bands might have had a quick song here and there, but this was an album where every single song was so intensely fast—the speed and the simplicity were just a complete shock. It was clearly melodic music, and yet Joey's nasal, almost deadpan delivery was so unlike the typical rock singer's. The subject matter was almost completely foreign—I was sixteen and I didn't know about sniffing glue or hustlers on the corner of Fifty-Third and Third. It was a completely new language. The first side opened up new worlds as it went by in a fourteen-minute blur.

My brother and sister had moved out by then and I had the whole upstairs of the house to myself, spending most of my time in the partially divided double attic room. I put a speaker in each room, so when "Blitzkrieg Bop" kicked at the beginning of side one, I was stunned: the bass was on one side of the mix, the guitar on the other, and the drums and vocals were down the middle, just like so many of my '60s singles. And because the guitar was on one side, it was easier to learn how to play their songs.

The usual way of strumming is up and down, but Johnny Ramone's guitar style was almost all downstrokes, which gave his playing an aggressive energy, like he was punching the strings. There were virtually no guitar solos, which made it easier to concentrate on the rhythm and learn how to accent and anticipate certain beats. I started playing along with that album, and with as much new music as I could get my hands on.

Around this time, NBC ran an exposé of the UK punk scene that featured excerpts from the Sex Pistols' scandalous appearance on Bill Grundy's *Today* show. I taped the audio off the TV so I could capture their controversial first single, "Anarchy in the UK." I became even more fascinated with this new style of music, and I listened to that cassette over and over and over.

Punk rock was so unlike anything else I'd heard. Metal and hard rock bands were all about excess: groupies, jet planes, and vast arenas. By contrast, the Ramones were just trying to buy a PA at Manny's Music and stuff it into a van. My friends and I could build a float and pretend to be Kiss, but mimicking those larger-than-life cartoon characters wasn't punk rock. Punk rock was actually *doable.* I thought to myself, I could do this. And, after a few weeks, I could play those fourteen songs on their first album. I could stand on the side of the room where the bass guitar was loudest and play along.

Of course, the New York Dolls were from New York, like the Ramones, so I was instantly interested. They were the bridge band between Kiss and the Ramones. They started before the Ramones and had a punk spirit about them, yet their ramshackle androgyny, as I later learned, influenced Kiss's makeup-wearing ways.

So I'm sixteen, I'm in this remote farm town, and I'm up to my eyeballs in this new music. A few of my friends give the Ramones a listen, but most of them aren't interested, or are dismissive of "that noise." I'm trying to convert them. To me, it's the sound of New York City, four hundred miles away. I'm envisioning the streets of brick and dirt, and musicians and artists mingling at shows and parties. All of this reinforces a simple fact: I need to get out of this place.

Music kept building my resolve. In December 1976, during my junior year in high school, a teacher named Jim Denesha helped a group of us organize a bus trip to Montreal—a cultural visit, a way to use our years of French class. In actuality, the main purpose of the trip was to attend a rock concert at the Montreal Forum.

The headliner was Aerosmith, then at the height of their drug-fueled debauchery. Rush opened; I barely remember them, having found my seat just after vomiting on one of the Forum's escalators. My friends and I were trashed beyond belief, but I still managed to fire up a joint as Rush wrapped up their set. My only real recollection of Aerosmith was that they sounded terrible and that there was safety netting above the stage, which prevented the band from being hit by flying objects. For some reason, people threw lots of fireworks onto the stage during their set. This was what big-time rock and roll was like in 1976.

In the spring of 1977, I noticed the Ramones were playing at the University of Quebec in Montreal. They were billed as the special support act for Iggy Pop and were promoting their second album, *Leave Home*. My friend Kevin Heath and I went to the concert, and it reaffirmed everything I suspected. The Ramones took the stage with clear focus: Joey quickly introduced the band, Dee Dee counted off the first song, and away they went. They played the songs even faster than the album versions, in unbroken packs of three and four, without speaking to the audience. I made a mental note of this. Iggy, in sharp contrast, appeared to me to be a total disaster. Iggy was supporting

The Idiot, an album I got for ten cents as a promotional incentive for joining the Columbia House record club. After the surgical efficiency of the Ramones, Iggy appeared to be completely lost. That night, the Ramones showed me what a rock concert could be.

After months of serious self-application, studying the Mel Bay instructional books and playing along with my new punk rock albums, I realized that I was going to be a guitarist. But the eighty dollar Sears SG copy with the burrs in the saddle, the high action, and the shoddy tuning pegs was holding me back. I asked my father if I could upgrade; he could tell I was serious about the guitar and agreed to let me pick out a new one.

We wound up at Bronan's Music in Potsdam, where there were some decent music stores. I would have preferred a Les Paul, but that was out of our price range, so I settled on an Ibanez Rocket Roll Flying V, the same guitar Syl Sylvain played with the New York Dolls. The guitar and its V-shaped case cost $250.

When we got home, I plugged it into my Electro-Harmonix Mike Matthews Dirt Road Special, a relatively simple amplifier: one channel, solid state, one twelve-inch Celestion speaker, and a built-in Small Stone Phaser. The sound was close to what I was hearing in my head, but it needed a more overdriven feel. The last step: the MXR Distortion +, a small yellow pedal with two knobs (output and distortion), originally designed in the '70s. Turning up the distortion knob cuts some bass from the signal, exaggerating the graininess of the high-frequency harmonics. Imagine the sound of someone starting up a chain saw in preparation for clearing a parcel of overgrown land.

In July of 1977, I took another concert trip to Montreal, this time to see Cheap Trick open for Kiss—and completely blow them off the stage. Cheap Trick's sound, heavily influenced by '60s Britpop, was familiar to me from my early childhood singles collection, and it would play a big part in informing my own songwriting many years later. For me, Cheap Trick's set was one of the final nails in the hard rock/heavy metal coffin.

Visits to A&A Records in Montreal opened my ears to great Canadian punk bands like the Viletones and the Diodes. There was Record Town in Plattsburgh, but they had little beyond the major label releases. But in the spring of 1978, it was in Burlington where I found the Suicide Commandos' *Make a Record*. In their *Rock Scene* photo, the Commandos had been this unassuming-looking three-piece: singer-guitarist Chris Osgood with his bookish glasses, singer-bassist Steve Almaas with his Kewpie doll look, and drummer Dave Ahl—this tall, Nordic-looking fellow with a big grin on his face. These guys looked different from the New York street punks and the nihilistic Cleveland bands; they exuded an endearing Midwestern wholesomeness, but who knew what they'd sound like?

Turns out I liked the Commandos' music—it had elements of first-wave American punk and '70s hard rock. There were melodic vocal harmonies, modest guitar solos, and tinges of '60s garage rock. I grew up listening to all those things, and could relate to their sound.

*   *   *

Getting out of town, for me, was attending Macalester College in St. Paul, Minnesota, with the intention of earning a master's in engineering. Macalester had a reputation as one of the nation's foremost hotbeds of liberalism, but I didn't go there for its politics. I went because I qualified for an underprivileged scholarship package. My parents would pay only $300 a year for a school that cost well over $5,000. In 1978, $5,000 was a lot of money for most families. But even $300 was a lot for my parents.

It was the typical scene: a parent driving his teenage kid to college. My dad and I did the two-day, 1,200-mile drive in a car filled with oversize stereo speakers, my Ibanez Flying V guitar, my amplifier, and a bag of clothes. For me, it signaled the end of a turbulent and sometimes confusing childhood. But as the two-day journey rolled by, my feeling of liberation gave way to concern over whether my mom would be OK during those spells when the darker side of my dad's personality made its appearance.

One of the first things I do once I move into my dorm room is get the free weekly paper. I see an ad for the Longhorn Bar—and the Suicide Commandos are playing. I find out the drinking age in Minnesota is nineteen, and when I pick up my student ID, I give the wrong birth date so I can go see them.

The first time I walked into the Longhorn, the Commandos were onstage, and it felt just like what I'd read about in *Rock Scene*. There were probably five hundred people there. We all knew the words to every song, and after a few minutes of surveying the situation, I threw myself into the excitement. All of us, standing on the battered floor of this ramshackle steak house, gathered up and unified in the moment unfolding before us.

I was the new kid in the room, so I was looking around the club, trying to see who was doing what, who I needed to meet, who I needed to know, and how to get close to those people. I did a little asking around and learned that a guy named Peter Jesperson was the DJ, Chris Osgood's then girlfriend Linda Hultquist was doing lights, and a fellow named Terry Katzman was running around, looking after the band.

I figured out a way to belong at college too. Physical proximity is the mother of all acquaintances, and my initial friendships at Macalester weren't formed around music, but on the sheer randomness of dorm room assignments. My first roommate was a Japanese-American fellow named Phil Sudo. Phil was a quiet, soft-spoken guy, which was in sharp contrast to my wilder, punkier demeanor, but we became great friends and wound up rooming together for two years. Next door, there was Ken McGrew, a buttoned-down kid from the Chicago suburbs. Ken's roommate was Geoff Klaverkamp, a tall, lanky, cheerful fellow who'd lived in Japan. I'd grown up in an all-white farm town, and as one might expect, I was raised on racial slurs. All this cultural diversity required a lot of adjusting on my part. But the four of us got along well and started to run in a small pack.

One night my freshman year, a whole bunch of us piled into a car and went to a multiplex to see *Quadrophenia,* the film based on the Who's 1973 rock opera. We were drunk, crazy, and pilled up, just like the guys in the movie, which centers around a gigantic riot between two rival youth gangs in mid-'60s Britain, the Mods and the Rockers. On the drive back, another car cuts us off—and we're pissed. We chase their car up a narrow hill and finally force them to pull over. We all pile out and start this huge fistfight in the middle of the road. We're living it.

Some guy took a swing and whacked me upside the head, a really good shot. I reeled back for a second, then started laughing at him, then lunged at him. I'm shit-faced, and I don't feel a thing. Geoff is throwing martial arts kicks, clocking people left and right. Ken is getting pounded, so we run over and pull a guy off and backhand him. Finally, the other guys tucked tail, got in their car, and left. We got back into our car, a little beat-up and bloody, and went back to the dorm.

Still jacked sky-high on adrenaline, we cracked another case of beer and listened to punk rock, then went into the hallway and smashed all the bottles. It was nuts. It was like *Animal House* but with punk rock as the sound track. I remember people looking at me as if I were John Belushi, like I had that kind of craziness. No one was stopping me; they may have been scared shitless. We ended up playing hockey in the hallway with a case of empty beer bottles. The broken glass slid under the doors, so the next morning, some of the guys in the dorm were walking around with bloody feet. So then you have a hallway full of blood. It was fucked up.

A healthier (and more civilized) way of finding community was by immersing myself in new music. Oar Folkjokeopus (Oar Folk) was the Twin Cities' preeminent record store. They had

all the latest import singles, the UK music magazines and weeklies like *NME, Melody Maker,* and *Sounds,* as well as free local
papers and flyers for shows. I'd pick up a copy of each paper,
park myself on one of the seats over the radiator next to the
window, and go through the papers cover to cover. Then I'd
return the papers to the rack and riffle through the import singles bins to find a couple to buy, based on what I'd just read in
the weeklies. Then I'd get back on the bus and do the hour-long
ride back to school, excited to gather up my friends, buy a case
of cheap beer, and listen to the new purchases. Rain or shine, it
didn't matter—that was my ritual. I was constantly reading
about music: the Oi stuff, the Manchester scene, Irish bands
like the Undertones and Stiff Little Fingers. Every week there
was the chance to discover a new band that might end up being
the best new band in the world.

At the time, punk came in a lot of flavors. There was a fashion component to it. There was the studious bohemian look of
Television and Talking Heads, with their white polo shirts and
khakis. There was the New York street punk look of the
Ramones and the Dictators, with their leather jackets, jeans,
and high-tops. There was the high-fashion Malcolm McLaren
look, with bondage gear, safety pins, and stenciled letters on
clothing—the way the Clash or Siouxsie Sioux looked. There
was Oi, there was ska, all the various subfactions. These dis-
tinctions were very important to me as a seventeen-year-old
looking for an identity. Being into a certain type of music was
like belonging to a gang. And I eventually found my gang in
St. Paul.

One day in late 1978, I stopped by Cheapo Records in St. Paul.
A PA set up on the street outside was blaring stuff like X-Ray
Spex and Pere Ubu. I was like, wow, this is cool, and I started
talking to the guy behind the counter. He was a pudgy, hippie-
ish guy, barefoot. He might have been wearing something tie-
dyed. And I'm thinking, Who is this frumpy guy? Not being a
Greek god myself, I wasn't making a judgment—it was more

like a feeling of solidarity. He told me his name was Grant Hart, and we started talking about music. Somehow the conversation gets around to the subject of marijuana. He says, "I got some Thai stick." So he closes up the store for a bit, and we go down to the basement and get stoned. I can't remember if it was that day or a subsequent meeting, but I eventually mentioned to him that I played guitar. He looks at me and says, "Sure you do," challenging me.

"I play guitar," I say again.

"What kind of stuff?"

"You know, like this kind of music that we're listening to. *Good* stuff."

"I wanna see you play," he says, challenging me again. "I'm gonna close the store right now and I wanna go see you play right now."

So Grant closes the store, and we walk up to my dorm, just a couple of blocks away. We get to my room, I take out my guitar, plug in, and start playing, probably a bunch of Johnny Thunders riffs or something. And he's like, "Yeah...we gotta play together...I play drums...we gotta play."

And I say, "Well, cool, whatever."

Then Grant says, "I know someone who's got a bass. He works at another record store called Northern Lights down on University Avenue."

I hadn't even contemplated the notion of being in a band so soon upon arriving in Minnesota. The Twin Cities were gigantic compared to Malone, and I'd gone from having an entire floor of a house to myself to living in a multistory dormitory. On my dorm floor alone, there was my Japanese-American roommate, there were inner-city African-Americans, as well as privileged suburbanites. I was fresh from the sticks, learning to adjust to this melting pot while trying to create my own identity amid all the other activity at Macalester. A band would be great, but at that particular moment it wasn't a top priority.

But I met Grant's friend — his name was Greg Norton — and

sure enough, he had a bass. I think he even had a strap for it too. Greg wasn't the same type of outsider as Grant or me; he had the air of a connoisseur—a hep cat, a *skiddly-bop-bo* kind of deal. He was into Sun Ra, Ornette Coleman, outside stuff. I thought, What is this jazz bullshit? Greg was also a big fan of new-wave cult favorite Gary Wilson and his album *You Think You Really Know Me*. We all enjoyed that album, but I think it eventually had a big influence on Greg's singing style.

Grant lived with his parents in the stockyards suburb of South St. Paul; his dad was a shop teacher, and his mom worked at a credit union. Greg's parents were separated, and he lived with his mom in a small '60s-style tract home in the nondescript middle-class suburb Mendota Heights. The house had a semifinished basement. That basement would soon prove to be key.

But I needed a push. Shortly after I arrived at Macalester, the Suicide Commandos broke up and I'd heard that Chris Osgood was giving guitar lessons. I thought the world of the Commandos and I wanted to hang out with Chris, so I figured I'd take a couple of guitar lessons from him. It didn't matter that I already knew how to play. Chris says he still remembers seeing me step off the bus with that Flying V in front of the house—this big historic mansion where he lived on the top floor with his girlfriend. (I found out much later that his girlfriend would hide in the closet and read a book while I was getting lessons, so as to not disturb us.)

After the second lesson, Chris just looked at me and said it: "You know, you need to go start a band."

CHAPTER 3

We weren't a band yet. But the chemistry among the three of us was built around our love of music, and Grant, Greg, and I started going to shows together, hanging out, drinking and smoking weed, bonding, and generally just getting to know each other.

Personally, I felt more of a kinship with Grant. Both of us were the youngest in our family, and both of our families had tragically lost an elder son; Grant's brother Tom had been killed in a car accident. We both viewed music from a melodic perspective, whereas Greg was more a fan of dissonance. Equally important, Grant and I were both attracted to other men. Grant and I never spent any time dwelling on the subject—and he wasn't exclusively interested in men—but at the time I sensed that was his preference.

I may have been dealing with my own self-loathing, but there was never any doubt as to my homosexuality, no matter how much I repressed it at the time. I was coping with the confusion that began with puberty—discerning between love, sex, and friendship. The differences and overlaps were unclear to me then, and I am not sure if they are clear to me now. But as far as I was concerned, there was never a doubt as to the nature of the relationship between Grant and me. We could be friends, but we would never be in love, nor would we have sex.

I don't remember explicitly telling Grant I had no interest in him, but I'm certain my behavior made it very clear. Establishing that boundary was important to me. Grant could be very persuasive: I'd seen him in action, and I wanted to draw the line as clearly and as early as possible. Neither of us expressed any of this verbally, but I felt there was no doubt as to the parameters of our relationship, so there was no need for deep discussion.

But we were all close, and of course, Grant, Greg, and I had these instruments. It made sense for the three of us to play music together. Enter Charlie Pine, a chatty fellow of medium build, medium-length hair, and medium personality. I think Charlie worked part-time at an investment firm. His aspiration was to be a broker, while the three of us had little to no financial hope. But Grant had a Farfisa organ and Charlie could play keyboards, so he was in.

Charlie got us our first gig at Ron's Randolph Inn, a bar one mile from Macalester. We had to come up with two sets of music, so we learned all kinds of stuff, including the old rockabilly tune "Sea Cruise," Pere Ubu's "Non-Alignment Pact," the Buzzcocks' "Fast Cars," and the '60s surf standard "Wipe Out."

Charlie was up there with these mirrored sunglasses, looking like Lou Reed on the cover of *Live,* but with a crack in one of the lenses. He starts to lay a rap on the crowd: "I'm Buddy, these are the Returnables. We're Buddy and the Returnables." And I'm thinking to myself, isn't that nice—we're returnable. We were Buddy and the Returnables, and Charlie was Buddy.

We're all up there playing like pigs in shit, having a blast. And yet I'm thinking, are the other guys noticing how out of sync Charlie is with the rest of us? Turns out the answer to that question was yes. Sometime during the second set, a friend of the band named Balls Mikutowski yanked the cord out of Charlie's organ, pointed at Charlie, and gave him the thumbs-down. He then pointed at the rest of us with the thumbs-up. We finished the evening as a trio, blazing through some original songs that likely included "Do the Bee," "Uncle Ron," and "Don't Try to Call."

The truth was, Grant, Greg, and I had been rehearsing without Charlie, writing songs in the basement of the Northern Lights record store. The songs were fast and quick, but light-hearted. Grant was a big surf music fan so the songs had that uplifted surf beat, and I'm throwing my Johnny Thunders–meets–Johnny Ramone style on it. I wasn't really sure what Greg was doing, but I know he was plugged in.

Buddy and the Returnables were history, so the three of us had to come up with a new (and better) name for our little band. One afternoon, while joking around with fake foreign language lyrics for a Talking Heads song, someone posed the couplet: "Psycho killer, Hüsker Dü, fa fa fa fa fa..." Hüsker Dü was the name of a board game ("in which the child can outwit the adult") that was advertised on TV nonstop when we were kids. And there you have it. The beauty of the name was that it shared very little with the typical punk monikers of the day. Most other bands were named [insert adjective] [insert noun]. The name Hüsker Dü was an identifier, not a description. Despite the superficial inanity, the name had a certain timelessness, and that avoidance of conformity (now there's a band name) served us well.

*　*　*

One morning in May 1979, we put all of our gear in a car and arrived at Jay's Longhorn right before the lunch buffet. Besides being a punk rock club at night, the Longhorn was a steakhouse by day, replete with cattle-print carpet, longhorns mounted on the walls, and wagon wheel chandeliers. For lunch they served a businessman's buffet so the fat cats who worked downtown could get their steak on. We sneaked in, set up all our gear, and started playing our set right as people started coming in to eat. Hartley Frank, the portly, sweaty man who booked the club, came rolling out of the back, squawking, "Whaaat the fuck is going on out here? Who the fuck *are* you?" We stopped and said, "We're Hüsker Dü and we want to play your club." Hartley offered us an opening spot for Curtiss A that weekend if we'd just stop playing. We stopped and accepted the gig. Then we started playing again.

That was the start of a tradition with us—if you want to win someone over, do something obnoxious and leave an impression. Provocation was very punk rock; we had nothing to lose by doing these things. And if we'd gotten eighty-sixed from the Longhorn, no big deal, we would have found our way back in again somehow.

That weekend, on May 13, 1979, we played our first real gig as Hüsker Dü. It was a dream come true for me—*everyone* played the Longhorn. That's where I saw local bands like the Commandos, NNB, the Suburbs, and that was my punk rock. The Police, Blondie, all the big acts played there as well. This was to be.

The actual set went by in a flash. We tore through our entire repertoire in about thirty minutes to a warm but not overly enthusiastic response. Mission accomplished: the first show went without any major hitches. Hüsker Dü was now an actual band, and we'd played a show at the Longhorn.

In the beginning, our shows had the up-surf and elemental punk rock feel: simple, stupid lyrics that rhymed and maybe didn't mean a lot, but were funny and punk. Then, as the months went on, another side to the band's sound emerged, a slower, darker droning feel. A lot of that was my doing, and one huge inspiration was Joy Division's album *Unknown Pleasures*. You come across only a handful of records in a lifetime that have that immediate impact, where you never forget the sound. It gets embedded in your cellular structure, and it seeps into the work you create. Joy Division's music was sad and poetic, and I felt we needed to add those elements to the mix. I also played chiming guitar parts that were influenced by early Cure, and a warped and warbling sound inspired by Keith Levene of Public Image Ltd (PiL).

Another band that inspired us was Pere Ubu. The three of us went to see them play twice in one evening at the Walker Art Center in 1979. We sat in the front row for both shows, and after the second, we walked onstage and chatted with the band. We didn't want to sound like Pere Ubu, but they showed us how a band could have a unique sound and an unusual, less than glamorous look, and still succeed in every way that was important to us.

Tim Carr was a major influence on the Minneapolis scene; he organized shows with many of the happening acts from America and Europe (and later went on to become a big-time A&R guy at major labels). Tim booked the Monochrome Set, Devo, Cabaret Voltaire, Judy Nylon, the Fleshtones, and many other legendary, very influential bands for the M-80 Festival, at the University of Minnesota Field House on September 22–23, 1979. It was a rickety venue, but with all the assembled talent and the excitement that surrounded each band's performance, it felt like something historic was happening. In my mind, it was equal to Woodstock or Altamont or the Beatles at Shea Stadium. There was a great scene building in the Twin Cities, and Tim Carr was a big part of it.

For me, so was trucker speed. By now I had acquired a smoking habit, but this drug was a revelation of sorts. With trucker speed I was able to drink more than normal. It also made me feel invincible. The stockyards in South St. Paul were a good place to find the ephedrine pills, since there were so many truckers around. Smoking and speed changed the way I looked. When I arrived in St. Paul, I was still carrying baby fat and weighed 210 pounds; by the end of the school year, I had lost 45 pounds. I appeared thin and severe; my cheekbones were pronounced, and my body snapped around like a disconnected live wire. This would be the first of many times my weight and appearance would go through drastic changes.

The band was playing, and I was living this scene, but I was still in college. At the end of my first year at Macalester, June 1979, I could either go back home or stay in St. Paul. I had no interest in returning to Malone, especially after hearing a horrific story about something that happened there. There was this friend of mine, a quiet kid with blond hair and glasses who was a year ahead of me in high school. He had allegedly made an unwanted sexual advance toward another young man, and sometime later he was found in the woods, hung up like a deer. After that, I wanted nothing more to do with Malone.

Besides, the weekly phone calls with my family were difficult enough, especially the ones where my father threatened to sever my financial support or escalate his violence toward my mother. It was a constant offer/reward/punishment cycle, and now that I was 1,200 miles away, I never wanted to return. Grant suggested I stay with him at his parents' house for the summer — that way, we'd be able to continue with the band. I accepted.

Living with the Harts was what most people would think of as normal. I joined the family for most dinners, which were eaten at the kitchen table — unlike with my family, who ate in the living room off of TV trays. I offered to pay a monthly amount to help cover the day-to-day living costs, but they wouldn't hear of it. Grant's room was in the attic, actually two small adjoining rooms not dissimilar to the one in which I spent my high school years back home. There was a stereo, a bong, and enough space for two sleeping areas. There was only one bathroom in the whole house, and it was downstairs on the main level, attached to Grant's parents' bedroom, which could make things awkward.

I occupied myself with mindless temp jobs, mostly in offices: filing insurance claims, doing microfilm work for medical firms, soliciting subscriptions to the local daily paper. The trucker speed was suppressing my appetite, so I rarely ate full meals. Another unhealthy side effect of taking the pills was that it softened my upper palate, which made eating solid foods next to impossible. So after work, I'd usually head to McDonald's for a thirty-nine-cent hamburger because they didn't hurt like potato chips did. Once I realized that the steamed White Castle burgers were even softer, I switched to those.

It's hard to forget my Quality Park Products job from that summer—or what I did there. The office was located in a light industrial park on Highway 280. I got a weeklong temp job working eight hours a day, filling in for a vacationing employee. My role was simple: invoices came in and I would time-stamp each one, separate the carbon copy, and place them facedown in two separate piles. I was hopped up on pills, and on the first day, I was done with my work by lunchtime. I asked the supervisor if there was anything else to do. There wasn't, and even better, I could go home early with full pay. I picked up the pace a little more on Tuesday, and so on throughout the week. By Friday afternoon, I really felt great about myself. Forty hours' pay for twenty hours' work.

When I came in the following Monday to pick up my paycheck, the supervisor asked me if I wanted to meet the person whose job I had performed the previous week. I thought, sure, why not. The supervisor approached a middle-aged gentleman, slight of build, working with his back to us. The supervisor called his name and said, "I'd like you to meet the young man who filled in for you while you were on leave." The man turned around in the chair and reached out to shake my hand. The man had lost both his hands and was living with two prosthetic metal hooks. No wonder it took me half the time. I didn't feel so great about myself after that.

That summer, I was listening to the British art-noise collective Throbbing Gristle, whose albums depicted an apocalyptic world of suburban industrial parks and supermarkets. They mingled that imagery with grisly photographs of World War II atrocities, medical procedures, and barbarism to create a disturbing and psychotic visual landscape. They also eroticized their work, giving it an additional emotional charge, then manipulated layers of sound to the point of unrecognizability, and the result was unlike anything I had ever seen or heard. It fit well with my reading of William S. Burroughs's *Naked Lunch,* done in one sitting. It was dangerous, erotic, emotional art. I became obsessed.

I wasn't the only one. I befriended a fellow named Stefan Hammond who wrote for the *Minnesota Daily,* the University of Minnesota campus newspaper. Stefan was a big Throbbing Gristle fan and even went so far as to travel to the UK to visit them in their "factory." We published a fanzine dedicated to their work and mimicked their aesthetic.

With all this in my head, some evenings, I'd drive myself to the Minneapolis–St. Paul international airport to drink White Russians at one of the terminal bars. I think it was actually called "Terminal Bar." I would listen to the Muzak and slowly stir my drink with a straw, watching the solitary macadamia nut spin around in the milky liquid, and sometimes a traveler would catch my eye. I never actively sought out sex at the airport, but the transitory nature of airports brought with it the prospect of a random, anonymous, and somewhat detached sexual encounter. I fetishized impersonal spaces. I can remember one awkward sexual encounter when I tuned the radio to KEEY-FM, "the music of your life." It was strange to be having sex while listening to Muzak. It was as if I was creating a performance piece, living out the imagery of the industrial music I listened to, to a kind of sound that was totally divorced from it.

The bleakness of the literature and the heaviness of the music were steering me toward the darker side of life — notions of uselessness and death added up to thoughts of suicide. I was becoming nihilistic, and on top of it all, I was suppressing my emotions with nicotine and alcohol and the speed was curbing my libido. I was fucking with my metabolism and my mind.

Starvation was happening on all levels. I was concerned about being "found out" by my dorm mates, and I was finding no healthy outlet for my sexual urges. I didn't hate myself for being gay, but I hated myself for not dealing with what I now know to be natural and beautiful: the act of opening up to another person, and finding comfort in physical contact. Instead I found comfort in the ugliness of life. I found relief in destruction.

One afternoon back at school, in a fit of blind rage, I pitched an old Royal manual typewriter out the fourth-floor window of a dormitory, almost hitting a passerby. It crashed on the sidewalk, keys exploding in all directions. On another night, I was hanging out with some friends. I said something about suicide and someone questioned me, so I pulled a knife from my desk drawer and dragged it across the top of my left wrist. I clenched my fist, lifted my bleeding arm in the air, and proclaimed, "You know, it's really easy to do it on the other side too." My friends freaked out. I ripped some fabric off my white button-down shirt and wrapped it around my wrist. I got on the bus and went to see a band, blood running down my hand.

In those moments I didn't think I was behaving strangely. It was just another act in my existential play. The thought that I could so casually end my own life? I chalk that up to a blend of youthful immortality and indifference. I was living in a place where nothing would ever be right, nothing would ever do, and nothing held pure value. I only listened to my dark side. I had learned to identify with suffering. It held an attraction, a fascination. It was what I was born into, and I was finding solace in darkness and detachment.

*   *   *

Returning to campus in September 1979, I was no longer the pudgy farm kid, but a lean, angular, intense young man. I had my band, my nihilism, and endless amounts of energy.

I became the late-night Saturday DJ at WMCN-FM, the low-wattage campus radio station. Since the program directors wanted to keep getting free records, they required all DJs to play new major label releases, which cut down my options. But

I'd bring lots of my own music, whether British Oi, American punk, or '60s Motown singles, and mix it in with the major label "new-wave" stuff. On occasion, I experimented with sound collage by mixing and overlaying disparate records together at different speeds. Imagine *Music for 18 Musicians* by Steve Reich with an overlay of the Sun Ra Arkestra. Eventually I gave up trying to follow the rules, played what I wanted, and falsified my playlist logs.

During the day, my work-study job was at the library. I would move quietly through the aisles, restocking the returned books and observing people studying quietly—or discreetly pleasuring themselves in an obscure alcove. It happened all the time. I also lifted the library's lone copy of *Naked Lunch* for my personal collection.

Macalester was the perennial liberal haven, but even there things were changing. Around this time, the Republican Party began building a platform for Ronald Reagan, who was then well on his way to winning the 1980 presidential election. There were other students, "Young Republicans," who were completely getting under my skin, pseudoaristocratic sheep talking about this guy who's going to lift us from the Carter "malaise." I had an innate dislike for them: they didn't like the same kind of music I liked, they didn't drink the beer I drank, they didn't dress the way I dressed. They had this sense of entitlement. No one knew exactly what it portended at the time, but whatever it was, it wasn't good.

I befriended a fellow student named Duncan Stewart. He was a short, wiry kid from Ireland with cropped blond hair, a Popeye chin, and wire-rimmed glasses. We shared a love of punk music, especially Irish bands like the Undertones and Stiff Little Fingers. I also had a romantic interest in him, and I suspect he knew it, though we never directly addressed it. We acted like little terrorists. The high point of our naive activism was directed at, of all unlikely people, Ted Kennedy, who was running for the Democratic presidential nomination.

In my head, all politicians were suspect. Kennedy was scheduled to make a speech on campus, and we decided to make a collage of all the embarrassing moments of his life, add some questionable taglines in hostage-note-style punk rock lettering, and post hundreds of copies of the finished manifesto around campus on the morning of his visit. Hours before his arrival, we went out in the freezing, snowing dawn and covered the area with our creation. Turns out the Secret Service took everything down well before Kennedy was anywhere near the campus. So much for our art/activism project. (Little did I know how influential Kennedy would become in shaping the social progress of America in the thirty years to follow. Chalk this one up to the folly of youth.)

*   *   *

Early in my sophomore year, two concerts had a major impact on me. The first was at the Longhorn, where Gang of Four opened for the Buzzcocks. I was a huge fan of the Buzzcocks' approach to pop songwriting, and also appreciated the slashing guitar of Gang of Four. I was front and center for the entire Buzzcocks set, studying singer-guitarist Pete Shelley, watching his every motion. Legend has it that the entire band was tripping on LSD that evening—I don't know, but many times during the set, Pete did lean down, off-mic, and shout the chord changes at me. It left a deep impression, and I became an even more intent student of their work.

Minneapolis scenester Jody Kurilla's house was where all these out-of-town bands went after their shows. Since I was not yet a fully accepted member of "the club," I would get turned away from the more exclusive parties. After suffering this indignity a handful of times, this night, I decided to stay out in the driveway in hopes of intercepting the big bands. I managed to corner Gang of Four drummer Hugo Burnham for a brief moment, but he soon opted to join the party.

That same week, Hüsker Dü met the Clash. Joe Strummer

and Mick Jones were milling about the Longhorn and we introduced ourselves. They were nice chaps, but very intense, as if
they were very aware of their importance. They humored our
"we're in a band too" routine, and even went so far as to sug-
gest we organize an impromptu gig for the following day at an
African-American laundromat of our choosing. We mentioned
one, but suggested it might not be the best idea — St. Paul was
not quite as progressive as London. After that, they moved on
to the next conversation. They played two nights later, and all I
remember from the evening is how abrasive and political they
sounded, that and my rushing toward the front of the theater
and bowling over my boss from the library.

Bands were everything. My buddy Geoff came back to Malone
with me for the holidays, and on New Year's Eve we went to
Manhattan to see a show by a late-era version of the Heartbreakers. It was a great day and night — running around downtown, drinking and smoking pot, slumming in the club, being
as punk as I had envisioned from reading *Rock Scene*. We went
back to the Port Authority bus terminal at 4 AM and waited for
the 6 AM bus to Plattsburgh, where my father would meet us. In
the terminal, we ended up sitting next to a fellow who was
wearing filthy ripped clothes; he was passed out and bleeding
from a cut on his temple. In later years, I found out this was
simply the way things were at the Port Authority terminal at 4
AM. But at the time: This, I thought, was punk rock.

Minneapolis had a bit of an infatuation with New York.
Some folks even liked to refer to the city as the "Mini-Apple."
Maybe it just wanted to be like New York — sophisticated, arty,
cosmopolitan. There was a clothing store in Minneapolis called
March 4th, a direct clone of New York's infamous Trash and
Vaudeville stores. Twin Cities bands such as NNB were very
informed by Television, and the Suburbs adroitly straddled the
line between punk rock and art rock in a very New York way.
Some elements of the Suburbs might have brought David Bowie
to mind, but at their core, they were a hard-drinking rock band

that wrote clever Midwestern story songs played at medium to high speed. Once the Commandos ceased to exist, I found myself in the front row of almost every Suburbs show in the area. I became an acquaintance of the band, and the Suburbs and Hüsker Dü eventually played shows together.

Johnny Thunders's new band Gang War came to Minneapolis on July 29–30, 1980, and Hüsker Dü was slated as the opening act. Johnny was one of my guitar heroes, and I wanted to get close to him. I ended up becoming his de facto babysitter while he was in town. I'm nineteen, and he's a grown man with years of experiences. Do you think I learned a lot in those two days?

Johnny was incorrigible. "Get me some fuckin' Dilaudid or something, I'm sick," he said to me in that drawling Brooklyn sandpaper voice. He claimed his bandmate Wayne Kramer stole his junk. John was jonesing, and I'm like, Where do I get heroin? I don't know this shit. I knew there was a methadone clinic, but he wasn't about to go down there and register. Someone brought him painkiller pills, but he just scoffed. "Look at 'em. They're fuckin' synthetic, they're not gonna boil down." So we finally bargained it down to "Get me a fuckin' eight ball and I'll be OK." One-eighth of an ounce of cocaine seemed to stabilize him enough to play a classic (or at the least typical) Thunders performance, complete with him berating our sound man between every song.

Later that night, he tried to talk my guitar and amp off me. I got him back to his horrible shit-hole hotel room a few blocks away. He had been going into the bathroom to do his drug business, but by now I guess he liked me enough to let down his guard. So I'm in the room with John, and he's tying off, burning more coke down, the works, the water, *flick-flick-flick*, getting it ready. I'd been around other people in Minneapolis who were shooting coke at the time, so I'd seen all this before. But this is Johnny Thunders, one of my guitar heroes. *Flick-flick-flick*, gets the air out, *slap-slap-slap*, on the bottom of the bicep, and shoot. Pulls the works out of his arm, looks at me, says, "much better," and throws the syringe ten feet across the room. It lands point-down perfect in a stubby drinking glass.

I wanted to be around these people. I knew there was something to learn. I always showed deference to my elders, but it wasn't strictly an ambition thing—I was a fan. I worshipped the Heartbreakers, the Dolls. How could I turn down the opportunity to take care of Johnny Thunders? Or when Nico performed at local rock club Duffy's and the promoter asked me if I could help take care of her, how could I say no? Once a celebrated model and Warhol superstar, she was now broken down and jonesing, and saddled with an inappropriate side player, but she was still Nico. It was an honor, even if it was a touch depressing. It was part of my education, observing how people of status carry themselves. Maybe it wasn't their shining moments, but there was still something to be learned, even if it was what *not* to do.

* * *

Through persistence, stubbornness, and a better-than-average knowledge of the touring acts of the moment, Hüsker Dü became the willing and able opening band for many of the punk rock/new wave acts that toured through Minnesota, from DNA to Discharge to the Ramones. It probably helped that we were more than happy to play for little or no money. Hüsker Dü was scheduled to open for Joy Division at Duffy's on May 29, 1980—a great thing, and we were ready. But the band's singer, Ian Curtis, hanged himself the night before the band was to fly to the United States. It was upsetting news, but not a complete shock, given the dark tone of their words and music.

We kept opening for bands, once playing two nights at downtown music club 7th Street Entry in November 1980 with an up-and-coming Boston band called Mission of Burma. At sound check, bassist Clint Conley plugged his electric razor into the back of his bass amp and gave himself a fresh shave on the spot. I thought that was one of the most un–punk rock, and simultaneously coolest, things I had ever seen. After the first night of performing together, I felt an immediate kinship with them: another three-piece playing loud, fast, angular music.

One of my own trademarks was to touch the tuning pegs of my guitar to my vocal microphone before we started playing. That all began at an early 7th Street Entry show. I was sweating profusely, as usual, and when my sweat-covered face touched the microphone, I got shocked and blown backward into my amp. From then on, I would always touch my guitar to the microphone and see if there were any clicks or sparks, which would mean the polarity was wrong and I'd get shocked again. Once that was out of the way, we'd typically launch into our set, barely breaking between songs for extraneous banter.

The band always played with purpose—there wasn't a lot of goofing around in the live shows. On the faster material, Greg would start jumping in the air or do scissor kicks. I typically wore a grave, glowering expression, digging deep into my guitar when not singing. Grant was behind the kit, looking much like Animal from the *Muppet Show* band, except with longer hair and bare feet. When the tempos were high, we generated white heat in two places: my right hand strumming furiously across the guitar strings, and Grant's right hand alternately pounding and gliding across the ride cymbal. We were young and inexperienced, but we had tons of energy and were able to create a solid wall of sound without relying on effects and gimmickry.

As 1980 went on, we started building our own following, commonly referred to as "the Veggies." There was a core group of guys who came to every show: Kelly Linehan, Tippy Roth, Pat Woods, Tony Pucci, Dick and Mike Madden. Most of the guys wore leather jackets, and once the music fired up, the good-natured pogo dancing/mock wrestling would begin. It was a bonding experience for all of us. The Veggies eventually morphed into a fine band themselves, called Man Sized Action.

One afternoon in November 1980, we brought ourselves to

Blackberry Way Studios and recorded three songs, with assistance from Colin Mansfield and Steve Fjelstad, two early supporters of the band. "Statues" was a midtempo droning guitar piece, clearly influenced by PiL. "Writer's Cramp" was a brisker, simplistic punk-pop song, with a rudimentary sexual pun as the hook. "Let's Go Die" was a faster-paced song, politically naive in tone, set to a Ramones-influenced musical bed.

I was fascinated with all the studio technology: the large Trident mixing board, the multitrack recorder, all the outboard gear and microphones. I watched everything as closely as possible, trying to figure out how it was done. I was making mental notes, hoping that I would be able to produce records someday.

Our songs were recorded as demos in an attempt to get signed by Twin/Tone Records. At the time, Twin/Tone was the obvious choice for Hüsker Dü. They released the music of prominent local bands like the Suburbs, Fingerprintz, and Curtiss A. The label was run by three partners: recording engineer Paul Stark, Oar Folk employee and tastemaker Peter Jesperson, and local sportswriter Charley Hallman. Unfortunately, each of those guys claimed to like a different song and therefore could not reach consensus about releasing a single.

So we decided to release the single by ourselves. We shelved the two faster songs and replaced them with a live version of another slower, chiming song titled "Amusement." We named our label Reflex Records, as a reaction to our being passed over by Twin/Tone, and bankrolled it with a loan from Grant's mother's credit union. We printed the black-and-white covers—"Amusement" artwork by me, "Statues" artwork by Grant—at a local copy shop, bought 2,500 clear plastic sleeves, and when the vinyl arrived from the pressing plant in Arizona, we folded the sleeves and stuffed each one by hand. The single was officially released in January 1981 to a smattering of familial applause and a two-line mention in the national magazine *Trouser Press*.

Pretty cool stuff, but it was also my third year at Macalester and time for me to pick a major. I found a strong supporter in one of my sociology teachers, Professor McCall, and was thrilled when she offered to be my academic advisor, working with me to design a major in urban studies. Her mentor was an oft-published sociologist from Chicago named Howard Becker who studied subculture and language, and I was to write my honors thesis on punk rock as a subculture, based on Becker's writings on jazz musicians. His work influenced how I viewed the punk movement. I was to keep a journal on the road and base my thesis on the experience. (Sadly, I later loaned my marked-up first draft to Kelly Linehan and haven't seen it since.)

My project would have been a natural fit with the band's touring, but the only place of note Hüsker Dü had played outside of Minnesota was Chicago. It was home of the pivotal Wax Trax industrial scene, as well as great bands like Naked Raygun and Strike Under. Punk rock, fashion, and queer culture commingled and informed the vibrant music scene. Chicago was where we caught our first big break. With only our single as a calling card, we convinced a club called Oz to hire us for a two-night stand, March 22–23, 1981.

Grant persuaded a car dealer in South St. Paul to let him "test drive" a vehicle that weekend. I don't think he told the dealer that it would be one thousand miles of test drive. We got to Chicago and stayed in one of the trashiest motels I can remember, in a derelict area of downtown. There were bullet holes in the sliding doors. We didn't feel particularly safe. Greg befriended a woman our first night there, and she helped move us into a nicer hotel nearby.

Black Flag, the ruling and notorious kings of Southern California hardcore, had played earlier that evening at COD's. Our gig at Oz was booked as the after-show party. During the set, I was out of my skull on cheap speed and beer, swinging at the air with a hammer, breaking bottles, and throwing myself into walls. I was trying to upstage anything Black Flag might have done at their show, but turns out I wasn't the only one contributing.

There was a little utility closet behind the drum kit that we used as a dressing room, and after the set, someone threw a bucket of blue paint from behind the stage. The paint bucket exploded on the floor in front of the stage area, and then a woman in a head-to-toe leather suit started scooping up paint with one of Grant's downed cymbals, intending to pour it over his drum kit—the kit he'd inherited from his beloved late brother Tom. Grant ran out, tackled her into the paint, picked her up off the floor, and started bouncing her off the walls, leaving a series of blue butt prints around the club.

Greg Ginn, the guitarist for Black Flag and the head of Southern California punk label SST, was blown away by this performance turned spectacle. Afterward, we talked for a while and he told us to get in touch with Mike Watt, who was the bassist for the San Pedro, California, punk trio the Minutemen, as well as the main force behind yet another new label called New Alliance Records.

It was something else, having this kind of interest, especially since Twin/Tone had rejected us. Black Flag was already a major force on the national punk scene, so this was a very big deal. We promptly called Watt and began to set the wheels in motion. A long journey was about to begin.

CHAPTER 4

Getting on our way meant shedding the musical baby fat and developing our own sound. We did our first US tour, which was named Children's Crusade '81 — maybe because, despite everything, our parents had made it possible. Grant's mom's credit union had facilitated the release of our first single, we rehearsed at Greg's mother's house, and my father bought, and drove out from Malone, a used rust-colored Dodge Tradesman van that we took out on tour.

We were usually the opening act on multiband bills, so we quickly honed our ability to set up our own gear, tune our own instruments, and then race through a clutch of songs in our small window of opportunity. Because our sets were short, we whittled out most of the moodier songs we'd been playing in our two-sets-a-night performances back home. And in the circles we traveled, there was ample opportunity for me (and others) to procure and consume cheap amphetamines. All of these things conspired to change the band's entire approach. Before, we had space to delve into atmospheric instrumental passages; now, we were confronted with a number of much tougher local scenes than our own, where bands blazed through twenty songs in forty minutes and people responded with unbridled aggression. We started doing the same. We had our Veggies in Minneapolis, our group of drinking buddies who would come to the shows and mock-wrestle in the crowd or even onstage, but the sights we were seeing on this tour were of a vastly harsher nature. Guys wore spikes and chains, did drugs and drank, and headed toward the front of the stage with malicious intent. Their dancing went well beyond pogoing, and veered into the realm of premeditated violence. Broken bones and bloody faces were not uncommon. The mosh pit, as it was later called, was not a place for arty girls or wimpy boys—it was dangerous.

This tour was when we finally saw what the rest of North America was doing. Hüsker Dü had opened for the powerful Vancouver punk band D.O.A. back in Minneapolis, and we had hit it off with singer-guitarist and band leader Joey Shithead, guitarist Dave Gregg, and their manager, Ken Lester. Those guys were incredibly giving and helpful, and Ken arranged for us to play six shows in Calgary in July 1981. The idea was to work our way out to Vancouver, where the opening spot on some D.O.A. shows awaited us.

D.O.A. and Dead Kennedys were the two bands that were the most instrumental in getting Hüsker Dü to the West Coast. It was part of what I liked to call "convergent evolution," a biological term that refers to the phenomenon of two distinct species with differing ancestries evolving to display similar physical features. Many bands around the country had a similar take on underground music, lifestyle, and cooperation, and it was encouraging to find that we were not alone in our rejection of corporate rock music, our tolerance for kids who were outside the mainstream, and our anxiousness to build a new way of life through music.

There was a loose network, which we often discovered by chance, where like-minded bands would share a stage and the hometown band would offer accommodations to the traveling band. In return, when that band came to your town, you would reciprocate. There was a remarkable lack of ego in all of this. Sometimes you'd run into a band that didn't understand or appreciate the idea. When Bad Brains stayed with Grant and his parents, they took Grant's pot and left behind an antigay note. Some gratitude. But once people caught the drift of those bands, they were usually shunned, and eventually they faded away.

We lived and thrived off the generosity of the people who were kind enough to put us up. When a punk band came through Minneapolis, we'd offer them a place to crash and some beer to drink, and we'd sit up all night and trade stories. A lot of the places I stayed, people had no money—often they couldn't even afford to heat their homes. We didn't stay in many houses of opulence. I'm sure there were kids from wealthy families in that scene, but that's the kind of thing you wouldn't want to make known.

This door-to-door approach, what I call "preaching," was the main way all the various local scenes became connected. There were a few national punk fanzines, most notably *Maximumrocknroll* (*MRR*), that would publish reports from all the scenes around America. More often than not, however, information was traded hand to hand. Bands kept information in their notebooks, and when we played together, we would sit down and trade information to fill in the gaps. This is how we built our community: no fax machines, no cell phones, no internet.

When we set out to do that first tour, the three of us got in the Tradesman van and headed north to Canada. Greg did the lion's share of the driving on this and all subsequent tours. As Grant and I were the main songwriters, Greg's major offstage contribution to the band was driving.

We had several boxes of the "Statues" single with us; those singles and our ability to play music were the only currency we had. We bartered our single for anything and everything: food, gas, places to stay. We sold them at shows. We left copies on consignment in record stores around the country. They only fetched us a dollar apiece, but it was all we had.

The tour began at the Calgarian Hotel, which was a flophouse with a bar and lounge on the ground floor. We were booked to play Monday through Saturday, three or four sets a night.

I'd sat next to bleeding, unconscious people in bus terminals, I'd watched Johnny Thunders shoot up, and I'd watched drunk women attempt to vandalize our musical equipment; I'd experienced sketchy before. But this was a whole new level of sketchy. One woman who was a regular at the Calgarian was stabbed on Monday night, and then stabbed again that Wednesday. It was that kind of place.

Early in the week, we were playing our first set while a handful of local Native Americans were getting drunk. During the second set, some ranchers started showing up. Then the two groups started going back and forth at each other. A fair amount of fighting happened around the pool table between the cowboys and the Indians—those are crass stereotypes, but it was the reality. We would fire the music back up, and they would stop what they were doing and say, "What the fuck is this punk rock? This band sucks!" So now the cowboys and Indians were putting their beef on hold and uniting against the punk rock; not only against us, but also the punks in the audience. Of the fifty or so people in the bar, there would be a dozen cowboys and a handful of Indians, but the majority were the punks. You might think that ratio would have discouraged the cowboys and Indians, but it didn't. We'd finish a set, get off the stage, leave the drums and amps behind, run upstairs, go back to the rooms they gave us for free, and just sit there and say to one another, "We have to go back down there?" Fights were pouring out into the street, and since our room was in the front of the hotel, we saw everything. It was like a barroom brawl straight out of an old western movie.

This continued for six straight days. By the end of the week, we'd not only managed to keep ourselves out of harm, trouble, and jail, but we'd also become acquainted with several folks in the Calgary punk rock community. It was a hell of a way to start a tour.

After Calgary, we went to Vancouver for a week. Grant had an ear infection, so he stayed at Ken Lester's place, a proper apartment, while Greg and I stayed in an abandoned house in Chinatown. We had no money for food; we had nothing. Ron Reyes had just left Black Flag and moved to Vancouver, and at night Ron would go to the food warehouses in Chinatown, where there were flats of strawberries and twenty-pound boxes of precooked ribs. He would climb over fences and concertina wire, throw boxes of food back over the fence, and bring them to the house. He'd haul the food up to our second-floor sleeping loft, and we'd eat strawberries and precooked bone-in ribs, then throw the bones downstairs and fall asleep, with the remains of our dinner rotting on the floor down below. We did that for most of the week. Then we played Canada Day in Victoria on Vancouver Island. Since the ferry charges were calculated per head, we hid under the amps to save money. Days later, we played with D.O.A. at the premiere punk room in Vancouver, the Smilin' Buddha Cabaret.

Seattle was up next. We used a couple of houses in the University District as home base for our stay, one of which was occupied by local scenester/writer Dennis Brown. I had the ear infection next and was in pain for most of the week, but we played a handful of shows at nightclubs like Gorilla Room and WREX with bands like the Fartz, who were a circle-A anarchy band. Seattle was full of runaways and heroin addicts, and in one of the clubs, someone blew up the toilets with fireworks.

Somehow we ended up playing early on a multiband bill headlined by the Dead Kennedys at the Showbox, one of the larger rooms in town. Jello Biafra, the lead singer of the band, was impressed by our set. After the show he asked us where we were headed. Portland was next on our itinerary, but after that things were uncertain. We had little money and no real shows booked. He suggested that we just continue down the coast to San Francisco, where we could stay in his spacious apartment and he'd find us some gigs in the Bay Area.

So after Portland, we continued down the coast to San Francisco, which at the time was arguably the most gay-friendly city in the United States. I was twenty years old, I was in a punk rock band, and this was my first time in SF. Maybe I'll have some time away from the band, have a little fun, maybe even meet somebody, I'm thinking. That would make sense, right? Maybe not.

Around this time I began to see newspaper articles about a strange new disease that was killing gay men. At first it was thought to be a form of pneumonia. Maybe it was caused by using amyl nitrate inhalers, also known as "poppers." Nobody knew what was going on, and it was scary as hell. This information, or lack of accurate information, made me leery of messing around with other guys.

When we arrived in San Francisco on July 14, we went right to Biafra's place, a two-floor apartment in the Mission. Biafra, his then girlfriend Theresa, and visual artist Winston Smith all lived there. Biafra was beyond gracious, allowing us to stay for almost two weeks. We forged rent receipts to get food stamps, then went to a Safeway to buy food (and beer) to repay the hospitality. One evening, a pizza cook-off between Grant and Greg got rather competitive, with Grant's pizza being a little better.

Another evening a large group of us trundled off to the Roxie Theater in the Mission where the now-classic LA punk documentary *The Decline of Western Civilization* was playing. There was a rivalry between the SF and LA punk scenes, and it was interesting to attend the movie with Biafra and company and get his take on his Southern California counterparts. The film featured several LA-area bands, including Black Flag, X, Circle Jerks, and the Germs. The Germs played fast, sounded angry, and vocalist Darby Crash wrote some of the best lyrics I'd ever heard from someone my own age. Their album *(GI)* made a strong impression on me, and to this day it's still one of my favorites.

There was a taqueria named La Cumbre on Valencia between

Sixteenth and Seventeenth Streets that served up the largest burritos I had ever seen. The price was right, so we would eat there as often as money allowed. (I still eat there to this day.) As a way to drink cheap, we'd go to a gay bar that served fifty-cent beers and showed *Wheel of Fortune* on the TV during happy hour. It didn't matter that I was in a gay bar—what was important was that I was in a bar that had fifty-cent beer.

At this time, Greg was very fond of wearing lots of bandanas. The thing was, in the gay community, there is something called the "hanky code"—a way to signal to other gay men the type of activities you prefer, and the roles you prefer to play.

The first time we walked into this bar for happy hour, we all looked very punk—a look, mind you, that is not very far from some gay fetish looks. Boots, ripped jeans, leather jackets, T-shirts: that's all basic Tom of Finland stuff. Throw in a little camouflage and a few bandanas and you can easily pass as street trade. So we walk into the bar and Greg has at least four bandanas around each shin, one on each wrist, and probably another half-dozen protruding from Lord knows where. Every head in the bar turned to him with an expression of complete befuddlement.

We played the Mabuhay Gardens nightclub four times in eight days. The Fab Mab, as it was sometimes called, was booked by a wonderfully irascible gentleman named Dirk Dirksen, the self-styled "Pope of Punk." The first time we played the Mabuhay, Dirk came onstage to introduce us. His preamble went along the lines of "Jello Biafra, while touring in the Northwest, ran across these people and asked me to book 'em, so here they are, an addition to the program. Here's . . . [*sounds unsure of the pronunciation*] Hüsker Dü."

We set the stage ablaze that evening. By that time we'd gotten really good at pile driving as many songs into the set as possible, and this breathless approach left crowds a bit bewildered. No time to talk, think, or react. Good.

In photographs taken at those early shows, I look possessed.

People who saw me scowling and lurching around the stage back then probably wondered what was going on inside my brain. It just felt like loose electricity was flying through my hands and off the guitar, and it sounded like my head was being riddled with pellets of ice—it was almost like being locked in the trunk of a car during a massive hailstorm. The treble on-stage was frightening; people often comment on the shrill nature of some of the band's recordings, but they sound positively soothing compared to standing in the center of that stage.

There was white-hot energy emanating from the core. Greg jumped up and down a lot, doing kicks and twitching. Grant flailed wildly on a trash-can kit, replete with his trademark bare feet. The barely constructed stages in these busted-up venues always felt as if they were about to blow into a hundred pieces. I used as much duct tape a I could to hold down my MXR Dis-tortion + box, but invariably, stage divers would get tangled up in my guitar cables and I would have to either block them with my body, spear them with the headstock of the Flying V, or boot them back into the crowd.

I was also concerned with protecting my teeth. If someone in the pit hurtled toward me while I happened to be in midverse, that person would usually slam into the mike stand, which would then smash the microphone into my mouth. Occasion-ally I'd wipe my bottom lip with the back of my hand and find bloody chunks of skin, like small pieces of red grapefruit pulp.

There was not a lot of money to be made by playing clubs like the Buddha or the Mabuhay; on a weeknight, you might be paid with eight bucks and a plate of spaghetti. But none of this—the fear of getting assaulted by the audience, the stolen, rotting food, the illnesses, the fraudulently obtained govern-ment assistance—ever struck me as difficult or odd. It was what we were doing; there was nothing else to do. We got to play music.

We had quickly worked ourselves up into a lather. It took us less than two years to convince ourselves that we were the best band in the world and that all we had to do was find a platform to tell people. We created this blistering wall of sound—bright white radio static with occasional melody, with words buried deep in the storm, as if encrypted for shortwave transmission. The overall effect was blinding, bringing uncertainty and sometimes fear, not unlike emotions I had sometimes felt as a child. We were always grateful for the guidance and generosity of bands like D.O.A. and the Dead Kennedys—but when it was our time to take the stage, we were not going to let anybody get in our way.

I wanted Hüsker Dü to be the best band at all times.

And I could get anything done, maybe because I got myself so worked up about being the best. I had an incredible power of persuasion. If I got a thought in my head, I could make it happen—*to a fault*. I think that power came down to a mixture of testosterone, cheap speed, alcohol, and a lot of ambition. I could get people to change what they were thinking.

*   *   *

After San Francisco, we played an Indian reservation in Reno with D.O.A.; the flyer listed us as "Who Screwed You." There was a forgettable gig in Sacramento and then one last show with the Kennedys at the Mabuhay. After that we said farewell to San Francisco and began a forty-hour, 2,100-mile nonstop drive to Chicago.

One of the more memorable parts of that journey was entering Utah from the west on Interstate 80 and driving through the Bonneville Salt Flats. It was a vast expanse of light-grey salt, occasionally punctuated by signs reminding drivers to "stay on the road" (there were a few slushy areas). Since 1914, nearly all land speed records had been set at the salt flats, a fact not lost on us at the time.

When we arrived in Chicago, we went straight to O'Banion's, a punk rock club where DC's Minor Threat and their Ohio friends the Necros were playing. I thought these two bands were

something like oompah hardcore. They were missing the antici-
pation in the backbeat, and it sounded like polka music. We'd
heard about their straight-edge thing; Hüsker Dü was definitely
not a straight-edge band.

The Naked Raygun folks, Jeff and Patty Pezzati in particular, very graciously put up Grant and Greg for a few days. I
found other accommodations. The night of our first Chicago
show, I had befriended a handsome Hispanic fellow named
Richard. He was military, stationed at the Great Lakes naval
reserve outside Chicago. After the show, I went back to his studio apartment in Boystown, a somewhat seedy gay neighborhood. We spent the rest of the weekend together. He and I drove
together to Madison, where the band played the final show of
Children's Crusade '81.

Gays in the hardcore punk scene were much like gays in the
military: if the military says, "Don't ask, don't tell," the hardcore punk corollary was "Don't advertise, don't worry." If
someone made a disparaging remark about gays, I would
simply say, "That's not cool," or, "You're so ignorant." It was a
way to make my feelings known without broadcasting my
sexuality.

Generally, there was no more homophobia in the hardcore
scene than anywhere else in America, although as 1981 progressed, the media began reporting on the "gay cancer," and
homophobia escalated throughout the country. Numberwise,
the hardcore scene didn't seem any more or less populated by
homosexuals than most major cities were. Then again, the scene
attracted the margin walkers, the folks who were outside the
norms of society, so maybe there was a slightly higher ratio of
gays to straights. There were bands that were clearly antigay—
Bad Brains immediately comes to mind—but I don't recall a lot
of hostility toward the gays. There was a greater common
enemy: Reagan, the president who couldn't address the AIDS
crisis in a public forum until September 1985, three months
after his old Hollywood friend Rock Hudson was diagnosed

with AIDS. It only took him another two years to actually utter the word *AIDS*.

That first trip left a deep impact on a number of levels. We realized we weren't alone in the fight to change the direction of modern music. We'd learned how to travel together without agitating each other, which would be key to the success of future tours. We appreciated the kindness and generosity of other bands along the way. We became a really good live band—better than almost anyone else we'd seen. Most importantly, though, I had a three-day fling with a Navy guy. Kidding... sort of.

Our homecoming show was Saturday, August 15, 1981, at 7th Street Entry, and Steve Fjelstad recorded both sets on a reel-to-reel four-track. The first set comprised the faster, more aggressive material we'd been showcasing during our tour. If the Ramones were fast, and the Buzzcocks were faster, and the Dickies were even faster, that meant Hüsker Dü needed to be the fastest band in the world. After months of rushing onto a stage and packing fifty minutes of songs into thirty minutes, we accomplished that feat by necessity.

People absolutely came unglued during the first set. It was clear to everyone that the band had changed greatly in the past three months. Before we left, there was breathing room in our performances; now that breathing room had been replaced with a claustrophobic, frenetic intensity that reflected our eye-opening experiences on the road, our elevated ambitions, and our burning need to upstage any band in sight, including our local contemporaries, the Replacements.

The homecoming gig was the perfect way to wrap up that huge summer. We covered a lot of land. We took a lot of speed. And we made a record.

CHAPTER 5

After recording the homecoming show at 7th Street Entry, we spoke with Mike Watt and sent him a rough mix of the first set, the faster, more intense one. New Alliance was an upstart label, but we had a good feeling about Watt and he was eager to release our record. This was an important moment for the band—after meeting with resistance from Twin/Tone, we'd found acceptance in the punk capital of California. Equally as important, we'd begun to forge a relationship with Black Flag and, ultimately, that would lead us to SST Records. There was also the simple thrill of knowing we would have a full-length album release, even if it was only a live set recorded on a three hundred dollar budget.

I had no idea then how far the music I was playing had strayed from the music I'd enjoyed as a child. But we were young and full of testosterone. I was twenty turning twenty-one. The evolution was environmental as much as any sort of conscious choice. We had to adapt to survive, and this abrasive white-static roar was the new mutation. This is what we had to offer because it was what we had to work with.

But really, a song called "Guns at My School"? What did that have to do with "Happy Jack"? There was nothing happy in a song about firearms on campus—it turned out to be rather prescient though. "MTC" was a gripe about the bus routes of the Twin Cities. "Push the Button" was an obvious nod at the looming nuclear threat that was part of the collective consciousness in the early 1980s; many truly feared that Reagan was trigger-happy and were mortified that he actually had the power to obliterate the earth. "Bricklayer" and "Ultracore" were two of my attempts to raise the bar of hardcore—we were punker than punk. There's no lasting value to the words though. They fall into the "blind rage" school of hardcore. "Gilligan's Island" and "Do the Bee" just added a veneer of levity to our two-by-four-swinging approach to the set.

I took the tapes to a Christian mastering house in Gary, Indiana. I picked that place for two reasons: one, the irony of having a religious facility master the album, and two, to visit my Navy pal Richard in nearby Chicago. I went straight to Richard's apartment in Boystown and was greeted at the door by a rather large and ruggedly handsome jarhead. He looked as if he'd just woken from a deep sleep. He told me Richard didn't live there anymore, and was very short with me. It didn't take me too long to figure out that they'd been boyfriends, Richard had been sleeping around, and now I was left with nowhere to stay.

I headed to O'Banion's and ran into Ray Morris, singer for the punk band Six Feet Under. I told him a truncated version of my predicament, and he offered to let me stay with him and his girlfriend. I graciously accepted his offer. It took one afternoon to master the tapes, and I left the sessions with an acetate to play for the other guys. The sound quality wasn't stellar, but the finished recording had a vibrancy and spark that represented the band well.

That September, after Hüsker Dü played a show with Dead Kennedys in Chicago, John Cale appeared backstage, offering his production services. He was intoxicated and kept trying to hug us and lift us off the ground. Despite his undeniable influence on the previous two decades of modern music, we politely declined his kind offer, as we were a little surprised and unnerved by his behavior. But the fact that Cale had heard about the band was surprising, and it signaled how quickly our reputation was spreading.

* * *

In November 1981 a burly club bouncer named Fred Gartner came to me with the idea of opening a club in the upper level of a downtown bar/strip club called Goofy's. 7th Street Entry had found it difficult to book all-ages shows, so we aimed to fill that void. We named the room Goofy's Upper Deck and started promoting shows with UK hardcore bands like Discharge and US touring acts like Black Flag, the Minutemen, and Meat Puppets. We also tried to showcase many up-and-coming Minnesota hardcore and punk bands. 7th Street Entry was less than two blocks away, but their talent buyer and promoter, Steve McClellan, quickly made his peace with us. Steve was my primary mentor in terms of booking, and he showed me how clubs made deals with agents, how to spot false expenses, and how to make the most favorable deal for the band. (Goofy's lasted almost two years before getting closed down after a miniriot.)

At the time, I was living in southeast Minneapolis with two of the Veggies, Tippy Roth and Dick Madden, in the second and third floors of an old house across the street from one of the first Target stores in America. It was a place to hang my hat for the better part of a year. It was also the house in which I experienced my first Minnesota tornado. One summer afternoon the sky went still and turned an ominous grey green. Suddenly a funnel popped into view, and I ran for the cellar. When I came up moments later, the roof from a nearby house sat, nearly intact, in the middle of the street.

That Christmas I went to SuperAmerica, a regional chain of gas station/convenience stores, and bought turkey dogs for my solo Christmas dinner. The heater in the house had gone out that week; the water pipes froze, then burst, turning the stairwell into a solid sheet of ice. The landlord tried shimmying up the handrail, but it broke under his weight and he tobogganed down the stairs, crashing in a heap by the front door.

Nineteen eighty-two began with the January release of *Land Speed Record* on New Alliance Records. At the same time, Biafra offered us a European release on his Alternative Tentacles label, which we quickly accepted. The cover was a clear political statement: an archival photo of flag-draped coffins coming home from the Vietnam War. It also held an inside meaning: there were three caskets in the foreground of the photo, a subtle reference to how we felt at the end of that first national tour.

In a November 1980 issue of the Minneapolis arts weekly *Sweet Potato,* local critic Terry Katzman may have described Hüsker Dü's sound best: "A familiar guitar hook or riff occasionally surfaces, but before you place it, it disappears. The band exists on the sheer strength of its music, nothing else."

In February we went back to Blackberry Way Studios to record three songs—"In a Free Land," "What Do I Want," and "MIC"—for the *In a Free Land* single. The cover was a photograph of an actual flag-burning we staged at Macalester, thematically continuing the incorporation of the American flag. My two contributions, "In a Free Land" and "MIC," were political rants; I'd already reached the zenith of my "antiestablishment" songwriting phase. This was not only the most professional-sounding recording we'd made to date (out of two), but "In a Free Land," in particular, showed a huge jump in my songwriting quality from my typical white-hot noise to a melodic, anthemic statement of dissatisfaction.

New Alliance quickly released the single in May, and we planned another tour to promote the single. We were beginning to build a catalog of songs, in addition to having more records to sell at shows.

You can imagine that my attention span for college was waning, and my grades were hardly stellar. I was very close to getting my degree in urban studies, but it had become apparent that music was my calling. Music had gotten me through my childhood, music was the language I spoke with the other two members of my band—and people were listening to what we had to say. After traveling the country, performing music at a breakneck speed for what was arguably a lunatic fringe audience, and being accepted by our forefather bands, it was a no-brainer: it was time to drop out of college.

My parents were not thrilled with this news but understood my passion for music. My father was the source of so much turmoil throughout my early years, and yet he was also the one who helped bring music into my life; he was actually quite understanding about my musical ambitions. Maybe it was the former air force saxophonist in him, but he wisely chose not to deny or denigrate his son's desires—the chance he never had. But my aunt June, who had strongly supported my desire for higher education, heard the news and immediately concluded that I was driving around the country selling drugs.

That June we set off on a national tour, bringing along stage tech Robin Davies, a friend of ours who played bass with the Madison, Wisconsin, band the Tar Babies. We got off to a great start when the owner of a club in Lincoln, Nebraska, didn't want to pay us our agreed to fifty bucks. We took two of the club's microphones hostage and were planning to come back later and break the large plate-glass window in front of the club if he didn't settle up. He paid us.

We spent a few days in Boulder with local band White Trash, crashing in their rehearsal garage and eating free happy-hour food at an Irish-Mexican restaurant they worked at during the day. Then we went through western Canada, including two more nights at the Calgarian Hotel, and Seattle, where we played with the Fastbacks, who put us up too. Fastbacks drummer Duff McKagan, who eventually wound up as the bassist in Guns N' Roses, would come to the Fastbacks House, wanting to watch MTV. But we'd commandeered the TV room to watch pro wrestling, and we didn't relinquish control. I can neither confirm nor deny the ongoing rumor of a bed being broken by one of the members of Hüsker Dü—all I can say with certainty is that it wasn't me.

Back in San Francisco we once again stayed with Biafra and Theresa for a few days. For our last night, we were put up by the militantly political hardcore band MDC. They and some other punks were squatting at an abandoned Hamm's beer brewery called the Vats where they'd skateboard by day and sleep at night. MDC were nice guys, but a bit edgy—there was a lot of biker speed going around the San Francisco scene at the time. We slept in one of the large brewery tubs that evening, and Robin was out in the van with the equipment. The following morning, Robin came in to gather us up to leave and found himself in the hallway face-to-face with a snarling Doberman. The guy who owned the building had showed up unannounced, with huge dogs. He had a rather large tumor on one side of his head. He released the dogs into the vats, so now we're in this big cement bowl with the dogs. We got out of the vat as quickly as possible, just hightailed it out of there. That was adrenaline for you.

After playing a show in San Diego with Battalion of Saints, we arrived for the first time in Los Angeles and met the entire SST crew. We'd met Greg Ginn and Black Flag bassist Chuck Dukowski at the "blue paint" show in Chicago, but this was my first meeting with the band's singer, Henry Rollins. Rollins was an intense individual, a physical yet cerebral type of guy. He was into weight lifting, writing in his journals, being the newest lead singer of Black Flag, and not much else that I could see. Quiet and diminutive, Joe Carducci was SST's operations manager. Mugger, the notorious Black Flag roadie and zany lead vocalist of the controversial Nig-Heist, was around the office on a daily basis, and eventually became the label's accountant.

The SST office was a ground-floor space, no more than seven hundred square feet, located on a somewhat busy corner near Artesia Boulevard in Lawndale. There were several desks, their record stock, assorted musical paraphernalia, and, in the back, a small bathroom with a tiny shower. Carducci and Rollins lived there, sleeping under their desks. Rollins offered to sleep elsewhere so that one of us could sleep under his desk, which I found particularly charming and touching, adding another dimension to his personality.

Spot, a slightly eccentric yet affable guy, was Black Flag's recording engineer. We were thrilled to have him oversee the two-day sessions for *Everything Falls Apart,* which we recorded at Total Access Studios in Redondo Beach. When we weren't at Total Access, we were enjoying the California sunshine and eating chili fries, burgers, government cheese, and the various fruits and vegetables that SST would buy for the office. We played basketball with Greg and his brother, the artist Raymond Pettibon. Pettibon created the iconic sexually charged antipolice illustrations that would adorn many Black Flag records and show posters. Dukowski handled live bookings for SST bands under the name Global Booking, and while in the office, I asked him and Carducci lots of questions about the music business.

The Minutemen would drop by fairly often, and we always enjoyed spending time with those guys. George Hurley, the drummer, was more of a "ladies man" than anyone in the SST entourage; Mike Watt, the bassist-vocalist-songwriter, was always up for a heated political discussion; D. Boon, the guitarist-vocalist-songwriter, was upbeat and amicable, no matter what was happening around him. Watt and Boon were extremely giving of their time, energy, and resources.

But our tour rolled on, and after a quick stop in Tucson, we played the Ritz in Austin, and people threw beer cans at us, which may or may not have been a show of endearment— always hard to tell in Austin. We played that show with local punk / performance art group the Dicks and stayed with their flamboyant lead singer, Gary Floyd, whose house was decorated with kitschy tchotchkes and sex toys. Austin was a progressive place with plenty of colorful folks, like the Big Boys, whose guitarist, Tim Kerr, helped build a thriving skate scene in nearby Pflugerville, and whose hilariously provocative lead singer, Biscuit, was also a fine visual artist.

Then it was on to Dallas, where we stayed with the guys from the Hugh Beaumont Experience: King Coffey, Brad Stiles, and Phil Flowers. A couple of those guys would figure in my life later, and this is where the first connection was made. Then back to the Ritz in Austin, where people threw empty beer cans at us again. Then Houston, playing with CH3 and the Circle Jerks, and on it went.

We went back to San Diego for a multiband show with Battalion of Saints and Minor Threat, the straight-edge band I'd scoffed at back at O'Banion's in Chicago. I had not gone one day without a drink since the age of thirteen. In my adult life, it was a three beer daily minimum, and, on a long night, upwards of twenty beers. I had little time for rules, and straight edge was one of my early glimpses into the contradictions of hardcore punk. For all the anarchy, the "no rules" posture, there sure seemed to be a lot of rules: don't drink, don't smoke, don't fuck. This did not sit well with me. I was not going to conform to this notion. So after sound check, we scattered aspirin all over the stage, and when Minor Threat came up to play, there were pills everywhere. No one from their band said anything to us, but Robin Davies remembers things being a little tense. Spreading the aspirin around made a clear statement about what side of the fence I was on. A childish stunt, yes. Antagonistic, probably. Mean-spirited, definitely not.

Up next, the LA show at the Olympic Auditorium was a six-band extravaganza featuring Black Flag, D.O.A., 45 Grave, and the Descendents. When I was a kid, the Olympic had wrestling and roller derby every week, and I'd watch those matches on TV or see photos in the wrestling magazines. In the background of a lot of those shots was a sign that said THE OLYMPIC and listed the phone number RI9-5171. So when I walked in and looked at the place, I already knew that sign and the familiar array of blue seats. I felt like I was in one of the Seven Wonders of the World. We were on second, and people were climbing the PA and diving off fifteen feet into the crowd. It was very hardcore stuff. These days you don't usually go into shows where you feel like you might not come out alive—or even just different, somehow changed.

That show was a gathering of the punk tribes. D.O.A. was classic punk from Vancouver; 45 Grave were a Hollywood goth band; Descendents were a power-pop punk outfit on New Alliance; Black Flag brought their own rougher crowd. There was always a bit of tension around these large shows. For example, if TSOL were on the bill, then they'd draw the prone-to-violence Orange County crowd. The Olympic was neutral territory. There were maybe 2,500 people in attendance; the floor seemed filled.

For the remainder of the year, the band stayed in the Midwest, and in the fall of 1982, we signed a recording contract with SST Records, becoming their first non–West Coast artist. Due partially to our naiveté about recording contracts, our friendship with Greg Ginn, and our general awe of the SST scene, we signed without fully understanding the ramifications of certain passages. We were excited to work with SST and had no reason to doubt they were dealing with us in anything but an upstanding manner—and anyway, we were soon out on the road again, both in preparation to support *Everything Falls Apart* in December and to record twelve songs with Spot at Total Access for what would become the seven-song *Metal Circus* EP.

We headed through Texas for more shows, including a fine Christmas dinner at an all-you-can-eat Mexican restaurant called Poncho's. We had an affinity for buffets—if you lined the pockets of your coat with wax paper or plastic bags ahead of time, you could take extra food for later in the day. Also, if you walked to the exit, where the cashier was stationed, there was always the chance that a simple request like "Where's the bathroom?" or "Where's the cigarette machine?" might get you to the other side of the turnstile, thereby avoiding paying for the meal.

I had a romantic interlude in the last six months of 1982. It was a big deal for me, being one of the first times I'd had strong feelings for another guy and openly pursued him. After the show in Dallas, the band had gone back to Fort Worth to stay at Brad Stiles's parents' house. That evening I had a sexual encounter with Brad, the singer of the Hugh Beaumont Experience. We tore into each other like animals.

After we got back to the Twin Cities in August, I took a Greyhound bus back down to Fort Worth to see Brad and King and spent several days with King in his father's unfinished two-room house on the outskirts of town. Various friends would come by and drive us into Fort Worth so that I could get drunk and crazy with Brad. This went on for many days. I took the bus back to Minnesota, hoping that something might come of this budding relationship. But when it came to parsing the intersection of heart and flesh, Brad was a wise seventeen and I was a stupid and naive twenty-two. He was very young, I was very busy, and there were a thousand miles between us. By the time I returned to Texas months later, Brad had moved on to another warm body, and I was politely rebuffed. I was confused for days, but I moved on. The band was always moving, leaning forward, and as hard as it was, there wasn't time to stop.

The Crystal Pistol in Tulsa, Oklahoma, was always an interesting club to play. We were friends with a local punk band called NOTA (None of the Above), and we played three times with them at the Pistol. The first time, I saw an Oklahoma cowboy ride his horse onto the dance floor. The third time we played there, a young mohawk punk was getting roughed up by a redneck. I intervened, he thanked me after the show with a curiously long handshake, and we ended up spending a drunken night together in a semiprivate bedroom of the NOTA house. That's one way to get over the confusion.

Running parallel to this tomfoolery was the January 1983 release of *Everything Falls Apart*. The album cover featured band-generated Rorschach test inkblots, one for each of the twelve songs. My title track showcased a nifty series of chord progressions that foreshadowed the songwriting depth to come — I say that looking back now. "Punch Drunk" was a commentary on the sometimes mindless violence I saw from the stage, complete with this curious line: "Take a look right in the mirror / What are you, a fucking queer?" Who, me? "Target" and "Obnoxious" were aimed squarely at the artsy crowd who were beginning to thumb their noses at the punk bands. "Signals from Above" was a quick diatribe about the bygone expiration date of the hippie movement. Looking back, those words I wrote are filled with irony — not just "fucking queer," but I would also eventually embark on a hippie-esque musical journey.

Album or not, I led a minimalist existence: I had a sleeping bag, a duffel bag of clothes, a guitar, an amp, and not much else. I put my stuff in the van and I went on the road. All my other belongings were in a wooden crate in someone's basement. It was a very spartan life, and it's not for everyone, but there were a lot of people who chose to live this way.

Across North America, hardcore kids, old-school punks, some metalheads, skateboarders, and surfers were going to hardcore shows. The skateboarding magazine *Thrasher* was a big part of building the scene; they wrote about various cities, not just places to skate, but also places to see bands that had an affinity with the skate community.

Indie rock culture wasn't invented on the internet, or in Williamsburg, Brooklyn. I went to the record stores and I watched other people browsing through records. Nothing is more telling than when someone pulls that one-square-foot piece of cardboard out of a bin filled with hundreds of similar pieces of cardboard. You're definitely going to look at what he's chosen. You see him pull out the Pat Benatar record, so you blow right by that person. But if he pulls *20 Jazz Funk Greats* by Throbbing

SEE A LITTLE LIGHT

Gristle, you perk up and take interest in what he might pull next. We'd do this dance around the record store with each other, and that was one way to find like-minded people. We don't do that dance now. Now you read someone's blog or use a search engine or do social networking.

Most people are passive consumers, the ones who hear something all over the radio and then buy the record or see the band at Madison Square Garden. Then there's the questioning, investigative type of person, the type who seeks out the new music—and that was us. There was a subculture that was making up its own rules, codes, and signifiers, regionally. We developed an eye for it when we visited other towns. You learn how to spot it, just like in the gay community where a business might put a rainbow flag on the door. You learn the different signifiers. You could ask somebody where the record store is, and if they told you Sam Goody, they didn't know. But if they said, "Oh, Skull and Bones is out in the abandoned strip mall," you knew it was the right kind of store. On tour, even visiting places you've never been before, you could figure out where to go within an hour. It was the people in those towns.

Those people were nonconformists, freethinkers—the kids who were probably ostracized in high school for reading poetry, for listening to different kinds of music, for being artistic. A lot of them came from broken homes, looking for a surrogate family. This was our fan base, the people who launched us; they were dissatisfied on virtually all fronts and they were looking beyond the normal forms of entertainment. That stuff was exclusive in that it was invisible unless you knew how to find it. Finding the music meant finding like-minded people. Then networks got built, bands got put up, notebooks got shared. Infrastructure and community. Hüsker Dü benefited from all that, and we also contributed to it. We gathered information and knowledge and gladly shared it with people who would take good care of it. It's not the kind of information we would share with the cover bands at the local bowling alley, the bands that weren't doing anything new, copying other people's work. But the bands that came through with original ideas, it was for them. Sure, there was filtering and exclusivity in it. But it wasn't meant to be for everybody.

The Replacements didn't seem to be too concerned with that network. At the time, they were also coming to prominence in the Twin Cities. They had Peter Jesperson watching over them, the manager who signed them to Twin/Tone after one show and took care of them (until he could no longer do so). Hüsker Dü, we were out scrapping and keeping it real, as the kids say these days. The Replacements were modeled on the traditional rock and roll motif, and the two bands were quite different in that sense.

Regardless, we were all cordial with each other. Singer-guitarist Paul Westerberg spent a lot of time at Peter Jesperson's apartment, and on occasion I joined in for long nights of drinking and drugging while Peter played what he considered to be seminal rock and roll records for the two of us and any other folks who might be around.

There was a healthy rivalry between Hüsker Dü and the Replacements. There was friendship too, like when Paul and I did some utterly forgettable demos on a four-track reel-to-reel recorder up in the attic of the Target house. They were stolen out of my van, along with a guitar amp. Don't worry, the stuff wasn't very good.

One day, Paul, Replacements drummer Chris Mars, and I were hanging out, killing a case of cheap local brew—most likely Grain Belt. We were fucking around with Dick Madden's IBM computer, which would make blips when you hit a key. That got old so we started listening to some of my jukebox singles. I can't remember which song it was, but I played one and Paul just lit up and said, "I love this song!" and asked if he could borrow the single. I said, "Sure, take it. Just be careful with it, and don't lose it." So he and Chris got on Chris's motorcycle, having had more than enough to drink, and headed back over to South Minneapolis. Chris was driving, and Paul was on the back holding the single. Something happened and a police car flagged them down. Paul must have egged on Chris to run the light, and they both ended up getting cuffed and taken downtown for processing. (The Replacements' song "Run It" tells the story better than I can.) But Paul was still clutching the single. He said he never let it go.

It was always nice to hang out with our fellow Twin Cities bands, great folks like Man Sized Action, Rifle Sport, Loud Fast Rules (later to find greater fame and fortune as Soul Asylum), and so many others. We had a lot of pride in our hometown scene and we bonded strongly. But in April of 1983, it was time to get in the van once again and make our first pilgrimage to the East Coast. All our connections were in the West Coast, Southwest, and Midwest; we didn't have much of an East Coast notebook. But we were finally getting our chance, our moment. We'd be playing for new audiences, especially in New York City, home of all the bands I grew up listening to and admiring, from Johnny Thunders to the Ramones.

CHAPTER 6

We started the spring tour in the Midwest, with our four-year anniversary gig at First Avenue in Minneapolis. First Avenue was originally a bus depot in downtown Minneapolis. It became a nightclub in 1970, and 7th Street Entry was the coat check before becoming its own 300-capacity music room. First Avenue had been a cornerstone of the Midwest rock scene for years, and to play the 1,200-capacity main room was the goal of many a Midwest musician.

In Chicago we played the Cubby Bear Lounge, right by Wrigley Field; we stayed at a punk house nearby known as Big Blue—you would see it during Cubs games, a blue four-story house out past left field. That was the show where I noticed a skinny, geeky kid staring at me the whole time, watching everything I was doing. Turned out his name was Steve Albini. He was usually at those early Chicago shows, asking lots of questions after the set. He was a pleasant guy back then.

Our Chicago posse expanded to include the band Articles of Faith; lead singer Vic Bondi was a very astute individual, intense and learned, and he brought that same relentless focus that Rollins and Dukowski had. Vic was a force, always ready to make a statement, defend his position, yet he was able to listen to the opposition and parse their words for some shared belief. In the coming years I produced a couple of Articles of Faith albums.

Technically moving east, we then played at the Jockey Club in Newport, Kentucky. Squirrel Bait opened, an unbelievable band, tight, melodic, and energetic. It was an encouraging sign to see that bands like this could develop in places like Kentucky. And onward to Philadelphia, where we played the first of many shows to come at the West Side Club, which was an old row house. The show was a glorified keg party, but we made good money. It was a regular stop for many of the punk and hardcore bands, and every time we played there, we drew a bigger crowd—eventually to the point where we had to start beaming closed-circuit TV to the rest of the house. Jon Wurster, who went on to play drums in Superchunk, as well as my own band, was at those shows. After Philadelphia, it was time for our New York City debut.

It was April 17, 1983, a matinee show at a small hardcore dive called Great Gildersleeves—just around the corner from CBGB. A New York band called the Young and the Useless opened, then the Replacements, and Hüsker Dü headlined. Young and the Useless demanded, and got, one hundred bucks; the promoter said the Replacements were lucky to be on the bill and didn't pay them anything.

I'd been thinking and dreaming about New York City since I was a kid in Malone, poring through *Rock Scene*. Now, here I was, surrounded by the concrete and brick walls and leather jackets, the dirt and the grime and the violence. New York's music scene had left an impression on me, and now I wanted to leave an impression on it. Some people carve their initials in a tree or draw a name and date in fresh cement. All I had was my voice, my guitar, and a late afternoon audience in a quasi–biker bar on the Bowery.

All in all, it was a fine show. But all the pent-up tension came to a head at the end of the set. That's when I went off. Pulling my hands away from the guitar, letting the feedback build into a shrill wail, I pressed my head between my hands like in Edvard Munch's *The Scream* and let out an ungodly howl.

We played another show later that evening at City Gardens in Trenton, New Jersey, and I realized that my catharsis didn't debilitate me, or get me sent home for counseling—we'd carried on to the next place and turned in another solid show.

One of the bartenders at City Gardens was a funny guy named Jon Leibowitz. With that job, he must have seen a lot of cool shows. He eventually changed his name to Jon Stewart and got himself a TV show. And now he has a good theme song and I have a nice house. But more about that later. In fact, a lot of interesting people came out of that whole scene. Back in Minneapolis there was Lizz Winstead, who went on to become one of the creators of *The Daily Show* and was just starting her career; Tom Arnold, who was eating goldfish onstage between sets at 7th Street Entry; and Jesse Ventura, ranting and raving on TV during Sunday morning wrestling well before he became the governor of Minnesota.

We were quickly discovering that the East Coast had a unique mentality that might be summed up best in two words: college rock. A lot of it came down to the clustering of high-quality schools in the Northeast, particularly in the Boston area, where the tour took us next. There were many more college radio stations in the Northeast than in the Midwest, and they gave rise to the likes of the Bongos, Violent Femmes, and the dB's, bands who had a more accessible, more melodic sound than hardcore.

REM was another of those bands, and they were really starting to conquer the Northeast. They made pilgrimages from their home base of Athens, Georgia, all the way up the Eastern Seaboard to Boston. They came to Minneapolis as well. So many people that we knew were cutting their teeth in the underground music scene, particularly in the Boston area. Julie Panebianco was writing for the fanzine *Matter*. "The Mystery Girls"—Sheena and Spencer Gates—had an awesome radio show on WMBR in Cambridge, Massachusetts. Lou Giordano was an engineer at Radiobeat, a small recording studio. Gerard Cosloy was doing his fanzine *Conflict*.

After playing Boston we continued down to Washington, DC, where we debuted at the venerable 9:30 Club. The club was famous for many things: it was in the shadow of Ford's Theatre, it was surrounded by the largest rats I had ever seen in my life, and the music room, when packed to its 300 capacity, would turn into a gigantic sauna. I remember one show when it became so hot onstage I thought I would pass out. In a feeble attempt to cool myself, I reached up to run my hand across a large pipe that ran above the stage. I had seen the condensation on the pipe and mistakenly thought it might have been cold water. Instead it was condensed human sweat—not quite as tasty as the pizza that the club was famous for serving to bands after their sets. Seth Hurwitz booked the club, and he and I have good personal and business relationships to this day.

The underground music scene was small enough then that a band like Hüsker Dü could become friends with a guy like Rick Rubin. At the time, Rick was living in an NYU dormitory, playing in his band Hose, and running a new label called Def Jam. Rick was very kind to Hüsker Dü, even bringing us out to stay for a few nights at his mom's house in Lido Beach, Long Island. A few months later, Hose supported Hüsker Dü on a couple shows in Wisconsin. Later in 1984, Rick played me some demos of a rap act he was keen on; I remember him saying that this guy was going to be big, but I had my doubts. "I dunno, Rick," I said, "I'm not really hearing it." The track he played me was "I Need a Beat" by LL Cool J. So much for me recognizing one of the other main directions of the future of music.

* * *

April 25, 1983, was a big night in my personal life. That's when I met my first boyfriend. Hüsker Dü played Benny's, a typical college/punk rock joint a few blocks from the Virginia Commonwealth University campus in Richmond. After the show these guys came up to us and said, "We're going to have a party at our recording studio, come on down and record a few songs."

We were pretty drunk by this point and had no place to stay, so we went and recorded a few instrumental tracks. It wasn't exclusively a punk rock party, but a mix of punks and new wavers, more of an art/college kind of crowd, which may have been an indication of things to come.

After recording, I was having a beer when I made eye contact with this really cute guy. He was five foot nine, 155 pounds, and had shocking red hair and a boyish smile. We sized each other up and smiled. But I had no gay social skills, and I was trying to figure a way to break the ice. He left the room to take a piss, and when he returned, I noticed his zipper was down. I took my umbrella, pointed to his crotch, and said, "Your pants are unzipped." He looked up and smiled, feigning embarrassment. That's how I met my first partner, Mike Covington. Mike was a real sweetheart, and studied art at VCU. He also played drums in a local art-rock band. He had a boyfriend at the time, an older guy, but was unhappy in that relationship. We spent the night at his place and stayed up until sunrise.

The next morning Grant and Greg picked me up. Greg made some wiseacre comment that I shrugged off with a "Whatever, I'm tired." Then I slept all the way to New York City.

We were back in New York for a show at Gerde's Folk City, the place where Bob Dylan had first made his mark. With assistance from *New York Rocker* writer and future Yo La Tengo singer-guitarist Ira Kaplan, Michael Hill booked newer bands at Folk City for a series he dubbed Music for Dozens. We played a quieter-than-normal set due to the club's sound restrictions. Then, after finishing our normal repertoire, we stretched out with a bunch of covers, including "Look Through Any Window" (the Hollies), "Don't Fear the Reaper" (Blue Öyster Cult), "Paint It Black" (the Rolling Stones), "Blue Wind" (Jeff Beck), and "Train Kept A-Rollin'" (Aerosmith style). The show was in stark contrast to the primal scream of Gildersleeves only ten days prior—perhaps a first glimpse into the band's next stage of looking back to the classic rock and pop I'd grown up on, while still moving relentlessly forward.

After the Folk City show, we headed home to await the October release of *Metal Circus,* which had been recorded in December 1982. This break also gave us time to work on our respective relationships, as well as planting the seeds for the music that would eventually become *Zen Arcade.*

Mike wanted out of his current relationship, so I urged him to move up to Minneapolis. Within a couple of months, he got accepted at the Minneapolis College of Art and Design. So in late summer, before school started, I drove down in the rusted orange van and gathered his stuff out of his Richmond apartment. Then we drove to his family's farm in South Boston, in Halifax County, Virginia.

I met his mother, who perhaps didn't fully grasp what was happening. For a Baptist woman like her, it was probably more than enough to see her son go to school in Richmond; now, out of nowhere, this wild-eyed guy comes and sweeps him and all of his stuff away to Minnesota. Mike and I pile his possessions, his mannequin, and his dog, Coco, into the van and drive 1,100 miles to Minneapolis. That was the beginning of our six-plus-year relationship.

I was proud, I was happy — I had a boyfriend.

We arrived at the apartment in Minneapolis, where I was renting a bedroom. When my roommate (who held the lease) came home that night, he saw Coco and said there was no way Mike and the dog could crash at the apartment. Mike and I scrambled for an alternative. Mike stayed in a ratty downtown flophouse for three weeks until we folded in together in a basement apartment in South Minneapolis. Mike was very outgoing and made friends pretty quickly. Some of our friends were gay and some were straight; they were mostly painters and sculptors and musicians and filmmakers. We didn't have a gay life, we just had our life. One guy's in a punk rock band, the other one's an artist. You could guess they're probably gay, or at least I would have thought so. But it wasn't a case of "It's Friday night, let's go to the gay bar and see our other gay friends." Everybody knew we were a couple, but even then, in the depths of the Reagan years, it wasn't that big of a deal. We didn't hide anything, but we didn't advertise it either.

I was in a group of people who were first ignored by the government and then demonized by the public because of ignorance. People were dying of AIDS, and in those days, they were dying fast. That scared the hell out of me. Even as a gay man, I didn't understand what was happening. I wasn't living in the Castro or the West Village, I didn't go to Fire Island—a lot of what I was hearing wasn't coming from the gay community, it was from distorted and perverse representations in the media. I was uneducated and misinformed because I wasn't an out gay man, I wasn't integrated, and I didn't live what most people would consider a gay life. I didn't have anybody who could tell me what was accurate and what was not.

So for a gay man in 1983, there was a bit of calm to be found in being faithful. For the three years I was at Macalester, I didn't act out sexually for fear of being found out. Now that I had a boyfriend, did I feel any better about being a gay man in the Reagan era? No. But I had a boyfriend, a partner, and a safe sexual framework. At the time, that meant a lot to me. Later I came to learn that those aren't the most important things to having a full life. But back then it seemed pretty good.

Looking back, I can see that the truly upsetting part of this period was that, as more of an aggressive masculine figure, I had very little time for the effeminate gay stereotype. For better or worse, that was my ignorant and sheltered rural upbringing. I had no role models and no exposure to gay culture. So when I was confronted with certain variants of gay life, it made me hate the fact that I was gay—not the act of gay sex, but the image that the media would hype up, or the one I kept in my head, of what a gay man was: queer, effeminate, camp. That was so far removed from how I perceived myself. But I was terribly ignorant of the diversity in the gay community. All I had was me and the media stereotype of what gay was, and the two were so far apart, I felt no connection.

* * *

Right around the release of *Metal Circus* was the beginning of a lot of changes, both for me and for the development of the band. In the studio I'd started using the unreliable and glitchy Eventide H910 Harmonizer on my guitar to shimmer the sound and take up more stereo space. The warbled pitching effect of the Eventide had a very crystalline edge, and the amphetamines I'd now used for three years probably had something to do with why I liked the sound.

The Flying V had a P-90 style pickup, which makes an overdriven rock sound. The Flying V shape is a visual representation of the sound, that rocketing *whoosh*. A lot of the Hüsker Dü guitar sound was just me trying to cover two guitar parts at once—holding a note, droning, doing chord progressions around a single note—combined with the little yellow box, the MXR Distortion + pedal. That's where the tone comes from, that box. Guitars have come and gone in my arsenal, but that box is still there. I always use it. That's the body and soul of the tone.

It was also the beginning of an introspective time for me. I was doing a lot of thinking and growing, and the songs on *Metal Circus* started to reflect this. The kinship I felt for hardcore was beginning to wane, and I was feeling repelled by its dogmatic ways. Maybe it's no coincidence that my songwriting also shifted from commentary about politics toward more personal topics. I talked about it a lot in interviews, and with the song "Real World" I put my music where my mouth was. "Real World" was a statement of intent: We are not a strict political punk band. We are now a band. We are musicians now. Don't tell me about anarchy. I never thought anarchy could work as a social concept—the "scorched earth" theory, where you level everything and wait to see what rises from the ashes. That is an extreme social view. In music, however—as an idea that moves you—it is entirely plausible.

"First of the Last Calls" was a shout-out to the Replacements, based loosely on their song "Kids Don't Follow." "Diane" is one of Grant's finest songs ever and has been covered many times. "Out on a Limb," the exploratory closer, had angular and ringing guitars coming from all directions, disintegrating into layers of noise.

We were starting to slow things down so you could discern the melody. We weren't concerned how it would play in the hardcore world—it sounded right to us. We were beginning to march to our own unique beat and could only hope that the more enlightened fans might follow along.

CHAPTER 7

The basement apartment that Mike and I shared was as good as it had ever been for me: painted cement floors, a large rent-to-own console TV, and a worn-out padded black-vinyl rocking swivel chair. There was a sickly yellow kitchen, a bedroom with a mattress on the floor and clothes piled in boxes, one bathroom, and a couple of windows that looked out to the sidewalk.

I was still enjoying my drinking—as heavily as ever. Mike liked to drink as well, and we'd also smoke pot on occasion, but I'd gotten on a cheap wine kick and drank the better part of a five-liter box every day. After polishing off a box, I'd remove the shiny plastic liner and blow it up, then put it in a hammock that hung above the dining room table. The hammock was filled with dozens of blown-up shiny silver bags.

I was nearing the end of my speed phase though. I'd been using regularly for years, and it was starting to take a toll on me. Speed sent my energy level through the roof and made my thought processes incredibly intense, but it also lowered my libido. Now, with a boyfriend, speed wasn't my drug of choice.

I must say, amphetamines made me a pretty good interview subject. "Things can be changed by just making a few people wake up," I proclaimed to my old college roommate Phil Sudo for the Macalester student paper. "One way to do that is to kick 'em in the face, like we try to do with our music. If they feel threatened enough, they'll respond. The only way modern politics keeps forging ahead is by groups threatening the established order." That was the speed talking.

* * *

A place called the Church, in East St. Paul, played a prominent part in the development of Hüsker Dü in 1983. A couple of Grant's friends had bought a former church, and he ingratiated himself into it, living in a tent he'd pitched in the middle of the basement. The band rehearsed at the Church for free—a real sweetheart deal. It was a place where a lot of people lived and did LSD, and people were coming and going all the time, looking for a place to get their kicks: loners, kids with little or no money. Sometimes we had gigs there, but more often than not, the police would show up and it would endanger the somewhat illegal arrangement.

The Church was the place where we put together many of the musical ideas for *Zen Arcade*. There was a lot of improvisation, jamming, and switching instruments. Grant and Greg had a history of taking acid and mushrooms. I never had a desire to do acid; it seemed like speed plus color, and that didn't appeal to me. But I quickly realized that if I was around a bunch of people who were tripping, I didn't really need to take acid anyway. After a while, I felt a contact high—I could see it in the air. I felt a bit left out, socially speaking, but it was my choice. Outside of rehearsals I was spending most of my time with Mike and not socializing much with Grant and Greg beyond the work. At that point, we were listening to a lot of psychedelic music, garage music, music from the early Minneapolis scene, the fiery '60s Minneapolis garage band the Litter, in particular. I was starting to really dig into classic albums by the Byrds, as well as obscure bands like Fifty Foot Hose, Michelangelo, and H. P. Lovecraft.

I had strong feelings about the '60s counterculture, but they cut both ways. "We're doing the same thing that the peace movement did in the '60s, but the way they did it didn't work," I told Mike Hoeger of *City Pages*. "They sat in the park and sang with folk guitars. We take electric guitars and blast the shit out of them over and over again until the message sinks in. We're saying the same thing they did, that you're not going to screw us around, you're not sending me to war to fight for Dow Chemical or some outrageous reason. We're not going to be passive. We'll fight back our own way. We don't want to preach, we just want to pose questions and get people to think for themselves by reading and not watching the tube."

By openly acknowledging my '60s musical predecessors, and through deeper examination of their large-scale works (*Quadrophenia, Tommy, Sgt. Pepper*), I began to contemplate the idea of a concept album. Remember, I was twenty-two, and I was drinking, smoking, and still speeding. There was a lot going around in my head about trying to make a bigger statement, something of lasting value. And I went on record with these grand notions during an interview with Steve Albini for *Matter* magazine:

> *Right now we're at a stage where we have to think things through in a big way. We're going to try to do something bigger than anything like rock and roll and the whole puny band touring idea. I don't know what it's going to be, we have to work that out, but it's going to go beyond the whole idea of "punk rock" or whatever.*

We were not digging the punk rock rules and regulations. What better way to rebel than to make a double album? That would be a grand statement for us to make at a pivotal moment in the development of the band. We were ambitious—we'd done a single, a live album, an EP, an album, and then a long EP. We were seasoned and we were ready. The critical acclaim was starting to roll in. It was time to put up or shut up.

*　*　*

But we hadn't had a lot of time to sit around and conceptualize the next album. We just rehearsed, toured, and recorded. We might talk about it at the bar or over the occasional lunch. Mostly things would work themselves out during breaks at practice; we'd stop playing, start chatting, and ideas would develop. We would socialize under the guise of rehearsing. We were together almost all the time on tour. A lot of ideas came to me while traveling.

Album titles fall out of the sky. They come from non sequiturs, riffing and spilling words alongside the other two guys, word association, the freedom of thinking out loud. It's a neutral, communal way of conceptualizing things. Word association is absurdist, a noncommittal dialogue, but when an idea begins to resonate, it becomes part of the shared vernacular. When an idea works for everyone, becomes something that all three people feel comfortable saying, it sticks. For one thing, that's how we got the name of the band.

We would compose songs alone and come together later to learn how to play them. We'd learn the music and then the words would be revealed later, either late in the rehearsal stage, at the recording sessions, or even as late as the first public performance of the song. There were times we would do a tour and I wouldn't even know what Grant's songs were about. I really had no idea. It was almost as if the emotional content of the songs was a secret.

This was also a by-product of playing on stages with lousy monitor systems. If we learned the songs without relying on lyrical cues, we wouldn't get lost when we couldn't hear the vocals. Same with the harmonizing—Grant and I would rarely work those out. It was a very natural thing, the way we sang together. When recording, the lead vocal would go down and then the other singer would take shots at different backing vocals. Performances and ideas would be met with approval or indifference—we'd never come right out and say we didn't like something. Once we made our choices, we'd balance the layers of vocals and sit them back a little bit in the mix. It made the music seem louder, and, hopefully, the listener would spend more time with the lyric sheet.

Touring so much, we'd figured out various strategies for staying sane and on good terms with each other. Amid the noise and stink and chaos of the road, the van was our only sanctuary. Once we got out of the van, punk rock was all around us. So we kept the van very clean, for one thing. And while we drove from town to town, there was very little talking for hours on end. We barely even played music in the van. It was a time to recharge and rest. Greg drove while Grant and I often slept, just to save our voices.

The dynamic in the van was very respectful. We all smoked, so that wasn't a problem for anyone. And if someone saw something on the side of the road, some goofy roadside attraction, we'd always pull over and take a look, no questions asked. We had no money so we took our kicks where we found them.

Now and then we'd turn on the radio, which was very regional: in the Midwest you'd hear news about grain prices, in the South it was gospel music and obituaries. You got a sense of the way people lived, not just through the radio, but from everything on the road. Driving through the Northwest, you'd smell freshly cut wood. All that stuff is disappearing now.

Early in the October 1983 tour, we were driving through a winding mountain pass on I-84 on the way to Arcata, California. A major snowstorm had just blown through the area, and we were traveling behind a large slow-moving truck that was clearing the accumulation of snow and slush in front and throwing salt behind. Not being the most patient crew, we decided to overtake the plow. Greg signaled and accelerated, heading the van toward the apparent opening ahead of the plow. As we went by the truck, the flying snow landed with a thud on our van, covering the windshield with wet, heavy slush. The wipers stopped working. So now we're on a winding mountain road and we can't see a thing.

I was riding shotgun, and Grant was seated behind Greg. Instead of panicking, the three of us came together to overcome this dire situation. I could barely see where we were headed, but I was trying to describe the road ahead to Greg. Grant locked Greg's door and climbed out the driver's side window, clearing slush from the windshield. Greg clutched the wheel, and through this group effort, we somehow avoided skidding off the winding mountain pass. That may have been the band's finest moment—keeping that van on the road.

*　*　*

Zen Arcade started like all albums do: a few songs here, a few general ideas there. But at some point we realized that it could be so much more and ambition kicked in. We didn't sit down and say, "Let's write a semiautobiographical opera; let's amalgamate the fact that Greg's parents are divorced, Grant's situation is this, and Bob's conundrum is that, and weave it all together." There wasn't a conscious effort to construct a composite character, but that seems to be the end result of the writing for *Zen Arcade*.

The early '80s marked the beginning of video game culture, and we used that as the jumping-off point for the album's loose plot: a bright kid leaves his broken home and heads to Silicon Valley to design a computer game called "Search." We started writing songs and loosely creating characters: the kid who designed the video game, his girlfriend, Pinkie, his cigar-smoking boss. It built from late 1982 through most of 1983. Once we saw what was happening with the narrative, the flow of the album became clear, and it became easier to put things in order.

We recorded *Zen Arcade* with Spot at Total Access at the end of October 1983. Throughout the sessions I was operating in a blur of alcohol and a last dance with speed, but I know we spent forty-five hours for setup, basic tracks, overdubs, and vocals. The three of us were in the live room at Total Access, which felt like a big garage. One of the first things we did was brew a pot of coffee. For this first pot, we added a gram of crystal meth to the coffee grounds, for a little extra kick. After a cup or two, I was more than perked up and quite ready to get to work.

There was a hitch though. Spot had bought used recording tape because it was cheaper than fresh reels. The tape turned out to be the sixteen-track master from a TV broadcast by the Bee Gees, and it needed to be erased before use. The sixteen-track recording didn't line up with the twenty-four-track machine, so Spot had to improvise a little spacing gimmick using pencils. This process added hours to the initial session, which left me drinking more "coffee," some beer, and chomping even harder at the bit.

Since we typically recorded our basic tracks (drums, bass, rhythm guitar) in one take, we used the Byrds' "Eight Miles High" as the warm-up track, not wanting to wear out any of the original songs. My vocal performance on that track was beyond intense though. It was straight from the primal core—like the wailing of an abandoned child or a stricken lone coyote howling on the side of the road. Little did I know that this version, which appeared on a single and preceded the album release by a few months, would set the stage for so much of the attention that *Zen Arcade* would eventually receive.

Most of the tracks were indeed first takes. We always preferred those because you're not overanalyzing what you're doing. We moved quickly through basic tracks, then on to guitar overdubs, vocals, keyboards, and percussion.

We established the general sequence of the album before we recorded. On side three, we created two piano interludes to bridge songs in unsympathetic keys. "Somewhere" was in D, and so in order to get to "Pink Turns to Blue," which was in C-sharp minor, Grant and I constructed "One Step at a Time." Similarly, we needed a musical bridge between "Newest Industry" (in F-sharp) and "Whatever" (in G). This time, I wrote a descending piano motif in F-sharp, but instead of using composition to move the listener's brain up a semitone, we gradually increased the speed of the twenty-four-track machine while mixing the song to the stereo master. As the track plays, the gradual rise in pitch is barely noticeable, but listen to the first five seconds, then the last ten seconds, and the key change is surprisingly obvious.

The album was mixed in one forty-hour session. I suspect the main reason for this rather foolish move was that we had a show in Phoenix and we wanted to drive away with a finished version. Some of the mixes certainly suffered due to this marathon approach—there is no way anyone's hearing can stay fresh enough to mix a double album in one forty-hour sitting.

* * *

I wrote a lot of the words to *Zen Arcade* in the back of what we affectionately called "the pimpmobile," a tricked-out van done up with rust-colored shag carpeting and a collapsible purple velour platform bed. This was the second van that my father had driven the twelve hundred miles from Malone just so his son could travel safely with his bandmates.

Many nights, parked in front of SST while Grant and Greg were sleeping under a desk or in a corner of the office, I'd be writing beneath the dull dome light in the back of that van. I scribbled for hours and hours, filling notebook after notebook with uncertainty, anger, and self-hatred. Later I'd review what I'd written in the heat of the moment, then trim it down into two- and three-minute songs.

Right before I met Mike, I'd been hung up on a young guy in Minneapolis. He was beautiful and I fell for him instantly. We saw each other for a week, but it didn't work out. I was angry, thinking I was never going to get a break. I ended up with a wonderful boyfriend in Mike, but at the time, I felt a lot of anger and frustration, mostly at myself. I'd let myself fall head over heels for this kid, even though he clearly wasn't interested in trying to build on our week of young lust.

I had a lot of issues with my parents then. Since when hadn't I? But not being open with them about my sexuality was one of the biggest. During a phone call in 1980, my father acknowledged, in a hostile way, that he thought I was a "fag." In the same breath, he again threatened violence against my mother. Even from a distance, and despite the support he'd given me, he knew he could use this as a way to try to control everyone and everything.

My father was going to do what he was going to do, and my mother had made the choice to stay with him. I had to learn to separate myself from this dysfunctional family dynamic. That's the life they made for themselves, but I couldn't be part of it any longer. Maybe that was supposed to be the cinematic moment when the son rises up to the father, confronts and defeats him, and becomes his own man. I only remember thinking, You're a crazy person, and I don't have any more time for you. Boom.

A lot of this stuff—the blinding rage, the expression of youthful confusion, and the bumpy passage to adulthood—found its way to *Zen Arcade*. There's a poetic irony to all of this: writing those words, crafting them into these fiery balls of uncertainty, preparing them for what I knew would be a momentous recording session—almost all done in the back of that van, yet another gift my dad gave to me.

* * *

The upbeat but cautionary "Something I Learned Today" was a not-so-vague LSD allegory that set the psychedelic tone for what was to follow. It was grabbing at images that were going by my life's windshield: life in the van, the constant travel, my life on the road. Given that fact, "Chartered Trips" needs little explanation. "Broken Home, Broken Heart" was partly based on the fact that Greg's parents were divorced, and partly informed by my own family situation. "Never Talking to You Again" is clearly one of Grant's best songs.

A lot of side two is my blind rage and self-hatred, my failed relationships, and my confusing sex with love. That whole side was a blur while recording. It sounds like someone is being pounded into a gigantic pile of broken glass. Some of the words and ideas seem misguided now, but history has proven they're made of a lasting substance. Gay people have always pegged "The Biggest Lie" as a gay song, and it is, seeing as it was informed by a sexual misadventure with a straight friend. It was about me hoping an awkward physical tumble would turn into something more, and it not happening.

Before I went in to record the vocals, especially for the songs on side two, I really tried to take myself back to the emotional place where I first experienced those things. It was like what prizefighters do before a match—they go into this dream state, hitting themselves and babbling to get psyched enough to perform beyond their capabilities. I did stuff like that before I went in to record. To be blunt, I was out of my fucking mind, barking at people and scaring the shit out of everybody. It worked. You can hear the results on the record, but I'm sure it took its toll on the people in the room, Grant, Greg, and Spot.

"Whatever" dealt with my battles with my family, but less through anger and more through resignation.

Mom and Dad, I'm sorry
Mom and Dad, don't worry
I'm not the son you wanted, but what did you expect?
I've made my world of happiness to combat your neglect.

Grant's song "Turn On the News" made the Rock and Roll Hall of Fame's list of the "500 Songs that Shaped Rock and Roll," a great achievement for a song that I thought was a bit of a throwaway. In hindsight, though, the song's lightness and hope was the balance for the heaviness and despair that I so ably and amply dealt.

Side four, the thirteen-minute "Reoccurring Dreams," was certainly a stroke of luck. We were just jamming, improvising, playing the signature riff over and over again, and Spot reached over and turned on the two-track and happened to capture a really heady riff, with everyone just going off on alternating waves of tension and release. If not for that, we might have been short one side of a double album.

We recorded two additional songs of mine that didn't make the album, partly because they didn't fit into the narrative and partly because they simply weren't up to snuff, as well as that scorching cover version of "Eight Miles High." We could have used those instead of "Reoccurring Dreams," but it wouldn't have been quite the same, or as good, as the finished body of work that people know as *Zen Arcade*.

*   *   *

Zen Arcade is regarded as this momentous work that requires deep explanation. The fact was, we were rehearsing and touring nonstop, not spending a lot of time thinking about it. We were doing it. We were living it. It was a visceral statement. It felt right.

It's a very good record, but it's the sum total of the experience, of that moment, that grabbed people. Now I hesitate to say this, but here goes: *Zen Arcade* means a whole lot more to others than it does to me. I began to outgrow and move beyond those feelings almost at the moment I documented them, but the fact that they resonate so deeply with my audience, the critics, and generations of fellow musicians—there is the reward.

CHAPTER 8

We finished up the October 1983 tour with stops in Phoenix and Denver. In Phoenix we played a show with SST label mates the Meat Puppets at Madison Square Garden, a venue used primarily for local pro wrestling and boxing events. The ring was in the middle of the building, wrapped on three sides by a fifteen-foot-high cyclone fence, and served as the bouncy and unstable stage for music shows. Kids climbed the cage while bands thrashed through their sets. After the show, I recall riding around the back roads of Phoenix in the Meat Puppets' van while they chucked urine-filled mason jars out the windows.

In December we added a fourth member to the touring entourage. We'd met Lou Giordano, a lanky, brainy fellow with a wonderfully dry sense of humor, earlier in the year in Boston when we needed a last-minute soundman. Lou joined us for a short East Coast tour. At Lou's first gig with the band at Love Hall in Philadelphia, a kid fell from twenty feet above the stage and landed like a sack of potatoes in front of Grant's drum kit. The kid was in rough shape but made it off the stage alive. Welcome to our world, Lou.

Now that the touring party had grown to four, it was time to start getting motel rooms on a nightly basis. The band was traveling hard and making better money, and we needed more peace and quiet, not to mention sleep. Lou roomed with Greg and Grant roomed with me. I wasn't a neat freak by any stretch of the imagination, but I liked some semblance of orderliness. By contrast, upon opening the motel room door, Grant would toss his well-worn, wildly overstuffed hard-shell suitcase onto a bed, and it would typically spring open on its own, spraying its contents all over. It was comical, the exploding suitcase. When it was time for Grant to call home, I would retire to a long, hot shower, thereby giving him all the privacy he needed. Grant would always return the courtesy. We were decent roommates.

We toured sporadically in the first half of 1984, knowing we would work hard in July, when *Zen Arcade* was finally to be released. There were a handful of highlights, including two dates in March in Boston with REM. They asked us to open for them at the Harvard Field House, and the following evening, despite their ability to sell way more tickets than us, they supported us at the Rat, a smaller Boston punk club.

Starting in mid 1983, we became incredibly prolific and were always anxious to try out new songs, so we tended to play new material on tour, as it was written. This often meant we were playing music from albums that hadn't been released or even recorded yet, instead of the album we were promoting. The conventional wisdom is, you flog your latest album, but we didn't care. We weren't there only to sell records. That's just another thing that set us apart from other bands.

In April 1984 SST released the *Eight Miles High* single, which gained some attention from both the US and UK press, and by May we were already test-driving several selections from what would be the follow-up to *Zen Arcade,* which hadn't even been released yet.

In Norman, Oklahoma, just for the hell of it, we played a version of "Reoccurring Dreams" that lasted almost an hour; the last forty-five minutes, I played one E chord on my guitar. It was funny, watching people go from smiling to "OK, we get it" to "now we're pissed" to then being just plain stunned. In

Austin we played in the basement of Voltaire's bookstore; someone let off a stink bomb in the packed and airless basement, which not only ruined the show, but could have ended in tragedy. In June we played the Electric Banana in Pittsburgh, a club built precariously on the edge of a steep cliff. We arrived early and fell asleep on the vacant club stage, only to be awakened by the son of the club owner shooting at us with a pellet gun. After a sound check at the Rat in Boston, a young fellow showed up in a surgical halo, informing us that he had broken his neck while stage diving at our previous Boston gig.

On June 23 we played our very first show at the great Hoboken club Maxwell's, which soon became a standard stop on the indie rock circuit. The club owner was a very gregarious fellow named Steve Fallon. Steve's gaydar went off on me immediately, and I finally had somebody in a big city who knew gay, who knew I was gay, and who I could learn from. Maxwell's was gay-friendly, but it wasn't a gay bar. It was just a scene that happened to have gay people in it.

We kept playing shows, but July 1984 was a momentous month for two reasons: the long-awaited (and long-delayed) release of *Zen Arcade* and the recording sessions for the follow-up album.

Nine months was a long time for a record to sit, especially for SST, but apparently they wanted to release our album on the same day as the Minutemen's *Double Nickels on the Dime,* the double album they decided to make when they heard we were making one. (The Minutemen could have made a triple if they wanted to; they were that prolific.)

Zen Arcade comes out and right away there's a lot of critical acclaim. I felt validated. I'd been telling people that we were going to do something bigger than ever, and lo and behold we did. But even more than validation, I felt relief—relief that we actually delivered on all my hubris.

There was one problem though: no one could find *Zen Arcade* in stores. We got to the record-signing party at an indie music shop in Columbus, Ohio, and there were no records. So we had to go down to the local print shop and hastily design flyers so we'd have something to sign for people. Turned out SST had been worried about printing up more than five thousand copies or so—anything beyond that was uncharted territory for them—because if that pressing didn't sell out, they'd have to eat the cost. But the initial pressing sold out quickly and, in reality, the album wasn't widely available until September, when SST was able to do another pressing. We had warned them that this was going to be an important record and that they needed to press up more copies than usual. They were not at all prepared for what was happening.

It was a discouraging situation. We were out there trying to sell the record, and there were no records for people to buy. Turned out SST wasn't quite the utopia people thought it was. That was the first crack in the bond between Hüsker Dü and SST.

We were being the good soldiers, doing as we were told. The SST deal gave Spot 25 percent of the band's artist royalties, which was normal for SST bands. We understood that when we signed the contract. What we didn't understand was how music publishing worked, and how individual songwriters were entitled to mechanical royalties. Before *Zen Arcade,* Ginn had control of our publishing through his Cesstone Music. We complained, got our publishing back, and divvied up the songwriting credits through our own entity, Reflex Music. Everything was now in accordance with standard music industry practices.

But at the same time, we were also deferring our royalties from SST so the label could cope with cash flow problems. Still, SST somehow had enough money to release no less than four Black Flag albums in 1984.

Months earlier we informed SST that we were going to record our next album in Minneapolis. Mixing *Zen Arcade* in one forty-hour session makes for a great story, but let's face it, it wasn't ideal. We wanted to spend more time making this next album and have more control over the recording environment. And while sleeping in the van or underneath Rollins's desk was oddly romantic, we also thought it might be nice to make an album while sleeping in our own beds each night. Also, I wanted more time at home to further my relationship with Mike.

Making a life with Mike gave me some sense of safety and stability. But it was also a challenge for me, this being the first time I had someone to talk with about my thoughts. I was only twenty-three and still had some learning to do, especially when it came to love and relationships. The dynamics of our families of origin are easy to emulate and hard to erase. The less flattering aspects always seem to resurface when times are tough, or when one or both people are living in an altered state.

Mike and I were drinking a lot, but when we were together, I was a happy drunk. When I was working though, I'm certain there were moments when I was tough to be around. Some people who were close to the band circa 1984 have portrayed me as dour, overbearing, even baleful. I don't doubt those descriptions one bit—I'll leave it to others to fill in the ugly blanks.

Steve Fjelstad had coproduced and/or engineered all the Replacements albums, and he offered to help us with our Minneapolis sessions as engineer. We booked time at Nicollet Studios, an old vaudeville theater turned recording studio complex on Nicollet Avenue, near Twenty-Sixth Street.

Spot came to town in the role of coproducer. The first day, Spot came in, sat down behind the recording console, and said, "Something's wrong here. We're going to need to move this console three inches—it's in the wrong place." It was a ridiculous request. He couldn't move his chair three inches? It was a power move, designed to establish some sense of dominance over the rest of us. Without making an issue, we all lifted this fucking-huge board that's been in the exact place for a long time, and moved it three inches.

New Day Rising was a very different album from *Zen*

Arcade. They were composed only a matter of months apart, but when I look back, it seems like years. Before *New Day Rising*, it was words floating around in notebooks, and me sweeping them up and gathering them all together in my hands like they were snowballs or fastballs, spitting on them, and throwing these words at the listener. The songs were outbursts of confusion, dealing almost exclusively with problems, and rarely offered answers. But the new songs, and their imagery, were different—they addressed time, the transitory nature of emotions, and the passing of seasons.

"Celebrated Summer" was my first truly effective use of melancholy, a sentiment that was to become a core element of my future songwriting. "I Apologize" chronicles a suspicion-filled and explosive relationship, describing how something as seemingly minor as forgetting to take out the trash can highlight how easily a relationship can go silent. I still play those two songs in most every show.

And if *Zen Arcade* was the "gram of crystal meth in the first pot of coffee album," then *New Day Rising* was my drinking album. That's surely why the sessions don't stand out big for me. I'd been drinking heavily for a while, and you don't have to listen too hard to hear my inebriated state. "Perfect Example" was the sound of me sitting alone in front of an open microphone, a wee bit too drunk, muttering through a series of doubts, fears, and regrets. The words tumbled in free verse, and I don't think I listened to it after it was done. Then there's the mindless hardcore blast of "Whatcha Drinkin'": "I don't care what they say / I'll be drinking today."

New Day Rising was a little more delicate, the emotional palette a little deeper. I was almost twenty-four, more aware of time in general, and beginning to reflect on getting older. The music was slowing down and I was growing up. And I'd started writing some songs on my acoustic twelve-string guitar. I was becoming a little bit mellower. And what I didn't realize as I was writing was that the audience was getting older with me, as well as growing in number and becoming more diverse. It wasn't just a group of pissed-off guys in black leather jackets—we were beginning to see more women in the crowds, as well as the bookish music aficionados.

There was one song that didn't make the recording sessions. Until now, when songs needed to be cut, mine were always the first to go. I was more prolific than Grant and was fine with letting songs fall by the wayside. But for the first time, I questioned one of Grant's songs.

At one rehearsal Grant submitted a song, we played through it a couple of times, and after a moment, I said, "Grant, I don't know about this one. It's the same riff and melody as a Dream Syndicate song that's out right now." The song was called "2541." Later I realized it was probably about a failed relationship he'd had, that it carried a lot of emotional weight for him at the time, and that it was one of the best songs he'd ever written. But at the time, I just wasn't putting it together. I only meant to point out something. I think it really hurt him, and I think he viewed me as an adversary from then on. Years later I felt bad about it, and I often wondered if it might have been the beginning of the end.

Flash back to the summer of 1980 when Grant Hart quit Hüsker Dü. We played a show at a small theater near the University of Minnesota. The show was pretty bad, and both Greg and I were upset at Grant's performance. We were playing on borrowed gear, so that may have been a factor. I suspected some sort of overindulgence. Regardless, when we confronted him about it, he didn't apologize or defend himself—he just quit. We were astonished.

The next day Greg and I went to Grant and asked him if he really wanted to quit. He decided he didn't really want to, so we patched things up and moved forward.

Grant quitting in 1980 was a power move, asserting his ability to destroy the band. I think the "2541" incident changed our quiet peace, broke that four-year truce, and ignited a passive-aggressive conflict between us.

There was also some friction because I was literally running the show: booking tours, coordinating activities with SST, and generally acting as band manager. In the earliest days of the band, Greg did the booking; when I realized we could be doing so much better, I took that task away from him. I didn't ask Greg; I just said, "I can do better." I only wanted to make sure we were getting paid what we were worth.

I had an aptitude for this kind of thing. I had the adding machine brain, and later, I'd studied under Steve McClellan, learning the ins and outs of the concert business. No one in the band complained when lots more money started coming in.

As time went on, the business got complicated, and there were moments when I was the only one who really knew what was going on. I explained everything to Grant and Greg though, and we always moved forward in consensus.

But there were also implications to this arrangement. Doing all that stuff put me in a position where I had more sway over things. To me, it wasn't about needing to have power. I wanted to steer everything, but everything was Hüsker Dü and the fate of Hüsker Dü. It was taking what we had and making sure it was presented properly. I wanted the band to be as successful as possible, and every day I fought for that success. Even though I deserved it, I never asked for a management fee—I enjoyed the work.

There were times when I would get frustrated, such as when Grant would want to do side projects while I wanted him to stay focused on the band. If there was personal gain to be had, I thought it could most easily be achieved by making the band bigger. I always had my eye on the prize—that's the kind of person I've always been.

*   *   *

In October we headed east for a series of dates in support of the now in-stock *Zen Arcade*. The album had been getting impressive reviews from music journalists around the world, which created more interest than we had ever experienced. While the music world was buzzing about *Zen Arcade,* here we were with yet another album finished and queued up for release. (After the July debacle, SST had the sense to commit to a prompt January 1985 street date for *New Day Rising.*) But if that wasn't enough of a sign of how hard we were working, we were already playing three brand-new songs: "Hate Paper Doll," "Green Eyes," and "Divide and Conquer," material for what would be the next album, the one after *New Day Rising.* Not only had we lapped SST, but we'd managed to race past ourselves too.

* * *

Around this time I developed some sort of respiratory problem. One day in Minneapolis, I was very short of breath and went to a local emergency room. They put me on oxygen that contained a bronchodilator drug. The doctor who treated me decided that I had asthma and put me on prednisone (side effects: weight gain, facial swelling, depression) and gave me an albuterol inhaler (side effects: nervousness, trouble sleeping), which I soon started taking onstage with me. In the next three months, I gained fifty pounds. Even after this diagnosis, I kept on smoking two packs of cigarettes a day—on top of my substantial drinking.

I would have maybe three, four, five, six drinks a night, every night. Not very much binge drinking. I'd work hard all day, and around 5 PM, I'd have my first drink. I was very productive and had my act together. I was a high-functioning alcoholic.

Nineteen eighty-four saw the release of some classic albums by our peers: the Replacements' *Let It Be,* the Meat Puppets' *Meat Puppets II,* and the Minutemen's *Double Nickels on the Dime.* Sonic Youth was picking up a head of steam as well. And there was such a positive spirit among the bands, everyone playing together, helping each other out while still competing in a healthy way—like in December when we flew out to California for three shows and had the extreme pleasure of being chaperoned up and down the state by D. Boon of the Minutemen. Riding with D. was quite fun. He was always such an upbeat, intelligent, and thoughtful soul, and his demeanor made the time fly by. REM was particularly helpful and supportive of other bands as well.

In my mind it was no longer "I wonder if we're better than the Replacements." We were playing shows with REM and I was thinking, "Next?" I started to wonder if we were better than U2. I wondered if we were the best band in the world. Sure, I was cocky then, but for years I knew we were good, and now everyone else could see it too.

We stayed on the road, preaching our stories door-to-door, and those years of sacrifice were paying off—things were really starting to happen for Hüsker Dü. As for me, I'd bounced from Kelly Linehan's basement, where I slept on a mattress next to the boiler and pissed in the laundry sink, to a roach-infested prostitute haven near Loring Park, to somewhat more civilized digs with Mike. It was a lot of movement and not much constancy, but it was all worth it. We were on one hell of a creative roll. So now what to do? The smart thing to do was make another record without blinking.

I'm really glad *New Day Rising* was done and dusted before *Zen Arcade* really started to resonate. Can you imagine if we hadn't had another record ready? We'd have been sitting around with the earth shaking underneath us, trying to get settled and centered enough to make another strong album—but instead we struck while the iron was hot. If we hadn't have done that, we might have tried to make another *Zen Arcade*. When people are watching so closely, it's tempting to stay with the winning formula. After all, that's what brought us to the party, that's the work that took us from nowhere to somewhere. So do it again. But really, the best way to survive is to mutate. When you've made the fourth most important record in the world at the moment, you ask yourself, what do I do now? If you're smart, you go with your gut.

And it paid off. We celebrated the release of *New Day Rising* with two hometown shows at First Avenue on January 30 and 31. Then we headed west, including a Seattle show with openers the Melvins and a new band called Sound Garden, who had yet to condense their name into one word. In early March we headlined "The Tour," a four-city SST package with the Minutemen and the Meat Puppets. The Los Angeles show, at UCLA's Ackerman Ballroom, was the night the major labels showed up.

Around this time, the *Village Voice*'s Robert Christgau was the most powerful critic in the country, and when he anointed Zen Arcade—"I get a kick out of the whole fucking thing," he wrote, giving it an A– rating—a lot of music biz types, critics, and civilians starting coming to the shows. The Ackerman Ballroom concert was the first A&R parade: Mark Williams from A&M, Karin Berg from Warner Brothers, and Anna Statman from Slash. Sure, the major labels were flirting with us, but why would anybody want to leave SST? From the outside, SST looked like the greatest label in the universe. They had the hippest bands, the hottest tours, and the most provocative artwork. It was a great brand.

But we were growing tired of SST, stemming from the distribution problems and the publishing dispute. The major labels had a strong case: they could keep our albums in the stores. There were other pieces of the puzzle that needed to fall in place—creative control and financial compensation, for instance—but the simple fact was that we couldn't sell records if they didn't exist.

We recorded our next album at Nicollet Studios in the spring of 1985. The "2541" situation had changed the dynamic between Grant and me but we were lifted up by the fact that Spot was now no longer producing our records. Greg stayed out of the way, Steve Fjelstad was a steady and helpful engineer, and we homed in on the pop sensibility that was my entry point for music, going back to those jukebox singles I had as a child. It's no coincidence that *Flip Your Wig* was the best album we ever did.

With *Metal Circus* we'd distanced ourselves from the sound and dogma of hardcore. *Zen Arcade* was a sprawling conceptual piece that broke further from established punk conventions. *New Day Rising* began to emphasize melody over noise. Now we wanted to make a full-on pop record, and we went for it. *Flip Your Wig* was easily the most melodic record we'd made to date.

Early on we had songs where everybody wrote a line, but from *Everything Falls Apart* forward, we wrote songs separately. Grant and I had cowritten mainly through jamming, not sitting together and concocting the essence. But we cowrote the title song from *Flip Your Wig* that way. It was an homage to '60s pop music — we tried to recreate the feel of the Monkees' theme song, and the title refers to the old Beatles board game.

Flip Your Wig had plenty of pop songs, like my trusty show-closer "Makes No Sense at All," "Hate Paper Doll," and "Games" (a song we never played live, but was amazing). "Green Eyes" and "Every Everything" were two of Grant's best songs ever.

On the sociopolitical front, "Divide and Conquer" was a Marshall McLuhan–influenced look into the future, but with even more detail and accuracy:

We'll invent some new computers
Link up the global village
And get AP, UPI, and Reuters
To tell everybody the news

Around this time, Grant and I made a business decision that would have repercussions in the future. We had a standard deal with SST: a 12 percent artist royalty rate. Out of what the band earned through those artist royalties, 25 percent went to the producer, who up to now had been Spot. But when Grant and I decided to produce *Flip Your Wig,* we agreed to split that sum. I was writing at least 60 percent of the songs, so we split the production money sixty-forty in my favor. In cash terms: if we sold 50,000 records at $10 a pop, we would get paid a $1.20 artist royalty on each unit, which comes out to a total of $60,000. So Grant and I split $15,000 of that: $9,000 to me and $6,000 to Grant. Three thousand bucks difference, which seemed fair and of little consequence. At least that's what I thought at the time.

Over in California, in SST land, Ray Farrell was our new hope. In April Ray joined on as promotions manager at SST, and he was making things happen with college rock. Ray understood the business and assured us things would run right for *Flip Your Wig.* Ray was the major reason we stayed at SST for as long as we did.

Then we met David Savoy. David was a Hüsker Dü fan, he was tied into the Boston-area music scene, and he knew a lot of the same people we did. We all took a liking to him—he was a very pleasant guy, well-spoken, and with a nice, easy demeanor— and he promoted two shows of ours in Massachusetts. After the December 1984 show in his hometown of Concord, we went to an all-night restaurant where David pulled a little prank on me. He gave me a Christmas present, this Hawaiian shirt that was way too short so that when I put it on, my gut hung out the bottom. Everyone was laughing, and I thought, This guy's got a good sense of humor, how dare he do this? I still chuckle at the memory. I thought, He's someone we want to keep an eye on.

In 1985, when the business workload became too heavy, I told Grant and Greg that we needed to bring someone in to help. I suggested David, and they were fine with that. David moved to Minneapolis in April of 1985 and promptly found himself smack-dab in the middle of the storm known as Hüsker Dü. He was thrust into the role of parent, peacemaker, and messenger. And he was only twenty-one.

We rented two office spaces in the Nicollet complex. Grant had his space, with his mysterious safe in the corner to do artwork for Hüsker Dü and other Twin Cities bands. David and I worked side by side in an adjacent office, addressing the more mundane tasks: monitoring record company activities, balancing the books, and—my favorite—routing and booking tours. Get out the calendar, check the mileage wheel, route the dates. What towns need to be weekends for us and which ones can be weekdays? How much ground can we cover? Logistics is not artistic work, but there is an art to it and I enjoyed mastering the skill. I still do the same tasks with my current agents and management.

In addition to writing, recording, and touring, I was in the office eight to ten hours a day. Chris Osgood, who at that time worked at Twin/Tone, told me how David was energized by being around me and excited by watching the business grow. I didn't realize that at the time—we were simply plowing through ever-growing piles of work. In addition, I was producing Soul Asylum's *Made to Be Broken* album, and Grant was producing a record by Otto's Chemical Lounge. Everything was rolling.

We kept touring, moving, giving back, and continuing that sense of community from when we were sharing our notebooks and our couches. We kept helping new bands with Reflex Records, releasing the *Barefoot & Pregnant* and *Kitten* compilations, as well as albums by Twin Cities bands Man Sized Action, Rifle Sport, and Ground Zero. We also worked with Midwest bands Mecht Mensch, Tar Babies, and Articles of Faith. That new blood helped keep the whole scene fresh—a rising tide lifts all boats. It was good energy, our way of countering and complementing Twin/Tone's influence over the Minneapolis scene. Minneapolis was the "it" city, and the buzz was deafening. South side, you had Hüsker Dü, the Replacements, and Soul Asylum. North side, there was Prince, Jimmy Jam and Terry Lewis, Alexander O'Neal, and Morris Day.

* * *

In 1984 we had scrapped a run of European dates opening for Black Flag. In hindsight it was a wise move. Playing in the shadow of Black Flag might have cast Hüsker Dü as a second-tier SST band, especially since Black Flag's 1984 lineup was not its best. But eventually we made it across the big pond.

In the middle of the May 1985 East Coast tour to support *New Day Rising,* we canceled a show in Raleigh, North Carolina, and made a big detour. We had been invited to play an afternoon show at the Camden Palace in London, for a taping of the popular *Live from London* television series. It was our first trip to the UK, not to mention my first trip overseas.

We played Washington, DC, on May 12, then flew to London for the May 14 gig. The London show went well, despite the fact that we played on rented equipment: we had no work papers, so bringing instruments would have drawn attention to us at immigration. The UK music press, which I had grown up reading and following word for word, finally got their look at Hüsker Dü, and they liked what they saw. The *NME*'s Richard Cook wrote, "This bitter metal howl is a sound that seems to literally pour over our ears, a glittering river of savage harmony." In the wake of such glowing praise, we made plans with Paul Boswell, our new European booking agent, for a headlining tour in September. (Paul and I have worked together ever since.)

The day after the London show, we flew back to the States, played a ferocious show that night in Cleveland, and finished up the tour as originally planned.

Far from the grey fog of London (or Cleveland, for that matter), we flew later that month to our first shows in Florida. This was a high point in the cocaine era of Anita Bryant's Sunshine State, and we brushed up against the drug a few times. After one show we witnessed a domestic squabble in the middle of a busy street—a coked-up guy bashing his girlfriend's head into the hood of a Camaro Z28 and then embracing her. It was perfect, in a perverse way, so *Miami Vice.*

May 1985 was also when we first crossed paths with William Burroughs. Famed Beat wordsmith John Giorno had a small record label called Giorno Poetry Systems and asked

Hüsker Dü to be part of a compilation album called *A Diamond Hidden in the Mouth of a Corpse,* which also featured Cabaret Voltaire, Sonic Youth, and Diamanda Galás. We gave John an outtake from *Metal Circus* called "Won't Change." I told him we wanted to donate our royalties to charity, and he suggested a new organization in New York City called God's Love We Deliver. The organization was made of a handful of volunteers who drove around town and delivered meals to people suffering from full-blown AIDS. I said that sounded great, and we challenged everyone else to do the same. John was excited, went to everybody, and they all agreed. Then John scheduled a photo shoot for us, himself, and William at the infamous "Bunker," Burroughs's writing room on the Bowery. That was our first meeting with William.

I thought back to working in the library at Macalester, reading *Naked Lunch* cover-to-cover in one sitting, and how much the drugs, the sex, the transgressive grittiness of the book affected me on so many levels. And how, amazingly, the path I had started on six years prior had led me to William Burroughs himself.

And now we were hanging out at the Bunker, which is still maintained like a shrine. William was a striking figure, and I was very much on one knee the whole time. We sat around the big table, smoking pot and drinking coffee, and he asked questions of us in his slow and deliberate voice: "So, you're from Minneapolis? What do you want to do with your music?" He was stoic and revered, dapper and proper—I watched his every move and listened to his every breath.

At William's side was James Grauerholz, his faithful custodian and amanuensis. James was a strikingly handsome man, proper and caring, and very good at keeping William current by bringing new and relevant people to him. And John Giorno was this wild, energetic Buddhist Italian, oozing sex and words and positive spiritual energy. What a crew—all so different, all so welcoming, bringing us into this sacred place.

In the years that followed, I would always stop by to see William at his modest home in Lawrence, Kansas. There was a fair amount of land around the house; James had purchased a number of adjacent parcels so it was somewhat buffered. James had his own house nearby. Locals would come in to have lunch with William once a week, then take him to town to run errands and get his hair cut. It was amazing. I can only hope that in my later years, I fall into a similar situation where there's this super-smart hot guy who oversees my estate while bringing in new people to keep it fresh. (Don't think I wasn't taking notes.) And always, after smoking a bunch of weed, William would bring up the possibility of going out back to throw some knives. You went along with it, because it's William.

I think back to something else that John once told me. He and Ferlinghetti and Ginsberg used to get into leather jackets and pants and go running for hours through these huge marijuana fields in the Midwest. When they came back, they'd be covered with resin from the plants. They'd scrape the resin off the leather with knives and end up with this sticky substance that was stronger than hashish. As different as our backgrounds, ages, and art forms were, we shared similar experiences. They're the same crazy stories, with different names and places. I'd never run through fields to gather hashish resin, but I had fled from Dobermans who were chasing me out of abandoned beer vats in San Francisco. It was all part of the same tradition, the same sensibility. I never would have said it at the time, but in some strange, cosmic way, as an American outsider/storyteller, I was in the same lineage as those guys.

CHAPTER 9

After seeing Hüsker Dü at the Ackerman Ballroom, Warner Brothers A&R person Karin Berg flew to Minneapolis to meet with us. Karin had worked with many great artists over the years, including Joni Mitchell, Television, and the B-52s. At Nicollet Studios we played her *Flip Your Wig*. She loved what she heard and told us in no uncertain terms that Warner was interested in this record. It was surprising that Warner was so eager to sign the band. Then again, college rock had sprung up in the Northeast and was now spreading all over the country. Media outlets like *CMJ, Rockpool,* and even MTV were all starting to move in our direction, as was the rock audience in general. Turned out the whole thing was just a few years away from exploding.

We knew it was time to go to a major. We saw a larger audience that was ready for what we were doing. And if we were to address that audience, the records had to be available—all the time, everywhere. There were other labels in the running, but we were impressed with Karin, as was everyone we talked to about her. Karin was maternal, calming, and perceptive about music. We decided to sign with Warner.

Although Karin was very interested in *Flip Your Wig* and we were frustrated with SST, we still felt some loyalty to the label that had done so much for us, so we decided to give them one more record. *Flip Your Wig* would be their last. In hindsight, it may have been a misstep in terms of reaching a bigger audience, but at the time it seemed like the honorable thing to do. Like I said, we were the good soldiers. Karin was disappointed, but she understood—and we assured her there would be another strong album right around the corner.

Somewhat ironically, now that Ray Farrell was on board, SST was doing some great work for us. Ray was willing to exploit the band's pop potential. He serviced college and commercial radio with a twelve-inch promo single of "Makes No Sense at All," as well as finding outlets for the video, which recreated the intro of the Minneapolis-based '70s TV sitcom *The Mary Tyler Moore Show*. It was a genuine expression of regional pride—the kind of regionalism that was largely swept away by MTV, which did much to homogenize the mystique of musical outbacks like Minnesota.

Jumping to a major label had huge political repercussions in our community. We were acutely aware of it, that we were the band. It's true that the Replacements were still on an independent label, but they weren't really a part of the community— they were a rock band in the classic sense. In hindsight, a key difference between the two bands becomes very clear: the Replacements never started a label to help out their friends' bands. They didn't give back the way Hüsker Dü gave back.

We kept our plan to move to Warner under wraps for as long as possible. It was easier to keep a secret back then, pre-internet. With an important career move like that, it's best not to tell people until the ink is dry. And we had to prepare for a backlash not just from SST but from the staunch anticorporate factions of the underground community.

Going on our first European tour helped, and September 1985 started with a ripping performance at the famed Marquee in London. We were in peak form. The rest of the tour, however, is a bit hazy thanks to stronger-than-American beer, plentiful hashish, and a bottle of scotch on the hospitality rider every day. Most of my memories revolve around our modified bread truck bouncing down the highways of northern Europe, overnight ferry rides with groups of Scandinavian men drinking and fighting among themselves, and late-night cards at the hotel. At Rock City in Nottingham, a group of Hell's Angels came backstage to meet the band and present us with a large bag of crystal meth. I snorted some of the sulphury powder off a switchblade that was held under my nose by one of the "friendly" bikers.

The following night we performed at the legendary Hacienda in Manchester. I was scouring the venue, hoping to find some remnant of the bygone energy of the early Manchester scene, but all I found was a surly lighting director who would not capitulate to Grant's request not to be rotisserie-cooked by the hot white lights behind the drum riser. We were informed that we were playing "the fucking Hacienda" and that there would be no back talk. Three songs into the set, Grant simply turned the lights away from himself.

After wending our way through Scandinavia and Germany, we finished up the tour with a blazing performance at the Electric Ballroom in London. In the back of the room, there was a lighthouse-shaped device that displayed the decibel level in ascending colors, almost like a rainbow thermometer. If it got too loud, the top of the tower would light up and the PA would shut down. During our set I was transfixed by this thing, wondering, "Is Lou going to push it over the edge?" We were definitely a loud band, but it was more about our claustrophobic clustering of songs—a Hüsker Dü show was an assault, slamming sonics together to shock people.

Then we returned home and toured the West Coast yet again. On November 1, we played the Santa Monica Civic Center with the Meat Puppets and DC3. This big-room multiband bill would be the last of the SST punk rock shows for Hüsker Dü. We informed SST that we were leaving after they put out *Flip Your Wig*. For a moment, Greg Ginn tried to make a case for us staying, and when that fell on deaf ears, he moved on to other interests. So much for the backlash from SST.

We signed with Warner on Veterans Day, November 11, 1985. We threw a huge catered party at Nicollet Studios, complete with a champagne fountain built out of drinking glasses. Many of our friends and family attended, along with fellow Minneapolis musicians and the Twin/Tone crew. Both my mom and my dad had supported my career, but my father never liked flying, so he stayed home while my mother flew in. She had the time of her life, overjoyed to be part of this celebration. Even some local TV stations covered the party. It was only a contract signing, but we'd contacted the press and made it into a newsworthy event. People had a good time and thought all the celebrating was cute.

We hoped that if we could succeed on a major label without compromising our integrity, it might open the door for other bands to follow suit. We weren't the only alternative band signing with a major, but we were probably the most vocal about creative control and autonomy. We wanted to reach a larger audience, we knew Warner would give us a bigger platform, and we were confident they wouldn't try to reshape our look, sound, or message.

Our Warner deal was pretty standard, with a solid advance that we knew we could earn back. All those years on the indie circuit had made us a strong touring act and so efficient and thrifty that we didn't need any financial help from the label to go on the road, which put us in Warner's good graces. We were very concerned with being charged for video and indie radio promotion, and we did our best to protect ourselves from decisions made beyond our control. Warner agreed to let us self-produce our records. Karin didn't meddle in the creative process, whereas other A&R people were notorious for acting like frustrated producers. They'd want to get into the specifics: "You know, if you just cut that first chorus in half..." They would say things that would make our eyes roll. Karin never did that.

If you can't tell, I felt particularly defensive about the move from SST to a major—I'd been so brash, so vocal, so dogmatic in the past, railing about large corporations. We'd set an outspoken example. We were just asking for it, right?

So I wrote a long piece in the respected punk fanzine *Maximumrocknroll*. We'd met the *MRR* folks—Tim Yohannan, Ruth Schwartz, and Jeff Bale—when we first went to San Francisco in 1981. We'd played Risk with those guys and watched with amazement as these radical leftists got so intense about a game of world domination. *MRR* was the natural choice for my little manifesto, not just because it flew the flag for punk rock values, but because I knew Tim would give me the page and not make a mockery of it.

It was a tricky piece to write. I could have complained about the fact that SST hadn't always been supportive, not to mention diligent, about paying us on time, but the punk community held SST in high regard. So I tried to put a more positive spin on things. The 1,350-word piece made it clear that we'd retained complete artistic freedom in the Warner deal and that the next Hüsker Dü album would be, in the best sense, just another Hüsker Dü album. "We haven't gone through a new image change," I wrote, " 'cause we've never had one."

But I also took the opportunity to address other sensitive issues, like why the band had abandoned political lyrics after *Metal Circus*. Basically, we didn't feel qualified to speak about politics and we weren't comfortable with hardcore's knee-jerk embrace of anarchism. I also talked about why we strongly discouraged stage diving at our shows: "It has nothing to do with elitism; we're concerned about ourselves staying in one piece, and not endangering unsuspecting people in the audience. Everyone has a right to see Hüsker Dü, not just the slammers in the pit."

And then I got down to reassuring the underground community some more:

We're still conscious of our audience, we're trying to play all-ages shows, we're trying to keep the ticket price down....Just because we've signed to Warner Brothers doesn't mean that there won't be ten new bands next week. If anything, it might be a sign that something is happening, that some people are finally listening to the underground, and they might even respect what's going on. Nobody at Warner has asked us to tone down; they haven't asked us to sound like U2, they're completely happy with the high end distortion and tons of ride cymbals and people yelling and singing pretty and writing any kinds of words they want. They signed Hüsker Dü because they liked Hüsker Dü and not because they think we will be the next Rick Springfield.

And after all that, there wasn't actually much of a backlash. Maybe our audience understood. Or maybe it just wasn't that big of a deal after all.

Still, I was extremely sensitive about the situation, and I remember Grant making a comment that left a sour taste in my mouth. We'd signed with Warner soon after the Replacements had signed with Sire, a Warner subsidiary. Grant said something to the press about it, something like "They were worried they were going to have enough money to buy cars. With Hüsker Dü, we're just worried about how many cars we're going to buy." Now we were twenty-five at the time and we all say some dumb shit when we're twenty-five, but I thought it was one of the dumbest things that could have been said. It was just another one of Grant's kooky pronouncements, but it irked me. Not only did it amplify this artificial and unnecessary acrimony with the Replacements, who were our friends, but I feared the comment would annoy some of our core fans. Another telling difference between Grant and me.

The two of us were a lot alike and a lot different. The parts that were alike is where the battle was. We had both been gifted, smart, golden children, and as a result, Grant could never take no for an answer and neither could I. So when I started to take charge, it didn't sit well with him. He was the flamboyant, free-spirit type, and to retaliate he started painting me as a square.

This was also around the same time that I began my "briefings." I'd have the three of us sit down, especially before the Warner Brothers record, and get focused on what we were going to talk about to the press. That was a sore spot for Grant. (In retrospect, though, it was visionary—now bands develop their talking points and even do media training.) In one briefing, I wanted to discuss what I knew was going to come, the backlash due to moving to a major. I said to the other guys, "Can we all sit down and make a conscious effort to stay on course?"

Grant said, as if to be a clever cat, "Should we talk about being gay?"

I just looked at him and said, "That's not really what I'm talking about here. We just jumped from an indie to a major, let's get this straight."

And I know he didn't like that. His response was along the lines of "Why don't you do all the fucking interviews and put words in people's mouths?" That's the dynamic that was now in full effect. I'm trying to steer the band, keep it focused, but it felt like Grant never missed an opportunity to be contrary. And if it weren't me proposing these briefings and business meetings, it would probably be a Warner employee.

I was becoming even more single-minded about what I wanted the band to achieve, and I thought we could best do it by being professional, responsible, and accountable. On the other hand, Grant was becoming even more of a free spirit. And between the heavier workload and the new label arrangement, I had neither the time nor the interest to include Greg in serious discussions. Ultimately, Grant and I were the songwriters, and we were dealing with the creative and business sides of the band on a daily basis. We had our frictions, but both of us knew that this was our destiny, so we needed to agree on the major objectives and move forward in unison.

Thankfully, working with Warner was less adversarial than anyone had anticipated. We had instant allies in the alternative marketing department: Mary Hyde, Jo Lenardi, Cathy Lincoln, and, later, Julie Panebianco. Steven Baker was our product manager, and he worked with Grant on the visual side of our projects. I worked on the audio side with Howie Weinberg at Masterdisk in New York. Greg was free to pursue his newest passion: playing a daily round of golf in rural Minnesota.

But our biggest booster and ally at Warner was Karin Berg. Karin was also able to focus on bands' strong suits, as opposed to picking apart things that just didn't matter. She had a bigger picture in mind, which was good because as an A&R person, it was her job to champion her bands to all the different departments of the label.

In late 1985 we began recording what would become *Candy Apple Grey,* our first album for Warner. Karin Berg was virtually the only Warner employee who stopped by the studio. Sadly, my memories of those songs are colored by a verbal hand grenade that Grant directed squarely at me. During the wrap-up of the sessions, he and I were alone in the large recording room of Nicollet's Studio A, and out of nowhere he blurted, "I'm going to have the first fucking single or else!" I thought, well, you don't have to tear my head off about it. It was clear he had written the singles on that record.

I had written an abrasive opener in "Crystal," a conscious attempt to maintain some kind of punk credibility. If the old fans put the record on and it began with some sweet little love song, they'd be gone. If we could at least hold them for the first three minutes, maybe they'd listen to the whole thing. (And yet the converse was also true: the abrasiveness would probably turn off a lot of new fans.) After that: Grant's "Don't Want to Know If You Are Lonely," great song, first single. "I Don't

Know for Sure," *not* a great song. Grant's "Sorry Somehow," great song, second single. Then, my two "downer" acoustic-based songs, "Too Far Down" and "Hardly Getting Over It." Ironically, these songs have endured well beyond the first single off many albums I have written and recorded. To this day they're two of the strongest songs in my repertoire. One key line of "Hardly Getting Over It" is "What do I do when they die?" That's how death was for me—I didn't know how to deal with it. In third grade I didn't attend the funeral of my classmate; when my grandfather died, my parents didn't tell me until weeks after the fact.

The first verse of "Too Far Down" illuminated my early bouts with clinical depression, a condition I wasn't aware of until ten years later:

I'm too far down
And I don't know how to tell you
But maybe this time I can't come back
because I might be too far down

The song was cathartic, and I just didn't quite realize why at the time. To this day, when I feel depression coming on, I don't want to be around other people because I don't want it to spread. And that's probably the real message of that song. To the folks around me, it looked like I was being sulky or stormy, but really I was just trying to stay away from other people—because depression is contagious.

We did songs in packs of three and four when we performed live, and we found that alternating Grant's songs with my songs on albums allowed both of us to catch our breath.

But in the end, *Candy Apple Grey* was an incomplete album. After "Too Far Down," the quality suddenly dropped. And two songs foreshadowed the problems to come. "Too Far Down" was my solo endeavor, "No Promise Have I Made" was Grant's. We were both very protective of our "solo songs." We worked alone and didn't share the results until the tracks were finished, allowing no input from the others. In hindsight, it was as if we were jockeying for position with Karin Berg, like two kids competing for a parent's affection. There had been a healthy competition between Grant and me, but with these solo endeavors it had taken a lousy turn.

We used our major label money wisely. Besides getting a box truck for the road crew, we bought a new van, which we had former Suicide Commando Dave Ahl customize with sound-proofing and a sleeping loft. Grant and I invested forty thousand dollars each, Steve Fjeldstad kicked in a decent amount of money, and we formed a recording studio partnership called Massive Leasing. We invested in a new recording console and multitrack tape machines for Nicollet Studio A while remaining a separate business entity from both Nicollet and Hüsker Dü. We kept track of the hours Hüsker Dü spent recording, and Massive Leasing billed it back to the band. We were dipping, so to speak, but Grant and I were investing in the studio business. Greg wasn't interested in being part owner of a recording studio, so he was investing his money in his record store in Red Wing.

One other goal was to buy a house for Greg and his longtime girlfriend, Jeri, as well as one for Grant, who now had a girlfriend and a baby on the way. I wanted a house too, and I also wanted to pay off my student loans and buy a piano. In order to get all that, you have to make trade-offs. So if Greg wanted to play golf and get a house, we had to sign to a major and tour harder than ever. It worked: Greg and Jeri got a house down in Red Wing, Grant bought a house just outside Minneapolis, and I purchased a small three-bedroom house with a backyard and a garage for me and Mike in South Minneapolis. I also paid off my student loans and bought a new piano. Then I went back to Malone and bought a car from my dad: a 1970 Pontiac Le Mans SS convertible, maroon with white interior, with a New York State Trooper Interceptor engine. What an awesome car.

Around this time I also found a stupid way to spend some of my newly earned money: I got into cocaine for a few months. I guess my 1980s wouldn't have been complete without briefly succumbing to the then trendy white powder. What a lousy, awful, terrible drug—it really causes creepy behavior. For example: when you run out of coke, you look for the person who still has some, then ingratiate yourself to that person in hopes of catching a few final whiffs off his mirror.

The cheapest way to pay for a coke habit is to buy in quantity, then shave off grams to sell to acquaintances so you can toot for free. That surely sounds like a slippery slope downward into coke addiction. So after selling an eight ball of blow to the Jets' session guitarist (think the dance hit "Crush on You"), I sensed it was time to get away from that drug.

We did extensive touring in February 1986 to support *Flip Your Wig,* and the Wig Out East tour was the band's finest moment in terms of quality songs, enthusiastic audiences, and consistently good performances. A typical set would start with the first three songs from *Flip Your Wig,* then a handful of gems from *New Day Rising,* and once we were settled in, we'd roll out material from the as yet unreleased *Candy Apple Grey,* songs like "Hardly Getting Over It" and "Sorry Somehow." We were building on three consecutive great albums, and after playing together almost nonstop for six-plus years, we were at the top of our game. The music had all of its usual raw, aggressive power, but to us it seemed incredibly fluid, almost effortless—even the brief pauses between songs held an exhilarating rush for band and audience alike. We were playing like we really were the best band in the world.

Another bright spot on this trip was our support act, Soul Asylum. I had produced their just-released *Made to Be Broken* album, which a lot of people feel is their best work, and this tour was a great opportunity to showcase our longtime friends' band. In a matter of weeks, they went from a band nobody had heard of to a known quantity. I was really proud. We'd made

records together, and to hear them refine the material throughout the tour was a pleasure. Soul Asylum was on fire every
night; we had to follow them, and that upped our game.

We brought along my friend Jim Melby as tour manager. Jim
worked in pro wrestling, mainly as a journalist and historian.
Jim also worked at Northern Lights, the record store where we
had our early rehearsals. Jim didn't drive, which is basically a
prerequisite for tour managing, but he made up for it with a
firm hand in dealing with promoters and club employees. He'd
gotten an ear pierced for the tour, presumably as a nod to rock
and roll, a small, shiny post in his ear, so we quickly dubbed
him "Diamond" Jim Melby—in the wrestling world, that would
be his gimmick name. Jim wore a suit when he settled the bigger
shows and had also taken to smoking cigars. It was priceless—
he was having the time of his life.

During the first leg, four consecutive shows in the Midwest,
Grant became a father. His then girlfriend, Kristen, bore him a
son. We had hoped that the baby would be born while we were
home, but so it went. We were in Wisconsin when the news
came; Grant passed out "It's a Boy!" cigars to everyone, and we
returned to Minnesota for a few weeks of rest and family time
before resuming the tour.

On February 13 we had our inaugural Athens, Georgia, performance at the Tate Center on the campus of the University of
Georgia. Rumor had it that most of the crowd was tripping on
LSD; whatever the truth was, it was definitely a mind-bender,
one of the loudest, shrillest, and most psychedelic shows we had
ever played. It reminded me of the energy that used to fly around
the Church in St. Paul, where most everyone but me was hallu-
cinating. Not only could I sense the energy, I could see it: sometimes bright white lines connecting people, other times loose
white matter hovering above their heads.

A week later, on February 20, at Mississippi Nights in St.
Louis, someone from the club came back to the dressing room
to inform us that Chuck Berry would be in attendance. We were

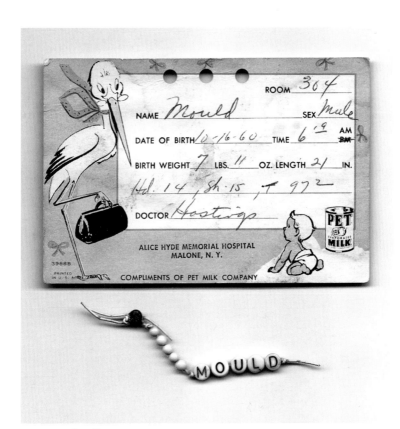

(Personal collection)

One of these things is not like the other. *(Personal collection)*

Birthday cake, October 1964.
(Personal collection)

Me and my grandmother, who took care
of me for years, 1965. *(Personal
collection)*

My brother Brian, me, and my sister
Susan, Christmas 1964. *(Personal
collection)*

I look like I'm about to cover "Wichita
Lineman," 1967. *(Personal collection)*

The first official Hüsker Dü press photo, 1980. *(The late Minneapolis photographer Steven Hengstler)*

Minneapolis all-ages show, December 1982. *(Shelley Hawes)*

Chicago, 1984. *(Gail Butensky)*

Boston, 1984. *(Photo © Laura Levine)*

Chicago, 1984. *(Gail Butensky)*

Peter Buck is trying to teach me a song on the Flying V. Boston, 1984. *(Photo © Laura Levine)*

My first meeting with William S. Burroughs and John Giorno. The Bunker, New York City, 1985. *(Photograph by Sylvia Plachy © 2011)*

Clearly I was inspired by this meeting. Minneapolis, 1985. *(Daniel Corrigan)*

I always played better guitar riffs when not singing. Minneapolis, 1987. *(Daniel Corrigan)*

Me and Mike Covington at the farm. Pine City, Minnesota, Christmas 1987. *(Personal collection)*

A rainy festival in Europe, summer 1987. The last of eight years of service for the Flying V. *(Personal collection)*

A light went off in my head—play a Strat instead. I haven't put Blue down since buying it. Minneapolis, 1989. *(Daniel Corrigan)*

John Lydon, Jello Biafra, and me, October 1989. This was after a Pixies / Bob Mould show at the Warfield in San Francisco. A real punk rock summit. *(© Jay Blakesberg)*

caught off guard by that, but didn't dwell too much on it. Mr. Berry was indeed in the crowd, seated at a VIP table no more than fifteen feet from my microphone. He lasted five songs.

Candy Apple Grey was released in March, at the conclusion of the US tour, to generally favorable reviews. We were always aware of what the press was saying, but tried not to let it affect the creative process. The next order of business was a UK tour that spring, which coincided with the release of the album there. It was twelve shows in thirteen days, and the tour cemented our reputation as a powerhouse live act. The press was ebullient, as this was only our second proper trip to Europe, and our first full UK tour.

This was the zenith of my alcoholism—I was drinking almost nonstop—and the trip was a complete blur. I wasn't alone in this, as Lou was hitting the booze rather heavily as well. In addition to the usual beer and scotch, we had made the mistake of adding several bottles of red wine to our hospitality rider. Those beverages never went to waste.

But to the casual observer, the band appeared to be fueled by amphetamines, and that was the case for a few years. One wouldn't normally associate that kind of music with alcohol. But as with the lyrics from *New Day Rising,* my writing was definitely shaped by my heavy drinking.

We returned to the States and played two shows at Irving Plaza on April 12. Our special support act for those two shows was country rocker Dwight Yoakam, who had just signed with Reprise Records, another Warner label. The punks down front were yelling at Dwight to play faster, and he handled the situation very well—by playing faster. Then we headed to the West Coast in May to promote the album and played three nights of showcase gigs at the Roxy in West Hollywood. Warner bought many of the tickets, so the audience was mostly executives and office employees, which is why industry showcase gigs are generally dull events. The Roxy show wasn't far in space or time from the big multiband punk fest we'd played at the Olympic

Auditorium in 1982, but it felt light-years away. Instead of playing for rabid fans who hung on every note, word, and movement, we were playing for corporate employees, including some who probably didn't want to be there in the first place.

On May 10 we played our first show at the august Fillmore in San Francisco, where classic rockers like the Who, the Grateful Dead, and Led Zeppelin once played. We had two strong support acts that night, and there was a bigger-than-usual buzz around the show. Anna Statman, the A&R person at Slash Records who'd checked us out the previous year, had been proclaiming earlier in the day that she was going to sign one of the two support acts to a record deal. The band she signed: Faith No More. The other band: Camper Van Beethoven.

We were making better money than ever through touring. Concert promoters were (and still are) my lifeblood, and guys that we maintained longtime relationships with — regional promoters like Chris Monlux and Mike Quinn at Monqui, Seth Hurwitz at IMP, and Mark Pratz at Liberty Lunch — were growing right along with us. Since the venues were bigger, ticket prices were slightly higher, but our amenities remained essentially the same: no fancy fruit bowls, no bowls of M&M's sans browns, no masseuses. The "rock star" trappings, groupies and such, didn't figure into my touring life. I had a boyfriend, I wasn't looking, and on top of that, I was an unattractive homosexual. The ladies could probably sense I wasn't interested. The Warner connection did give us greater access to other "rock stars" though. We threw a party for Depeche Mode after their concert in St. Paul in 1986. I remember a birthday being involved, as well as a sexy and thuggish German roadie who held my fascination for a few hours.

* * *

Then there were nine months when everything changed. We'd kept moving forward for seven years, from March 1979 to May 1986, without a break, without stopping to think about anything. Then everyone went their separate ways. That's the first time the band basically stopped working. And that's when everything started going to hell.

When you're in a rock band, a lot of your life revolves around drinking and smoking and partying. In the early days, I'd hang out in Peter Jesperson's apartment, watching people do drugs, listening to the Only Ones, drinking scotch on the rocks, learning that whole thing. Or I'd hang out with the Oar Folk crew—Terry Katzman, Jim Peterson, and Mark Trehus—and after the store closed, we'd head across the street to the C C Club, a neighborhood drinking joint with a cranky-ass jukebox, ratty bathrooms, and vinyl benches. On any given night, you'd run into Paul Westerberg, or Lori Barbero from Babes in Toyland, or Chris Johnson from Rifle Sport. The music scene in Minneapolis revolved around getting together at the end of the day and drinking.

For a good chunk of the year, Minnesota is pretty cold. I've always said the Minneapolis scene was so fertile because you were indoors so much and you had to find an occupation or hobby or something you could do inside. Lots of us built our lives around playing music, hanging out, and drinking. I enjoyed beer as a kid, boxed wine in and after college, and was definitely a scotch man by 1986.

And then, that summer, I stopped drinking.

Greg's wedding was the last time I drank to get drunk. I'd been drinking beer, then some champagne at the reception at their house. The morning after, I woke up, looked in the mirror, and said, "Oh, my God..." I saw the reflection of my father. And I thought to myself, if I continue drinking like this, I might end up exactly like him.

Like my father, I was yelling—but onstage. Like my father, I had my paranoid moments, although they weren't consuming my thoughts. And like my father, I was being abusive, if only to myself.

I love my dad, but not *that* dad.

It was a vivid and sudden realization: I had to catch myself and stop this addiction before it escalated any further. I was twenty-five years old and I said to myself, I've had a drink every day for twelve years. If I keep this up, I will not make it to thirty. I was a high-functioning alcoholic. I had the scotch in my desk drawer, started drinking straight from the bottle at 2 PM, and could still complete a full day's work. It's great to be a high-functioning alcoholic—I could drink a fifth of scotch and drive just fine. It didn't interfere with my work, so why wouldn't I do it? No one ever pointed out a problem to me.

When I was younger, I felt immortal. But the stupid things I did when I was trashed... One day when I was at Macalester, I got drunk and raced my early-'70s Chrysler New Yorker, a tank of a car, right down the main drag through campus, saw a parking spot out of the corner of my eye, hit the brakes, and executed a perfect U-turn at 60 mph. I got away with it. Another time, I was driving around with my college roommate, Phil, and some other friends. I crank up Phil's favorite song, "Born to Run," and speed up to 100 mph, with everyone but me yelling hysterically, hiding under the seats. I'm laughing my head off. It's a miracle I'm still alive—and didn't kill anybody.

There was no program, no AA, no handbook. I didn't get the shakes or the DTs or anything like that, I did no twelve-step program and had no counseling. It was an act of sheer willpower, a testament to my ability to scare myself straight.

How? I had a drink a week after Greg's wedding—and made myself throw up so that I would never drink again. That was it. I haven't had a drink since.

As soon as I went sober, friends were hesitant to invite me out to the bars. I stopped doing the things friends do when they base almost everything around drinking. Instead of going to the C C Club or Liquor Lyle's every night, I stayed home, wrote music, and spent more time with Mike. He still drank but tried to be supportive. It was tricky for Mike because he enjoyed the social aspect of drinking.

So, through the back end of 1986, as I'm writing songs for *Warehouse*, the next Hüsker Dü album, I'm beginning to fade away from the scene—and from the band.

Our personal lives were spreading out. Greg was an hour away in Red Wing with Jeri and his new record store. Grant was hanging out with the notorious Minneapolis band Run Westy Run, had started a romantic relationship with their friend Ivan Daniel, and this new crowd drew him away from the band. Meanwhile, I was sober, spending more time with Mike, and working along with David Savoy to keep the office on track. What little interaction there was between the three of us wasn't going very well, especially the now counterproductive competition between me and Grant.

We got the recording sessions for the new album up and running in August, but there was tension in the air. For the first time, it felt like a chore, the one you knew had to be done, like cleaning the refrigerator—not a terrible chore, just something you didn't look forward to. In other words, it began to resemble a normal nine-to-five job. Never before did anything involving the band feel like work. All the years on the road, the long hours in the office, the near-to-actual poverty, none of that ever seemed like a hardship or a burden. Now, with the vibe getting heavier all the time, and whatever level of camaraderie we had waning, the words that would eventually be cast on the wall began to form in my mind.

We just didn't really care to be around each other. Greg barely showed up to the sessions, and Grant and I were hardly in the studio at the same time. He wanted time to experiment; in contrast, I would come in, bang it out, and it was done.

One thing Grant and I did come together on was replacing some of Greg's bass parts. We were listening down "Charity, Chastity, Prudence, and Hope" and next thing I know, Grant goes in, picks up the bass, and plays the part better than Greg did. As we listened through more tracks, if I heard a questionable bass track, I'd recut it myself. We replaced Greg's bass on at least four songs.

I was working late one night when Mike came by. After wrapping up the recording session, we drove home in our respective cars—Mike in his old, broken-down MG Midget and me in my beloved Le Mans. Mike was two car lengths in front of me when I got blindsided by a stolen Ford LTD. The driver had held up a gas station and was fleeing the scene. The LTD practically tore off the front of my car, then careened into the front room of someone's house. One or two seconds sooner and the LTD would have killed Mike, in front of me in that little MG Midget. I went to the hospital for X-rays and showed up the next morning at the studio in a neck brace, all junked out on pain pills.

Grant's song "You Can Live at Home" was to be the closer for this album, so it was one of the final tracks to be polished. Grant called for a freak-out at the end, like a "Hey Jude" finish, so we recorded the basic track with that in mind. In tracking, I laid back on the finish, playing simple rhythm parts to leave a nice, wide space for the guitar solo. The guitar solo that I over-dubbed later turned out to be the last notes of music I ever recorded in a studio with Hüsker Dü.

* * *

The healthy competition had finally turned against us and reared up when neither of us wanted to cut songs from the album. I was always more prolific, but my songs always got cut first and I was tired of that. I felt like Grant was throwing stuff together just to see how much he could get on the record. That could have been fallout from the "2541" incident; maybe it had something to do with publishing money. Wisely, Karin wouldn't get involved. It was out of David's league as well. There was no producer. There were no parents. It was all coming to a head.

If we'd only cut some songs, it might have been a decent single record. Looking back, *Warehouse: Songs and Stories* was no *Zen Arcade*. It was a less-than-stellar finish to our recorded output.

"Could You Be the One?" was written specifically to be a single—there was no heavy meaning to the words. "Bed of Nails" was a study in how I react when I perceive lies and betrayals around me (not well), and it set the stage for my future explorations into religious imagery. "No Reservations" is a nice series of lyrical images, like a handful of found antique post-cards. The song is like a soundtrack for driving cross-country—the birds on a line, the broken-down shack. Sometimes the things we notice in passing are as important as the big thoughts we remember so clearly. "Never changes the things I feel inside / Sit by a lake and cry"—things might not get any better, and maybe they won't get any worse either.

We were feeling some pressure from Warner to shine up the production so we could sell more records. Sometimes Warner would hint that if you guys can't shine it up, maybe we'll get someone else to do it for you. It wasn't overt, but you could feel it. Karin would just say little things here and there. So we did it ourselves and Warner was more than patient with us. We spent a lot of time on the sounds. For instance, we recorded the cymbals separately, which is totally weird. We recorded on one two-inch twenty-four-track and then we would reequalize everything and send it to another machine, sort of premixing. Production values had gotten pretty high by that point, and we were trying to hang in there.

We turn in the record and Warner is not thrilled with the idea of trying to sell a double album to mainstream music fans. The only way they'll do it is if they pay us as if it were a single record. Grant and I agreed to the reduced royalty, and our attorney, George Regis, negotiated this arrangement with the label. Even with deals like this, we still made more money with Warner. They gave us advances and cut us a more generous deal than SST did, and we got paid on time.

The cover of *Warehouse* was as fun to make as it is to look at. Inside a classical setting of stairs and pillars, Grant assembled several bunches of twigs and branches that had been sprayed with fluorescent paint. A camera was set on long exposure, and we illuminated the darkened set with flashlights and black lights, effectively painting in the ultravivid colors.

We appeared on the back cover, making *Warehouse* only the second record to feature a photo of the band. How we looked was never a key part of our aesthetic—our image was in our music and the artwork. Despite all that, this anti-image wound up being part of what we were about—the barefoot hippie drummer, the gas station attendant guitarist, the bass player who looked like he might be gay. The proof is that people always talked about it.

Daniel Corrigan took that back cover photo of us in the garden of Lakewood Cemetery—very fitting with the front cover, which, in retrospect, looks like a psychedelic funeral parlor.

* * *

By the fall of 1986, the mainstream was flirting so much with underground music that the USA Network staged a "New Music Awards" show at the Apollo Theater in Harlem. I presented the best new band award to Big Audio Dynamite, and a fully intoxicated Joe Strummer came to the podium to accept the award on behalf of his former Clash bandmate, BAD leader Mick Jones. The part that was not obvious on TV: I was standing behind Strummer, as instructed, with my right hand holding him upright so he wouldn't topple over.

By this time Frank Riley of Venture Booking in New York was on board as our new booking agent. Frank was great to work with and totally understood where we were coming from. When it came time to do a tour, Frank and I would get together on the phone, route it out in less than an hour, and say *go.* He booked the dates, getting us more money than ever before, with the routing exactly as we wanted it.

Very few bands ran this tight an operation. We came from nothing, worked hard for years to build our brand, and, along the way, we didn't waste a lot of time or money. We learned how to succeed without a bankroll behind us; now that we had one (Warner), we were careful not to become too beholden to the bank. I knew the worth of money. And through years of doing it, we knew that touring was our bread and butter.

We only had a couple of real differences of opinion with Warner. The first was Karin telling us we needed a "real" booking agent. She set up a meeting with one of the really big agencies. I went, and they were not the nicest people I had ever met. I came back and told Karin no way. Karin replied, "Frank comes over to this record company with a backpack on. You need a real booking agent." I said, "Sorry, we're not budging on this. We're staying with Frank Riley." Time has proved me right—Frank has long been one of the most prestigious agents in the business, and he and I have a great working relationship that continues to this day.

The second was Karin saying, "We all love David Savoy, but you need a real manager." At that time, record companies were averse to doing business with artists or the artists' handpicked mouthpieces. (A classic example would be Peter Jesperson's experience with Sire, after the Replacements signed with the label.) Admittedly, David could be a little flighty. Besides being inexperienced, he was bipolar and was on medication. Sometimes he stopped taking it, which exacerbated his problems. One day in the summer of 1986, he disappeared for a week, then called me and said something like, "I'm in San Francisco, in a halfway house, sweeping floors." When David returned, the four of us never addressed or resolved the episode.

Nor would we ever properly address or resolve the final time David disappeared.

CHAPTER 10

Grant and I were in a pattern of passive-aggressive, non-communicative behavior. As usual, Greg stayed neutral. Karin Berg and Warner were still questioning David's abilities as a manager. The label was on us to replace him, and had suggested Cliff Burnstein of Q Prime Management. Cliff was a nice enough guy, and a fan of the band (as were his main clients, Metallica), but we didn't like the idea of anyone coming from the outside to run the show.

Under this cloud of dysfunction, we booked the most ambitious tour we'd ever attempted: a trip of nearly fifty shows around North America to begin a few weeks after the release of *Warehouse*. For the first time, we took a full production—PA, lights, and staging. We planned to perform the twenty-song, seventy-minute double album start to finish, then encore with the hits—"Makes No Sense at All," "Pink Turns to Blue," "New Day Rising." It might have been a lot to ask of the audience, but that's what we chose to do.

Big rock bands made tour programs, so we did too. Ours was in an 11" × 17" format, printed on glossy heavy card stock. It had tons of great live photos, spin art, and images we created by hand painting small glass slides. We all kicked in text to accompany the images—short stories, prose, and parables, similar to the liner notes for *Warehouse*—although I wrote the lion's share of it. With little communication between the band members, there was no quality control, and yet the program ended up a fairly attractive package, though maybe out of tune with our original punk aesthetic.

A bit ironically, after Grant's blowup, Warner chose one of my songs as the first single. For the video for "Could You Be the One?" we took the color slides from the tour program art and projected them behind us on a large curved wall, painted with 3M road paint, made with tiny glass beads, which made the projected images glow even brighter.

*　　*　　*

The day before leaving for the first show of the *Warehouse* tour, Grant, Greg, Mike, and I were hanging out at my place. I was waiting for Pete Fleming, a local guitar tech, to stop by with my refurbished Flying V. David still hadn't shown up.

Then the telephone rings. I answer and the voice on the other end says, "It's David Savoy's mother. My son is dead." Right at that moment, Fleming walks in with my guitar. I get out my wallet, take a twenty-dollar bill and hand it to him, point to the door and wave good-bye, and continue the phone call. She continues. They found his body on the Mississippi River; he'd thrown himself off the Lake Street Bridge. It was winter and the river was frozen solid. A jogger found his body. She'd called the coroner and was going to have the body sent back to Concord. She was just trying to get a picture of what things were like in David's life, because she really didn't know.

I flashed back to that time in third grade, when one of my classmates suddenly fell ill and left school. I never learned what was wrong, and then he'd died. I didn't attend the funeral. That left me with no sense of closure. When my dad's father died in 1984, my parents didn't tell me for almost a month because they didn't want to upset me while I was on tour. I'd never had to deal directly with death and was completely unequipped to comprehend the pain or offer proper consolation to his family. All of this has resurfaced and haunted me many times later in life.

Meanwhile, I'm trying to manage an explanation to David's mother, having no idea what the right words are. David never spoke of his family much. I didn't know anything about their relationship, or what they knew of his personal life. I'm having this conversation, the other guys are watching me, and they know that something is up. I'm thinking, Yes, now we are totally fucked. This whole thing is definitely fucked up.

I'm also beginning to realize how little I knew of David's life outside the hours we worked together. Similar to my personal relationships with Grant and Greg, David and I rarely socialized beyond the office. We worked side by side in a room for eight hours a day, and by the end of the day, I naturally wanted to get away from all of it, no matter how much I liked David. I wished I could have told David's parents more about his life, but I just didn't know very much.

The night before David committed suicide, he met up with the road crew and wanted to go out for a ride. According to the crew, David showed no signs whatsoever, no behavior that would lead anyone to think he would throw himself sixty-six feet from a bridge onto the frozen Mississippi only hours later.

Why did he do it? I don't know. I will never know. I can only speculate. David had a history of emotional issues and had stopped taking his medication. It might have been something personal, perhaps a relationship went off course. It may have been the increasingly toxic environment in which we all worked. It may have been a crisis of confidence, brought on by the label questioning his ability. It was probably a combination of all those things. That's where I live with it. That's what gets me through.

I was devastated. I grieved. We didn't go to the funeral, which was held a week later in Concord, because of a blizzard. I felt terrible that I wasn't there. Instead we held a memorial service in the live recording room of Studio A at Nicollet Studios. Grant walked around burning sage. Friends shared stories of David. We were trying to keep things as upbeat as possible.

The folks at Warner were great through this. Julie Panebianco and Mary Hyde immediately got on a plane to Minneapolis and stayed for a week; Karin came in as well. Everyone who worked at Twin/Tone and for the band rallied around us and did everything they could to make sure we were OK. Without that help and support, I don't know what I would have done.

It's impossible to overstate the effect suicide has on the survivors. It shatters you, it shakes everything around you, it puts a scar on your psyche that never heals. All balance is lost, and the routines of everyday life start tumbling out of sequence — eternally out of order.

We chopped off the first two weeks of the tour and added it to the back end. What happened in those two weeks off? Greg drank like a fish. Grant seemed more distant and preoccupied than usual. As for me, I dived even deeper into the office work. It was as if I was still somehow working alongside David, as I had done for so long in that room. I think David's death amplified everything that was already happening. I've noticed that when people are traumatized, their true nature comes out because they are seeking refuge in what makes them feel most safe. The office work was a great solace for me.

One major change in the tour was my rooming arrangement. For years I had roomed with Grant, and Greg had shared a room with Lou Giordano. I didn't care to be around Grant any more than necessary, so I chose to room with our stage tech, Josiah McIlheny. Grant roomed with our lighting tech, John Henderson. Greg and Lou continued to room together, and tour manager Casey Macpherson roomed with monitor engineer Bill Batson.

Grant's personality had changed once he began hanging out with the Westies, although I didn't yet understand why. His old whimsy began to turn me off. Now his off-the-wall nonsense came with a hint of bitter and a dash of sour. At this point I was sober, pragmatic, and shell-shocked, and just didn't have time to humor Grant's increasingly vague behavior. Between shows and sound check and traveling in the van, I had quite enough of Grant. Maybe it was mutual, since Grant didn't bat an eyelash when I told him that after all these years I wanted a new roommate.

I bought a typewriter for the upcoming tour, for writing short stories and journaling. Warner Brothers was now using a primitive e-mail system called Telex, and since I was once again responsible for day-to-day communications with the label, I also had a Tandy 102 portable computer with these rubber couplers that you'd stick an old-fashioned phone receiver into. I packed both the computer and typewriter into a gold Halliburton case that I carried everywhere.

From late February through early May, we did a cloudy, grey tour of North America. It was a routine trip, save a few moments. One night we sold a couple thousand dollars' worth of merchandise at a show in the Northeast. Afterward our stage tech, Josiah McIlheny, went back to the venue's office and asked the promoter why the money wasn't accounted for in the settlement. The promoter slowly opened the top drawer of his desk, revealing a pistol, and said, "I don't recall any merch money, do you?" This kind of thing was common in those days—thankfully it seems to have faded away.

Then there was an episode before a show in Chapel Hill, North Carolina. I was sweating and shaking uncontrollably as if I had a terrible flu. I thought I was having a nervous breakdown, but looking back on it, I guess I had a clinical anxiety attack. I've rarely had such a massive crisis of confidence. I've had stretches of self-doubt, but it doesn't usually get to the point where I feel like, "Oh, my God, I'm paralyzed, I can't move or think or do anything." It was one of the first shows after the cancellations, and I was feeling so much stress about virtually everything: David's suicide, trying to get back out and do it, grief mixed with guilt—not to mention internal band tensions. Should I even be doing this, after everything that's happened?

I asked myself that again on Easter Sunday when we played a show in Lubbock, Texas. At the after party, the local metal kids made a videotape of a live rabbit being fed to a giant python. And sometimes on this tour there was a little comic relief. In Denver local music publication *Westword* came up with a brilliant idea—introduce the members of Hüsker Dü (the band) to the designer of Hüsker Dü (the board game). That afternoon we all played a round of the game against the inventor, and were soundly trounced.

Another funny thing happened the first night that opening band Christmas played. We had these big white columns and wooden stairs onstage, which mimicked the album cover. At one point in the show, Christmas singer-guitarist Michael Cudahy was running around and accidentally knocked over one of the columns, which weren't properly secured. It was funny, but in retrospect, those rickety pillars were sadly symbolic.

*　　*　　*

Despite the increasingly obvious internal band tensions and the concerns Warner had about selling a double album to the masses, more and more the mainstream media was paying attention to us. The first exposure that prime-time network TV–watching Americans had to Hüsker Dü was on April 27, on *The Late Show Starring Joan Rivers*, which was broadcast on the brand-new Fox TV network as an ill-fated competitor to *The Tonight Show*. We were to perform the single, "Could You Be the One?" then be interviewed by the brash, sassy hostess, and finally close out the show with a second song as the end credits rolled.

We arrived on the set in the early afternoon to find the stage area decorated almost identically to the *Warehouse* album cover. This made the three of us very happy. Soon Ms. Rivers appeared, we all introduced ourselves, and she promptly put us at ease about being on live television. She asked a few humorous questions, then moved on to the other guests: actor Ian McKellen and an eighty-five-year-old marathon winner.

Eventually showtime rolled around, Ms. Rivers introduced our song as "You Could Be the One," and we kicked in. Looking back on the footage now, my singing is tentative but, for once, I nailed the guitar solo on that song; I looked back at Grant and we shared a laugh about it.

After the song we walked over to the interview area. All three of us appeared a bit nervous at first, and as the two-minute interview crawled along, we started to loosen up a little. "You used to be much more of an underground group, much more radical," Rivers said to us. (So it wasn't *Maximumrocknroll* we had to worry about, it was Joan Rivers.) "As you get older," I answered, "your emotional spectrum becomes a little wider and it's not just screaming about how messed up the government is and how much you hate your parents." Rivers wanted to know who was the calming one and who was the wild one. I volunteered that I was "the calm one" (yeah, right). True to form, Greg took the neutral stance ("I'm sort of halfway in between the calming influence and the wild influence"), and Grant, Rivers presumed, was "the wild boy." The segment was done, and we were free to leave the set, return to the stage area, and play as much of "She's a Woman" as the credit roll allowed. We'd made our national TV debut with no grievous errors. How far we had come—and how far we were falling.

We played *The Today Show* on May 20. For that week, the show was touring the country, with a local musical guest at each stop. In Pittsburgh it was George Benson. Our show was in downtown Minneapolis, and we were to play several songs, one of which would air live on NBC. We hired a Jimmy Jingle truck to come to the site and provide coffee and donuts to our fans. Bryant Gumbel briefly interviewed us, then we performed "Could You Be the One?" There were several "grips," or technical crew, holding small portable heaters below Gumbel to keep him warm, even though it wasn't that cold. (By the end of the day, a few of the grips had serious burns on their hands and were taken to the emergency room.) We again played under the end credits, and onward through a short set of favorites to an appreciative and chill-swept crowd.

*   *   *

By now I was seeing the band in a different light. For one thing, I had lost respect for Greg. Despite our differences, Grant and I were the ones who were making this thing go and we knew it. We really didn't listen to Greg. So I just thought, let's keep him out of this. He'd check in maybe once a week, but Grant and I discouraged him from even doing that much—"Go play golf, go do your thing." It was just easier to move forward without his input.

It was like any office environment: if three people are working together and one day someone doesn't show up but the work-day goes as expected, well, maybe that third person isn't essential. I don't know how or when this dynamic with Greg started, but it did. The dynamic shifted, the balance tipped, and before we knew it, everything was different. But the audience never saw this. They only saw the excitement of the live show— and everything was fine onstage with Hüsker Dü.

Because Grant and I were partners in the studio, the more recording time we racked up, the less money it was for Greg. With songwriting, it was clear: Grant and I were the writers, and we deserved more money. Without the songs, there would have been nothing. Sadly, it also contributed to the race to write as many songs as possible on *Warehouse*. But beyond that it wasn't quite so easy to determine who should get what. Grant deserved to be compensated for doing the most of the band's artwork. I should have taken a 15 percent management fee and a 10 percent booking fee. Do we start paying Greg by the mile for driving? Where do you draw the line?

Things between me and Grant were strained, but we both

knew it was in our financial interest to keep the band on track. That wasn't the purest of motives for making music, but after years of struggling to make ends meet, we all wanted to make money, and Grant and I had tapped into a steady stream of cash. Despite our different philosophies, or what we did with our shares of the money once we made it, the financial compensation became the main motive for keeping the band intact. Hüsker Dü had become a job.

And a big part of that job was touring. We began a European leg in June 1987, hitting clubs and a few large outdoor festivals, sharing the bill with the likes of New Order, Robert Cray, and Elvis Costello. It was a bus tour, and for the first time we had the luxury of bringing our significant others on the road. I brought Mike and Grant brought Ivan, but Greg did not bring Jeri. Lou Giordano was still house engineer; we had a friendly yet no-nonsense British tour manager named Zop, and his workmate Mick Brown was our stage technician. I still work with Mick on occasion; he's a great guy.

The double-decker bus was large enough that one could avoid the others if necessary. There was the main lounge, and then, down the back stairs, there was a second smaller lounge. This is where I spent most of my time, alone, writing short stories on my typewriter. Mike would come down to visit, but by this point, all I wanted was to get away. I was tired, I was depressed, and I wanted to be alone. I was slowly cutting myself off from my band, my workmates, and even my partner.

This tour was also where I saw my first major fracture with Mike. He disappeared for the better part of a day at the massive Glastonbury Festival, then turned up later with some guy; he was sloppy drunk and they'd swapped T-shirts, so it was pretty clear that something had happened. I was very upset, but I was in the middle of a tour so I tried my best to block it out and let it go. Funny, I suppose—I'm the rock star, I bring my boyfriend along, and then *he* starts fucking around. That kind of tension is impossible to hide. What else could I do? Piss, moan, cry, or throw someone out the window of the bus? I was at work. I just wanted to finish the tour.

Things were in rough shape. The band was shaky, I was questioning Mike's faithfulness, and I was retreating from everything that was familiar. And then in late summer we started rehearsing for the next album. I started playing an Ibanez Artist, a guitar with the same pickups as the Flying V I'd used throughout Hüsker Dü, but a double cutaway body. It sounded the same but looked very different. A theme?

Historically, we would have torn through and learned a pack of new songs in about a week, then headed right into the studio to start recording. Now, we were struggling to come up with a coherent direction. I'd brought in a number of new songs but wasn't getting any positive feedback from the others. I suggested using strings and horns, doing bigger arrangements, and Grant and Greg would just shrug. Grant brought in songs, but I didn't find them interesting or inspiring. So the silent friction between me and Grant escalated.

Another source of friction was my home recordings. I had bought a drum machine and used it to lay out rudimentary beats for demo versions of my new songs. Grant mocked the demos by emulating the stiffness of the drum machine when we ran through the songs. Drum machines were uncool, and maybe Grant thought I was cutting out his creativity, but they were sketches meant to demonstrate the arrangements. So much for trying to move the sound of the band in a new direction.

Often we'd work for a half hour, then Grant would become really fidgety and distracted and say, "I gotta go do some stuff...I'll be right back." So I'd be left sitting in the room with Greg, twiddling my thumbs, working on logic puzzles, reading the newspaper, anything to keep myself occupied, seeing as I don't have a lot to say to Greg at this point. Grant's gone ten, twenty, thirty, forty minutes. Then he'd return in a completely different state of mind from the one he'd been in when he left. He'd leave seeming anxious and would return in a state of bliss. At the time I didn't recognize why.

* * *

Warner had tried to get us to replace our booking agent and failed. Then they tried to get us to replace our management, and they mostly failed there too. Now they wanted us to get a producer. Grant and I had done just fine producing the last three albums and weren't about to give up that seat without a fight. But we had to at least humor Warner.

We started at the top: George Martin. Warner came back and said he couldn't do it, but his former engineer Geoff Emerick was a possibility. Karin Berg suggested Pete Townshend; other names included ex-Feelies drummer Anton Fier, as well as Hugh Jones, who had worked wonders with Modern English. Hugh came over to meet with the band, but there was no chemistry. So the producer discussion was temporarily tabled while we went out to play an event called River City Reunion in Lawrence, Kansas.

We were one of two bands, the other being the legendary '60s underground group the Fugs. It was a celebration of Lawrence resident William Burroughs and several writers/performers/artists with a connection to the Beat movement: Allen Ginsberg, John Giorno, Anne Waldman, Peter Orlovsky. Edie Kerouac-Parker, Timothy Leary, Jim Carroll, Keith Haring, and even our longtime friend Jello Biafra were also part of the celebration. The Beats were a huge inspiration and influence for me, and it was an honor to be in the presence of all these great writers, these American outsiders/storytellers.

A month later, in October 1987, we did a quick run around the East Coast in what's called a "victory lap"—you do the first tour to draw attention to the record, then another tour to clean up when the record becomes popular. We made good money, around five grand a night. On Sundays we would treat ourselves to something nice, which usually meant a band and crew meal at Red Lobster.

We'd given up on playing *Warehouse* in its entirety. Compared to trying to get a lukewarm record over to people, playing the hits was a lot easier. It was like hitting the play button on a tape machine. All I had to do was start the riff of "Celebrated Summer" and everyone went berserk. It was much more fun than rehearsing and working on new material.

In the moment, during the actual sets, it was still fun to look out and see people go crazy for the band. That kind of reaction is never a problem. When all the volume is up and I'm facing the crowd and I don't have to look at the other two guys and I see the audience immersed in the music, that is still the moment when everything is right. No matter how silent or troubled the daily journey, that noise could make it all go away, even if only for those minutes onstage. To borrow a line, it can take a nothing day and suddenly make it all seem worthwhile.

But at the same time things were changing, and not for the better. My neighborhood in South Minneapolis was quickly deteriorating. The crack cocaine was coming toward me. Then one day I heard fire truck sirens, looked out the window, and saw that someone had set fire to my garage. That was a cue for me to start thinking about moving out of the neighborhood—and maybe even out of town. I didn't know how bad it would get or how else it might manifest, but I can feel when the juju is fucked, when it's time to move on. So on three main fronts—the band, Mike, and now my own home—I was starting to disconnect.

Another major change, one I would have once thought unimaginable, was the hiring of outside management for Hüsker Dü. At the beginning of this October tour, we finally conceded to Warner's request and brought in Linda Clark, who also managed Los Lobos and Violent Femmes. Linda had been a product manager at Slash Records, a Warner subsidiary that specialized in punk rock, so she was a known entity inside the Warner machine. Linda's assistant, Rick Bates, was a supernice guy. He rode with us in the van for a couple of dates, and I showed him how we did our business.

I was a little uneasy about no longer driving the Hüsker Dü train, but I wasn't getting paid extra for the amount of time and effort I was putting into keeping the train on the tracks. Grant appeared to be oblivious to the situation that was clearly unfolding in front of him. The train was changing tracks at a rapid clip, and not everyone was on board for the next destination.

CHAPTER 11

Right before a short Midwest tour in December—the Christmas Money Tour, as it was referred to on the inside—I made a big life change. Mike and I had talked about doing something different with our lives, and our neighborhood was starting to go downhill, crack and fires and all. It was time to leave South Minneapolis. We both grew up in rural settings, so we packed up and moved to a farm town.

Mike and I found this beautiful two-story brick farmhouse just outside rural Pine City, Minnesota, about an hour's drive due north of the Twin Cities on Highway 61, the old main road that ran from the Twin Cities north to Duluth. The place was nearly one hundred years old, on ten acres of land, with three bedrooms up top.

I bought the house in late November from a schoolteacher who had lived there with her now ex-husband, an African-American man; for rural Minnesota, I'm sure that was quite unusual. The one thing that was strange about this beautiful house was that the heavy wood doors upstairs were all split in the same spot, looking very much like they'd been punched through, hit with a fist.

One of the upstairs bedrooms was quite similar to my old upstairs bedroom in Malone, where I spent most of my high school years, hearing the Ramones for the first time and learning to play guitar. That became my studio room. The main outbuilding was a two-story granary that was once used to cure hops for making beer, and that became Mike's painting studio. Between the traces of violence, the similarity of the bedrooms, and the granary, there was a lot of symmetry between my childhood home and this farm.

Grant came up once to look at the place right after I bought it. He seemed a little anxious when he arrived, but, just as he did at rehearsals, he dismissed himself, walked the grounds by himself for half an hour, and returned in a much better mood. I didn't think anything of it at the time. Later that night, when checking on the large outbuilding, I found a leather belt that looked quite familiar lying on a haystack.

*　*　*

This short tour felt different from October—there was an unidentifiable tension and uncertainty. Everyone seemed on pins and needles, as if there were something secretive going on; I just didn't know what it was. In Champaign, Illinois, Grant stormed off the stage, claiming someone had thrown an ashtray at him. Eventually we went back out and finished the show, but I suspected that perhaps nothing had been thrown and that something else was eating at Grant.

The next day was St. Louis, Missouri. We had a night off before our show at the Mississippi Nights club, and we were staying at an Embassy Suites near downtown. We were spread out across this hotel, with its interior courtyards, all doing our own thing. At one point in the evening, I spotted Grant outside his hotel room door with a stereotypical druggie hippie chick—she had a shaman-lady vibe, like Stevie Nicks or the Dance of the Seven Veils. It struck me as bizarre—people who looked like that were rarely around our entourage.

For the life of me, I don't recall this, but two people who were on that tour say they came to me that night and explained the situation: Grant was addicted to heroin. The hippie chick had been flown in, presumably by Grant, to bring him methadone so he could get through the rest of the tour. The story makes sense: it's highly unlikely that Grant, in the midst of a tour, would have had time to locate a drug clinic, go there, register, and get methadone.

But all of that is beside the point: Grant was a junkie. It might sound ridiculous that I can't remember being told this; it's actually kind of embarrassing. The only explanation I can come up with is that I was so shell-shocked by the news that I buried how it was delivered, just pushed it aside. We still had a tour to finish and I just couldn't deal with it yet. The following night's show at Mississippi Nights ran without incident, and it wasn't until a week or so later that I was fully able to process the information. That, I remember.

The next show was Columbia, Missouri, December 11, 1987. Grant was jonesing or trashed on booze—or both—but either way, he was all messed up. We were trying to get through the set but were stinking up the joint. Bill Batson was running monitors by the side of the stage, yelling at Grant to stay awake. Lou Giordano was at the front-of-house position, practically hiding under the soundboard in embarrassment. I was doing my best to distract the audience, but it was an intimate room so there was no way to hide what was happening. Hüsker Dü didn't play bad shows. But this was a terrible show, simply awful.

At the end of the set, I headed back to the dressing room. I was livid. What the fuck was going on? Then it all started to fall out. Grant said he was sick—dope sick. He was a wreck, and needed methadone. I said, "We've got one more show in Omaha, what are we gonna do?"

Grant said, "I can do it, I can do it."

Greg then informed me he'd known for months but said nothing. I thought, Greg Norton, you would knowingly let Grant dig this trench in his life just to keep the band together? That's just excellent. Lou was in the room with us, shaking his head, saying, "I can't fucking believe this is happening."

That was it. I wasn't about to roll this shit out one more time in front of an audience. We didn't need to do any more damage to ourselves. Let's go home. I canceled the following evening's show in Omaha, and we drove eight bleak hours straight back to Minnesota.

Grant was a wreck—irritable, sweating then freezing. We kept changing the temperature in the van to try to satisfy him. At one point he said, "I'm hot, I'm cold, get me ten candy bars," so we pulled over to a gas station. Beyond this, there was nothing but total silence for the entire five-hundred-mile drive. I'd never been in a funeral procession, but this sure seemed like one. It was death. It felt like the end.

Everyone went their separate ways when we got back. I retreated to the farm, confused and disgusted. As the days went by, all the pieces started falling into place. Grant's distant and erratic behavior of the last eighteen months, the time spent away from the band hanging out with Run Westy Run and Ivan Daniel—now it all made sense. Between maintaining my sobriety, David's suicide, moving to Pine City, and trying to salvage my relationship with Mike, I'd been so preoccupied I didn't even notice what had happened to Grant.

You can't kick yourself for not realizing someone's a junkie. Junkies hide it really well. Even people close to them might not see what's happening. It's not like all junkies are scabby messes—many function at a high level for years, before they eventually unravel and reveal themselves. I'm not kicking myself for being oblivious.

And now that I knew, what could I do? My assumption was that Grant and Ivan were using together. But since the beginning of the band, I tried to keep a respectful distance from Grant's personal life. Now I was in no position to say anything about that, without appearing to be meddling. The professional friction had added yet another dimension of distance between us. I didn't know how to repair or address any of this. And I wasn't even sure how much I cared about the future of Hüsker Dü anyway—by this time I had lost a lot of interest in the band.

All of us have been in relationships or situations that have slowly turned toxic. We know they'll end sooner or later, but we stay, partly out of habit, partly out of fear of change, and partly through false hope, that things might change somehow for the better. Our gut tells us it won't get any better, but we hold on anyway. Then that one single incident happens, the one that shows you the open door, the one that gives you clearance to walk away.

We all make our own beds, and when the alarm clock goes off, it's time to wake up.

*   *   *

Hüsker Dü was scheduled to play an acoustic miniset as part of a benefit show organized by our old friend John Giorno for the AIDS Treatment Project. It was to be at the huge old Beacon Theater in New York, alongside Laurie Anderson, Philip Glass, William Burroughs, and host John Waters. But I called Giorno and explained the situation to him, and said that we couldn't do the show. I knew John was very disappointed, I could hear it in his voice. The next thing I knew, Grant had started driving to New York City—for what reason, I don't know. I called up our attorney, George Regis, and said, "Under no circumstances is he to be allowed in that building." I wasn't sure if that could actually be done, barring him from the theater, but if I had any control over the outcome, I wasn't going to let it happen. I wanted to stop him from getting on that stage—Grant wasn't Hüsker Dü. It turned out to be a moot point: he didn't even make it to the show on time.

After Christmas the Hüsker Dü family was at a crossroads. Casey Macpherson, our tour manager, suggested we organize Grant's family and friends and stage an intervention. Casey had experience with people with drug and alcohol problems, and he mentioned Hazelden, a world-class substance-abuse facility in nearby Center City, Minnesota. The intervention sounded promising. I'm not going to pretend that my sole motivation was to get Grant healthy; it was also a way to address the problems within the band. I sensed things were over, but there was no way to know for sure unless we confronted Grant directly.

We gathered up a handful of key people in Grant's life, like Abbie Kane, who worked at Twin/Tone, and other people Grant confided in and was close to. We didn't include the Run Westy Run crew, since I felt they were part of the problem. I thought Ivan was part of the problem too, so he wasn't going to be part of the solution either. We didn't call Grant's parents, but we talked to a couple of his siblings, which turned out to be the big mistake: his sister stooged it off; the intervention never happened; the opportunity was gone, and so was Grant.

I was upset, disgusted, and disappointed. I felt let down, both personally and professionally, by a partner who could no longer hold up his responsibilities to the business we'd worked so hard and so long to build. But Hüsker Dü was not only the livelihoods of the three people onstage, but of several people who depended on us for their paychecks. Grant was also letting down Lou, Casey, Bill, Josiah, everyone who worked for and cared about the band. My bottom line: Are we closing up shop? Are we going to take a vacation to heal? What are we going to do?

*   *   *

January 26, 1988. Greg and I decide that we need to sit down with Grant and talk, to figure out our collective future. This is the story that has never been told. This is the story of the last time the three members of Hüsker Dü sat together in a room.

Greg and I drive separately to South St. Paul to meet with Grant at his parents' house. Greg and I arrive and Grant's there, but so are his parents. So we're having a band meeting with the five of us around a homespun oval wood table, tucked up against the window of the small kitchen. Is this an awkward situation? Yes, most definitely. Grant's mom is being cordial, his dad a little cranky as usual. Beverages are offered, How was everybody's Christmas?, small talk, *blah blah blah.*

We open it up with "Grant, how are you doing, what are you doing, what do you want to do, what are we doing here?" Grant takes a hard draw on his cigarette, and slowly says, "Well..." That was always Grant's tell—this sort of pensive cigarette draw and then "Well..." Anytime he did that, I prepared myself for a bunch of words that wouldn't really add up to anything.

He says, "You know, I just, you know, I really want to get back to work."

I say, "Well, there's this problem. Have you talked with your parents about what's happening?"

Grant's mother takes the floor. His dad is just sitting there, not adding anything, just grousing a bit. "I think everything's OK," she says. "I think it was sort of like—it seemed like a cold almost. I think he's been good—he was sick for about a week, but, I think, it seemed like a cold or something."

At this point, Grant wants to have a sidebar with me, so he and I go from the kitchen into the dining room, leaving Greg to sit with the parents. Grant asks, "What's the advance for the next record?"

"One hundred seventy-five thousand, Grant."

"We just need to get going. We need to put all of this behind us," he says in a shaky but hopeful tone, "and we need to get back in the studio. That's going to be the best thing for us."

I flatly reply, "I think we should go back into the other room." We go back in, and the next statement from his mom is the one that does it for me.

She says, "You know, what I think might be really good is if—I just think that there's too much work. I think if you just played on the weekends and weren't working so hard..."

I flash back to that summer after my first year of college, when I didn't have anything going, didn't have a steady job, didn't have a dorm room, and I stayed with Grant's family. I ate at that same table with these people many times, and the poetry of it is not lost on me. The same exact table. And now it's come to this.

By this time Greg is turning three shades of grey. I'm just sitting there like, Oh my fucking God, this might be the most dysfunctional situation I've ever been in, and I grew up in one hell of a dysfunctional home. I push away from the kitchen table, begin to rise, and say, "I think I'm done here. Good seeing everybody. I'm going home to Pine City now."

Greg follows me out and asks what we're we going to do. I say, "I'm going to come down to Red Wing and get my stuff in a day or two. I'll talk to you then. I'm just going home now."

That was it. It was over.

*　　*　　*

On the long drive back to the farm, I kept thinking, I can't believe that just happened. This was the most absurd ending possible. It's definitely not very punk rock, and not even very rock and roll. It's just pathetic. As soon as I got home, I called up George Regis and firmly said, "George, I'm done."

After the Beacon phone call, George had to know something was coming. He understood the gravity of the situation. This was not just an impulsive "I'm pissed, I quit" that happens so often with bands and then blows over. No, the weight, he could feel it coming down the phone line. He didn't try to talk me out of it.

My first question was "What do we do?"

"Well," he said matter-of-factly, "the vehicle is that you are the leaving member, and under the terms of the agreement, I will draft the letter that states you are no longer a member of Hüsker Dü. Warner can act in one of three ways: they can keep you as a solo artist, they can keep the remaining two members and replace you, or they can terminate the agreement."

I understood and asked him to send the "leaving member" letter to Warner, Grant, and Greg.

The next day, I drove down to get my equipment from Greg's place in Red Wing. Greg asked me, "What do you think?"

I said, "I'm done with the whole thing."

"What about replacing Grant, what about the two of us continuing on?"

"I don't think so. I'm taking my stuff and I'm going back to the farm. See you."

The last order of business was dialing Grant's phone number at his parents' house. This was a day, maybe two, after our band meeting. Grant's dad picked up the phone. I said, "Hello, Mr. Hart, it's Bob. Is Grant available?"

"No, he's not available; is there anything you want me to tell him?"

"Yes, you can tell him that I'm leaving the band, and I hope he gets better soon, and to watch the mailbox for a letter that should show up in a couple of days."

And that's how it ended.

By 1988 Hüsker Dü was a no-win situation and I had to walk away. I was ready to move on to the next part of my life, even if I didn't have one clue as to what that might be. And, selfishly, I wanted to keep my professional reputation intact.

Because the breakup of the band was so public, some people paint Grant's heroin problem as the reason for the end of Hüsker Dü. Sure, it was part of it, but the writing had been on the wall for eighteen months. The Columbia incident was just the moment that made me realize it was time to walk away.

I had zero interest in dealing with the other guys ever again. The Hüsker Dü estate needed to be liquidated. Most of the physical assets—mainly T-shirts—went to Linda Clark's office in California and were sold to other vendors. Memorabilia, press materials, and office documents ended up in Greg's garage in Red Wing. It's funny—after all those years of work, when it was all over, I couldn't be bothered to keep track of all that stuff. I just let it go.

Massive Leasing had piled up some significant assets. I kept my vintage Pultec equalizers while Steve Fjelstad sold off the larger pieces and disbursed the proceeds among the three partners in the company.

The band was done. All of a sudden, it was mighty quiet. I hunkered down at the farm with Mike. I didn't answer the phone. I just let the people from the newspapers leave messages. I bought a satellite dish and watched a lot of pro wrestling. I went to the grocery store every few days. I cooked a lot of fishcake casserole. I even applied for a day job at a nearby state park working at the gift shop and giving guided tours. I started losing my mind a little bit, wondering what the fuck I was going to do with the rest of my life.

Eventually I had a breakthrough.

CHAPTER 12

I was doing a lot of creative writing, journaling, playing music, just trying to come up with ideas to keep myself going, to stay occupied. Mike was commuting daily from the farm to his job in St. Paul. As time went on, he came to dislike the two hours of driving each day and began spending two or three nights a week with friends in the city.

By March 1988 I had recorded a fair amount of music and put together a demo tape I titled, strangely enough, "Demonstration Tape." I used a Roland R-8 drum machine and a Roland D-50 synth, and was experimenting with new sounds and arrangements. Some of the songs that I composed during the summer of 1987, "Compositions for the Young and Old" and "Trade," eventually saw the light of day, but other songs were misguided. The best thing on the demo tape was an electronic cover of "A Sign of the Times," a 1966 hit for Petula Clark that I rediscovered while digging through a box of my childhood jukebox singles. The majority of the stuff wasn't focused; it was work ideas. It was me trying to find a sound that had nothing to do with my past.

Boston band the Zulus signed to Slash, Linda Clark got me the production gig, and in March I went out to Massachusetts to work with them. The Zulus were drummer Malcolm Travis, guitarist Rich Gilbert, singer Larry Bangor—the three of whom had all been in the Boston post-punk band Human Sexual Response—and bassist Rich Cortese. That turned out to be an important connection. Malcolm was a great drummer and easy to work with, but Rich Gilbert and I were at loggerheads much of the time. He was a good guy but was always challenging the direction in which I was steering the project. I think Rich saw the band as contemporaries of the Pixies and Throwing Muses; I thought they were a heavy band, closer to Led Zeppelin than anything else. And in the end, that was how the record came off. I thought it sounded great—and it got me out of debt.

I'd been in a successful band, but nowhere near the Springsteen level, so my income had been middle-class at best. Not only was I was having trouble selling the Minneapolis house because the neighborhood was going downhill, but my adjustable rate mortgage had ballooned and I was in danger of defaulting and losing the house. I just didn't have the money. Linda Clark loaned me $10,000 and the Zulus project repaid the loan within three months.

Professionally, things started to get back on track. I'd wrapped the Zulus project in May and gone back to the farm, and there was a slight bit of sunshine. I made it through the cold winter, I had this production gig under my new belt, and my debt was paid off.

It was spring and the fruit trees around the house were starting to blossom. Mike had gotten two dozen chickens—some show birds, some work birds—and I'd go out at noon and feed and water them. My favorite thing to do would be to go out in the yard with a paring knife, pick up the fallen fruit, cut it into little chunks, drop it to the ground, and keep walking. Soon I'd have this trail of chickens following me. I would sit in the middle of the field, and the birds would gather around me in a circle, waiting for more fruit. Another favorite pastime was riding my small yard tractor, mowing the two acres of level ground. I would sit in the middle of the field, hearing the train go by once or twice a day and seeing the Amish buggies moving by on the main road.

One day I went down into the city to run an errand. Driving back I saw a sign for a music store in Forest Lake, a town on I-35 halfway between Minneapolis and Pine City. I have no idea why, but I pulled off the highway, went to this music store, and saw this blue Fender Stratocaster up on the wall. I asked the guy, "Can I play that guitar?"

"Sure. What amp do you want?" he said.

"I don't need an amplifier, I just want to play it for a minute."

This guitar had the most amazing feel. The body was so dead-tight solid, the sound was resonating; it was a maple neck, not rosewood, a completely foreign instrument to me. It sounded amazing even without being plugged in. I turned to the guy and said, "I'll take it."

He said, "You don't want to p—"

"No, I don't need to plug it in. I'll take it."

It was 750 bucks. At the time, that was a lot of money for me to be spending on a guitar. But between the new Yamaha APX acoustic twelve-string I'd just bought in Boston and this blue Strat, it was the beginning of a whole new sound.

Everything started to open up. I'd written about two hundred pages of poetry and short stories that year. I experienced this outpouring of work. It was an amazing period; I could do no wrong. I still don't know what the hell was going on. One day, "Wishing Well," the next day, "Sinners and Their Repentances," three days later, "Brasilia Crossed with Trenton." It just didn't stop—it was an eye-opening experience.

For so long I had dealt in a wall of guitar distortion. Now I was writing cello parts on the synth, laying out string arrangements on top of acoustic guitars playing these huge open droning chords. The Yamaha twelve-string had an enormous sheen, filled with twinkling overtones that floated above the fundamental tone of the guitar. I called that sound the "bag of dimes" because it sounded like someone shaking a Crown Royal bag full of dimes—*thththththth*.

The acoustic guitar instrumental "Sunspots" was an accidental piece of music. I was trying to learn how to fingerpick, and the passages fell out of my hands and into my lap. It was so different from anything I had ever done before, and that's why it was the perfect opening track. It was a clear signal of the changes I'd made in my writing and playing style.

There would be days when I would write words and days when I would write music. The music days, I would start to strum and a motif or pattern would begin to unfold. As soon as that happened, I had an eight-track reel-to-reel ready to go. I'd find the right tempo, lay down a simple click or a standard beat, and hit record.

As far as lyrics, I'd have a sheet of free verse in front of me, which might contain several thoughts on a general theme: weeds, grass, water, dreams. When I improvised on the guitar, I would begin to sing, rarely sticking to the words in the order they appeared on the sheet, just grabbing lines as they went by: "Strum and sing, wishing well, runs wet and dry, I wish for things I never had. Surrounds and wells up in my eyes, the screaming voice, it lies." Before, it was four lines to a verse, and they may or may not rhyme clumsily, usually in an A-B-B-A or A-B-A-B scheme. This was more of a spiritual compositional style, with little concern for structure or rhyme.

I was becoming more aware of the use of vocal sibilance and consonance. Sibilance functioned as percussion, and consonance worked when *esses* landed on cymbals, and *tees* and plosives and percussives landed in spots that fell in with the guitar. Now I was more in tune with the smaller details, the spaces between words and sounds. This new approach was like nothing I'd ever done before, and it appeared out of nowhere. It wasn't like I sat down and said, OK, I'm going to work with drones, alternate tunings, free poetry, and plosives as rhythm.

Environment has always had a great effect on my writing

style, and my new rural setting was the spiritual and lyrical basis for this new group of songs, with their open fields and jackrabbits and hens.

The song "Lonely Afternoon" speaks volumes about my existence up there:

Well, the silence in this house
It echoes in this house
I pull myself together, say, 'Today I will get out.'

Mike was spending most of his time working in St. Paul. I was often alone and sometimes depressed, but I was kind of reveling in it. I was making great art, but I had no friends and no social life. My life was living in that house and working on music. I knew no one in town. My only regular human contact came when picking up groceries or going to the post office to pick up mail. Once it snowed two feet in twenty-four hours and the neighbors came by and plowed my driveway; all I said was thank you. I knew the chickens better than I knew my neighbors.

So I'm sitting up on the farm, watching wrestling and listening to Amish buggies and trains. I'm making shit up, trying to find something that makes me feel good about myself. I'm winding myself down to zero and then spinning back up, gathering energy and momentum. Some nights, I would sit upstairs in that workroom with the sound up so loud I felt like those speakers were as big as the earth and the moon. Closing my eyes and feeling myself shrink as the sound got bigger, I felt as if I were a speck of dust floating in space. The sound was taking me away from everything.

But back on planet Earth, I didn't have a record deal. I talked with Karin Berg and we came to the conclusion that she shouldn't sign me to a solo deal, no matter how bad or good the music was. This was a concerted effort not only to divorce myself from my past, but also not to live off of my past accomplishments. Had I pursued a future with Warner Brothers, everyone would have said I quit the band to have a solo deal. It was the wise move, even though it would have been very comfortable for me to continue working at Warner.

One sunny summer afternoon, the Soul Asylum guys and their manager, Dave Ayers, all came up to the farm. I hadn't seen them in ages and a lot had changed—I was a far cry from the howling alcoholic of years past. They all walked around the property, checking out the buildings. I played a song or two for them, and they appeared to like the music but were more concerned with getting back to town in time for a Minnesota Twins game. Dave pulled me aside and said, "We need to get together— come on down, I want to hear more of this music, if you don't mind playing it. I won't talk about it." Later the following week, I went down to his apartment, played him most of the new stuff, and he sat there stunned.

He said, "Have you ever heard of this guy Richard Thompson?"

I said, "No, who is that?"

He pulled out *I Wanna See the Bright Lights Tonight* and *Shoot Out the Lights*, two classic albums by Richard and Linda Thompson. He hands them to me and says, "I'm not going to say any more, just take these records and listen to them." Once I got home and listened to them, I got really self-conscious. I was like, Uh-oh, I think I see what Dave's talking about here: the Celtic melodies and chord progressions, the dark, introspective lyrics, the nasal singing voice. My new music was similar to Richard's, despite my being unaware of his work. But I didn't think for a minute about changing what I was doing—if people made the comparison, so be it. I had faith in my new musical course.

To stay engaged with the current scene, I cofounded Singles Only Label with Steve Fallon and WFMU DJ Nick Hill. The 45 was a cheap and easy way to give new musicians exposure. And, of course, I loved my jukebox singles when I was a kid, so this project was a natural for me. We put out great singles by Moby, R. Stevie Moore, and years later, a collaboration by Kurt Cobain and William Burroughs. Soon, the 45 single would become the coin of the indie rock realm.

Earlier this year, I met Anton Fier through Steve Fallon. Anton had been in consideration for producing the follow-up to *Warehouse,* and had drummed in bands like the Feelies, the Lounge Lizards, and his own band, the Golden Palominos. Anton's style was rooted in classic rock drummers like John Bonham and Ginger Baker. It was expressive, yet very methodical in how it advanced a song. Anton offered his services — "If you need a drummer, let me know. And I have a bass player that might work too, a guy I played with in Cleveland — he's in Pere Ubu."

I said, "Tony Maimone? I love Pere Ubu, I saw them at the Walker Art Center in 1979. I sat there in the front row for both shows, walked around the stage talking to everybody in the band. That sounds really great, thank you."

That summer I went back to Hoboken to visit Steve. Anton wanted to hear the music I was working on, so he rode back with me in my pickup truck from Hoboken to the farm. It was a two-day drive, it was ninety-five degrees, and we were riding through Ohio and Indiana with the windows down, no air-conditioning. Anton was a dry-cleaned guy — all pressed suits and crisp white shirts — but the only way he could keep his hair in place on the ride was to wear this dirty baseball cap of mine backward. This was not his style at all. Once we arrived at the farm, we spent a day and a half listening through the music I'd been writing. Anton had kind words for the work, and his measured praise was an additional boost for me.

At the same time, Linda Clark was shopping the demos to various labels. The first demos included "Wishing Well," "If You're True," "Sinners and Their Repentances," and "Poison Years." Interest built at Atlantic, Geffen, and Virgin. Late that summer we sent out the second batch, which included "Walls in Time" and "Brasilia Crossed with Trenton." By October it was clear I would have a new major label home.

A&R guy and longtime fan Mark Williams, previously of
A&M, along with label copresidents Jeff Ayeroff and Jordan
Harris, brought me to Virgin Records. The Virgin deal was
much better than the Warner deal—two albums firm, with
three single-album options. A $225,000 advance for the first
album, $250,000 for the second, and additional escalations for
subsequent options. I could have bought all the cars I wanted.

* * *

In December 1988 I began recording *Workbook*. Anton, Tony
Maimone, and I recorded the basic tracks at Prince's Minneapolis studio, Paisley Park, with Lou Giordano as engineer. Lou
had a very difficult five days—Anton was being unduly hard on
him because we weren't getting the exact drum sound Anton
wanted. I'm not certain why Anton was challenging Lou so
much, but it was constant. One extreme instance was in regard
to a "drum punch"; there were two bars in a song that Anton
wanted to record over. To do so with drums is very difficult on
both player and engineer; it takes an incredible amount of trust,
skill, and timing. The drums took up eighteen channels of audio
on the twenty-four-track tape, and punching in and out on that
many tracks at once is a major chore. "Get me in at the top of
bar sixty-one and out before the downbeat of bar sixty-three,"
Anton told Lou, adding ominously, "and if you erase the downbeat of bar sixty-three, I'll kill you."

The last day or two, we were in Prince's main room, working
on bass overdubs. Tony got his bass parts finished fairly quickly.
Outside of Sheila E.'s drums and Prince's scarves on the wall,
Paisley had an antiseptic vibe, a blend of airport terminal and
hospital waiting room, complete with a twenty-foot-high by
two-foot-diameter birdcage, presumably for a dove.

I was done with Paisley Park, and in January 1989 my longtime stage crew member Bill Batson drove all my equipment
from Pine City to rural Willow, New York, near Woodstock,
where renowned jazz musician/composer Carla Bley had a stu-

dio in her home called Grog Kill Studio. I hired engineer Steve Haigler, who had worked with producer Gil Norton on the Pixies. Steve and I hunkered down in the middle of the woods for three weeks of recording.

I had all my guitars, amplifiers, and other equipment set up in the live room. I was surrounded by vintage microphones and warm wood surfaces. As I sang and played, I looked out the large studio windows onto a pastoral January landscape of snow, trees, and more snow. Other than the music I was making, everything was still.

This was my first major recording project after being tied to a band for eight years, and I had this incredible freedom to express my thoughts in any way possible. But I also had the responsibility to make a great album that would highlight my rhythm section, as well as prove that I was capable of much more than recreating my past or skating on my laurels, that I was a serious artist in my own right.

I brought in New York–based cellist Jane Scarpantoni, who had recently worked on REM's *Green* album. I sent Jane my work tapes, which laid out the string arrangements in audio form—I'd never learned to notate with sheet music. Jane loved the arrangements, and beyond those parts I gave her latitude for improvisation, most notably on "Brasilia Crossed with Trenton" and "Poison Years." Jane went on to perform or record with many notable artists, including Nirvana, Sheryl Crow, and Bruce Springsteen.

Those weeks of singing, playing guitars, and recording cello at Grog Kill were exhilarating. The cellos brought the music to life, adding a new voice, a depth that had never existed in my work. All the time on the farm, the emotional investment, the months of solitude—it was all coming to a head and I could see the album coming together. I was shedding my former skin, forging a new sound, and I was quite pleased with what was on tape.

In February Haigler and I went to Blue Jay Studio in Carlisle, Massachusetts, to mix the album with assistance from house engineer Mark Tanzer. This was the biggest record I had made to date, in terms of arrangements, the sophistication of songwriting, and studio costs. I was thrilled with the final result. My first solo album was done and dusted, and I hoped that people would give it a fair listen—and not simply hold it up against my previous band's daunting discography.

The title *Workbook* was influenced by Chet Atkins's 1961 album *Workshop*. The cover of *Workshop* shows Atkins, wearing a sweater, holding his guitar, appearing to be working in his elaborate home studio. The back cover photo of *Workbook* is a reference to that photo, with me wearing a sweater too. That photo was taken in the granary on the farm in Pine City. I was sitting in the middle of the ground floor where the grain trucks used to back in to catch the cured hops that were poured down a funnel from the attic. Mike designed the Joseph Cornell–inspired memory box cover, which I still look at every day. Among the artifacts in the memory box were small shells, arrowheads, and antique typeset pieces he'd found in various places. The centerpiece was Jesus removed from his cross.

I love the liner notes to the Atkins album, which were written by David Halberstam, who went on to become a legendary Pulitzer Prize–winning journalist: "This is the lonely man's room and Atkins when he is working is a lonely man. 'Can't take my time in the studio. We're making money there and when you are making money you can't really take your time.'" I sure could relate to that.

I was very aware that I'd been in a band that made a lot of great records and left a deep impression. I told everyone at the new label, please, no mention of my old band, no sticker on the record, let's downplay it. I was taking away my own ace card, the one thing that could have made it easier. I was starting over.

I had probably been the first of my generation of American underground musicians to step away from a well-known band to begin a solo career. I wasn't aware of that at the time, but I think I made the move with grace. I sensed there was a part of the punk audience that would feel betrayed, but it was important to move beyond the sound of the past eight years. In the generation prior, Pete Townshend's *Empty Glass* would have been the model—the Who were a bombastic group, but Pete tackled difficult emotional matter with a more mature view.

The album got very nice reviews, which was a real relief. And when I heard that *Rolling Stone* was going to give it the lead review, and a glowing one, I knew things were going all right. "The road to success and maturity can indeed be treacherous for anyone who ventures onto it," wrote critic David Browne, "but *Workbook* is proof that every once in a while, it's worth it."

Critics and fans have often assumed that many of the lyrics of *Workbook* are aimed at my former band mates. But the words were mostly stream of consciousness, although inside those streams are rivulets of bitterness. The only song that consciously spoke to the breakup was "If You're True," which didn't make the album. Virgin eventually released a live version recorded at a May 1989 show in Chicago; the words spoke directly to the final year of that band. A sample stanza:

No more friends that lie and hide
No more games to play to get to know the answer
No more lazy days, unproductive days
Inspiration haze that every artist seems to know

* * *

For the first time in my life, I handed over almost every aspect of the business to other people. Linda Clark and Rick Bates were managing my career. At their suggestion I was now represented by renowned music attorney Alan Mintz. They hired a large accounting firm to handle my finances, which was a big deal for me—I'd never let go of the checkbook before. Now I was free to be purely a bandleader, the focal point of all praise and criticism.

But if I had been managing myself, I might not have followed the label's suggestion to spend $75,000 on the video for "See a Little Light." All the numbers were at least double anything I had ever spent before. The album advance was also double, but still, the video was crazy expensive. Videos were 50 percent charged back to the artist, which increased my debt beyond the advance.

I put together a band of expensive hired guns to do a limited run of dates and present the record: Anton, Tony, and Chris Stamey (formerly of the dB's) on guitar and synth guitar. Anton had toured with Herbie Hancock, so he had very high standards. He came in with a list. He needed dry cleaning and a nice hotel—not the best, but much nicer than anything I was accustomed to. Anton brought his digital recording rig in two large flight cases. I do things on a most-favored-nations basis, so Tony and Chris got whatever Anton got, and up the budget went. The salaries were pretty high for a small club tour as well. All this was new to me, but this was a different caliber of musician I was working with and I wanted them to be happy.

The first show was at Maxwell's, and I was a complete fucking nervous wreck. It was my first show since everything fell apart in Columbia, Missouri. Thankfully Maxwell's was a familiar stage for me. Steve Fallon kept me calm as best he could. Before the show I was coming unraveled, much like the Gildersleeves show back in 1983, but for different reasons. Back then I felt invincible and wanted to make sure no one forgot the show. But in 1989 I was out of my comfort zone, uncertain how the band would sound, even unsure as to how I should portray myself onstage. New musicians, new guitar, nothing felt the same; for the crowd, nothing looked or sounded the same. All my identifying marks were erased, and it was my first step toward creating a new public identity as a musician. Even my physical appearance was different—I'd lost a lot of weight in 1988 from a combination of stress and not eating road food, so my pudgy, rounded features were gone.

Walking onstage that night, it was the strangest feeling, as if I were trying to fill my own big shoes. Maxwell's had been the site of several classic shows in my past, and here I was going back to the scene, so to speak. But it turned out the worry was all for naught—the set went well, the band played great, and the crowd was behind me all the way. All the precision drills that Anton hammered into us paid off. It would have been hard for the four of us to fall apart on that small stage. Even still, in the basement dressing room after the set, I started hyperventilating from the stress; I must have looked like Dennis Hopper's character in *Blue Velvet* with an oxygen mask strapped to my face.

So we continued on this short club tour, and the shows went pretty well. The press kept getting better, my confidence grew, and I became comfortable in my new incarnation as singer–songwriter–band leader. We went back out in the fall, doing a full loop around North America, but without Stamey. Chris is a great guy, but the setting was too loud for him. He was very honest about it. In rehearsals I wanted him to get louder and turn up, because I kept turning up, getting more physical. I told him we needed to step it up and hit people with it. He said no. I said, "What do you mean?" Then he pointed a finger toward one of his ears and said, "Alex Chilton took this ear, and you're not taking this one," the pointing to his other ear.

After that comment, it was as if I was looking at a calendar in my mind, thinking, It's seventeen days until Chris gets sent home. Like a prisoner putting Xs over the dates as they pass, waiting to get out. It just wasn't going to work. Make no mistake: Chris is a very good player. But after hearing his concern, which was more than valid, I'm thinking, No, this is only going to get louder as time goes on. I didn't hold it against Chris, but I knew he had no future in the band.

During this tour I performed my first-ever solo acoustic shows at McCabe's Guitar Shop in Santa Monica, California. I'd seen Rosanne Cash perform there the year before and was a bit intimidated by the history of the room. I quickly got over it and turned in two solid shows that evening. I was learning on the spot: how do I make this voice and solitary guitar sound like the raging storm? What I learned: if the song is good, it will resonate, no matter what the orchestration. This was the first time I had no distortion in which to wrap my sound; I had to fill in the percussion with my playing; I had to sing clearly. It was a bit frightening at first, alone onstage delivering my words and music, but once I found my footing, it felt very comfortable—as if the words were meant to be delivered in this almost-solemn setting. At the time, I didn't see it, but this was a formative night for me, and the experience would be one to stand on.

*　*　*

Back in 1988 Mike had begun working for a scenic company down in St. Paul, designing and building sets for TV commercials. He rented a small loft in a building in Lowertown, St. Paul, so he wouldn't have to drive back and forth every night. At the time I thought that made sense. As it was, we only saw each other a couple of times a week—and in my mind, we were still a couple. I had been faithful throughout the relationship. But I was getting so busy, I wasn't noticing that he was slowly detaching. We were drifting apart.

Mike had a beat-up pickup truck and was missing payments on it. I happened to be standing in the parking lot of the scenic company where he worked in St. Paul when the bank came to repossess his truck. I ran and got my checkbook out of my truck and wrote a check for whatever the amount was. But when I told him what I did, Mike was pissed off and I couldn't figure out why.

As 1989 wore on, the disintegration continued. I was losing my mind on the farm. There was nothing left for me—I'd simply worn the place out. Then the house started getting overrun by box elder bugs. By late spring 1989, they covered the south-facing walls of the house. Infestation. I couldn't get rid of them;

they were everywhere. It was like a swarm of red locusts. I took it as a sign that it was time to move on.

After a business trip to California, I had a panic attack about flying home to Minnesota. I got all the way to the gate and flipped out. I had convinced myself the plane was going to go down, which is weird since I'd flown for years with no fear whatsoever. It was probably all about the prospect of heading back not just into my hermit-like existence in Pine City, but back to a relationship that I knew in my heart of hearts was broken. I ended up staying in Burbank an extra day to compose myself.

In July I put the farm up for sale and moved back to the Twin Cities. I rented a top-floor loft in the same building as Mike's space in St. Paul. It was hard to get Mike interested in coming up to spend time with me; we had grown apart. I wasn't acknowledging or processing this very well. I planned a birthday dinner for Mike and a few of his friends, but he couldn't be bothered to show up. No one showed up. Someone with more relationship experience might have seen the handwriting on the wall, but I was blind to what was happening.

Early Saturday morning, September 9, 1989, there was a farmer's market kitty-corner to the building. I bought some cheese and fruit and a cockscomb—a bloodred-burgundy flower with the appearance of rippled paper. I put the cockscomb in a vase and went downstairs. I knocked on his door—there was no answer. For the first time, I used the key Mike had given me to let myself in. I was sitting alone with the cockscomb, waiting. Then I heard someone fidgeting with keys outside the door. In came Mike—in his underwear.

I asked, "What's going on?"

And he fell apart. It all tumbled out: "You know Tim who lives next door?" he said. "Well, I was over there last night."

"Are you guys...?"

"Yeah," he said.

"All right, don't let me interrupt."

I went back to my place. I didn't feel angry about what had just happened. I knew things had been over for a while, but I wasn't facing up to it. I knew why Mike avoided me when I moved to his building in St. Paul. He wanted the distance for reasons beyond the commute. He had a second life that he didn't want me to be a part of. Now I had opened the door, faced the situation, and could walk away. I felt sadness, but even more so, a sense of relief.

The decay of my relationship with Mike had been right in front of me, but I was so busy in my own little creative world that I hadn't even noticed that he'd checked out. I paid no attention to the warning signs. But if I had paid attention to all the signs, my head would have exploded. Sometimes the eraser is your friend.

I had no boyfriend and I had no house. Anton and Tony lived in New York City. Steve Fallon, my best friend through these times, lived across the Hudson River in Hoboken. It hit me then. Why should I stay in Minnesota? There was nothing left there but history.

Once I move I don't look back. I move forward and away. And that's what I did. Over the next seven days, I gave away the possessions I didn't need and put the rest in storage. I packed all of Mike's remaining possessions in a trunk, took a copy of *Workbook,* inscribed it "To Mike, thanks for everything. Love, Bob," placed it on top of his items in the trunk, closed it up, and brought it down to his space. I packed the rest of my belongings in my Subaru wagon and drove eighteen hours straight from St. Paul to Hoboken.

CHAPTER 13

I arrived in Hoboken around 3 AM. I figured I would stay up all night and meet Steve in the morning. I was exhausted and hungry, so I headed to Malibu Diner on Fourteenth and Willow. I walked into the diner and a guy named Mark Zoltak recognized me. Mark was a Maxwell's regular and quite familiar with the music scene.

"Bob, what are you doing here?" he asked.

I replied, "I just left Minnesota. I think I'm going to move here."

"Where are you staying?"

"I don't know," I said. "I'll probably stay with Steve until I get a place."

He says, "I'm a realtor—there's an apartment a block from Maxwell's on Twelfth and Washington that just opened up. It's a railroad apartment on the fourth floor of a five-floor walk-up; we can look at it tomorrow. If you like it, you can rent it."

I said, "I'll take it." Sight unseen and serendipitous: an affirmation that I did the right thing by leaving Minnesota.

Bill Batson drove all my possessions out to New Jersey and put them in a storage space in Secaucus. I settled into the Palace Hotel on Tonnelle Avenue in North Bergen for three weeks until the apartment was available.

It was September 1989, and I was rehearsing the band every

day at a studio in Weehawken. Anton and Tony were once again the rhythm section, and I hired an old Minneapolis pal of mine named Jim Harry to play second guitar on this tour.

Almost every night after rehearsal, I made the five-minute drive to Maxwell's to eat dinner. Most of my friends and acquaintances either worked or spent evenings at Maxwell's: Steve, Nick Hill, bartender John Bruce. I started meeting new people, including this one guy named Ray, who I was really fond of. We spent a little time together. He was a handsome and sweet guy, but any potential romance was soon preempted.

One of the guys milling about Maxwell's late one night was Rick Phelps, who was a painter/visual artist. He was an acquaintance of Steve's, originally from Georgia, and he moved to New York City to work on his art. There was also this younger blond-haired, tall, skinny fellow; we started looking at each other. His name was Kevin O'Neill. He was with Rick. We introduced ourselves and made some small talk. Right away, it was obvious that there was a mutual attraction.

A few nights later, just days before I left for tour, Kevin and I reconvened at Maxwell's for dinner. We sat at a small table for two, ordered food, and observed each other's behavior. He asked, "When did you move here?"

"Earlier this month."

"You were in Minneapolis, and you had a boyfriend there, right?"

I said, "Yeah, well, that's over now. I'm here and I want to start over."

"Yeah, I just moved to New York a month ago myself. I just broke up with my boyfriend of four years."

I asked him, "Where did you move from?"

"I grew up in Athens, Georgia." Then he paused a moment and added, "I know who you are. I worked at Wuxtry Records with Pete Buck. I grew up around Jim Herbert and the B-52s, I was in *Inside/Out*," and on and on, making his case. I'm thinking to myself, this guy is interesting.

"I'm so happy to be single," I said. "I don't think I would ever want a boyfriend again, I'm so sick of relationships." And Kevin's echoing my thoughts, telling me, "Yeah, me too, never again."

The conversation continued for less than an hour before we were together in bed at the Palace Hotel.

Right away people were commenting on us. Kevin was six foot three, full head of blond hair, sparkling blue eyes, and a winning smile. He had charmed me and could do the same to anyone with whom he came into contact. I was no shrinking violet either. The two of us together made an impression on people. We couldn't help but be noticed.

Steve Fallon didn't approve at first. Less than a year before we met, Kevin had a brief run-in with heroin while spending a season in Amsterdam; now he was sharing a studio apartment in the East Village and working at a Kinko's. Steve was being protective of me, and I appreciated that.

Kevin remembered seeing me around Athens in 1985, when Mike and I visited for a week. We stayed with Michael Stipe for a handful of days, and it was a bit odd at times. For instance, Stipe requested that certain friends enter through a window instead of the fully functional back door. Maybe it was an art project. Who knows? (I used the door — I don't do windows.) After a few days, we moved over to Pete Buck's place. Kevin said he had noticed me around town and steered clear. I was drinking a lot on that trip and making a bit of a scene. Kevin also claimed he was the one boy in Athens that Michael Stipe pursued but never "got."

Both Kevin and I were of the "still waters run deep" disposition. Whereas Mike had been a happy-go-lucky type who may have grown tired of my emotional cross, Kevin not only understood, but seemed ready to tolerate — and even facilitate — my sometimes heavy soul.

In one month I had closed up a six-year relationship, left the town where I'd lived for eleven years, and fallen in love with a beautiful young man. It was now October, and I had to go on tour just as the apartment became open. While I was away, Kevin moved in all of my stuff, set up the apartment, and started spending time there.

Three weeks into the tour, Kevin joined me in San Francisco. He had been around musicians for years and fit right into the tour. Kevin enjoyed smoking marijuana at the time, as did Anton, so they got on wonderfully. It worked out well—I would go do press, Kevin and Anton could hang out and have fun, the band would play the show, and everybody got along.

I played a handful of gigs with the Pixies right as the Bay Area earthquakes happened. I had a few conversations with Charles (aka Black Francis) from the Pixies. We treated each other as equals, a very cordial interaction. Kim was a touch eccentric, but always charming. At the time, I wasn't fully aware of the influence I'd had on the Pixies. I hadn't yet heard about the legendary 1986 want ad placed by Charles in a Massachusetts music paper: "Bassist wanted for rock band. Influences: Hüsker Dü and Peter, Paul and Mary." All I knew was there was an artistic kinship. I enjoyed their music and thought they were a solid live band.

My job was to go out and make sure people knew I was dead serious about my presentation. During my performances on that leg of the tour, I went out there and gave blood, screaming and stomping across the stage. I was breaking all the unwritten rules of the support act—you should not do this, do that; less production, lower volume. I was trying to steal the show. It had nothing to do with them, personally; it could have been anybody. It was having the crowd in front of me, I wanted to get my point across. And, yes, I wanted to show off, just a little, for my new boyfriend. During the cathartic album (and set) closer, "Whichever Way the Wind Blows," I'd fall backward off the stage, over the barricade, into the crowd with the guitar and microphone, screaming bloody murder.

After the San Francisco show, Kevin and I rented a car and drove together up the coast to Arcata, where we stopped to walk the magnificent craggy cliffs. North to Eureka, through the Redwood Forest, and on to Portland and Seattle. It was a very romantic week, tour activities notwithstanding. I kept wondering to myself: How did I end up with this incredibly handsome guy?

I finished the six-week tour with two well-received (and sold-out) headlining shows at First Avenue. I made my name in Minneapolis, and to this day, am still thought of as a native son. With these shows, I wanted everyone to know I was tearing it up more than ever and at the top of my game.

After Minneapolis I stopped home in Hoboken for nine days before the European leg of the tour began in Cardiff, Wales. When I walked into my apartment, I saw it was set up perfectly. I was touched and thrilled at what Kevin had done with the place. After this I was in a hurry to tear through the Europe dates so I could get home and spend time with Kevin.

Not that the tour didn't have its moments. As the band and crew tried to enter an after-hours nightclub in Copenhagen after our show there, my second guitarist Jim Harry got sprayed with mace. People were getting kicked, punched, and pushed, so the security guards grabbed us and skirted us into this upstairs room. We get there, the room was very quiet and still, and there, sitting quietly in a chair, is none other than Boy George. He's like, "Hello." Two minutes ago people were kung fu fighting and getting sprayed with mace, and now I'm sitting in a quiet room with Boy George. I'm like, "Hey, George, what's up?"

*   *   *

After returning from Europe in December, I finished the writing for *Black Sheets of Rain*. Half the album had been written in Minnesota before the breakup with Mike and the second half was written in Hoboken. I would sit in my little room and work, and Kevin would be next door in the bedroom watching TV.

Black Sheets of Rain was a dark record. The first group of songs (including "Hear Me Calling," "Out of Your Life," and "The Last Night") made up the "write it and it shall be so" part, the self-fulfilling prophecies, and the remainder of the album was "yeah, and that's what happened." So the album ended up a combination of the prescient and the pensive.

February 1990: it was time to make the record. I wanted Anton to be happy with the drum sounds, so I asked him where he wanted to record and he suggested the Power Station, a place on West Fifty-Third Street in Manhattan in a former Con Edison power plant. It was one of the most famous studios in the world, and people like John Lennon and Neil Young had recorded there. Tony was excited at the prospect of working there too. We worked with house engineer Steve Boyer and, sure enough, Anton loved the drum sounds right away. Everything was sounding big—that was the nature of the main tracking room.

This was the biggest-budget record I ever made. I had a quarter-million 1990 dollars to work with, and I spent three months and $125,000 of my advance making that record. It was rock and roll fantasy land, unlike anything I'd known before. This was not working at Total Access from 11 PM to 9 AM, recording on used tape. Not even the experience at Paisley Park could match these sessions. The Power Station was a world-class studio, with some of the best gear in the history of recording.

Whitney Houston was working upstairs for much of the time. Even though she appeared to weigh about ninety pounds and seemingly never ate a morsel, Ms. Houston had an extensive hospitality rider with fresh fruit and deli trays every day. After she left, our second engineer would go upstairs to retrieve the leftovers. We dined like royalty on the scraps of the then reigning queen of pop.

I piled on so many layers of electric guitars that it felt almost claustrophobic. Then in the final mix stage, Steve Boyer and I enhanced the drums—already thick and huge from recording in Studio A, a cavernous wooden room with a churchlike peaked ceiling—with samples that made them sound colossal. Every part of the sound spectrum was saturated to maximum capacity.

I turned in the record in late April, and the label became concerned about how to market such a dark album. This thing was beyond the "wall of sound"—listening to it felt like being trapped in a large factory that was quickly filling with motor oil. What can I say? I wrote the songs during a troubled time and the record reflected that. It was that and having all the technology at my disposal—the loud room we recorded in, combined with equipment that could layer and bolster every aspect of the sound. And we'd just come off a year's worth of very loud, very physical performances. It had altered my perception of the quieter songs, and not necessarily in the best way.

I wish I'd done some things differently. The demos for *Black Sheets* were more delicate; the album versions were sheer bombast. "Hear Me Calling" was intended to be a tempered plea for revisiting a failing relationship, but the album version turned somewhat bellicose. "Stand Guard" had worked fine without all the layers of distortion, but these snapshots of a dissolving life, conceived as elegiac, suddenly became a constant chorus of pile drivers leveling everything in sight. The only song that escaped relatively close to the original vision was "The Last Night," which held true to its compositional tone of resignation.

The lyrics of the title track are torturous and relentless:

Is there an upside to every downside?
Keep it inside, it's a downward slide of broken glass, it
    keeps building in piles
And I don't know if the sun ever smiles
It's the black sheets of rain, following me again
Everywhere I go, everywhere I've been, following me
    again

The song was partially inspired by a trip Mike and I had taken in 1987 while on tour in Europe. We had a day off between Munich and Vienna, and I wanted to visit Dachau. Dachau was one of the first Nazi concentration camps, and besides Jews, the prisoner population included political dissidents, Catholic clergy, and homosexuals. We entered under a large archway emblazoned with the infamous words "Arbeit Macht Frei" ("work makes you free"). The sun was beating down and there was little shelter to be found. One image that sticks in my mind was the sight of a group of Carmelite nuns, praying and worshipping in the middle of the barren work field.

As far as dealing with David's suicide, "Hardly Getting Over It" forms a matched pair with "Hanging Tree." The former was about how I perceived death and the latter was about how I actually dealt with it. When I sing "Another bridge I cannot bear to cross alone," that's about David. But that song is also about a lot of other stuff that was going on in my mind at the time. "And above my head, all that's left are footsteps of some kid too young, too far away from home," that's Mike. And "I've been on the mend, I've been getting ready to change my name again," that's me.

* * *

Sandra-Lee Phipps was a photographer/documenter of REM and the Athens scene who was living in the New York City area. She took the album cover photograph of the door of a rusted-out, abandoned car over on the Brooklyn waterfront. Less than ten minutes after Sandy got the shot, the car was towed away. The remainder of the package was photos she had taken on a trip to South America and included shots of Anton, Tony, and me on the back cover.

Kevin and I left Hoboken in June 1990 due to a problem with the neighboring apartment. One morning I heard a commotion in the hallway. I stepped out and saw the father—drunk, yelling, and waving a pistol at his kids. I called up Kevin and said, "We have to get out of here." We moved to a 1,600-square-foot loft in Tribeca, a somewhat unsafe neighborhood at the time. Kevin got mugged one night while I was on the road. I felt helpless—but at least the thieves let him keep the cheap sterling ring I had given him.

Black Sheets of Rain was released in August 1990 to mixed reviews. It didn't sell as well as *Workbook* and wasn't getting much support at commercial radio. Still, I didn't let it get to me. I had a job to do: go out and play the shows and beat myself up every night, hands and throat bleeding, head ringing all the time.

We were down to a trio for this album's tour. Jim Harry was a good player on the fall 1989 tour, but his presence inadvertently helped me make an important realization: most fans don't want to hear a second guitarist competing for the same sonic range and tone as my guitar.

The tour became demoralizing to me when I realized that my business had gotten away from me. It wasn't that I was being taken advantage of, but I had lost control of the finances and logistics. I wasn't writing the checks, I wasn't monitoring what was happening. And I paid greatly for that in 1991. Everybody I was employing was making more money than I was, and it was starting to piss me off.

After the last show in San Diego, we were staying in a nice hotel, much nicer digs than any of us lived in. I looked around, shook my head, and decided this was it—no more touring like this. Even in the most spartan of days, touring would break even. But this tour had lost money. So this was the end of the Bob Mould Band, version one. Anton went on to the next well-paying gig. Tony went home to Brooklyn. There was no European tour for *Black Sheets of Rain*.

The thing is, I loved playing with Anton and Tony—I learned so much from playing with them. The main lesson: how to stay in time. In Hüsker Dü the three members were in a constant race—the tempos went faster, and the beat became a blur. But

Anton dug in, and if I tried to pull ahead, I would know because he would do something to remind me where the tempo was. And Tony was fixated on Anton's bass drum. His job was to hit those bass strings at the same time as Anton kicked the bass drum—that's how tightly they played together. With Anton and Tony, I realized the punch that a rhythm section can create when they're totally in sync. I heard it, and more importantly, I felt it.

Those lessons resonate to this day; they set me up to be a long-standing player. Still there were lessons left to learn. The final lesson from the Virgin era would be an expensive one. It would bring about yet another change.

CHAPTER 14

Our loft space in Tribeca was across from the loading dock of a *New York Times* distribution center, so Kevin and I had a built-in 4 AM alarm every morning. I set up my recording studio in the back bedroom. Two windows in the rear area were boarded up; as the weather turned cold, so did the room. It was a dodgy setup, but we worked hard to make it our home.

One night over the Christmas holidays in 1990, the electricity in the entire building blew out. The fireman who responded pointed to an old-fashioned on/off switch—imagine a normal light switch you would flick—and said, "Here's the breaker for your whole building."

Most of the electronic devices in the apartment, including some of my studio stuff, were fried by the power surge. Kevin and I went to our landlord and said, "We have to move, it's not safe here." He apologized, wrote us a check for $5,000, and in March of 1991, we moved to Williamsburg, Brooklyn.

We signed a lease on a 4,400-square-foot loft on Richardson Street—a former clothing factory, complete with several left-over boxes of Frederick's of Hollywood–size tags. There were dozens of orange 220-volt electrical cords hanging down from the ceiling to supply power for row after row of sewing machines. The first few months we lived there, women were knocking on the door every day looking for work.

Kind of pioneering, yes. Back in 1991 the only people with blue hair in Williamsburg were the grandmothers who shuffled daily through the pockmarked streets. We shopped mainly at a shabby supermarket over on Metropolitan Avenue—we were living on the cheap. I parked our Omni on the street and the neighborhood Dominican kids repeatedly busted out the windows. After the third time we replaced them, they started to stop and say hello, because they realized they weren't going to drive us out.

It was a huge place. The living room alone was the size of the entire Tribeca loft. There were windows around two sides facing north to McCarren Park and westward over the industrial landscape of Williamsburg. We built a bathroom and kitchen, and Kevin refinished the floors with an old-fashioned sander; it almost killed him, but it looked beautiful. Again, he was working hard to make a comfortable home for us.

Sometimes we would climb the fire escape to the roof, where we had parties of a hundred people or more, with wonderful views of the entire East Side of Manhattan.

*   *   *

I'd learned so much about the music industry from running my own affairs for eleven years that my fellow musicians often called me for advice about the business side of things. I was familiar with the folks in Sonic Youth, both as a fan from our SST days and from playing together in Paris in 1987, as well as through mutual friends in New York City. So when they were negotiating the jump to Geffen in 1989, guitarist Thurston Moore called me and grilled me about what to do, what not to do, and how to do it. Like the old days of sharing notebooks, I relayed my experiences, both good and bad; I hope that my conversation with Thurston helped them strike a good deal with Geffen. (Given the amount of time they stayed, and the uncompromising nature of their Geffen output, it seems like it went well.)

I wish things had gone so well for me. I'd given Linda Clark limited power of attorney to sign off on certain business decisions. One decision she made was to sign away my songwriting royalties for both records to Virgin in exchange for tour-support money. She never told me about it; I only found out about it from the label. I knew I was getting tour support but I had thought it was getting charged back to the general artist account, which is separate from the songwriting account.

I found this out at the beginning of solo touring in March 1991. I discovered my mechanical royalties for the two Virgin albums were gone forever. This was especially traumatic for me, given the careful way I'd handled my career myself until 1988. This was the first time I'd trusted someone else to look after my business interests, and this is what happened. Even worse, it triggered my latent paranoia, and the whole thing made me suspicious of ever again allowing anyone else to have power over my finances or major business decisions.

Linda Clark did some good things, but signing away my publishing without consulting me was unforgivable. The only thing a songwriter has, in the end, is the publishing. To sign that away, to get tour support that they could then commission, was terrible. I was furious. I got on a plane to Burbank, showed up at the office, and said, "How dare you do this to me? You're all fired. What in the fuck were you thinking? Where are my boxes? Give me that roll of tape. I'm boxing this stuff up and shipping it UPS to New York City. You're *done*." Next stop, Alan Mintz. "Sorry, Alan, you did a great job as my lawyer, but you're fired." Next stop, the accountants. "Any money left in the account? Give it to me right now. Oh, and you're fired." I get back on the plane and go home. It took two afternoons to fire the entire lot.

After this it was time to reckon with the label. By now Virgin was unsure of what to do with me, and I was equally unsure as to how to proceed with them. I went back home and talked with Steve Fallon, who said, "I don't want to get involved in your business, but here's somebody you should call: Josh Grier."

Josh was a young lawyer, just up to New York from North Carolina, where he'd been the general manager of the indie label Dolphin Records, working with Let's Active, Tommy Keene, and Corrosion of Conformity. Now he was building up his music-law practice. I liked Josh right away. I explained my situation. His recommendation: Walk away. Management screwed up your mechanicals, you're in debt to the label on the artist side, and you'll never see any money. They'll write off the losses and you can start over. Walk away, play some shows, do something. I thought about it for a moment, and quickly realized Josh was right: walk away and don't look back. It was an easy decision, it felt right, and it was time to move forward.

I called my agents, Frank Riley and Paul Boswell, and asked them to continue booking solo acoustic and electric shows all over the world. I did a run of solo dates in March and loved it — it was a good way to work out new material, and the low overhead was a joy after the *Black Sheets* tour. I ended up being on the road for close to nine months in 1991, winding around the States a couple times, driving a rental car an average of three hundred miles each day. I'd show up in a town, play long sets, then find a cheap motel to lay it down for the evening. All I brought was my guitars, a bag of clothes, and a jug of water. I was netting five to seven thousand dollars a week, building up funds to bankroll the next project.

One of the more memorable shows of the year was in March at the annual South by Southwest music conference in Austin. I played a brief and energetic set in a small, sweaty room called the Cannibal Club. The mix of older material and works in progress was typical, but this was one of those special nights: I had an enthusiastic crowd, I was in a particularly good mood, and I had the great fortune of working with a sound person named Jim Wilson, who would resurface a few years later as a creative collaborator.

It was also on this trip that I was introduced to Vic Chesnutt, a gifted singer-songwriter from Georgia. Vic and Kevin were old friends from Athens. Vic was promoting his Michael Stipe–produced debut album, *Little*, as well as readying the follow-up, *West of Rome*. We played dozens of shows together in 1991, including three shows over two nights, March 30 and 31 at 7th Street Entry in Minneapolis—a dozen years, to the day, since the first Hüsker Dü shows in St. Paul.

These stretches of time on the road were both lonely and inspiring. Driving for hours every day, I had plenty of time for reflection; consequently, I was writing a lot of songs. I'd come home for a week at a time and head straight for my studio. My studio room was right next to the Brooklyn-Queens Expressway, and lots of dirt, fumes, and noise came through the solitary window. A large section of the floor was covered with sheet metal, while the walls were brick, which made for a very reflective sound. Despite these less-than-ideal conditions, I did some of my best work in that room.

I was trying out the new material during the solo shows, and people loved the songs. It created a great feedback loop where the positive response to the music would inspire even more songs. I'd write "A Good Idea" one day, "If I Can't Change Your Mind" the next. I was getting back on track. I'd come home with all this good energy and record elaborate demos with bigger production touches. The simpler home recordings that started in 1986 with the four-track were now eight-track recordings, and were approaching album quality. I was in my most fertile period to date.

Kevin came along for the Australian dates, then we went to Europe for a month. That was when the documentary *The Year Punk Broke* was filmed. In one fleeting shot, you can find me smiling like the *Mona Lisa*. Maybe I knew something was about to happen? The tour started with a week of club shows in Holland, opening for Dinosaur Jr. The shows were held in community centers. During the day senior citizens ate their government lunch; at night the space turned into a rock club. The crowds were mostly stoned squatter kids, and they were right

BOB MOULD

up in my face yelling, "You suck, get off the stage. We want Dinosaur!" There was a certain irony in that, considering Dinosaur was one of several key bands who had followed in the footsteps of Hüsker Dü. It was a little unsettling at first, but by the end of the week, I'd gotten used to the banter from the crusties and, as a parting gift, dialed up the distortion boxes and cranked out waves of noise, both to torture them and to drown them out. The crowd reactions got better as the weeks went on, particularly at the festivals with Sonic Youth and Nirvana.

At one show in Germany, an afternoon outdoor festival in front of 7,000 people, Nirvana played their set and then trashed the joint. That was the way they were the entire summer: ripping drunk, trashing things, all building up to the release of *Nevermind* that September. Having to follow them, pounding away on a twelve-string acoustic by myself at an outdoor festival in the middle of the afternoon, was no easy feat. Nirvana destroys the stage, then it's me carrying on like Richie Havens at Woodstock, then Sonic Youth comes out with their army of guitars. It was a lot of work, but great fun, and it was the constant challenge of capturing a festival crowd's attention with only my guitar and my voice that made me a better player in the long run.

There was something in the air; we all knew something big was about to happen in the world of music. Boswell was smart to book me on those shows, and it was the right place to be. The year had started so poorly, but after the summer dates in Europe, I felt hopeful. Seeing bands who may well have been influenced by my earlier work, watching them flourish, gave me a sense of pride and accomplishment. Now I had a bunch of great new songs, and the stage could not have been set more perfectly for me.

I went back around the States by myself in October. I played the Trees club in Dallas, a warehouse building in the Deep Ellum section. That night there was a big thunderstorm—heat lightning and a torrential downpour. Behind the stage, the huge

184

roll-up garage doors were raised so the crowd could see the raging storm hitting the street. Appropriately enough, I was playing lots of songs from *Black Sheets of Rain,* and with the combination of the lyrics and the elements outside, people still talk about that gig.

Again, I was following Nirvana's stage-trashing act. Those guys were a day ahead of me in some towns, and they'd played Trees the night before. When I walked in, the monitor board was trashed. I'm like, "What happened?" "This fucking band Nirvana was in here last night, and the bastard singer tomahawked the board with his guitar." I understood why the whole crew at the club was upset at Nirvana. But I also know what it meant in the greater scheme. Nirvana was turning things upside down. They were going to be huge, and things were going to change in a big way.

And it's funny — well before playing those shows that summer, I'd heard the demos for *Nevermind,* courtesy of Gary Gersh, their A&R person at Geffen. According to Linda Clark, I was in consideration for the production job, which went to Butch Vig. When I heard *Nevermind,* I knew they'd made the right choice. I highly doubt I would have gotten the job, and if I had, their album wouldn't have sounded as crisp and concise as what was released. But that's all right, another door was about to open.

I'd been going around to prospective labels with my portable digital audiotape (DAT) machine, playing five songs, and then leaving. People were interested but also a bit hesitant, likely due to the limited success of *Black Sheets of Rain.* My longtime friend Julie Panebianco liked the demos, and in November she made a suggestion — one that would have a lasting effect on my career. I was about to play some UK gigs, and she urged me to meet with a fellow named Alan McGee while I was there. "Alan runs this label called Creation Records and is a huge fan of yours," she said. "Take the demos over, see if you can meet with him, and see what he thinks of your songs."

Kevin and I headed to the Creation offices in Hackney, in East London. Alan's Scottish accent was so thick I could barely understand what he was saying. Hüsker Dü was "the fookin' best," he said. "The Jesus and Mary Chain and my band wouldn't exist if it weren't for you." He was an intense character, clearly in love with music. He had a passion in his eyes when he spoke.

"Are you going to play me some fookin' music?"

I played him a five song demo—he thought it was genius and wanted to put it out right away. "What do we need to do?" he said. "Look around this office. Creation is a small label, we don't have a lot of money." The vibe of the office reminded me of the good times at SST, but Creation was a bigger operation with grander ambitions. Signing with them immediately felt like the right thing to do. It was one of those moments, like falling in love or winning the lottery—you might not see it coming, but when it happens, instinct tells you to go with it. I asked for time to go home and speak with my attorney, but I knew Creation was the place for me.

The second major event on this trip happened one night after a show. Neither Kevin nor I liked driving in the UK, so we traveled with the support act, Heather Frith, and her manager, Abbo, who'd started a British label called Big Cat Records. Abbo also managed a few artists of note, including EMF and Jeff Buckley. Abbo was driving when he looked back at me and said, "Have you ever heard this band My Bloody Valentine?"

I said, "The name is familiar, but no. Why?"

He said, "They're on Creation, they just put out this record called *Loveless*, and you really should hear it."

We had a nice rental car—it could top out at 110 mph at least and had a great stereo system. Abbo put the CD in and cranked it as we blazed down the motorway in the dark of night. I was astonished. I couldn't believe what I was hearing. This was *the* record I thought was never going to be made. From the opening notes of "Only Shallow," it sounded less like music and more like a herd of wild elephants stampeding through the rental car. The slightly warped feel of the music, created by the gauzy combination of Belinda Butcher's oft-whispered vocals and Kevin Shields's pitch-shifting tremolo effect on his guitar, was unlike anything I'd heard in popular music. By the last hypnotic swoons of "Soon," I was hooked. I was still wet from performing, we were racing to get back to London, and the whole thing was a religious experience. No one spoke a word for the entirety of the record. When it was done, I was both exhausted and exhilarated. *Loveless* had a profound effect on me.

* * *

The US label that showed the most serious interest in my new demos was the prominent independent label Rykodisc, which had enjoyed success with reissues of the David Bowie and Frank Zappa catalogs. Jeff Rougvie was the A&R person at Ryko; he was a longtime fan and an easy person to spend time with. Jeff really liked the demos and arranged for further meetings with other key Ryko personnel. I asked marketing head John Hammond to make up a plan, and he came back with pages and pages of detail, way more than I ever saw from Virgin.

Josh Grier and I constructed parallel deals with Creation and Ryko. For instance, if we did a single with one label, the other had to follow suit. That way they would naturally compete, but also benefit, as long as they kept up with each other in terms of setting up tour dates, press, and other promotions. It was a really smart move. We negotiated small advances since I didn't really need the money to get up and running. By now I'd done a year's worth of solo shows and socked away enough to make a couple of records without any loans from the record label. By asking for less money in advance, I was able to do licensing deals for the albums, meaning I retained ownership of the master tapes. Win, win, and win.

Now I had to put together a rhythm section. I remembered drummer Malcolm Travis from producing the Zulus back in

'88. Malcolm was a sweet guy, easy to work with, and an excellent player. And the Zulus had just broken up, which meant he might be available. I called and asked if he was interested. He was. That filled one spot.

Kevin knew David Barbe from the Athens band Mercyland. He and Kevin had been friends since attending journalism school at the University of Georgia. In the summer of 1991, Kevin visited his family in Georgia and David drove him back to the Amtrak station. Kevin took it upon himself to cue up "Hoover Dam" on a Walkman and play it for David. David loved the Beatles as much as I did, Kevin knew that, and so he had picked the most Beatlesesque song to play for him. The song finished, he took the headphones from David, boarded the train that had just pulled into the station, and disappeared down the tracks. A few months later, Mercyland was over, and David and I had serious discussions about the future. He signed on for the job and became the first person beyond Kevin to receive copies of the demos I'd been working on.

The majority of the new material was pop songs, simpler in structure than the material from the solo albums, with a more driving beat. *Loveless* had left a big impression, but the other album that informed this group of songs was Cheap Trick's *In Color,* a favorite of mine from my high school days in 1977. I wanted Malcolm to approach the drums with the undeniable power and economy of Bun E. Carlos.

I knew that Lou Giordano was a hard worker, a quality engineer, and would be perfect for the job of helping me make a record, so I asked him. Lou wanted full producer credit, to which I said, "Come on, Lou, you know better." The songs were fully formed, and I was just looking for technical expertise and a valued outside opinion about the quality of the performances. We agreed to coproduction and coengineering credits.

We packed up and went to Athens. Kevin, Malcolm, and I set up camp at a motel on the edge of downtown. We worked in this ramshackle storage space David found, with a couple of power cords and a crap-ass PA, a chewing-gum-and-duct-tape type of setup. John Bruce, who I knew from Maxwell's in Hoboken, came down to film the rehearsals and daily goings-on. I was putting us through the paces—we had thirty songs to learn in a few short weeks. We threw ourselves into this new relationship, with nothing guiding us but a notebook full of songs I'd written trying to make sense of yet another turbulent period in my life. I'd taken back control of my career; now all I hoped for was a decent third solo album.

CHAPTER 15

There were lots of reasons it ended up being a *band* called Sugar. Right away I had the sense that these guys were willing to do what it took to make things work. I wanted them to be paid well, but I could also tell they weren't going to make unreasonable requests. David had done van tours practically his whole life. Malcolm was looking for a gig since the Zulus were over. We were all in this spot, and we gave in to it.

I also realized that the average indie rock fan in 1992 didn't want some guy's name on the T-shirt—they wanted a shirt emblazoned with a band name. These days many solo projects have a band name because it sells more T-shirts. But more important than the marketing, it just felt like a band. David and Malcolm were not hired guns, we were in this together, building this project in a very punk rock manner.

Still, I was the band leader, the main songwriter, and the guy who directed the traffic. There wasn't a lot of room initially for David and Malcolm to steer the creativity. Their job was to interpret my ideas as powerfully and concisely as possible. But as the rehearsals went on, everyone started to add small personal creative touches, while staying true to the blueprint. Shuffling a drum fill, adding an additional bass run while turning the corner on the end of a verse, realigning an anticipatory beat—it was a lot of small, small touches, but over the course of learning thirty songs, they defined the overall sound.

While rehearsing in Athens, 40 Watt Club owner Barrie Green asked us to play a show, so now we had to come up with a name. The four of us usually met for breakfast at Waffle House. One morning I noticed a sugar packet on the table and thought, That's as good a name as any.

The first Sugar show was on February 20, 1992. The Athens music community turned out in full force to see the band, and the show was even covered by a writer from *Spin* magazine. In just those few weeks of rehearsal, we had constructed a formidable set of songs, and we blasted through the new material in an hour. We opened with what would become the first three songs off the first album, then played a few more upbeat pop songs, then a four-song suite that was a work in progress, then four cover songs that included the Monkees' "The Door into Summer" and the Who's "Armenia City in the Sky," and finally an original closer. We clicked well as a unit. It felt natural to all three of us. The crowd cheered loudly as we left the sweat-soaked stage with a successful debut gig under our collective belt. It was time to pack up the gear and leave the temperate Georgia climate behind.

We trekked northward to snowy Massachusetts to begin the recording sessions for the album with Lou Giordano. We set up shop at the Outpost, a modest studio built in a barn-like garage in suburban Stoughton. Lou and I were very demanding of David and Malcolm. We were constructing the basic tracks in a very methodical and unorthodox way. We laid down a click track, David put down some guide tracks on bass, then Malcolm played the drum parts without hearing guitar and vocals. He did a great job, although it took considerable time. Once the drums were finished, it was time to put down the "keeper" bass tracks. David had done a magnificent job of studying for the sessions, but his bass itself was another story. The intonation was off, and when I started adding guitars to the tracks, some of the bass parts were out of tune. We would address this problem later.

This wasn't the Power Station and we weren't staying at hotels. I'd learned, $125,000 later, that if the songs are there, money shouldn't matter. And I just wanted to get back to a simpler way of doing things. David and I slept in sleeping bags in the attic of the studio. Malcolm typically went back to Boston, but occasionally slept in the lounge on a couch. Lou lived not far from the studio and drove home each night. There was a supermarket on the other side of the fence—we took one of the boards off the fence so we wouldn't have to walk all the way around the block in the freezing cold. We had a hot plate, a coffee maker, a microwave, and a dormitory refrigerator. We were a long way from Whitney Houston's deli tray.

After two weeks it was finally go time for me. I dug through the thirty completed rhythm tracks, discarded a few songs that weren't feeling right, and focused on the remaining twenty-two. Once the guitars were done, I moved on to day after day of recording vocal after vocal. Once I had the lead vocal I liked, the process would begin: making double, triple, sometimes even sextuple layers, then I'd start on the harmony vocals. This was before Pro Tools, so I'd do it over and over until it was perfect. If there were a couple of *esses* that didn't land together, I did it again. It's tricky business.

I had put those guys through it, and now I was putting myself through it. The stacked vocal arrangements became larger than ever, but after several long days of heavy singing, my voice was wrecked. All I could do was sit in the control room and play solitaire on the computer, waiting for my voice to come back. Those were frustrating days: I was still on the clock, paying for the studio. Lou would find things to do with the recorded tracks, but if I had no voice, we couldn't make much progress. After several weeks of waking up, drinking coffee, working very intensely for fourteen hours, then crashing and doing it all over again the next day, I was physically exhausted and questioning the whole project.

I didn't know it going in, but we were actually making two very distinct records at the same time. I was plowing through the songs and the fluff was starting to fall to the side. I relegated a half-dozen songs to B-side or outtake status, leaving me with a ten-song pop album and a six-song suite that had a heavier feel. Those six songs had very few words, but I had a sense of what they were all going to be about—a religious theme, questioning religion. The religious references first surfaced in *Workbook,* and even Mike Covington had, without any prompting from me, included religious artifacts in the memory box for the *Workbook* cover.

My Catholic roots crop up from time to time in my music, like on "Sacrifice/Let There Be Peace," the last song on *Black Sheets of Rain,* with its images of self-flagellation, martyrdom, heresy; the struggles between right and wrong, blessing and blasphemy, and sinner and saint. I assume the role of a character wandering through the fire, trying to both find my way into the hottest core of Hell and an exit to Heaven, for which I might be rewarded with oxygen.

At the time of the Sugar sessions, I was not religiously observant. But if there was an earthquake and the only building left standing was a church, don't you think a lot of people would go back there? I didn't have an earthquake, but I could sense something coming. It was nothing that I could particularly identify; it was just instinct, like animals that sense the ground shifting before humans do, or the way car alarms sound in the distance moments before the first tremor arrives.

Then one evening I had a phone call with Kevin, and the conversation went poorly. Somebody said something, which led to something else; nothing major happened, nothing to call it quits about, but it flipped a switch and everything in my brain got turned upside down. I went into a self-destructive rage. I sent Lou home, and I stayed in the studio's attic by myself for a day and a half, writing and writing and writing. My imagination was on fire; I was out of my fucking mind with white-hate-light-energy-noise. I was trying to purge the frustration with Kevin, the exhaustion, and the self-doubt by writing. I was spilling it all out, trying to boil it down to an essence.

One song to come from that time was "JC Auto," which was (up till then) the ultimate in self-destruction and desecration. As a way to humor myself, I placed an acrostic, a hidden reference to its predecessor, "Poison Years," in the second bridge: "Parts Of It Seem Over Now / You Expect A Real Solution." "Feeling Better" attempts to re-create a mind that's carrying fragments of many personalities—the call-and-answer game in all corners of the mix, themes refraining, fractured pieces of the song recombining and mutating. It was the musical equivalent of the sound of throwing a box of glass off the roof of a house, running downstairs to spread out the pieces on the pavement, and trying to glue them back together.

"Walking Away," the song that would become the closer of this heavy suite of songs, was clearly influenced by *Loveless*—the warbled synthesizers, the slow tremolo pitching that Kevin Shields popularized. There were layers of keyboards, particularly the D-50 synthesizer (the Van Halen "Jump" sound) run through distortion boxes. It resembled the sound of someone rising from sleep, someone fading away in the morning fog, or someone regaining consciousness in a hospital after being pounded for hours with bare knuckles.

I like to close the darker albums leaving the listener wondering if I'm all right. A strange analogy would be the *Batman* TV series. If the story stretched out over two episodes, we would always see the hero in peril at the end of the first installment. Imagine Robin, hog-tied by the villainous force du jour, dangling over a boiling vat, waiting, hoping, praying for Batman to come and save him. The suspense was intended to make the viewer come back for more, to see how it ended.

One would think, with everything going so well in my personal life, that I wouldn't be experiencing this questioning, this doubting, this insanity. Was it self-sabotage? Not really. Was it an unpredictable blend of religious doubt and a perceived loss of a companion, mixed in with thoughts of suicide, both by others and myself? Maybe. Once the questioning starts, it spirals in all directions. All these emotions, doubts, and fears start colliding and piling on top of each other, and I want to destroy everything around me. The eighteen-year-old kid, the nihilist who dragged a rusty blade across his wrist in front of his dorm mates, he never went away.

Growing up in a violent house makes you hypervigilant—you do everything in your life to make sure the egg doesn't break. The vigilance, along with the depression and the demons I battle, it all mixes together and shows up in my work. I beat myself up when things get out of control. I was supposed to be watching over it. Even more disturbing is the realization that I alone can create an utterly hopeless catastrophe. The only way to control it is to create it. Write it and it shall be so—the prescient thought. People don't fully understand or appreciate the power of the mind, the power of thought, and the power of the word as self-fulfilling prophecy. We can all create the catastrophe, but we can't control the outcome, even if we imagine the scenario from start to finish.

Sometimes I can misconstrue and amplify the simplest thing, and that can set it off. It can be as simple as a lack of perception, or as complex as a complete miscommunication. It's like going into the woods, surrounded by dry brush, with a lit cigarette. You thought you stomped it out, but you actually flicked it into the brush. Suddenly half the state is ablaze. Maybe there was a lot of dry brush that wasn't necessarily visible to the eye. Maybe it was waiting to burn. Maybe the phone call with Kevin was perfectly normal.

So I'm screaming all of that into the songs. As they were happening, I felt gigantic, bigger than the room, like I was ten feet tall. The speakers felt like they were the size of the earth, and I'm listening, not believing I created it. If other people get it, great, but at that moment, what does it matter? Making a living and getting your validation is really important, and it all needs to be attended to later on, but at the moment you make the work, you're sitting there and taking it all in. Who cares what happens? Who considers the fallout? I guess I don't, not always. I feel untouchable, I feel invincible. It doesn't happen that many times in your life, where the sound is coming out of the speakers and it's as big as life gets. That's when it's like religion: you give yourself over, you take the journey, and you take the pain with the joy. Very few of us get that many chances to make that big a statement.

*   *   *

When we started up again, David came back to Stoughton to rerecord his parts with a new bass. He was doing quite well, but a few songs, "Feeling Better" in particular, were eluding him. One day there was a lot of tension in the air, and I sensed that David might be ready to walk away from the project. I calmly said to him, "I can tell you're getting really frustrated with doing this, and I think you're about ready to just want to go home. And if you do, I understand, and there's a train that leaves here later today." But David didn't give up—he stuck it out. Lou was very helpful in building David back up, assuring him that he was the man for the job and that he could rise to the occasion. And he did.

Lou and I spent four weeks mixing the finished songs at Carriage House, a rural estate on the outskirts of Stamford, Connecticut. We stayed in a large apartment above the studio, and there were long stretches, sometimes five days, when Lou and I didn't leave the property. Once the two albums were mixed and assembled, we headed to New York City for a long, loud, exhausting mastering session with Howie Weinberg, with whom I'd worked since *Flip Your Wig*.

When we were done, I went home to Williamsburg. I was in

bed for three weeks. I didn't leave the house and barely even left the bed. I was wrecked. I had a rash all over my hands and arms and blisters popping on my hands. I thought I was dying. I'd completely fallen apart. The months of nonstop creativity and intense emotional purging had caught up with me. It was psychosomatic, and it manifested itself in physical form on my body, like stigmata.

It was early June, the weather was beautiful, but I wouldn't even open the window for fresh air — the walls were closing in — and Kevin finally said, "You have to go see a dermatologist. And you're not going to die." I agreed, and when the doctor examined me, she said, "You have a stress rash running along your nerve lines. Have you been under a lot of pressure lately?"

A little ointment took care of the rashes in a few days. But that just treated the symptoms. I still had to deal with the underlying problem. I had to learn how to relax. With the emotional state I had worked myself into, that seemed nearly impossible.

The word that always dogs me is *catharsis,* and in the most classical sense. People often use it to describe my work, and it's probably apt, though I'm not the one to ask. It's not necessarily that I feel *better* after creating or performing, but simply that I *feel.* Either way, it's not necessarily a fun word to drag around. What am I supposed to do with it? When do I get to be happy? Maybe someone can adapt this book for Broadway: *CATHARSIS!* starring Bob Mould. The hit play with no ending.

Finally the albums are done and both labels are thrilled. David and Malcolm are happy with the results. We run through a two-week warm-up tour in July 1992, hitting clubs in the South, Northeast, and Midwest with just the three band members, Kevin in a car, and stage tech Barry Duryea and tour manager Bill Rahmy dragging the gear around in a van — doing it old-school. In Morgantown, West Virginia, there was barely a stage to play on, so we used our flight cases to extend the stage.

John Bruce, who had been documenting the early rehearsals,

produced two inexpensive videos. The first, "Changes," was a fairly primitive collage of rehearsal footage. The second, "Helpless," was a blend of lip-sync footage shot atop the Puck Building in Soho and slow-focus portraiture vignettes filmed both on the streets of Soho and in the meat-packing district of Manhattan.

UK journalist Keith Cameron, who was one of my biggest supporters, came over to join the tour. He rode in the car with us for a few days, including an afternoon visit to Heritage USA, Jim and Tammy Bakker's religious theme park. I picked up a couple of T-shirts in the gift store; one was something about "Jesus, Saint or Sinner, Repent." We listened to the six-song suite at earsplitting volume in the car, with me driving, Keith riding shotgun, and the other three in the backseat. His stunned-silent response was not dissimilar to the one Peter Buck would display months later after hearing the same tracks at the Williamsburg loft.

In late July we made our first appearance in the UK. We debuted with a Virgin Megastore in-store, played a few songs, and blew the power out. That night we played the Clapham Grand. The following day we recorded a handful of songs for Mark Goodier's show, which aired on BBC radio. Following those sessions, we played a show at University of London Union. And this is all in one weekend.

The set was strictly Sugar material—and people are going bonkers. Part of the PA system fell into the crowd at the ULU show, but once we realized that no one had been struck by the heavy speakers, we kept right on going. There was a communal energy, there was stage diving, and the rest of the night bordered on the edge of a beautiful insanity. Sugar didn't have to provoke people into that state of frenzy; they were already waiting to let it go. Same with the band. It wasn't the "we're going to fuck you with this thing until you fight back" approach of the underground punk scene in the '80s. It was more of a celebration.

And this was my payoff. This was my receipt for everything. The crowds had seen Nirvana's cheerleader video and they knew where it came from. And then I was right there, with the right record at the right time. I didn't have to provoke; I just arrived with a smile. All the fighting had been done, Nirvana had won the war, and I showed up to rightfully claim some of the spoils.

After we got through those tough sessions, everything fell into place for Sugar. We would go to London for two weeks at a time and Creation would rent us a three-bedroom apartment. Laurence Verfaillie and Andy Saunders, our publicists at Creation, were great at whipping up attention for the band. We would sit in that apartment seven days a week, twelve hours a day. They would parade the journalists in, we'd talk, they'd leave—over and over again for days. Kevin and Kle Boutis, our day-to-day liaison at the label, would go down to the corner to get us sandwiches; we'd eat and then get right back to work. It was hard work, and we didn't stop.

Friday afternoons the music journalists would all come 'round the pub near Creation's office, and the bands would show up as well. We would sit and drink with Keith Cameron, Steve Lamacq, Dave Cavanaugh, Everett True; these guys were the major music writers. Everyone (except me) would enjoy a pint, and the stories would begin: which band is in which studio, who is dating whom, what really happened backstage at this or that show. As the afternoons turned into early evening, the boundaries of public and private stories would slowly blur. People would break away and head to either play shows or see bands. There was camaraderie between the musicians and writers—it was a great British rock tradition. I'd come a long way from sitting on the radiator cover at Oar Folk.

* * *

It makes sense that the resulting album, *Copper Blue,* is one of my sunniest. After all, it was inspired by music I loved.

"Helpless," with its straightforward sixteenth-note snare fills, recalls Cheap Trick's "Surrender"—it's that power-Ringo, power-pop feel, without any of the heaviness of *Black Sheets*. "Hoover Dam" came to me fully formed in a dream. From the Beach Boys–informed organ intro to the Left Banke–inspired baroque harpsichord solo to the backward guitar swirls straight from the Byrds' "Thoughts and Words," it incorporated several touchstones of my days as a student of '60s pop music. ("Brasilia Crossed with Trenton," from *Workbook,* was another fully realized dream song—I sang the first version of it into a portable recorder while I was in the shower.) There was an unconscious homage too: I didn't realize the similarities between "A Good Idea" and the Pixies' "Debaser" until Sugar was riding around America during the summer 1992 dates. I simultaneously laughed and gasped at the horror of having accidentally pilfered Kim Deal's bass line.

The only real dark moment on *Copper Blue* was "The Slim": a song in 6/8 time written from the perspective of a survivor, a person remembering and wondering when he will meet his deceased mate—a mate who died of AIDS.

* * *

Copper Blue came out in early September and went top ten in the UK national charts. We did two weeks of touring and the responses were getting stronger, as were the demands on our time and energy. We came back to the States and toured heavily there. The Boo Radleys, another Creation band, came along as special support act. We were the headliners but they had the tour bus. I wanted the first date of the tour to be in a smaller city so we could run the full show before taking it to the bigger stages in Minneapolis and Chicago; Columbia, Missouri, fit the bill perfectly. And, of course, there was my history with the Blue Note there—it was the same club where Hüsker Dü played its final performance. In October 1992 Sugar more than made up for that dreadful swan song in December 1987.

The next night was Lawrence, Kansas, and as always, we stopped by to smoke pot and throw knives with William Burroughs and James Grauerholz. I celebrated my thirty-second birthday by playing the Riviera Theatre in Chicago, a key city for me. We barreled through the Midwest and East Coast, ran through Texas, and on to Las Vegas. We were deep in the land of vice. The Boo Radleys enjoyed Vegas on one level, but at the same time, their singer, Sice, was complaining about how decadent and perverse it was. I agreed completely, and suggested they get more free drinks. We ran into Sonic Youth at Binion's Horseshoe that evening. They had a night off and were playing roulette. I was playing blackjack, and David and Dewitt Burton, our stage tech, were on mushrooms.

By the time we hit the West Coast, the Ryko campaign was finally beginning to match Creation in terms of gathering press and radio support. They were really enthusiastic—no label had ever gone three singles deep on a record of mine before. The fourth single would be the upbeat and catchy "If I Can't Change Your Mind."

We toured Japan for the first time in early 1993. As is customary, our first night in Tokyo we went out to eat with a group of people from the Japanese record company, Nippon Columbia. We were seated on mats, enjoying the meal, when suddenly the building began to shake. I'd been in a few earthquakes in Southern California, but being in a very foreign country on no sleep, we were all a bit rattled. Everything soon settled down, but it was quite the welcome to Japan.

Our hosts enjoyed watching us try exotic food. I figured it was some sort of cultural test, and since I have an iron stomach, I was game for it. They did a live sushi presentation: the restaurant had a tank filled with live fish; they catch a fish, bring it to the table, the fish still flopping around, and place it on a wooden board. Then they whack the head off with a sushi knife, flip it over, slice the body in half, skin it back, and chop it into pieces of sashimi. The disconnected fish head is tipped upright, mouth still gurgling, eyes still darting. They pick up a piece of sashimi with chopsticks, and proceed to try to feed the fish to itself. They're laughing and the fish is still dying. It's so fucked up. This is only the first night of the trip.

I was expecting the Japanese audiences to be reserved. I had this vision of finishing a song and looking out to see hundreds of people standing still, giving me the golf clap. I was very wrong—the Japanese audiences were very attentive, cheered as loudly as any Western audience, and were physical, even crowd surfing. But for all their boisterousness, the crowds at the end of the shows would file out in an orderly manner, gathering work possessions from the wall of lockers at each venue.

We returned home, and I arranged for the making of the video for "If I Can't Change Your Mind." After two previous videos, it was our first big shoot with 35mm film, a real stage set, lighting directors, and craft service. And at $35,000, it was a much larger investment for me, but I sensed the time was right to take the financial plunge.

The whole point of the video was this: all relationships are valid. "If I Can't Change Your Mind" spoke about relationships and incorporated all different kinds of couples: a man and a woman, two women, two men, some with children. There was a quick shot toward the end where I'm holding up a Polaroid of Kevin and myself, and when I flip the Polaroid over, the writing on the other side says, "This is not your parents' world."

I had teased with outing myself during the Kevin Kerslake– directed "It's Too Late" video in 1990, where I was tied to a barbed-wire fence with the American flag, had my hands set on fire by the LA County fire department, and was framed by a spray-painted "Silence=Death" message on the wall. And once again I played with outing myself in the new video. I thought most people knew I was gay, and this was a "wink, wink, yes, I am gay" action, without having to specifically identify myself as a gay artist. This was the constant struggle at the intersection of my work and my sexuality, the same struggle that led to the gender-neutrality of my previous relationship-based songs. I never defined them as being about a man dealing with another man; they were always presented in a universal, non-gender-specific way. They could mean something to everyone, straight or gay.

This was the grunge era, the three years where MTV took a chance on indie guitar music. I had hosted MTV's popular and influential alternative rock show *120 Minutes* a number of times, and the show regularly featured the videos for "Helpless" and "Changes." But now "If I Can't Change Your Mind" was in regular MTV rotation, and the music was being exposed to a mainstream audience.

Back then MTV's programming choices informed the programming choices of Los Angeles's KROQ, at the time the most influential alternative radio station in the country. Only thing is, KROQ wasn't playing my record. So *120 Minutes* host Lewis Largent went to bat for my work. Lewis told Gene Sandbloom, the assistant program director at KROQ, that the station was missing the band and that KROQ needed to get on it. Soon, "If I Can't Change Your Mind" was getting the push at both MTV *and* KROQ, and the floodgates finally opened in America.

It was the perfect storm—quite unlike the one in January 1988 that washed away Hüsker Dü. Sales jumped from 30,000 to 100,000 to 300,000 — the most copies of any record I'd ever made. It doubled the sales of the best-selling Hüsker Dü album, *Zen Arcade*. Ryko was pushing the band hard and had the distribution juice and the marketing dollars to keep it going. Ryko deserved a lot of credit for capitalizing on the popularity of the song and video.

All the while, though, those other songs were burning a hole in my back pocket. I was anxious to have the six-song suite, now formally titled *Beaster*, released to coincide with Easter. Alan McGee agreed wholeheartedly. We'd already gone through four singles and had *NME*'s Album of the Year—what could be more interesting than putting out a six-song follow-up three months later? That was classic British music business thinking, as opposed to '90s US major label music business practice, where you milk it for two years. The rapid-fire approach was the old-school '60s Britpop and '70s punk rock way. Keep hammering it, and when you're on fire, throw more petrol on it. It was time to do it.

Creation released *Beaster* on Monday, April 6, the week before Easter, and Ryko released it the following day. Sure enough, *Beaster* entered at number three in the UK charts, my highest national chart position ever. This brutally dark piece of work was the third most popular record in the United Kingdom. I was amazed.

In late April of 1993, we began a four-week US tour in support of *Beaster*, covering the whole country as quickly as possible. We'd be hitting venues with capacities of 2,500 to 6,000, the level right before the jump to arenas: the Aragon Ballroom in Chicago, the Roseland Ballroom in New York City, the International Ballroom in Atlanta, the Warfield in San Francisco, and the Palladium in Hollywood. Many of these were ballrooms that David's parents had played when they were big-band musicians in the 1950s.

We convened at Minneapolis–St. Paul International Airport the evening before the first show. We headed to the dimly lit garage and piled into our rented Lincoln Town Car. Four hours and three hundred miles later, it was time to stop in rural Iowa and gas up. We pulled into a Pump 'n' Munch and, under bright fluorescent lighting, piled out of the car. Simultaneously, we gasped and stared at our car. One of America's hottest rock bands was touring the country in an iridescent-lavender Mary Kay Cosmetics car.

At each venue we'd play forty-five minutes of upbeat songs, then break it down to an acoustic setting—me sitting with the twelve-string, David on acoustic bass, and Malcolm playing percussion. We finished the shows with *Beaster* en suite. Spiritually, those final thirty minutes were a loose approximation of

Hell. Every time I played *Beaster,* I relived the writing of the material and, in a smaller sense, the events that inspired those songs. Consequently, playing those songs every night really fucked with my head and wore me down faster than a normal show. I didn't see that coming when I wrote them.

Jeff Rougvie, the band's A&R person at Ryko, told me a story about the local theater group in Salem who, every day during summer months, reenacted the Salem witch trials for tourists. The actors portraying the witch and her accuser were actually mother and daughter in real life. After the experience of playing *Beaster* every night, and how it made me feel, I wondered if, after weeks of portraying their scene, the daughter actually began to believe her mother was a witch.

After our run of theaters, we performed the first of two nights at First Avenue in Minneapolis. Returning to the Twin Cities was always bittersweet and familiar, but this time there was an extra twist. Grant Hart showed up, trying to be congenial, as if nothing had happened. This was the first time I'd seen him since the discussion at his parents' kitchen table. I let him into the dressing room, he sat down, and I sat in the room not facing him — listening, nodding, and talking occasionally. I was being cool — not cold, but cool. I was suspicious because I always felt Grant was the kind of person who, if he saw the smallest opening, would try to take a mile's worth of road. After a few minutes of cautious interaction, mostly small talk about the *Beaster* tour and Grant's projects, I asked him to leave our dressing room. It was getting closer to showtime, and I needed to be with my band.

After the show, as we're driving to the hotel, David said in a mix of hilarity and incredulity, "What the fuck is up with Grant Hart?" I asked what happened and David said, "He was hitting on me. You know I don't have a problem with that, but I told him no and he wouldn't stop." I started laughing and told David to forget about it.

Later that evening, my laughter turned into deeper reflection.

I'd heard stories about Grant having affections for my ex, Mike Covington, back when I was leaving Minnesota. And now he's coming on to my bass player? This was a continuation of a pattern of behavior I had recognized at the beginning of the Hüsker Dü days, and to me, that behavior was inappropriate. So by the end of that evening after the First Avenue show, I resigned myself to building a thick wall between Grant Hart and me. I wasn't going to let him anywhere near my life again. I didn't see him, nor speak with him, for many years.

CHAPTER 16

Living in Brooklyn was great, but I was on the road so much now and it started to dawn on me: Why am I paying all this money basically just to store my things in New York? But there was another reason to move. At some point I'm done with a place, spiritually and creatively, and I have to move. I'm sure that sounds crazy to people who have families and worry about school systems and are stationary and taking care of relatives. But Brooklyn wasn't buzzing for me anymore. I'd done a lot of great work in Brooklyn, but I wanted to try something different. Even though we could have purchased the entire 15,000-square-foot Williamsburg complex for $150,000—which would have been a heck of an investment—the vibe just wasn't there anymore.

We were making good money at the time, but the taxes were killing us. Texas, on the other hand, was income tax free. Kevin and I both had a long-standing connection in Austin. We both knew Butthole Surfers drummer King Coffey from our past lives: Kevin from the Butthole Surfers' six-month stay in Athens, and me from the early punk days in Dallas–Fort Worth. And I always enjoyed Austin; it was a player's town, so it was easy to plug in. It made sense to move there, so we took a weekend trip to look for a new home.

Our realtor showed us a beautiful house in the tree-lined

Hyde Park neighborhood, ten minutes from the airport. It was a Craftsman bungalow that had been greatly expanded and encased in brick, then fitted out with big stone-arched porches. King lived a few blocks away, other friends lived a little bit farther, and the whole town felt like hipster central. We immediately made an offer on the house, which was accepted. Between the American and European tours in May of that year, we packed up everything in the Brooklyn loft, threw it into a big truck, and went off to Austin. We didn't look back.

But life has a way of catching up with you, and this was also when Minnesota attorney Doug Myren got involved with Grant Hart and his Nova Mob project, and then wanted to handle the Hüsker Dü estate as well. Myren had gotten the financial books from Greg, who had been grousing about the production money. After talking with Greg and Grant, Myren called me and proposed redoing the books. Those three had reached a consensus: the sixty-forty production split that Grant and I had agreed upon back in 1985 wasn't fair, and they wanted to redistribute the production money equally among the three band members.

This was the moment when it became clear I was the odd man out. The business and legacy of Hüsker Dü was now firmly in the hands of a small-town attorney and two disgruntled ex-bandmates.

To break it down: When we sold 200,000 albums for Warner, the band grossed $300,000. A quarter of that, $75,000, went to the producer—that is, Grant and me. With a sixty-forty production split, I would get $45,000 and Grant would get $30,000. But once Myren redid the books, all three members would split the $75,000 equally—$25,000 each. So I'm out $20,000, Grant is out $5,000, and Greg gets $25,000 for doing virtually nothing on the two Warner albums.

At this point in my life, I was euphoric. *Copper Blue* had been named *NME*'s 1992 Album of the Year, and Sugar was playing in front of thousands of people every night all over the world. And now I'm presented with this nonsense. I called Josh Grier and said, "What is going on?"

Josh asked me, "What's it worth to you?" He then offered the same advice he originally gave me in 1991 about dealing with Linda Clark and the Virgin publishing debacle: walk away. And I reacted the same way as before—I didn't give it any further thought, and simply walked away.

So Myren went back and redid the books. Now all future royalty money would go to Greg until the new set of books reflected parity between the three of us. Myren proceeded to look for loose money in the field and arranged for the release of a live album on Warner Brothers, culled from the recordings of Hüsker Dü's October 1987 tour. He called me, asking if I had any ideas for a title. I said, "Yeah, why don't we call it *Seventy-Five Thousand Dollar Advance*?" They ended up calling it *The Living End*.

With those financial shenanigans behind me, Sugar headed to Europe to begin what was to be our most successful tour to date. We all convened in Stockholm for our first festival show, performing on rented gear and no sleep. It was a bumpy start, but we powered through. We then traveled to Helsinki and caught a commuter flight to Vaasa, a northern Finnish town inside the Arctic Circle, where we played the Seinäjoki festival. The accommodations for the festival were in a former mental asylum. The buildings were beautiful, but difficult to navigate since the hallways were laid out in such a way as to confuse the patients. It also worked well for confusing a touring musician operating for sixty hours without sleep—I kept getting turned around in the hallways. It was difficult to sleep there anyway because the sun barely sets in the summer and it was light outside at midnight. Another interesting component was the Finns' nonstop drinking. I saw an inebriated local approach one of the festival agents and, mistaking him for a tree, begin to urinate on his leg.

Third day of the tour, we had an afternoon show at Finsbury Park in London with Green Day and the Cure. Robert Smith sent an emissary over to our dressing room, asking if I would play "Purple Haze" with the Cure. On no sleep for seventy-two hours now, I politely declined the invitation. Then we walked out onstage in front of thirty thousand people—and my amps didn't work. People were yelling and cursing at us while Dewitt feverishly tried to fix the problem. I walked to the microphone and let loose with twenty seconds of foul language, which only made the crowd hotter. Objects rained down on the stage: drink containers, sandwiches filled with stones, and bags filled with (I think) mud. It continued through the better part of the set, with me egging it on. I would be in the middle of a song and see an object heading toward me. Being that high up over the crowd, I had time to react, so I either caught the objects, or blithely spun to the side to avoid being hit. I loved it.

On to Amsterdam. We traveled by sleeper coach from London to Dover, then a ferry to Calais, France. Upon our landing there, customs took it upon themselves to thoroughly search our stuff, presumably for illegal drugs. Bill Rahmy was our tour manager/sound engineer, and his wife Vanessa was carrying jars of unmarked nutritional supplements. Customs ran them through an assay test, possibly looking for ecstasy. They dismantled some of our musical gear. After they found nothing, the night manager woke from his nap and started yelling at the agent who had ordered the dismantling. I understood enough French to know what he said: "You stupid fuck, they're going *to* the Netherlands, not coming *from* the Netherlands!"

Once we arrived in Amsterdam, Kevin, David, and I made up for it and spent all evening and a fair part of the next day walking the streets, smoking hashish. The show at Paradiso, a beautifully converted old church, was much better than our stoned-as-fuck sound check earlier in the day. It was one of the rare occasions since 1986 that I went onstage in even a slightly altered state.

After Paris we played large clubs in Germany, as well as festivals in Ireland, Denmark, and Belgium. I was playing in front of the largest audiences of my life—crowds of up to seventy-five thousand people.

At festivals we'd often play in the middle of the day. We'd usually have no sound check, which meant that the first time we'd see the stage was when we started playing. When that happened, the first song was spent just trying to sort out the onstage sound—while we were trying to make our case to tens of thousands of people. I've always kept in mind that to present an effective show, you find the last row and sing to them. But how do you do that when the last row is a quarter of a mile away?

After those shows David and I would look at each other and say, "What happened?" We were never quite sure. I just hoped we'd held it together. Did playing to those massive crowds make me feel all-powerful? Not quite, not like Bono—especially when ducking all the shit people were throwing at me.

Of course, some of my colleagues did embrace a certain amount of grandeur. Metallica had two identical sets of full staging (including washer/dryers with their own flight cases), and would fly the entire production from show to show, one planeload of equipment leapfrogging the other. Lenny Kravitz had a six-by-twelve-foot tent completely dedicated to wardrobe. The brothers Robinson of Black Crowes fame had a chill-out tent, complete with Persian rugs, a big '70s-style home stereo, and a large hookah. At one festival Iggy Pop decided he didn't want anyone seeing him walk from the dressing room to the stage, so he had the crew build him a sheltered walkway out of large black garbage bags.

These were levels of excess I had never seen before, and I found it amusing and ridiculous. I wasn't like that. Sugar lived on the tour bus, eating off the hospitality rider and playing Strat-O-Matic fantasy baseball; our only real indulgence was daytime marijuana to help ease the boredom of life on the bus.

At some point on the tour, a tape of the Hüsker Dü live album showed up for my approval. I said to our guitar tech,

Dewitt Burton, "Damned if I'm going to listen to this thing. D, you know Hüsker, right?"

Dewitt said, "I *love* Hüsker."

"Would you listen to this and tell me what you think?"

So he took the tape and listened a couple times and said, "It fucking rocks."

If Dewitt liked it, it was good enough for me. I looked at Kevin and said, "Tell them it's approved." I still haven't heard it to this day.

*   *   *

The tour was almost over, and I was exhausted on all fronts. The combination of the nonstop schedule, the physicality of playing on larger stages, and the emotional content of *Beaster* had worn me out. I thought back to 1990, when I sang on a track for Anton Fier's band the Golden Palominos called "Dying from the Inside Out." I only wanted to sing those harrowing words once, so I gave it my all. I screamed so hard that I popped some blood vessels and gave myself black eyes.

So why do I write these words? I couldn't help it. By the last show, headlining Brixton Academy in London, I had sung *Beaster* twenty-seven times. I was sick of it. My head pounded all day. I was so beat up I was taking ten Advil a day. I had become rather irritable, and had lost my ability to suffer fools as gladly as I usually would.

Out of nowhere Greg Norton shows up at the Brixton sound check. He's in London, studying at a culinary school to become a chef and restaurateur. In a voice reminiscent of Batman's Penguin, he says to me, "Well, I just want to do a little bit of business." He's got this stack of papers in his hand, shaking them toward me. "This is the contract for the Hüsker Dü live record. I need you to sign this, I need you to sign this now."

Have you ever seen the Brian De Palma movie *Phantom of the Paradise* (1974), with Paul Williams as Swan, the evil record producer? I was reminded of the scene when he's got the deformed composer Winslow Leach (wearing the Daft Punk–looking helmet) boxed up in the control room, writing his cantata, and Swan is yelling, "Sign this! *Sign this in blood!*"

I looked at Norton and said, "Send that to my lawyer and get out of here. Enjoy the show. What are you *thinking?*"

We take the stage at Brixton. There's over five thousand people stuffed into the room, and the energy is sky-high. We get into *Beaster* and the energy goes over the top. The floor is shaking and the whole room seems ready to collapse. The meltdown that precipitated the writing of *Beaster,* the triumph of will to make this band succeed, and the knowledge that this was the final reading of *Beaster* en suite meant I held nothing back. It was raw, visceral, and—dare I use the word—cathartic. It put Great Gildersleeves 1983 in the rubbish bin for good.

In the middle of "JC Auto," I'm out of my skull and I lock eyes with Norton, who is standing in the sea of humanity. Everything in the world is coming unglued except for him, standing there with his mouth open. I was like, Yep, that's what it feels like. Send that contract to my lawyer and leave me alone. After the show I asked David, "Did you see him out there?"

He asks, "Who?"

"Norton," I said. "He was standing there like he pissed his pants."

David laughed.

* * *

That was the end of the tour, and everyone went home for a much-needed break. Kevin and I headed back to Austin. Kevin's involvement with my career was increasing. In two years he'd learned a lot about the business and was handling a fair amount of the day-to-day coordination of schedules, tour logistics, and record company activities. I was directing traffic, but Kevin did a lot of the heavy lifting.

But now that we were on break, we were having an idyllic time, eating fish tacos and smoking weed, doing the Austin thing. It was *Slacker* 1993, quite a change from Brooklyn. We started calling the house the Compound. I bought a couple of cars—you have to have cars in Texas.

I began my working relationship with Jim Wilson, who became my engineer and go-to guy in Austin. He did sound for me at that great South by Southwest show I played in 1991, and we had hit it off right away. He was super peaceful, a high-intellect guy, and a great person. He was a staff engineer at Cedar Creek Recording, a small but well-equipped studio in a ramshackle South Austin house.

Years before we met, Jim's brother committed suicide at his parents' house in Dallas. Once you are touched by suicide, you can sense others who have gone through the ordeal. You have a kinship, even if you don't know why. Jim and I shared that, as well as a love of music and sound and numbers, and it made for this real bond—we had that hypervigilant thing in common. We had a good working relationship from the start.

In August 1993 Jim and I recorded the second album by Magnapop, a smart punk-pop band from Athens, Georgia. Magnapop came out to Texas and we worked at Pedernales Studio, Willie Nelson's place. Tracking the album was a chore, and although Jim and I had a few trying times while mixing at Bobby Brown's studio in Atlanta, the band wound up with a pretty good record. It was trial by fire, but it showed that Jim and I worked well together.

The rest of 1993 was a series of small acoustic shows, a big contrast from those vast European festivals. I was trying out new material for the upcoming Sugar album and just reconnecting with the core fan base, not to mention picking up some extra money for the holidays.

Christmas brought Kevin and me an unexpected gift. In December our next-door neighbors had twins, at the same time that their dog began escaping the fenced-in yard and showing up at our front door. He was an intense dog, physically strong, but with severe coat problems. We began paying attention to him, eventually bringing him inside and trying to nurse him back to health. Within a few weeks, the neighbor suggested that if we wanted, we could adopt the dog, and we took him up on it. He brought over the dog's registration papers and bed, and we were now the proud owners of a full-blooded Australian cattle dog named Domino Deemo Dingo Dundee. Kevin and I were getting on fine, and Domino brought us even closer together. Domino was a great addition to the family.

After a February 1994 solo acoustic tour of Japan, it was time to record the follow-up to *Copper Blue* and *Beaster*. I'd outfitted one of the bedrooms in the house with a greatly expanded home studio and was writing songs between tours. David came to Austin to demo three songs as well. These high-quality demos were essentially finished works.

In March I gave the keynote address at South by Southwest. I showed up with a forty-eight-ounce travel coffee mug and delivered a "welcome to Austin, get trashed and see bands" speech. Kevin and I hosted a large party at the Compound and most everyone who did business with the band was there. During the party I played the demos for both Ryko and Creation, and everyone from both labels seemed pleased with what they heard.

Shortly after SXSW the band began the sessions for what would eventually be titled *File Under: Easy Listening* (FU:EL) at Triclops Studio in Atlanta, where Smashing Pumpkins had recorded *Siamese Dream* and Hole had done *Live Through This*. I was producing and David was engineering. That was a lot for us to bite off.

On paper it was a great studio, but we struggled to find a sound. The drum room was a big open industrial space, and it was so loud in there that Malcolm couldn't hear himself, the click track, or anything else. We built him a set of isolating headphones, using shells from the noise protection muffs that airport runway workers use, and he still couldn't hear. We spent two months trying to get basic tracks, and an undue amount of time searching for the guitar sound. They had tons of guitar amps and loads of vintage equipment, every doodad known to mankind. I tried every amp with every pedal—to the point where I was so confused I didn't know what anything sounded like. I had totally fucked myself.

Triclops had a weird energy. David and I were struggling— we were in this dark hole, not making headway. Nothing we did worked. Then, one day, we were watching CNN and heard that Kurt Cobain had killed himself. A lot of people would have thought, Wow, that's really awful, and moved on. But a lot of people didn't. I was really upset for days.

I had first met Kurt at the HUB Ballroom in Seattle in 1986; I remembered Courtney Love's short stint in Minneapolis in 1987–88; I had heard the demos for *Nevermind* and was in the running for producing the album; I had shared a bill with Nirvana in Europe in the summer of 1991. And there was no doubt that Kurt's music follows the lineage of my work. So I felt very close to this. And now I was sitting in the lounge of the studio where Courtney Love's album *Live Through This* had been recorded, watching the first news reports about Kurt's death.

Maybe I was overpersonalizing it, but Kurt's suicide made me start questioning a lot of things about the business. I'd been struggling with these sessions, then this terrible news just amplified things—not only the frustration with the work at hand, but my concerns about one of the darker sides of the business.

It almost seems like the more you show of yourself, the more people want. People gravitate to the artist, wanting to see deeper pain, higher joy, brighter light. And once you become successful, the business won't let you stop to catch your breath. I experienced a small taste of it with *Beaster*, going out and performing that music every night.

I knew there was a record to be made, one way or the other. I knew that Ryko had expanded partly as a result of the success of the two Sugar records. And after *Copper Blue* and *Beaster*, the labels were looking at me to deliver something even more successful. But I was having big problems getting this record to work, and I didn't think the industry machine would have the patience for me to sort it out.

We spent two months filling up a two-inch tape with music, and none of it was satisfying to me. One day I abruptly said, "The session is over. I'm taking all this stuff back to Texas and I don't know what I'm going to do with it."

I went back to Austin, completely deflated. I felt bad that David and I couldn't get a sound together. I think there were just too many options and I lost my ability to make clear decisions. Seeing as David and I were in the band together and were good friends as well, perhaps it would have been better to have an outside voice, like the role Lou Giordano played in 1992. It was hard for me to be critical of the job David was doing, and I wasn't being a very good captain of the ship.

Both labels had laid grand plans for this release, and Ryko in particular was betting big on it. There was a schedule already in place on both continents, and I needed to keep this project on track so that the entire marketing plan wouldn't have to be recalculated.

But the misstep in Atlanta was a major problem — the sessions were useless. I wasn't sure how to proceed. I called up Jim Wilson and asked him if he could help me out of this predicament. He cleared his schedule, and we got to our first order of business: erasing the Atlanta masters, reel by reel. Everything we'd done in Atlanta for two months, more than an album's worth of music, gone forever.

Jim suggested constructing the album the other way around, similar to how I'd been working at home: start with a drum machine; then add bass, guitars, and vocals; and save live drums for last. We were starting to get close to our deadline, so we needed to find a studio and get working quickly.

Our first choice for the new sessions was Cedar Creek, but studio owner Fred Remmert had already booked the room. Luckily, Fred's brother Travy had a multimillion-dollar home studio called Meridian in nearby Boerne. This place had all the bells and whistles. And there was no regular clientele because it wasn't a commercial studio, so Jim and I could have the run of the place. We started the new recordings there.

I went in with the drum machine and programmed and recorded the patterns for those same sixteen songs. Then I spent a few weeks recording guitars and vocals to the drum machine tracks. Jim and I worked long hours each day, usually without taking breaks for food—we were running on nicotine and caffeine, and not much else. At the end of each night, Jim and I would go to a Taco Cabana drive-through, the only restaurant that was open at 2 AM. I would order four large bean-and-cheese burritos, scarf them down, then fall into a food coma for eight hours. Then we'd get up and do exactly the same thing the next day.

After the majority of my part was done, I called up David and said, "It's your turn, come to Texas." It took David two days to do all the bass and his vocals, including recording for three of his own compositions: "Company Book," "Frustration," and "In the Eyes of My Friends." I hadn't finished the vocals for "Explode and Make Up," the album closer, so once David was done, I took another shot at the song. The performance was harrowing; Jim recalled the stunned silence in the control room after I finished my caterwauling. I said something to the effect of "I hate the person who wrote that song," then went into the kitchen area to sit alone for two hours.

Now it was time for the wild card, Malcolm. We didn't know if the drum problems in Atlanta were Malcolm's fault or whether it was just impossible for him to hear anything in that large live room. So instead of putting him in that room down in Boerne where we didn't really know what was going to bounce around, we took him to Cedar Creek (now available), which was a smaller studio, in stark contrast to the palatial home studio in Boerne.

We set up a kit in the living room, and Malcolm blasted

through all sixteen songs with no problem—in the smaller room, he could hear everything. Turned out we were unfairly questioning Malcolm's ability. He gave a lot of blood to get those tracks right; by the end of the second day, his hands were completely shredded and he was soaking them in buckets of ice water to numb the pain. He had redeemed himself and things were starting to feel back on track.

After the drums were finished, Jim and I went back down to Boerne and mixed the entire album in two hectic weeks. By the end of the Texas sessions, I was both startled and disappointed to find I had gained forty pounds due to my late-night Mexican food binges. I looked puffy and felt sluggish. My jeans didn't fit anymore. But we finished the album just in time for the Ryko and Creation promotional machines to stay on track with their grand plans for the fall 1994 campaign.

FU:EL didn't have the high drama of *Beaster* or the deep melodies of *Copper Blue*. After thirteen months of nonstop Sugar touring, moving 1,700 miles to set up a new home, producing the Magnapop album, and doing a solo acoustic tour, I'd had maybe twelve weeks to write as opposed to twelve months. And it showed. In the midst of all the hullabaloo, I wasn't astute enough to notice that I had produced some of my best work (*Workbook* and *Copper Blue*) during periods of relative and sustained quiet. If I had taken more time, it might have been a stronger record. But the machine was rolling and wouldn't slow down for anyone. This was a case of trying to capitalize on momentum, and in hindsight, the music suffered for it.

I again called John Bruce, this time to make videos in the scorching heat of an Austin summer. "Your Favorite Thing" was filmed on a concrete overpass that was under construction, and "Believe What You're Saying" was shot at an abandoned airstrip outside of town. We couldn't have found two hotter locations. After twelve hours of standing out in the sun, I was miserable. John's production assistant wore the hell out of me with his misguided ideas, and it strained my professional relationship with John. In fact, making those two videos soured me on working with John ever again—a shame, really, since he'd been documenting the band from its inception.

Despite the difficulties with the recording and videos, there were a few bright spots on the horizon. I loved the artwork for *FU:EL,* which was created by an Athens artist named Lou Kregel. Lou had spent time in north Texas and was also somewhat connected in the entertainment world. The colorful retro designs that made up the core of the *FU:EL* packaging were originally created for a clothing line that was to be sponsored by River Phoenix, before his untimely passing. I saw the artwork in a coffee shop in Athens, and it ended up being recycled for the packaging of the album.

Also, the publicity machine was revving up, and I was hopeful that the positive momentum of the previous two albums would continue. The key national pieces were falling into place, and the centerpiece of the campaign was to be a multipage feature in *Spin* magazine. That article would become more of a historical talking point than anyone could have imagined.

CHAPTER 17

The writer Dennis Cooper was a huge Hüsker Dü fan. He'd even touched on the band in one or two of his novels. Now he was trying to build a name for himself as a journalist. Dennis Cooper is gay. So in the summer of 1994, *Spin* magazine asked Ryko, How about we send Dennis Cooper down to Austin to spend some time with Bob?

I knew what was about to happen. This was to be the "Bob is gay" story, and I could do this the easy way or the hard way. I wasn't thrilled about it for a number of reasons, beyond personal ones. My first concerns were that this news would make it tough for my family, and that my fans and peers would recontextualize everything I had done with my work. I also knew that the press was always going to write whatever they were going to write. I could try to steer the story the way I wanted it to read, but ultimately, editorial always wins out. It's the business.

I talked about it at great length with Kevin. This article would have a lasting impact not only on my professional life but also on our personal lives and our private relationship. Once my story was public, everything in our lives would be viewed in a different light. Kevin would be viewed both as a part of the operation and as my partner in life. We were fine with that, but it was a big decision to make and agree upon. I went back to

Ryko and said, "If this is what everyone thinks is best, I'll do it, and we'll be done with it." Ryko was happy, of course—it was a large feature that would certainly get people talking about me and the album. I had made my decision. Kevin and I agreed to open our home to Dennis for two days.

The first day was relaxed. Dennis arrived from Los Angeles and the three of us bopped around Austin, chatting about music, sexuality, and people we knew in common. Dennis was a modest sort, flattering and quite ingratiating. All pretty innocent stuff.

The second day, Dennis and I sat down in the TV den for the formal part of the interview. For the first time in those two days, he brought out his tape recorder, and for the first time in my life, I spoke publicly about my sexuality. We talked for an hour. I had rehearsed certain parts, but in the heat of the moment I was pretty candid. Though I'd been interviewed many times before, I felt odd this time, knowing that anything I said about my sexuality would be out there for everyone to read— including my family.

Dennis turned off the tape recorder, said he had what he needed, and headed back to the airport. I thought it had gone as well as could be expected, but one never knows with a piece this big. It's easy to say things that can be taken out of context and blown out of proportion.

As it turns out, that is exactly what happened. For a single moment, on one specific line of thought, I made a very awkward choice of words: "I'm not a freak." Those four words were the highlight of the article. That statement haunted me for a long time. The context was in talking about gay-pride parades, and how it really gets to me that the mainstream media always focuses on the more outlandish characters and not the folks who dress in everyday clothing. I'm gay and I'm a normal person like everybody else, I maintained—or so I thought.

A month or so later, the tear sheet from *Spin* came through on the fax machine. I read the pull quote, "I'm not a freak," and knew I was in trouble. I'm thinking, All the things that Dennis and I talked about, and *that's* what they zero in on? I was beside myself, not happy about this at all. I slipped up on one line and now it was about to be this huge mess. Kevin tried to reassure me that everything would be fine.

Ryko publicist Carrie Svingen could sense how upset I was. I took it upon myself to call *Spin* editor Craig Marks and ask, "Craig, do you realize what you're doing here? Do you realize how you're portraying me? Is this really what you want me to look like?" He basically said, "You know, I really can't do anything about it at this point. My hands are tied on this." I was incredulous. "You know what? Fuck you. Fuck yourself, and take fucking Dennis Cooper with you." I didn't talk to *Spin* for fifteen years.

I saw Dennis Cooper a few months later in Amsterdam. He came to the show and was sheepishly trying to ingratiate himself to me. I forget exactly what I said, but it was something to the effect of "Dennis, you did a hell of a job on me. All those years of writing fiction have really served you well." And then I walked away.

In the end, though, Dennis Cooper was just a pawn; my anger had little to do with him. He just happened to be the one who showed up to do the job. I was more upset with *myself*. I was upset that it took me so long to acknowledge what most everyone already knew.

In professional circles my homosexuality had been an open secret for years. Generally, I figured most people knew, but since I wasn't drawing attention to it or living a double life, I never thought much about making a proclamation. But now it was to become a big thing. It was to put me in a different public light. Coming out is never quite as graceful as in an ABC after-school special, but this was the most awkward coming out I could imagine.

I told my parents about the *Spin* article before the street date. I said, "You're going to hear things about me, they're true, and you might feel some repercussions." I always sensed my mom knew I was gay; we didn't talk about it, but I knew she understood what I meant. My dad never acknowledged I was gay other than the one episode when he blew up on the phone. He still does not acknowledge my homosexuality.

For years I had lived in a fearful yet protective state. My parents were in a small town where people didn't accept or understand homosexuality. I didn't want to cause any undue stress in their lives by coming out. I remembered what happened to my high school acquaintance who ended up slaughtered in the woods. My coming out might create a hardship on my brother's kids too—Syracuse, New York, where he now lived, was not a progressive bastion.

I had looped all the different possible fallouts and fears in my mind, a big one being that for fifteen years I had gender-neutralized my work so that it would be all-inclusive; as a result, my music was highly personal, and yet it affected a lot of people, whether they were gay or straight. But my fear was that 90 percent of my audience would have the meaning of my songs ripped out from underneath them. A song that straight people related to, now they find out it's about two guys? The flip side, or what I now know to be the upside, was that I had a large audience who might not have known about my homosexuality, were very attached to the work, and could now see that love and loss and hope are universal emotions that can't be owned, controlled, or denied by law or religion.

I had my suspicions as to how the gay community would react when they saw the *Spin* article, and some of the reactions were well founded. I got mail from a few gay fans saying, "How dare you portray us like that!" The gay press neither condemned nor glorified me. I never sensed I was going to appear on the cover of a magazine, sitting in a barber chair, getting shaved by someone of my own gender, like k. d. lang did the year prior when lesbian chic was all the rage.

And later on I felt some professional backlash. A handful of radio stations in the Southeast pulled their support of my music, simply because I was gay. I understood completely and I didn't care. I know how the game goes. The people who advertise to keep that station in business are going to say to the program directors, If you continue playing this guy's music on the station, we're going to pull our money. There are things in life that I personalize, but this was not one of them. I knew this was business. So I didn't tour the Southeast as much as I normally might. It hurt my pocketbook a little—so what? I wasn't going to let one interview, or a handful of Bible Belt radio stations, decide the fate of my music.

* * *

As a kid I'd always feared the consequences of my actions. If I made a wrong move, chaos would ensue. It's hard to shake that stuff. And that dynamic played out in my public life too. When Hüsker Dü signed to a major, I thought the repercussions would hurt us. I was wrong—it hardly mattered. And same with the *Spin* piece. In the end it didn't actually amount to much. But I still think this way. I worry too much about the potential fallout of what I say or do. I hoped to have gotten past those worries when I quit drinking, but apparently not. I keep trying, but I haven't yet finished the work.

The other side of the issue is inaction, not doing or saying anything—not telling people the things they might need to hear for fear it will send everything spiraling. But not doing anything can hurt people as well. I'm still working on that too.

I now recognize that walking away with no explanation is likely related to whatever abandonment issues I was feeling from my early childhood. My father wasn't always emotionally or physically available, and I became the same when I felt betrayed or hurt by people I cared for. Instead of confrontation, it was easier for me to walk away, avoid the conflict, and spare everyone more pain. What I didn't know was that by leaving, say, the closing of a relationship open-ended and unexplained,

I was causing more anguish than would have been created by actually talking through it.

* * *

Amid the confusion of the *Spin* article and the problematic recording sessions, Creation asked me to perform a solo acoustic set on June 4 at the Royal Albert Hall. The event was called Undrugged, in celebration of the label's tenth anniversary.

As soon as I stepped out of the taxi, I was awed by the size and history of the building. Kevin and I were met at the stage door by a hobbled old gent. He led us to the conductor's dressing room, which was my inner sanctum for the evening. The farther we went into the bowels of the building, the lower the ceilings became. In the conductor's room, the ceiling could not have been more than six and a half feet high. I felt completely oversized in the room, and not in a good way—I was already under pressure, and the low ceilings added more weight while subtracting oxygen. When I walked onto the stage for sound check, I was again struck by the sheer size and beauty of the building—the rich red and gold colors, the large oval shape, and the thousands of empty seats.

At one point I was introduced to a guy who said, "I'm Liam, I'm in Oasis, and we're the best band in the world." Bold, I thought to myself. Turns out that, for a moment anyway, he was right—they went on to become huge.

Toward the end of the evening, I walked onto the stage to a strong response and sat down to play. I started with a shaky version of "Walking Away" from *Beaster*. I'm not sure why I chose a song that was written and recorded on keyboards and had no previously existing guitar part. Moving along, I went to "Hoover Dam" and froze up in the second verse. I lost track of where I was in the song, or more likely, where I was, period. I abruptly stopped, looked up, and apologized to the audience. I then lurched into a positively harrowing version of "Too Far Down" from *Candy Apple Grey,* a strange choice for the party-like vibe, and I ended my set with an offering "to the boss" (Alan), a solo electric version of "Makes No Sense at All." I felt terrible about my performance, and barely remembered the rest of the evening. I left the building as quickly as I left the stage. That was a high and low professional moment, all wrapped in one.

*　*　*

During the first half of 1994, Ryko retooled certain departments of the label in preparation for, among other things, making *FU:EL* a huge record. They brought in a new director of marketing named Bob Carlton to replace John Hammond, who I thought was great at his job. Though well intentioned, Carlton turned out not to be the best fit. This change was one small piece of the beginning of Ryko's downfall. But I was merely an artist on the roster, and all I could do was continue marching forward.

The songs from the *FU:EL* sessions broke down to three different styles: perfectly good pop songs, acoustic-flavored sprawl, and punkier songs like "Mind Is an Island" and "In the Eyes of My Friends." But I needed to grow, so I changed things up and dropped the punk stuff in favor of the acoustic material. "Panama City Motel" tied together images of a house in my neighborhood being transplanted to Barcelona. Living in Austin, being around the country cats and roots-rock players, I wanted to do a country song; I thought "Believe What You're Saying" had a real good shot at country radio. Among the pop songs, "Gift" was loosely based on the effects pedal that kicks in on the guitar at the twenty-five-second mark. I had spent an evening with Kevin Shields of My Bloody Valentine, and he gave me the Octavia pedal he used on the band's legendary "You Made Me Realize." I wrote "Your Favorite Thing" to be the single, and it occupied the number three slot—where I always put the single. The pop songs opened the record, and had I closed the album with the punky stuff, I would have given the people exactly what they expected and wanted. Maybe that would have made it a more commercial record, but artistically speaking, it was time to move on.

FU:EL entered the UK national charts at number seven, a decent showing. I was hoping for better, having seen *Beaster* enter at number three; Creation must not have been too disappointed at that chart number though. In late September we did a big three-week tour of the UK and Western Europe. We did very good business, playing venues comparable to or larger than those on the previous tours, but it was an uneventful trip. We returned to the United States and embarked on a tour of large clubs, small theaters, and ballrooms. Everything was proceeding according to plan: the first single was getting lots of airplay, there was plenty of press (including the *Spin* feature, naturally), and tickets were selling well.

We continued for a few more months, but Sugar was essentially finished on November 13, 1994, the night after we played the cavernous Roseland Ballroom in New York City. We were staying at a Motel 6 outside of New Haven, Connecticut, planning on a quiet night off. We checked into the motel and David said, "Bob, I need to talk with you, can you spare a little time tonight? Just me and you." I said, "Sure, David, of course. Let's get checked in, let me take a shower, and then I'll come knock on your door, and we can go for a walk."

We walked along a quiet road, chatting about the weather and other nontopics. When we were far enough from the hotel to have privacy, David turned serious and said, "Look, I've been on the road nonstop, I'm going to miss baby steps, my kids are acting out, my wife is ready to kill me. I can't keep doing this." I knew it was coming—I could sense it.

I stopped, looked at him, and said, "I'm right there with you."
He was like, "Wow."

"David, I'm a wreck," I said. "I don't even know if I'm coming or going. The last two years have been so busy, I don't even know where I am. I'm completely wiped. What we went through trying to make that record, all the shit this year, I'm right there with you. How do we want to do this?"

"How much more work have we got?"

"We have the rest of North America, home for the holidays, then the one week in Japan. Can you at least give me the stuff that we're booked for?"

"Absolutely," David said. "That's what I signed on for, and now that I know there's an end date, when I go back to Amy, everything will be fine."

After that the rest of the year was a breeze. All the pressure had been lifted. We finished the US tour, took a break for the holidays, and in January 1995 convened in Los Angeles for one day to shoot blue-screen performance footage for the "Gee Angel" video. Immediately after filming, we flew to Japan, played seven shows in eight days—going up and down the entire country—and had a great time. The pressure was completely off.

This trip, the Japanese-food test came in the form of a small ceramic container filled with hot oil, with stuff floating on top of the oil. You would eat the floating substance with a strainer. It was bad enough I had to say no to the drink, the act of which can be taken as offensive, so I couldn't really say no to any of the food stunts.

They asked how it was. I politely replied, "It is a . . . different taste."

"It's whale sperm," I was informed. "Very good for the libido."

I thought for a second, and then pretended to be grossed out, seeing as the record company folks were heterosexuals.

The tour wasn't all giggles. We visited the Peace Museum in Hiroshima, a depressing and moving experience that reminded me of my 1987 trip to Dachau with Mike Covington.

After Hiroshima we flew north to the island of Hokkaido to play in Sapporo, where the 1972 Winter Olympics had been held. This was in January, and even though the rest of the country has temperate weather, almost like San Francisco, we were coming in for our landing with a blizzard going on, a total whiteout. Actually, the landing turned out to be smooth as silk. Once we got settled in Sapporo, the four of us broke off from the promoter reps and went out to a birthday dinner for a friend of a fan who had followed the entire Japanese tour. It was one of the best meals I've ever had—the fish and vegetables were so fresh, and it was unbelievable. Nobody spoke English except for us, so we had to order in Japanese. No stunt food was served.

The last Sugar show was in Sendai. Only David, his wife, Amy, and Kevin and I knew the band was over. Malcolm didn't know. I told him we were going to take a really long break.

David and I had made the call to keep the decision to ourselves. The press campaign in 1994 had lasted long enough for me, particularly with the *Spin* story, and I just wanted to finish the tour without another round of uncomfortable questions from the press. But it wasn't right to keep it from Malcolm. I made a bad call.

After Hüsker Dü broke up, I wondered, Does anybody out there have a handbook for how to do this? Does anybody have a handbook for how to end a really intense relationship? What's the proper way? Do I tell people everything they shouldn't hear? Do I shake hands and walk away? To this day I've found no good way to end a band. People get bruised and feelings get hurt. Sometimes people become vindictive.

I tend to be identified most with Hüsker Dü, because that's where I started. But few know the half of how much fun I had with Sugar. Hüsker Dü was an eight-year ground war that started with me and some guy smoking Thai stick in the basement of a record store, and ended with that guy's mom suggesting we should only play on weekends. Sugar, in twelve months, went from three men building a stage extension out of road cases for a punk rock show in Morgantown, West Virginia, to playing gigantic European festivals with Metallica. Which part of my life do you think I enjoyed more? Sugar was intense. The band was not enormous, but we were mighty close to the top. We had a good view of the valley below.

After that final show in Sendai, David and Malcolm flew back home to the States while Kevin and I stayed in Japan for an extra three days. We woke up the morning after the Sendai show to the news of the Great Hanshin earthquake, which killed over six thousand people and caused massive damage in the Kobe area. Despite this tragedy, Kevin and I continued with our vacation as best we could. We didn't talk about the end of Sugar—we just shopped, ate, and traveled with friends. We loved Japan, and it was a nice way to unwind before heading back to Texas, where Kevin was all I really had.

CHAPTER 18

Thinking back to the summer of 1991 and the European and Australian solo tours, through returning from Japan in early 1995, I'm hard pressed to remember a moment longer than two hours when Kevin and I were not in each other's company. We were deeply in love, there was a greater good, and there weren't a lot of explosions. We were alike in some ways, but the biggest difference was that Kevin had a calmer head than me. If I started to vent about something on a business level, he would listen, repackage it, and go defuse it. If I got upset at a certain aspect of a marketing campaign, Kevin would go to John Hammond and make it work. If I went ballistic over a misquote in the British press, Kevin would go to Creation and arrange for a redaction. Had it been me dealing with people, in my agitated moments, things might have been uncomfortable. Maybe that's why record companies don't like dealing directly with artists.

My business philosophy boils down to three basic points: don't promise what you can't deliver, know what you're worth, and show up on time. I imparted this philosophy to Kevin (and others who worked with me) more through deeds than words, and mostly just left him to execute the work. Starting in May 1992, Kevin was the one keeping track of the schedules and details. I was directing traffic, and he was alongside me the entire time. We were rising together, eating together, working together, and sleeping together. Everything we did, we did as one. We were glued together for the better part of four years.

It wasn't like Kevin built tables, then all of a sudden walked into this position. He grew up around the Athens music scene. He knew the lay of the land. He might not have known the specifics of how to get the business done, but he learned quickly. He was a much better "people person" than me; he had the charm that goes along with good looks, and a solid product to sell.

But the workload in those three years was unrelenting. There were many days when both of us rolled out of bed, headed immediately for the office, and didn't leave our desks for at least twelve hours. On the road it was constant movement, endless requests for interviews and appearances, and exhaustion from the physical wear and tear of traveling the globe on a regular basis. There was no off-season, no vacation, and the constant topic of conversation was the task at hand.

There were times when our relationship could have turned destructive, due to the complete overlap of work life and home life. Kevin could have his moments of anger as well. But we took good care of each other, for the most part. We thought the world of each other. And we were both long-term relationship guys.

Still, the smart money says one shouldn't work with one's significant other. And sure enough, work had begun to take a toll on our relationship.

Mike Covington and I never really worked together, so we didn't have those inherent stresses and strains. The only overlaps were few: a couple of video shoots, a failed photo shoot at the farm in 1988, and the *Workbook* art box, which I adore to this day.

Over the years, I'd lost touch with Mike. He sent me a letter in early 1990 expressing his sorrow for all that happened and how he never meant for the relationship to end so poorly. It was very thoughtful of him to send the letter, but by then I was over it. When I'm done with something, I'm done with it. When Hüsker Dü was done, I walked away and never looked back. When Mike and I were done, I walked away and didn't look back. Not looking back is a recurring theme in my life — for better and for worse.

The one time Mike and I reconnected in person was in the spring of 1993. He was living in Atlanta building customized boutique furniture, and I was on tour performing at the International Ballroom. He brought me one of his creations: a hand-weathered, whitewashed CD case that stood thirty-six inches high. The front panel was constructed out of a recycled plantation shutter. I was so proud of him, that he had created this beautiful piece of work, and thankful that he had given it to me.

Mike said, "I think I just met your boyfriend. Is that him over there, the tall blond guy?"

I said, "Yeah, that's Kevin."

"Wow! You *go*."

I was like, "Yeah, he's great. Thank you." That's the last time I saw Michael Allen Covington.

* * *

In doing research for this book, I found Mike's obituary online in the newspaper from Halifax County, Virginia, where Mike's family still lived. It was very plain: "Michael Allen Covington, 40, of Atlanta, died January 29, 2003, at his home. Services will be held at South Boston Baptist Church, Windy Hills Cemetery."

That's pretty much it. There were no details, no cause of death listed. Steve Fallon last saw Mike in 2001 and said it looked like he'd been burning it pretty hard on both ends. It shook me badly to learn that Mike was dead. It was all I could think about for weeks. I thought about our time together, mostly the good times. Sure, it ended badly, but it takes two people to end something. Mainly I was stunned to realize my first lover and I had drifted so far apart that it took me six years to find out he had died.

*   *   *

Five weeks after the last Sugar show, I played a run of solo dates in my strongest towns. There were two shows I remember well. February 26 was the second of two successive nights at First Avenue, and within ten minutes I had completely lost my voice. So I had the sound person set up another vocal microphone, and I asked audience members to come up and help me sing. It was great that people took the chance to come up onstage and sing with the singer, so to speak. Those fans really listened hard to the words, knew them well, and obviously felt them deeply. It was a wonderful way for the fans to salvage what would have been a miserable show.

The other memorable show was on March 4, at the Academy Theater in New York. The room was packed and steamy, the crowd was enthusiastic, and things were clicking. I finished my set, walked off to the wings, and waited for the din to get loud enough to return for an encore.

Suddenly a stagehand grabbed me and said, "You have someone upstairs who wants to see you—Pete Townshend." Without missing a beat, I said, "Could you go up and tell him that I'm not quite done yet?" I finished the show, headed up the narrow staircase behind the stage, and walked to my dressing room to meet my distinguished guest.

I was soaked with sweat and still charged up from the performance, just starting to process the fact that I was now meeting one of my formative artistic influences. In deference, I had to dial that energy back so I could have a civilized interaction with him. Once I downshifted and felt a comfortable energy between us, I began to take notice; he appeared younger than his years would belie and had a familiar focus in his eyes, the knowing gaze of someone who holds the answers.

Pete said, "I'm a big fan of yours." I was caught off guard for a moment, then responded, "I know your body of work as well, and I've been a big fan of yours since childhood." He started naming off some of my songs he liked, "Celebrated Summer" in particular. Pete was accompanied by Michael Cerveris, who was playing the title role in the Broadway production of the Who's rock opera *Tommy*. We all talked about the Broadway show, my new album, and projects that Pete was working on. After a few minutes, we wrapped up our casual meeting with a typical "Let's stay in touch."

It was the high point of the tour, but after the last solo date, April 13 in Boston, I was back home in the big, beautiful house in Austin—and left completely to my own devices. I was in my own head space and it wasn't always the healthiest one. I was usually alone in one of two rooms in the house, isolated and ignoring what was going on around me. One of those rooms was the office, where I was spending way too much time on the computer; AOL, SimCity, and Usenet binary porn had infiltrated my life. When I wasn't distracted by the flashing pixels, I was in my studio room, writing a record about the end of a relationship— and it may have been about my relationship with Kevin.

With no Sugar duties, Kevin didn't have much to keep him occupied. He'd sit in the front den with his friends smoking pot and listening to music all day, and I simply didn't care. Kevin and I were at opposite ends of the house, rarely coming together beyond dinner, sleep, and sex. Perhaps it was a by-product of having been coupled for five years and joined at the hip for at least three of those five. We'd begun to create separate lives, and we weren't keeping each other apprised of, or inter-ested in, our individual situations. I don't know if it was the beginning of some unspoken yet mutually assured destruction or a simple case of relationship negligence, but I lay claim to half the blame.

I was composing this dark breakup record, and once again, here was the prescience—write it and it shall be so. In years past I played everything for Kevin, even works in progress. This time, as I was writing the record, I kept him away.

Kevin started spending even more time away from me and befriended Austin musician Alejandro Escovedo. Al was a pleasant enough guy, but beyond being musicians, he and I had nothing in common. I didn't approve of the friendship, but I also didn't get in the way of it. When Kevin wasn't burning it down in the front den, he was in South Austin with Al's kids. Kevin was making a whole new social life separate from me. The distance between us grew as 1995 went on. I turned away in isolation, and the only person I was really communicating with was my engineer, Jim Wilson.

Jim would come by the house to listen to the demos, and he loved both the songs and the homespun recording approach. He'd say, "Don't overthink it, just do it." At the time, I was listening to artists like Sebadoh and Guided by Voices. There was an immediacy, charm, and simplicity to their lo-fi recordings that made me realize I didn't need to always spend weeks recording single parts, which can sometimes suck the life out of a song. I'd overthought myself into a hole with *FU:EL*. The idea that the first time is the best time wasn't so much a discovery as a rediscovery — after all, it was the way I'd made records for the first eight years of my career.

A perfect example would be "Thumbtack." I had the words for the song pretty much written. Then I sat down with the lyric sheet, my Yamaha twelve-string, and a DAT machine, hit record, and "stumbled" through a few chords. As I opened my mouth to say the first line ("Here's the town we live in..."), I unconsciously settled my left hand on a first-position B-5 chord, almost randomly setting the key for the song. The next five minutes were completely improvised, and the version that made the album was that first and only attempt at recording — and, in fact, writing — the song.

As the years continued, I further explored that elusive spot, that magic moment lying between unconscious creativity and conscious performance.

During my solo album recording sessions with Jim, we spent a lot of time detailing sounds and ideas, using different amplifiers and miking techniques, and I learned a lot from this experimental yet methodical approach. I programmed the kick and snare patterns on my Roland R-8 and played along on cymbals and toms. After that I began piling on the remaining instruments and vocals. Between experimentation and recording, we spent about six weeks at Cedar Creek. It was a lot of time, but we had great fun — more than I was having at home.

The emotional content of the songs was a lot to contend with, but Jim's upbeat personality kept the sessions from turning into a wrist-slitting party. I kept people away from the project without contemplating what might result from my hermit-like behavior. Kevin is out of the loop. Emotionally speaking, the writing is on the wall.

Jim and I spent two weeks mixing the tracks at Carriage House in Stamford. Once the record was mixed and mastered, I went back to Austin. I took the CD into the front den and played it for Kevin. This was the first time he was hearing these songs, even though they'd been written three rooms away. When I'd composed this music, I wasn't sure of what was happening elsewhere in the house, but the silence and indifference resonated throughout our home, informing my doubts, my fears, and my perhaps-unconscious desire to end something. After his initial listen, Kevin had no comment.

Kevin was managing Vic Chesnutt but earning no money. And for most of 1995, I didn't mind — and I didn't care. I never once went to him and said, "Why don't you help out with the bills?" Instead of dealing with Kevin head-on, I was funneling my feelings into my music. It was really good music, but once again, I was minimizing chaos in my daily life, avoiding confrontation, and accepting the shaky status quo. I'd mastered this trait as a child, and now I was doing it with Kevin.

In December of 1995, I traveled to Syracuse to see my brother and his wife and kids for a few days. Neither Kevin nor I had cell phones yet. I couldn't get hold of him for two days, which had me both bothered and worried. Normally, when either of us traveled, we had our ritual, our usual times to talk, and we talked a lot. I didn't know how to reach him, which showed me the fracture was deeper than I'd realized.

The night before I was going to fly home, I was asleep at my brother's house. I was woken from my sleep by a psychic jolt that shook me to the core. I jumped out of bed and had a moment of sheer panic and terror. This wasn't the feeling of waking from a bad dream, but the feeling of a lightning bolt, tearing and exploding everything as it passed through my being. I was in a cold sweat and never got back to sleep that night. I was scheduled to leave the next afternoon, but after this experience, I opted to take a morning flight. I had a strong sense that, by switching flights and not mentioning anything to Kevin, I was about to get my answer. I arrived at the house that afternoon, and a short while later, Kevin showed up with some guy I had never seen before. He was startled to find me at home.

Everything started to make sense. He met this guy through Al and started seeing him. I confronted Kevin, and he admitted they were romantically involved. His explanation was that this guy wanted to have children and I didn't, so Kevin thought there was more of a future with him—even though the other guy also had a partner. I was having a hard time processing this situation. I couldn't understand why Kevin would get involved with someone else without ending our relationship first.

Christmas was always a crap-shoot holiday for me because of a couple bad ones from my childhood. Sure enough, this holiday season was blowing up right in front of me. The timing couldn't have been worse. I asked Kevin to leave as quickly as possible. But he just lounged around on the couch for two days until I finally went in and said, "You don't seem to understand. You need to pack your belongings and leave this house now. *I don't want you here anymore.*"

He finally realized I was actually throwing him out. He

packed his books, records, and clothes, took Domino, and moved into a motel-style apartment. Our codependent relationship had come to an end.

I sat there over the holidays and had a miserable time. The only person offering any real support was Ann Guidry. I met Ann at Little City, a downtown coffee shop I'd been frequenting in the months leading up to this. Ann was a lesbian, soft-spoken yet firm in personality, and also had an artistic temperament. She was able to listen and give measured advice about taking care of my own soul. I always looked forward to spending time with Ann, and she kept me alive over the holidays.

As 1996 began, I was trying to build a new life, reaching out and meeting a few new people. I was in no rush to have a relationship of substance with anyone, but I was keeping an eye out for new acquaintances and, dare I think it so soon, potential dates. Again, with next to no courtship skills, I was petrified at the thought of dating. My two previous partners were all I really knew.

I went to both of my labels and explained the situation. It was devastating to tell them that not only is Kevin not working with me but that we're no longer a couple. They'd always thought of us as "Bob and Kevin," but that was no more. I was humiliated.

I was an emotional wreck, but the next album was already on the release schedule. Both labels were very understanding and accommodating. Ryko said they would work with anything I chose to do, including postponing live dates and doing minimal press. Creation figurehead Alan McGee wrote a long, thoughtful, emotional letter to me about family, crisis of confidence, and his own personal struggles. The reactions from both labels made me feel better about myself and restored some of the faith I'd lost in the music business after my management debacle in the spring of 1991, not to mention Kurt Cobain's suicide in 1994.

I found another unexpected source of faith in music while

One of six sold-out Sugar shows at First Avenue. Minneapolis, November 1994. *(Daniel Corrigan)*

A candid shot of Sugar, circa 1994. We accomplished so much in three years. It started, it exploded, then it was over. *(© Jay Blakesberg)*

Me and Jim Wilson in front; Jason Narducy, David Suycott, and Alison Chesley of Verbow in back. Austin, Texas, April 1996. *(Personal collection)*

Me and Kevin Nash slumming around downtown Las Vegas after a WCW pay-per-view, October 1999. Big Kev always made me feel like I was "in the band." *(Ross Forman)*

My two guys—Kevin O'Neill and Domino. Washington, DC, October 1997. *(Scott Stuckey)*

Kevin and me, New York City, circa 2000. When things were good, we were a formidable duo. *(Personal collection)*

(© Catherine McGann)   (Lisa Pearl)

(Todd Franson)

What a difference ten years can make on a person. I've always battled with body issues and weight fluctuations. In 1996 I was rail
thin and worn down from the first breakup with Kevin. By 2002 I
had three years of gym discipline under my belt and actually dared
to make a shirtless photo. And in 2006 I was a heap of muscle.
Rich Morel was no slouch either, but damn I was getting big.

Backstage at WedRock. Washington, DC, April 2004. Henry Rollins was such a champ to emcee a same-sex marriage benefit, and I was thrilled that my gym crush Will Hiley showed up as well. *(Personal collection)*

Me and my parents visited my sister in Roanoke, Virginia, in summer 2004, just weeks before my mom had her heart trouble. *(Personal collection)*

Great American Music Hall, San Francisco, 2008, after Jon Wurster's third show on drums. He was kicking major ass from the minute he joined the tour. Jason Narducy and Rich Morel look as pleased about Jon's presence as I do. *(Peter G. Whitfield)*

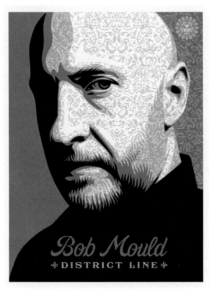

Shepard Fairey created this wonderful illustration, based on a photo taken by Peter Ross, 2008.

The torch gets passed at the ATP Festival. Playing with No Age was such fun. I didn't do too badly for an old guy. Just ask Dean Spunt and Randy Randall. Monticello, New York, September 2009. *(Abbey Braden for ATP New York)*

Hold this image up against almost any photo of me from the ages of eighteen to forty-five and tell me I'm not having the time of my life. I love this gig. Blowoff, Highline Ballroom, New York City, 2009. *(Michael Alexander)*

Micheal and me in the parking lot of the Boatslip, after one of many afternoon tea dances. Bear Week, Provincetown, Massachusetts, 2010. *(Michael Alexander)*

mastering the album in New York with engineer Howie Weinberg. Howie could sense that I was preoccupied and upset, so at one point he suggested we take a break and listen to something else. He disappeared for a few minutes, then returned with an album-size box containing a reel of quarter-inch tape. He handed me the box. I read the label and was speechless. It was the US masters for *Sgt. Pepper's*, complete with handwritten changes to song titles. We listened to the first side at full volume, wide open with no equalization or compression. I'd never heard music sound so majestic. It was a real pick-me-up to hear the pure version of an album I'd memorized in 1967, at the age of six. It reminded me that music can truly soothe the soul, if only for a precious moment.

I'd been alone for three weeks, trying to regain my footing to move forward as a single gay man, when out of the blue, Kevin called and said, "I really want to talk with you." Even with all that had happened, I still thought that we were supposed to be together forever. So without hesitation I said OK, but told him I didn't want to meet at the house and preferred to meet somewhere neutral. We met at the Botanical Gardens and spent hours walking and talking.

The upshot of the conversation was Kevin saying, "I don't know what I was thinking. This guy had a boyfriend, but we both love kids — and I know you're not big on the idea of having kids. Somehow I thought he might leave his boyfriend, and then he and I could have kids."

I had no interest in having children. I didn't think I had the proper tools to be a good parent. But Kevin wanted to have kids. So I asked, "What are we doing here? What's going on?" He said, "I'm done with that guy, I'm done with that whole situation and I want to come back."

We wanted to fix the relationship, knowing we were supposed to be together. We tabled the kid issue, kissed and made up, and he moved back in. I made two concessions. One was that I would go into therapy. I guess he felt he didn't need to go.

Still, I was thirty-five years old and a loud, emotional person—this screaming hulk on stage—and I was supposed to sit down with a therapist and talk calmly about my feelings? I couldn't quite see it.

Secondly, Kevin wanted a large chunk of money for a separate bank account. I didn't care; it was only money. If these two concessions would help heal the relationship, so be it. Kevin was asking a lot of me, and I stepped up to his requests. In hindsight, I probably didn't get the good end of this deal.

CHAPTER 19

My therapist, Jeff Hudson, ran a gay-friendly practice. Not that the breakup and the issues involved with it were exclusively gay, but I figured a gay-friendly therapist might understand the whole thing a little better. The work we did together is called regression therapy, which deals with early memories and family issues.

It was during the third session that Jeff posed a question to me — one that rattled everything I thought I knew about myself. Out of nowhere, Jeff paused for a moment, looked me squarely in the eye, and asked, "Do you have any knowledge of having been sexually abused as a child?" I was speechless. How could he ask such a thing? I told him I didn't think so, but still I was reeling from his suggestion. He went on to explain that, given the information I had shared about myself, it was not out of the question. He suggested that I ask my parents if they knew of any sexual abuse. I had given him the dots — he was simply connecting them.

I drove home, numb and confused. I had no reason to think that anything had happened to me, but I was trying to make sense of my life, so I called my parents and asked them if this was so. My father fell silent. Only my mother spoke.

In early 1962 I was sixteen months old. My mother was both working full-time at the phone company and tending to us three kids. Before leaving for work, she would call the local cab company, a taxi would arrive, my mother would put us in the car, and it would take us to a babysitter's house nearby. Once my mother finished work, a taxi would return us to the apartment on Main Street.

One day my mother went to change me and noticed black-and-blue marks on the inside of my upper thighs. She didn't know what to do and she didn't know if it happened to any other children, but that was the last time I was sent to that babysitter.

By the end of this story, my mother was sobbing and distraught. She blamed herself for allowing this to happen. I quickly assured her that it wasn't her fault, and that there was no way she could have foreseen what happened. My father remained silent. I'm not even sure he was still on the line.

The following week, I took this story to my therapist. Jeff looked sad at hearing the news, but not surprised. We began digging deeper into my childhood. I had stayed home from school to protect my mother. I had abandonment issues. I had intimacy issues. The list of what I perceived as defects kept growing. For weeks I was ashamed, confused, and uncertain of how much to share with Kevin.

But this information began to shed some new light on my childhood. Not only had my parents lost their eldest son right after I was born, but now, their youngest son had been violated by a babysitter. Perhaps this helped to explain why I'd been treated as the "golden child."

My parents had moved from Malone to north-central Florida in the early 1990s. My brother and sister had visited them and told me of the conditions in which they lived—a trailer park with no paved roads or streetlights. It wasn't the nicest neighborhood. I visited them in 1995 and saw it for myself. Clearly something had to be done. I was in a position to help and it would have only a minor effect on my bank account, so I offered to buy them a new house, as long as it was reasonably priced.

I was able to put aside all the difficult childhood memories—the paranoia and passive-aggression, the shame in bringing friends over, the weekends of violence—to make sure my parents were safe. They'd put me through college and supported me financially through my first few years in Minnesota. My dad had even driven two band vans out to St. Paul. Alongside all the unhappiness, they had always done the best they could, and I was glad to pay it back. When they found a modular home in a much safer community along the St. Johns River, it made me feel good about myself. It was a step toward personal happiness, but I still had plenty of work to do.

Jeff Hudson started me on a path that was key, and as life goes on it's become a mantra to me. It's that you're born into a family, your family of origin, and you're stuck with it. Once I recognized that, it freed me up to have a different kind of family: a family of *choice*. The people I surround myself with, spend holidays with, look to for support and comfort and validation—that's my family of choice. It's by no means a situation that's unique to gay men, but often there's the extra layer of not being able to comfortably share your life with your family of origin. I was bound up in those old family constructs and used so much of that dysfunction as the guideline for all kinds of relationships that I had. But Jeff didn't open the door, he just showed me where the door was. It's taken years—and it will continue to take years—to get through that door. But at least I'm on my way.

Therapy or not, Kevin and I soon lapsed into our old routine of spending our days in separate parts of the house. The only difference was, we'd now chosen different rooms—me on the ground floor of the garage apartment, still on the computer, and Kevin in the one-bedroom apartment above me. At night we reconvened in the main house to have dinner and try to resume our relationship. But the next morning we went right back to our new hideouts. Things were better, but not by much.

* * *

Running parallel to all this personal upheaval were the recording sessions for the first Verbow record. I'd originally met the band's leader, Jason Narducy, in the fall of 1990 at the 9:30 Club in Washington, DC. The following year, he came to a sound check at Metro in Chicago, reintroduced himself, and gave me clippings from the past few years of my Chicago press. There's also a video of a young Jason covering "Wishing Well" while wearing a Who T-shirt—what else can I say?

Jason formed Verbow with cellist Alison Chesley, expanded the lineup, and signed a rather huge deal with Sony 550 Music, becoming one of the many beneficiaries of the alternative rock gold rush then sweeping the music industry. I was pretty happy that all that grunt work I'd done in the '80s had, in an indirect way, helped get them the deal, and perhaps happier still that I was going to produce their album.

A few days after I'd caught Kevin with that other guy, I was in the studio with Jim Wilson, trying to produce the Verbow record. But I was useless—my mind and heart were consumed by my personal crisis. On the third day, I stepped back and the sessions were postponed. We reconvened in Austin in March 1996, just as my next solo album was about to come out. This time we were much more productive.

While finishing the Verbow album, I got a phone call from Ryko. They said, "We know you don't want to tour on this record, but we just got a call from Pete Townshend's management. Pete wants you to play two shows with him in New York at the Supper Club. He wants you to do a solo opening set each night. His shows are booked for May third and fourth."

I mentioned the request to Jason, adding that I had no intention of playing live any time soon and that I wasn't going to accept Townshend's offer. Jason said, "Bob, you absolutely have to do those shows. Are you nuts?" I thought for a moment and said, "Yeah, I guess you're right. I have to do the shows."

Bob Mould was released in April 1996. The album cover was a digital scan of a hubcap I'd found, ironically, while walking around Austin with Dennis Cooper in 1994. The album became informally known as the "Hubcap" album. The release was met with a moderate amount of fanfare in the States, less-than-normal interest in Europe, and a fairly scathing letter from Malcolm Travis. He mocked my use of the drum machine and laid into me about how I both publicly and privately mishandled the end of Sugar. I deserved it, but wrote him back to respectfully disagree with his album review. I don't have any lingering resentment toward Malcolm: he's a good guy, a fine drummer, and a proud parent.

That weekend, I went to New York for the two shows with Pete Townshend. The Supper Club was a great venue that was on two levels, with table seating around the perimeter of the main floor. The room was rather ornate, almost formal, yet had the feel of a well-worn nightclub. Given the setting, I blazed away as best I could. The first night, after his third song, Pete stopped to chat with the crowd and said, "I went to see Bob Mould at the Academy last year, and I couldn't believe it. Just a man and his guitar, a bottle of water, and a rental car. I thought to myself, I've got to do that." Never in my wildest dreams did I think I would get Pete Townshend off his ass to do some solo shows.

Afterward, Richard Butler from the Psychedelic Furs stopped by to say hello and had very complimentary things to say about both my work with Sugar and my ability to reinvent myself. Jason was also there to witness a great moment: Joey Ramone showed up with a big stack of Who records, headed straight for Pete, and started the "I'm not worthy" routine. Pete tousled Joey's hair a little, gave him an affirming nod, and started signing the pile of records.

That was truly adorable, but it was also a beautiful collision of many important things in my musical world. Playing these shows with Pete Townshend and witnessing that touching moment between Pete and Joey, two people who had such a profound and lasting impact on my life and work, got me really excited about playing music in front of people again.

It reset and mended my freshly damaged and distorted view of life, and made me recognize that this thing we call music, this primal expression that we reshape and refine and define ourselves with, is the gift I was given. The ability to communicate what others feel but cannot fully express, the passing down and around of songs and stories, from Pete Townshend to Joey Ramone to me, to the audiences who take the time and effort to support our work and give us a way to support ourselves—I'm thinking this is what I am supposed to be doing.

*   *   *

The video for "Egøverride," the first single from the album, clearly illustrated the emotional roller coaster I'd been riding. The video debuted on *120 Minutes*. I cohosted the show alongside Matt Pinfield, who is not only the most knowledgeable music fan I have ever met, but also one of the nicest guys in the business, as well as one of my biggest supporters. People remarked on how thin I looked—not as rail-thin as in 1989, but I had definitely dropped the extra forty pounds caused by those late-night burritos in 1994. I trimmed down on a home exercise bike, although the stress of my relationship problems with Kevin certainly had something to do with the weight loss too.

The video featured me walking and riding a single-gear bike around Manhattan. The experience rekindled my love of New York City. Maybe I was unconsciously mapping out a new life. If I know anything, it's the therapeutic nature of both pedaling away from what's behind you and toward what's in front of you.

Mentally and emotionally, I was beginning to fade away from Austin. The fracture had cast a shadow on the house. Austin was a good town, but it was a small town and everyone there knew what had happened. I thought it might be easier for us to put things back together in different surroundings.

So I started to think seriously about getting a pied-à-terre in Manhattan, and when I mentioned it to Kevin, he liked the idea. We loved Josh Grier's apartment on the east side of Manhattan, near the UN. It wasn't the hippest neighborhood, but it offered easy access to LaGuardia Airport, which would make it easy to get back and forth from Texas. So I looked to buy something similar in that area. And later in August, after looking at dozens of apartments, I finally found a 1,000-square-foot place in a nondescript apartment building at the corner of Forty-Eighth Street and Second Avenue. Eleven floors up, the place had a pleasant but uninspiring view of Midtown and overlooked the backyard of Stephen Sondheim's building.

But back in Austin I had made a new friend, a musician named Andrew Duplantis. Andrew was a sweet guy, very charming, and we immediately started spending a lot of time together. We both smoked cigarettes, and he also enjoyed marijuana, so I joined in on occasion. We would sit in my office, killing time by getting stoned and laughing at each other's corny jokes. In a way, this mirrored the relationship Kevin had with his Austin friends. Andrew had a boyish radiance that was attractive to me on many levels, and he was a wonderful distraction from the process of healing the relationship with Kevin.

Andrew was straight, but our time together was fraught with oddly tense moments. We would be talking about something innocuous, and if it had any undertone of sexuality, we would pause and look at each other as if to say, Yeah, and now what? Beyond those curious moments, it was a tight bonding, more of a big brother–little brother relationship.

We started to play music together, mostly my songs, and I thought it might be interesting to try performing material from my songbook as an acoustic duo. We had promotional photographs taken of us, and people commented on how similar we looked. I had deep feelings for Andrew, but there was little chance of anything physical happening between us—except music. Those feelings manifested themselves in a show we played together that July at Tramps in New York: the entire set was a barreling ball of energy. It was a public display of our private chemistry, and by the end of the set we were all drenched with sweat—Andrew, me, and even the audience.

One day in August, I was at Andrew's apartment, hanging out, listening to music. Kevin called in a panic and said, "You have to drop everything you're doing and get on a plane and go out to New York and finish Vic Chesnutt's record." Dave Ayers, who I practically grew up with in Minnesota, was Vic's A&R person at Capitol. This was to be Vic's first album for Capitol, *About to Choke*. I was being drafted into a chaotic situation, but given the people involved—Dave, Vic, and Kevin—I couldn't really say no.

In the span of eight hours, I drove home, packed a bag, went to the airport, landed at Newark International, and went straight to Waterfront Studios in Hoboken. I spent three days with Vic, ostensibly fashioning a cohesive album from sessions recorded in three studios. As it turned out, I didn't do any rerecording, editing, or remixing—all I did was sit around and reassure Vic that the album was good. When the record was eventually released, I couldn't hear a trace of my involvement. But I guess putting out the fires of Vic's uncertainty was worth giving up three days of my summer vacation.

* * *

Andrew and I did a run of acoustic duo shows in the fall, with me on guitar and Andrew on acoustic bass. Less than a week into the tour, I realized it wasn't working. One problem was that Andrew stomped loudly when he played; it wasn't always in time and it was very distracting. Also, personality differences get magnified on the road, and it turned out that Andrew and I weren't as compatible as I thought.

After a few shows of this, I decided it might be better if I just did the rest by myself. I drew this conclusion in late September, right before we were to play two weekend nights in New York. But his then girlfriend was coming to New York just to see him play, so I sent him home after that weekend.

Andrew didn't challenge the decision—I think he knew it wasn't working either. The feeling onstage never recaptured the magic of that show at Tramps two months earlier. He headed back to Austin with his girlfriend, and I spent the next week finishing up the East Coast dates by myself.

One of my major flaws is assuming that people are aware of what I expect. I should have just said, "Andrew, you need to lay off the stomping when we play." I also wasn't addressing the sexual tension between the two of us, for fear of losing him as a friend. By failing to address either problem, I cost myself a friendship, one that might have been healthier than the relationship I was trying to repair. The sad part of it is that Andrew was an unconditional friend who was there only to offer support.

After I wrapped up the dates, I returned to Manhattan, where Kevin was waiting for me. We quickly fell back in love with the city we'd left three years before, and within days decided to sell the Austin house. I was done with Texas and Kevin concurred. I made plans to put the house up for sale at the end of an upcoming run of West Coast and Texas dates. We had hopes of a speedy and stress-free sale.

Not only did I leave my house behind, but I left therapy behind as well. Somewhere on the acoustic tour that fall, when I would do therapy sessions on a pay phone at a rest area in, oh, say, central Ohio, I felt my time with Jeff Hudson had run its course. I was ready to walk away and resume my life without therapy. I said to Jeff, "I think I'm done here," and he said, "No, we have to wind this down in a four-week pattern." He asked me to stay on for another month in order to learn to say good-bye. That was insightful of him, and I didn't recognize what he was doing until years later. Now I know there is a healthy way that people can end relationships. Do I always do it? Not always, but I know that it's there.

But leaving places? Still no looking back. Over the course of three days in November, I filled a huge 20' × 6' × 6' Dumpster in Austin with my former life—a lot of my childhood belongings, boxes and boxes of wrestling magazines from the '70s, obsolete recording equipment, a ping-pong table, and the bed Kevin made of Brazilian hardwood, none of which would be of any use in Manhattan. I couldn't believe how many possessions I'd eliminated from my life—a twenty-foot Dumpster worth of memories.

During that week of physical (and emotional) purging, I played a solo acoustic show in Houston with Matt Hammon, a local singer-songwriter. The next night, another solo acoustic show—a farewell of sorts—at Austin's cavernous Liberty Lunch club, where I had played for fifteen years. I invited Andrew Duplantis and Matt to play solo sets as well. It was a great evening of music and a fitting end to the Austin years. Jim Wilson and I then drove a ten-foot box truck, filled with my pared-down possessions, to Forty-Eighth Street in New York.

*   *   *

Once again Kevin and I were becoming glued at the hip. We had a somewhat hermetic relationship. We had Domino and we had our 4Runner. We bought new furniture, kitchenware, and a bedroom set. We waved the magic wand—or more appropriately, the credit card—and tried to create a whole new life. We were trying to make it work, without truly working on ourselves or on the relationship. Maybe not the healthiest way to live.

But music work came quickly. I met up with my longtime Minneapolis friend Lizz Winstead. She and her creative partner, Madeleine Smithberg, were starting up a satire of TV news for Comedy Central, to be called *The Daily Show,* and they needed some theme music. I had two songs I'd decided not to put on the "Hubcap" album, so I submitted those. The one they picked was a song Jim Wilson called "Dog on Fire." (This original guitar-driven version ran on the show for a number of years; the theme has since been rerecorded and is probably my most heard song ever.)

The other outtake from the album would also prove useful and profitable. American Express was about to launch a new credit card in Asia, and a major New York ad agency was looking for signature music for the commercial campaign. They liked my song, but they wanted me to rerecord it. So Jim Wilson and I piled into a taxi with my bass, twelve-string acoustic, electric guitar, and drum machine, and headed seven blocks west to a studio in the Hotel Edison. Two hours later the session was done, and American Express subsequently renewed the rights to use the song two extra times, earning me triple the initial fee. It's nice to land one of those every few years—it really helps to keep the regular gig afloat.

And in December I was again asked to be a musical contributor to *The Daily Show*, this time as a caroler of sorts. Craig Kilborn, the show's original host, and I recreated the Bing Crosby/David Bowie "Little Drummer Boy" skit from Bing's 1977 Christmas special. Craig wasn't much of a singer and I wasn't really feeling the song that much either, but it was a fun piece of business.

In early 1997 I did a series of short solo acoustic tours, which covered virtually the entire country in four months. When I was home, I spent a lot of time riding around the city on a bicycle given to me by Josh Grier, who was an avid cyclist. I started riding every day, sometimes in Central Park, sometimes downtown, mainly by myself.

As summer approached, I spent many of my afternoons journaling at Peter Detmold Park, a sliver of green along the East River underneath FDR Drive, running from Forty-Ninth to Fifty-First Street. I was trying to write myself through this difficult time. I had this relationship with Kevin, but what was it I was really looking for, what was I attracted to, why was I uncomfortable in my own skin, why did I have abandonment issues, why did I cut people off so quickly? On and on. It was the first time that I thought long and hard about the things brought up during the eight months of therapy in 1996; I was on a self-exploration trip.

I created a second life down there. A homeless Israeli guy named Gadi was unofficially taking care of the dog park. He wasn't sitting in a corner in his own piss or rattling a tin can. He was probably in his midthirties, about the same age as I was, and I was intrigued by him. Eventually we acknowledged each other and started to talk. We spent the better part of three months, at least three times a week, sitting for hours and talking. Some days I would give him a little money, probably about twenty dollars a week.

I asked him, "How do you make it work?" He explained, "I rely on the kindness of others. I do volunteer work at the Catholic church in trade for meals. I do odds and ends for people. With the cash I gather, I'm able to have a gym membership. I go during the quiet times of the day, pretend I'm doing yoga, and that's when I can sleep." Through the work at the church, he had access to a washer/dryer. He had a locker at the gym where he kept his clothes. He had this veneer of credibility, yet he was homeless—and I was fascinated by this. I was in my own state of transition, some uncomfortable in-between, and maybe I was learning something I couldn't identify or recognize at the time.

It was helpful to have somebody who didn't know or care who I was or what I did. I didn't tell Gadi all about my career, not that it would have meant anything to a homeless man—it's not like he was watching MTV or reading *Spin* every month. And it was nice to have someone to sit and talk with, without the investment and intensity of a partnership. That's what people do. People have confidants and people have close friends that are private friends. I rarely confided in anyone beyond my partner, and I was very protective of my true emotions. The only time people got a look at my emotions was through my work. The music was the way I let myself be heard. My time spent talking with this homeless guy was a bold step for me. It was completely a second life.

I kept this up for three months. All of our interactions were in the dog park, or some other neutral public space. Then one day, instead of saying good-bye at the park, Gadi followed me home, and that's when I stopped meeting him in the park. I didn't see him until months later. He was working at OMG, a job-lot store that sold the previous season's clothes, three blocks down Second Avenue from my apartment building. I walked in, we locked eyes, said hello to each other, and I quietly congratulated him. "This is great," I said. He said, "Yes, it's good right now."

* * *

Pete Townshend and I got together again in 1997 for a dinner with Michael Cerveris, Kevin, and Pete's girlfriend. Pete was in town on business, and his girlfriend came to town to buy a VW Bug—because she wanted to have a vase on her dashboard. It was a great night, and as we ate outside at Restaurant Florent, I realized that Pete had a body shadow positioned one hundred feet away. The bodyguard followed us, at that fixed distance, for the entire evening.

As for me, I could walk down the street in Midtown or ride my bike down Second Avenue without being noticed. But if I went to a rock club in the East Village, I would instantly be recognized, and would feel most everyone in the room pointing and whispering about me.

Notoriety, or recognition, is like a diamond. You start to turn it, and when the light hits it, you see there are all these wild little facets inside. Things start to reflect and distort in unpredictable ways. Am I famous, notorious; do people recognize me? When is it to my advantage? Guys who try to get my attention, are they interested in me because I'm famous, or because they think I'm hot? It's an interesting yet vexing situation, and at this point in my life, I didn't have a clue as to what the answer was.

Being a public figure of slight note, but having deep resonance with a small group of people, is an odd position to be in. If you're a politician, it's implicit that people like you because they want money and they want the fruits of your power. When you're a musician, the connections with people are complex. How much do you give? How much do you reveal; when do you give it; when do you allow somebody to penetrate that first layer to even get an e-mail address or, God forbid, a phone number? Never mind about giving someone your home address.

This was the same level of protectiveness I extended across my sexuality. I was so hesitant to speak publicly about my personal life because of my perception of how it would change the work, or what people might think of me, or how it would affect my parents. Compared to other famous people, I've hardly come under public scrutiny or fallen victim to media sensation. Nonetheless, the complexities of protecting myself and those around me were exhausting.

I had also been protecting myself from getting in touch with my real emotions, which I'd been suppressing for years. It was coming time to confront and extinguish the nagging agitation I felt after concluding my therapy sessions in 1996. But first I had to put something big behind me. And little did I know how hard that battle would be.

CHAPTER 20

Jeff Hudson had made a big stink about my smoking — a habit I'd undoubtedly picked up from my father. Before our sessions I would smoke furiously, saturating my brain with as much nicotine as possible. He asked me to try not to smoke before coming in, just to see if the sessions would go differently. I tried, and it left me feeling more agitated than normal. It would be eighteen months before I quit.

Quitting smoking is the hardest thing I've ever done in my life, much more difficult than quitting drinking. The social fall-out from going sober was tough, but the physical act of stopping the booze was not so bad. I still can't believe how hard it was to quit smoking cigarettes.

It was Thanksgiving Day 1997. I woke up, and it was similar to the morning when I saw my dad in the mirror and said to myself, I have to stop drinking. Oddly enough, the tip-off came from my computer. I noticed that the screen appeared slightly warped from the center to the edges. I thought the monitor was going dead, but in fact, it was the screen protector that hung over the top of the monitor — it was covered with a sticky yellow tar from me sitting there and exhaling cigarette smoke onto it. I realized I was in trouble. Look at that, I'm viewing everything through a hazy yellow film, and it needs to stop.

I started smoking a pack a day at the beginning of college,

and by the end, I was up to three packs a day. Smoking had become both the centerpiece and timepiece of my life. Every cigarette was six minutes long, and I could practically mark out the whole day with smoking, like a sundial. Six minutes on, nine minutes off. Repeat sixty times a day. It was like playing Scrabble: when it's your turn, you turn over the egg timer and start thinking. I have an innate sense of time, but smoking was this additional timekeeper, like a wristwatch.

For me, there was no patch, no acupuncture, no therapy, no group hug, nothing. I maintain that nicotine is a much harder drug than heroin to quit. An ex-junkie once told me that very same thing, and I believed him. My dad smoked for fifty years before he finally quit.

I quit cold turkey. I had willpower, so not lighting up wasn't the problem. But it turned out that nicotine had suppressed my emotions. I could make it through the first ten hours of the day, but then I would turn into an angry baby. All this rage, frustration, and pain would come flying out of my body. At 6 PM of my first day without cigarettes, I said to Kevin, "I have to get out of here, I feel like I'm going to explode, I have to get out of this house." I walked up Second Avenue to around Eighty-Sixth Street, about two miles, turned left, walked the half mile to Central Park, and back down to Forty-Eighth Street. This is right after Thanksgiving, so the evenings are brisk.

I did that every day for at least three months, until I finally regained control of my system. The walk would last for an hour, give or take the amount of time I would spend buying a cup of coffee. Those six-mile walks kept me sane and also kept me fit. I didn't have the weight-gain problem that most people suffer from when quitting. It was the only thing I could do to stop from snapping at Kevin or killing myself. Cigarette smoking had been suppressing all that rage. Here I was, making this gut-wrenching music, brimming with anger, but still suppressing a lot of my emotions by smoking. Now I had to reassess how much rage was really in there.

In the 1960s and 1970s, before pop psychology became a more pronounced part of our social fabric, men (like my father) were not encouraged to be "in touch with their feelings." Men were to be tough, not show emotions, and dominate the family structure. Women (like my mother) were subordinate and demure, yet held great power over the family dynamic. Lots of kids (like me) were brought up in violent homes, and we weren't any the wiser. I was a child of my environment, and in adulthood I could have easily become that male figure of the 1960s.

My parents are still together, so whatever works for them is what counts. But now I was learning to identify the impression my childhood left on me, and that was the source of a lot of the anger I felt.

When I was a kid, I didn't think I was having a horrible childhood. For one thing, just about everyone I knew came from some kind of dysfunctional family — one with alcoholism, domestic violence, incest. But still I knew things were not right. Almost every weekend was the same drill: the calm before the storm, then the violence, then back to school on Monday morning. Growing up like that, week in and week out, established a cycle that never seemed to stop. More than twenty years later, I recognized it and slowly began attempting to correct it. It wasn't going to be easy, and it wasn't going to change overnight.

My father was a heavy smoker, and by quitting I was eliminating yet another piece of me that emulated the worst aspects of his behavior. To get there, I needed more than my long walks. I needed a new routine.

After finishing the "Hubcap" album in November 1995, I had stopped writing music. And since leaving Austin in October 1996, I had no home studio. Even if I had wanted to, I didn't have a place to write music. So in late 1997 Jim Wilson came to Manhattan and spent two weeks assembling an awesome little recording studio for me at a rented workspace in Soho. The room wasn't soundproofed and there were other businesses surrounding me, so I had to work at night, which I actually liked.

After months of journaling, I had a wellspring of ideas waiting to be tapped. I wrote what would become *The Last Dog and Pony Show* in less than a month.

I followed the same routine every night. I would take an early evening nap, then get up at 10 PM. I'd drive down Second Avenue to Fourteenth Street, west on Fourteenth to Broadway, and then park in front of the building. At the bodega next door, I'd pick up a cinnamon-apple PowerBar, one twelve-ounce coffee, black, and a one-liter bottle of Poland Spring water. Then I'd work from 11 PM to 5 AM before driving back home up First Avenue to catch a few hours of sleep. The next night I'd do it all over again, exactly the same way.

Rituals and routines—I need them. To this day, after walking the same six-mile route to help myself quit smoking, I still count my steps constantly.

Sometimes it's difficult to sort the healthy routines from the harmful ones. By this point I was thoroughly frustrated with the guitar rock paradigm. I had been doing basically the same thing over and over for almost twenty years—playing rock guitar. "I Hate Alternative Rock," from the "Hubcap" album, told the story:

Tired epileptic charade
Get on the plane and fly away
I knew you when
I knew you when
You had something to say

I wrote those words in 1995—a rough year for guitar music. Everything good about alternative rock had been exploited and ruined by the major labels, and the bands they chose to elevate. The musical subculture I helped create had descended into fashion shoots, groupies, and fabulousness. The music industry took a sound that was once pure and honest and true and heartfelt, and wrapped it in the glossy paper of fame and fortune. The whole thing smacked of commercialism. There was no struggle, no cause, no real reason for these bands to exist.

At the same time, I knew I had an audience with certain expectations about my work, and I was feeling trapped by my own history. I was tired of being the alternative rock guy; the art form had become useless to me. I was stuck in a spot, similar to how I felt at the end of Hüsker Dü. Just as *Warehouse* was the swan song of Hüsker Dü, I viewed this upcoming album as the swan song of my guitar rock existence. I started telling people that this was it, that I really didn't want to do it anymore. I wanted to be free of my professional history, free to experiment with sound and words. That's why I called the album *The Last Dog and Pony Show.*

I was tired of alternative rock, and you know what else? I was tired of not being gay. I was on the verge of something new, and it hit me that the longer I sat in a van, riding around the country with straight guys, playing rock music to mostly straight people, the longer it would be before I could claim my sexuality. I wanted to be a gay man with a gay identity. It was time for me to claim that identity, and in my mind, the quickest, easiest, and best way to do so was to abandon the professional identity I'd built over the past two decades.

I was starting to bicycle myself down to Christopher Street, which for decades has been the symbolic "gay street" of Manhattan, to a gay-friendly coffee shop called the Factory Café. I would duck in, grab a cup of coffee, then sit slightly away from the building, watching and observing how everyone carried themselves. I wasn't sure how to fit in. I could command an audience of sixty thousand people, but I wasn't sure how to act at the gay coffee shop. How weird is that, at the age of thirty-seven?

* * *

I recorded the last rock record in early 1998, back in Austin, again with Jim Wilson as my engineer. When we started up at Cedar Creek, it was business as usual. I brought the drum machine tracks, printed them to tape, and started laying down guitars and basses. By the fourth day, I was very unhappy. I told Jim I didn't feel like making "this record" again. I'd felt obliged to make another rock record, that's what people expected, and now it really was a grind—the same old routine.

In an attempt to shake things up, Jim brought in a bunch of equipment I hadn't used before. After a few days of experimenting with the gear, we had turned the studio into a rat's nest with wires running every which way. My favored piece of gear was an eight-bit Akai sampler, which yielded a strange yet appealing low-resolution sound. We sampled everything under the sun: guitars, vocals, and other people's recordings. We didn't use any unauthorized samples on the album, but we certainly had fun turning Linda McCartney's infamously out-of-tune background vocals from the monitor-board recording of "Hey Jude" into a large group of seagulls.

Hot 97 FM was all the rage in New York at the time, and hip-hop production was unique, far ahead of what was going on in alternative rock. It led me to recording "Megamanic," this white boy's lame attempt at hip-hop. We added small sampling touches to songs like "First Drag of the Day" too.

Even though the sound of my music was changing, the album's lyrics stayed close to the norm, but with a few interesting twists. "First Drag of the Day," lyrically, addresses my battle with cigarettes:

If I can get to the words before that first smoke
Everything seems to come out differently.

"Moving Trucks" was a clear reference to my problems with Kevin and, subsequently, leaving Texas. "New #1" was about my friendship with Andrew and the irony that the relationship turned out so poorly. "Skintrade" was a nod to William Burroughs, an attempt to write in his style with imagery of the forlorn junkie. "Classifieds" was about the ads in the back of the

Village Voice for "Men Seeking Men," and how, more often than not, they led to a fruitless chase.

Another key aspect of the experimentation was recording ambient guitar passages using an Eventide H3000 Harmonizer. As the minutes of improvisation accumulated, I realized I was more excited by these pieces than I was by the songs themselves. I decided to incorporate them as interludes on the album.

After a few weeks, we moved down to Boerne and brought in Matt Hammon, who, in addition to being a singer-songwriter, was a rock-steady drummer with a lyrical yet economical style. My unorthodox drums-last approach worked like a charm, and Matt tore through the twelve tracks in five days. Alison Chesley from Verbow played cello on a number of tracks, and her contribution was top quality.

Then disaster struck. Jim and I moved on to Carriage House to mix the album. After the first Friday night of mixing, we left the master tape that contained all the edited improvisational pieces in the machine. On Saturday morning there was a class in the control room, and someone had accidentally recorded over the entire tape. All the improv pieces, the music that sparked me and kept me interested in making the album, were gone. There was no way to rerecord them—they were borne of total spontaneity. I was devastated, angry, and supremely depressed. After that I lost interest in the album. Jim ended up mixing most of it himself while I sat upstairs in the studio apartment, numb from what had happened, hearing the dulled sounds vibrating from below. Regardless, the album needed to be finished and released on time.

* * *

In early 1998 I decided that I needed to be able to work at all hours of the day, which meant working at home. Kevin agreed and we began hunting for a new place to live in Manhattan. In March we bought a 2,800-square-foot loft in a former soap factory in Tribeca. It had a wall of east-facing windows that looked out onto Canal Street and Soho, and the southern wall was comprised of windows that had views all the way down the Hudson River past the Statue of Liberty to the lights of the Verrazano Bridge. We spent six months fixing it up, with Kevin overseeing the renovation while I worked on the album. He was winding down his management work with Vic Chesnutt, so the renovation project gave him something to occupy his time. The renovations were completed in October, right as I was getting ready to leave on band tour—for the last time.

The album was titled *The Last Dog and Pony Show,* and I promoted this tour as my farewell to rock, hoping that, after the tour ended, things would be really different. Still, I knew there would be skepticism. There's a long history of "farewell tours" in rock and roll, whether it was the Who, Kiss, or whoever. But I truly wanted out. I'm not sure I even wanted "in" as far as touring went, but it was an obligatory part of the album campaign.

The touring band was Matt Hammon on drums and Jim Wilson on bass. Against my better judgment, I added a second guitarist. Reenter Michael Cerveris, who had been with Pete Townshend at my New York solo show in 1995. Michael positioned himself in my line of sight, offered his services, and I gave him the spot. He was a charismatic person, a good singer, and a great Broadway performer. He had his own music career as well, writing, recording, and performing with his band, Lame. He'd studied my songbook, was very attentive, and seemed qualified for the job. He seemed like he'd be an asset.

Josh Grier suggested that I hire Mike Stuto, who at the time ran Brownie's, an influential East Village rock club, to handle the office duties for the album campaign. Mike and I were a good fit, and he represented my interests well to both Ryko and Creation.

I rehearsed the band and we played two small shows in New York City. The first, during the week of the album release in late August, was a showcase organized by Ryko, and it was held at Angel Orensanz Center, a former synagogue on the Lower East

Side. The premise of the show was to invite downtown celebrities to stop by, capture them on film, and incorporate the footage into a video for the first single from the album, "Who Was Around?" Very few VIPs turned out for the ridiculously loud show, so that idea was scrapped. The second show was unannounced and took place eight days later at Brownie's, where we ripped through a short set. Nine days after that, the *Last Dog and Pony Show* tour began in Fargo, North Dakota.

While the rest of the band would wear the same clothes onstage that they wore at lunch that day, Michael was stylized. Maybe it was the Broadway mind-set, but he was prone to gesticulation, which affected his guitar tuning and vocal pitch. His amps were loud, and despite the important lesson I'd learned from the 1989 tour, I had yet again allowed another guitarist to clutter up my frequency range. And just like in 1996, I said nothing about it. I slowly stewed. Beyond our initial rehearsals, where Michael showed great aptitude, I offered little criticism or direction. I had gotten myself into a rough spot—two months of touring like this. As a result, I have few memories of this final tour—almost as if it never happened.

But I know how I felt by the time we got to Europe—I really couldn't believe I was going out like this. This wasn't what I had pictured earlier in the year. I was holding in a lot of anger and I wasn't addressing it directly with Michael.

One afternoon while in the UK, after sound check, Jim, Matt, and I went for a walk. We were looking for a pair of shoes for Randy Hawkins, our tour manager and sound person. He'd worn down the soles of his shoes so far that they leaked when it rained.

One of the guys piped up, "Bob, do you mind us asking, what is up with Michael?"

It was as if someone had pulled the plug out of a stagnant bathtub filled with scum and turgid water. I said, "You guys, I'm dying up there. It doesn't sound right, and this is not what I envisioned."

Jim and Matt reminded me, "This is your band, you're the boss, and if you're not happy with something, change it."

I was like, "OK, there's no time to waste."

We went back to the venue and I gathered up the crew and the band. I looked around the dressing room and said, "I want to thank everybody for putting their best effort forward to make this tour as enjoyable as it could possibly be. You all know how much this has meant to me for twenty years, and I'm getting ready to walk away. Unfortunately, Michael, you're not working out. London will be your last show. I will make all the arrangements to get you and your stuff home. You tell me what I need to tell people. I want to make this as easy as possible for you, but I am not ending a twenty-year career this way. I started in a three-piece, and I'm going out in a three-piece. I'm sorry."

Michael took it like a man. I doubt anything like that had ever happened to him before—he was so successful in his stage career. I felt bad about dismissing him in front of the whole crew, but that's how it played out. After the Sugar breakup in 1994, where nothing was said, I went the opposite route and took it to the entire entourage. Clearly I had yet to find the best way to do this.

That night Michael had his best show with the band. He played as if a fire had been lit under him. If I'd said something sooner, maybe things would have been different. The last few shows were also better, including the London show, which was recorded for a live album. That show was emotional for me—I was saying good-bye to a town where I'd had lots of success over the years. Many of my press friends were in attendance, the Creation folks were very supportive, and the folks from My Bloody Valentine came by as well. Even Robert Plant was at the gig, though I didn't get to say hello to him.

The first show as a trio was at the Rex Club in Paris, a 250-capacity basement club, a bit of a dive. We arrived, walked into the back area, and came face to face with our catering, which consisted of a mound of white rice, maybe twelve by eighteen inches, with cockroaches running all over it. That was not the fine Parisian dining experience I'd had in mind. But we walked out on that stage and burned the place down. It eclipsed anything we had done on the tour. All the anxieties and discontent instantly disappeared. It was as if I'd started over with a new band.

Jim stepped up and, for the first time since we started playing together, showed his real stage personality. In the trio setting, Jim's playing completely opened up. He played with a confidence and authority I had never seen in him. Jim and Matt locked tightly to each other, and the entire set was one long, fluid motion. When we walked off the stage that night in Paris, the three of us were drenched in sweat, grinning from ear to ear.

The last week of the tour was great, particularly with Jim, with whom I'd been through so much. Jim was loyal, so helpful to me, and always giving, both personally and professionally. He showed me different ways to make records, which complemented the lessons I'd learned from Spot, Steve Fjelstad, and Lou Giordano. Jim brought another dimension of deeper learning. And he was so good, as was Kevin, at dealing with my rants, and he was able to defuse my darker idiosyncrasies.

The crew and the band were relieved, and all was good for the final week of electric touring. The final show, in Brussels on November 6, was a strong one, and I remember more about the party afterward than I do about the very long set and multiple encores. We all stayed late at the venue to celebrate the end of the tour. There was a local drunk who wouldn't get off our case and was getting everyone very agitated. Right before it came to blows, nature called the drunkard. The restroom was a single toilet in a closet-type room, with a heavy metal door. Once he was in the restroom, we jammed the door shut by stuffing coins into the door frame. We finished our drinks and left. The music in the club was loud, so it was unlikely his banging would be heard until the bar was closed.

More than the last show though, I remember the flight home.

I had this blue composition book, and on that plane ride home, I made a list of things I was going to do:

I'm going to fix my body.
I'll start going to the gym.
Maybe I'll get a tattoo.
I might change my appearance completely.

This was the list of things that I wanted to do now that I was free of the burden of being Bob Mould, the Rock Guitar Guy. I sat on that plane and I dreamed. Finally, I hoped, this weight can be lifted off my back. Bob Mould, the Angry Man. Bob Mould, the Miserablist. Bob Mould, the Pessimist. The Smoker. The Bad Ender of Things. The Self-Hating Homosexual. It was time for all of them to leave the stage, hopefully to make room for Bob Mould, the Gay Man.

A few days after returning home, I saw an episode of the Charlie Rose show on PBS. His guest was British-born journalist Andrew Sullivan, who had just published a book titled *Love Undetectable,* a memoir/study of homosexuality and culture. I was as fascinated by his eloquence as I was by the substance of what he had to say. Andrew spoke about being HIV-positive and about how his diagnosis made him consider the paradoxical bond between friendship and death, the concept of survivor guilt, and how to confront gay shame. Andrew said he had to "confront the shame, really face it, and come through it. And I feel stronger as a result." I really related to all of it.

I called my mother the next day and implored her to watch the show, which would air several more times that week, and I suggested that my father watch it with her. I thought it might help them understand some of my more intimate thoughts and concerns. Of course, it was my mother who had unknowingly showed me how to ignore things, turn away from big issues, not talk about big problems, and avoid conflict. I'm not even sure she watched the show. If she did, I don't know if she fully understood it.

But I wasn't waiting. I began to put the wheels of change into gear. As far as I was concerned, my "rock guitarist" career was over. My new gay life—I was going to have to build that from scratch.

CHAPTER 21

Early in 1999 I started going to the gym for the first time since high school. Kevin and I joined together, and we would go at least five days a week. Our particular gym was in the West Village and quite gay. The clientele was varied: from famous folks like actor Chris Meloni and comedian Sandra Bernhard, to musicians like Luscious Jackson's Kate Schellenbach. I'd also spot a plethora of male escorts — I recognized them (and their tattoos) from the classified ads of gay publications like *HX* and *Next,* which I was now reading every week to find out all the fabulous things that were happening around town. Seeing all these people with their well-sculpted bodies made me think, Maybe if I get myself into shape, I'll get noticed. I'll fit in and make some new friends.

After three months of running three miles a day, then working out for an hour, I looked in the mirror and was shocked to see a different person. I had lean muscle, the baby fat was gone, and I was looking more masculine. I said to myself, Wow, I'm sort of a hot guy underneath all this fat. I was also looking more severe, like someone you might not want to mess with. I began to carry myself differently. I wasn't walking in a defensive stance, staring at the sidewalk, or avoiding eye contact on the street. I stood up straight, lifted my chest outward, and walked with a brisk and authoritative pace. I felt more confident—it was a total mind/body/soul awakening.

A couple of things came to a head at once. One was that I didn't want to continue being the pessimistic, self-hating homosexual. I started allowing myself a little bit of enjoyment in life, a little latitude. I'd been out for five years but I still wasn't in "the life." I'd had a career that, to my mind, had little to do with being gay. I wasn't homophobic, but I was definitely self-hating, and not exclusively or necessarily due to my sexual orientation. I thought I was ugly, unappealing, unattractive. I had a beautiful man on my arm, but that didn't make me feel any better about myself. I'd been beating myself up, even comparing myself to Kevin, who everybody, straight or gay, threw themselves at. I decided not to do it anymore. (A small observation from personal experience: if you marry the gorgeous one, it might be hard on you.)

The second was that I'd never felt people were attracted to *me*—instead they were attracted to the person onstage. Now that I had walked away from my career, this was the moment to make it all about *me*. Sure enough, people started coming up and talking to me. I know that might sound shallow: They only talk to me if I look good? What about my esteemed career? What about my personality? They didn't know about any of that, which was perfect. I wasn't the rock guy. I was just a guy. Now they were going to be my friends because they wanted to be—because I looked like them or because we worked out together. It's like responding to a "band member wanted" ad in a college newspaper because it mentions your favorite bands. Every group, every situation that we enter into, has a code, rules of conduct, and markers and signifiers that attract or repel us.

Kevin and I would walk from the loft to the gym, work out, then have lunch at a little vegetarian place nearby or at Manatus, a longtime gay diner on Bleecker Street. After lunch we'd go to the Factory Café, which became the center of my social life.

From the beginning of 1999 until I left New York I don't think I ever missed a day going there. It was the center of the universe for me. That's where I made my first real group of gay friends—the experience was priceless.

I started meeting all these characters like Mark, this five three, 230-pound African-American flight attendant. He was completely worked out, busting out of his uniform. He would come from his Upper East Side apartment with his roll-aboard bag, sit in his seat by the corner window (we all had preferred seats at Factory Café), and tell stories of his exploits in foreign ports. Mark would make mix CDs of classic disco and new music for the shop to play. I learned a lot about dance music from Mark, and heard things like the Avalanches' album *Since I Left You,* which would later be an influence on my LoudBomb recordings.

There was also this fellow named Jack, a handsome, masculine, yet mysterious fellow. He usually dressed like a construction worker, with a Carhartt jacket, jeans, and work boots. He had short black hair, a goatee, and dark brown eyes—very strong Italian features. No one was quite sure what he did for a living, but like clockwork, he would show up each day for a cup of coffee to go and sit out front on one of the two wooden park benches. One day I showed up alone and, instead of sitting inside, decided to take my coffee to go and sit next to him on the bench. We sat quietly, not talking, for several minutes. Suddenly he looked up at me and said, "Do you like chocolate?"

It was the first time I had heard him speak, let alone speak to me. I said, "Oh, yeah."

"Come with me," he said. As we walked down the street to the old Li-Lac Chocolates shop, Jack asked me if I smoked pot. I said sure, and we proceeded, with coffee and chocolate in hand, to smoke weed and listen to music in his studio apartment a few blocks away. Nothing intimate happened—it was simply a moment that brought me a new friend and some new knowledge about how to be gay in the West Village.

One of my gym buddies was Michael Lucas, who is one of the biggest gay-porn stars/producers in the world. He lived in Chelsea with his Austrian-born partner, Richard Winger, who owns the two West Village brownstones that house the LGBT Community Center. If you walk up and down Eighth Avenue in the Twenties and see this Russian guy with big pouty lips and black hair, that's Michael Lucas. He would show up at the gym, lift his shirt, and reveal his tightly defined abdominal muscles. Then he'd run his hands up and down his torso, as if he were a model on *The Price Is Right* gesturing to a fabulous new vacuum cleaner, and proclaim, "Perfect." We would all nod and say, "Of course, Andrei, perfect." His real name is Andrei—Michael is his stage name. He invited me to his home office, where he had manila envelopes stacked in a corner. He explained that they were filled with résumés and photos of aspiring porn stars. Some afternoons he would hand me a magnifying loupe and let me go through a stack of envelopes in hopes of finding a suitable candidate for an upcoming film.

One night Kevin and I went with Michael to Bar d'O for a performance by legendary female impersonator Joey Arias. During Joey's monologue, he noted that Michael was in attendance. He asked the lighting director to turn the spotlight toward Michael, but the light landed on Kevin and me. Joey quipped that we were Michael's two newest Russian porn star finds. I heard a cackle of laughter from the other end of the bar. Turned out the guy laughing was Rufus Wainwright.

Back at the Factory Café, I only knew the guys by Bill or Tom or whatever their first names were, but we all hung out together and shared the stories of our lives. I would sit and listen as the older men told of what the West Village used to be like in the '70s and '80s. They would tell me about Stonewall, the disco era, the fetish clubs, and the advent of AIDS. I was all ears—this was not my personal history, but the history of the culture I had never known.

I learned how to harmlessly flirt with other guys, how to be bitchy without being hurtful, and how to look at other men without letting eyes connect for more than a half-second (lest you end up married—gay joke). I didn't know the details of tricking or open relationships, but I learned about those things and more, and rather quickly. I was getting a crash course in how the gay world turns.

These were the behaviors, routines, and rituals I had never experienced, the ones that most gay men learn at seventeen when they run away from Nebraska and move to Chicago. And here I am in the West Village, at the age of thirty-eight, finally experiencing and learning this stuff. I felt like Rip Van Winkle— I'd been asleep for years.

* * *

I had fallen in love with Christopher Street, the West Village, and my new romantic notion of gay culture. Although it had been nearly twenty years since the heyday of gay life in the West Village, it was thrilling for me. One thing I've found over the years is that no matter how hard new commerce and new community has tried to gentrify a "gay ghetto," you can still feel the old sexual energy there. Walk down into the Sheridan Square subway stop at Christopher Street, and you can imagine men of all ages and body types, cruising each other on the platforms. Look for the smallest of details in the buildings, and you will see traces of the struggles, the dramas, and the plague. All these things will eventually fade and disappear, but in 1999 it was still a very good version of the classic gay Christopher Street, right down to the smells: afternoon burgers with the old-timers at Julius, freshly mopped floors at the seedy adult book stores, the occasional whiff of poppers wafting out of a ground floor apartment window.

Within months I started hanging out in Chelsea, which at the time was the younger, hipper, more happening gay neighborhood in Manhattan. My main haunt was Barracuda, a bar on Twenty-Second Street at Eighth Avenue. There's no sign out front—it's next to the gay-oriented Unicorn bookstore. Barracuda was a fabulously gay place, playing Cher and Madonna and hosting drag shows. I had never been part of any of this before; in fact, these were the very people whom I felt alienated from for many years. Before I knew better, these were "the freaks" that rattled me. But now I saw how they embraced their "freak" and used it as self-identification and for self-empowerment. Another piece of the big gay puzzle fell into place.

Kevin and I had a nightly ritual: hike the mile and a half from the loft to the West Village, where we'd pick up an energy drink at the same corner deli, then continue up to Barracuda in Chelsea, arriving around 10:30 at night, ready to party. Everyone around me was drinking and carrying on while I remained a teetotaler, completely sober. I didn't care though—I was just happy to be there. I befriended Stephen Heighton, a handsome British chap who was one of the owners of Barracuda. I had crushes on the two main bartenders, Cole James and Darren Dryden. They were so sexy and hot, and I would sit at their bar and drool. Kevin would just be chuckling through all of this. We'd go in the back lounge and watch female impersonator Candis Cayne do her Pat Benatar tributes to raise money for her Mexican boob job. The best I could muster was a one-off solo acoustic-electric show in that same lounge on July 11, 1999, as a fundraiser for the Anti-Violence Project—one of my earliest and most direct involvements in the New York City LGBT community.

Another way of getting into the gay mix was at our loft, where we hosted fabulous dinner parties on our roof deck. We'd run an electrical cord out a window, up two stories to the roof, and into a lamp and a ghetto blaster, and we'd cook up delicious meals for Andrei and Richard and others while we all shared our life stories. Most of the guys at the dinner table had led much more typical gay lives; my stories, though, were mostly about my old punk rock life, and were as foreign to them as theirs were to me. Those conversations were illuminating, and we all learned from each other. The dinners were modest and intimate, yet just as meaningful as the wild smorgasbord I was about to encounter.

Andrei and Richard would have us out to Fire Island, a sandy spit of land running parallel to the east coast of Long Island, and I quickly realized there was another level to all of this. That level was the Pines, the vacation town for rich and famous East Coast A-gays, like David Geffen, who has a palatial estate there.

The trek from Manhattan to the Pines, and the gossip that goes along with the trek, is all part of the ritual: What is (s)he wearing that outfit for? What is that little tiny dog they're carrying? Didn't they break up last weekend? On and on. Most guys ride the Long Island Railroad to Sayville, then take the ferry to Fire Island. The Pines is essentially a series of dunes crisscrossed by plank walkways; there are no cars. You bring what you can carry in your arms or on little red wagons. The beaches are white sand and the water is the purest blue. It is simply stunning.

Andrei and Richard owned a large house on the bay side, not far from the center of town. I would usually be in the swimming pool that faced the bay. Over to one side, there's a big privacy fence. From time to time, I would see heads popping up over the fence. This would go on for hours. After a day of this, I said to Richard, "Your neighbors keep looking over the fence." Richard said, "Oh, that is my house too. That's for my exes."

If I thought I was A-list in the rock world and B-list West Village gay, I quickly found out I was a nobody at the Pines. I went to my first circuit party out there. A circuit party is a seasonal dance, usually a fundraiser for various gay organizations, and the DJs typically play diva remixes. This guy Beau threw a party one August where they built a dance floor that went out onto the water, and that was my first real exposure to "the clones": seven hundred shirtless muscle boys with buzzed heads, all wearing Levi's 501 jeans. None of them are shorter than five six, none taller than five nine, and they're bumping around against each other. Kevin and I are up on the catwalk, watching this spectacle, this party thrown by a multimillionaire for these boys. The next morning we go to brunch with the organizers, and they're dropping famous names and exotic places like nobody's business. I ask myself, What am I doing in this movie?

Circuit parties are usually themed parties: the White Party, Black Party, Cherry Party, Black and Blue Party, and so on. The White Party, for instance, is an all-night dance party where everyone wears white. If it's an outdoor White Party, people dance as the sun comes up, and continue until noon. The promoters typically hire a DJ like Junior Vasquez to do those parties. Tribal music, sounding like pots and pans banging in a busy restaurant kitchen, would be the evening music. Uplifting, more ethereal and melodic house music would be the morning music. So there was night music and morning music, and I'm trying to figure out all this stuff on the fly.

Then there's the Black Party. To begin with, the dance floor is not that different from that of a leather bar on a Saturday night, except it's filled with a thousand men and over-the-top sound and lighting. The music is more primal, more intense—harder sounds, hypnotic layers, what I refer to as "hunting music." I would never advise anyone to go to the Black Party unless that person has a strong stomach and a wide-open mind. It's a very dark S&M-oriented party. Imagine a thousand men or more, many dressed in leather, rubber, or other fetish wear, and some of them with absolutely no boundaries. If something can go into something else, it's probably happening in some dark corner. There's a lot of hardcore sexual experimentation, and not many people want to remember what they did the next day. My first Black Party was the first time I witnessed things I had only heard whispered about. Two fists aren't supposed to go into that hole at once. OK, turn away. What do you look at when you've seen everything?

Remember, I'd grown up in a farm town, then gone to

college, spent ten years on the road, then holed up at the farm, then spent several cloistered years nesting with Kevin in Austin and New York. These new experiences were a little surreal, but I was rolling with it, figuring out which parts I wanted to bring into my life and which didn't work for me.

If I wasn't out before, I was certainly out now. I immersed myself in gay culture and was having a great time. In my previous life, my miserablist state, the world was often cold and small and grey. I had the feeling I wasn't in Minnesota anymore. Now my life was filled with revelatory experiences, suddenly painted with vivid colors.

This was my new gay life.

Chapter 22

In September of 1999, my fabulous gay summer was pre-empted—I took a day job. I was going to work for World Championship Wrestling.

As a child in rural northern New York State, I had a number of interests and hobbies, but only two passions: music and professional wrestling. I discovered wrestling at an early age, and once I saw it, I was hooked. Some kids had Batman, others had the Lone Ranger, but pro wrestling was my action-adventure series. My first exposure to it was when I was eleven, through Montreal TV stations, and I've followed it ever since.

As a youngster, I was drawn to it for the obvious reasons: the drama spoke to the young man growing inside of me, waiting to be released. Not unlike most school sports, pro wrestling spoke to the desire to have contact and intimacy with others, not necessarily in a sexual sense, but in a healthy, competitive manner. Pro wrestling has always been predicated on good versus evil. The wrestlers on TV were larger than life, pitching and catching heated threats of destruction, humiliation, and retribution. Sometimes it was simply about who was the better man, other times it might involve a piece of stolen or destroyed personal property, and, on rare occasions, it was about the betrayal of a best friend.

I used to buy wrestling magazines at the neighborhood

pharmacy, and every few months my father would drive me to the matches at the Montreal Forum, an hour and a half away, with our usual stop for hot dogs and poutine. If there was wrestling anywhere within fifty miles of Malone, I would ask to go. I studied wrestling like other kids study baseball cards—immersing myself as deep as I could, gathering as much information as I could find. Some of the wrestling magazines focused heavily on match results, and I would read these results over and over until I memorized them—much as I'd done with the label copy on seven-inch singles.

My friends and I would reenact matches in the backyard, not certain of what we were doing, but it was a way to pass the time. I got my nose busted three times when I was a kid; the last time, at thirteen, I was play-wrestling with my friend Steve, who accidentally connected full force with an elbow-drop on my face. After the elbow connected, I sat up and cursed, more at the pain than at Steve. I felt the warm blood pouring down my lips and chin, and in a matter of seconds, my white T-shirt was covered in red. My nose still tips to the left, starting just below the bridge.

My last few years of high school, my interest in wrestling was superseded by sex, drugs, and rock and roll—or at least two of the three. Freshman year at Macalester, there was a television in the common area of the dormitory, and Sunday mornings at eleven, a bunch of us would gather around, hung over, and watch *All-Star Wrestling*. I instantly jumped back into fan mode, learning the new characters and following their story lines.

I watched Jesse "The Body" Ventura every week on television. Jesse was a charismatic figure who emulated 1970s wrestler Superstar Billy Graham. I got to be friends with him in 1982 when I helped book and run Goofy's Upper Deck. Jesse used to come to Goofy's and hang out a little bit. He had that wild look, with asymmetrical sunglasses, feathered boa, and ears pierced with large feathers. He appreciated the punk rock mentality, so there was a natural kinship. We gave Jesse a *Metal Circus*

T-shirt, which he wore on an episode of *WWF* on the USA Network. It was their highest-rated show to date, and the fact that he wore a Hüsker Dü T-shirt throughout the two-hour episode was hilarious, touching, and a real thrill.

This was also when I got to know Jim Melby. Jim was the guy who later managed Hüsker Dü's 1986 Wig Out East tour. Jim was one of the nicest guys in the world, and he always had time to help out a friend no matter what else was going on. He also happened to be one of the foremost historians of the wrestling business and wrote articles for the American Wrestling Association's monthly programs. He was a big music fan, I was a big wrestling fan, and we became good friends. Jim and I would talk about wrestling history, and from those conversations, he could tell I was a serious student of the business—but that I didn't know how they created the choreographed illusion of the physicality. Jim took me under his wing and taught me all about it.

Jim gradually "smartened me up," as they call it in the business. When you smarten up a "mark," or layman, you show him how it all works. Much of the wrestling business is an extension of carnival culture—basically, working the marks (that is, deceiving and manipulating the unknowing audience). Even the dialect, which is a type of pig latin language that, in later years, became mainstreamed through constant use in rap music, comes from the carny world. Jim taught me how to sp*iz*eak a little c*iz*arny, explained most of the insider terms, and started letting me see inside the business. He showed me a little bit of the dressing room, introduced me to a couple of the boys, and generally explained how things work behind the curtain.

In late 1985 Jim brought me along to a small show in northern Minnesota. Jim was the ring announcer and I was the timekeeper. After the show Jim and I went out to dinner with a bunch of the boys and were joined by one of the main promoters in the area, Wally Karbo. All the wrestlers who fought earlier in the evening were sitting together at this big banquet table, and Wally is buying us dinner. He's telling all these war stories about hookers and drinking, guns, stealing money, all this crazy shit. Old-time wrestling made rock and roll look like church. This was way cooler than I ever imagined. On the drive home, Jim said, "You have got to keep this to yourself. I'm letting you see this, but you have to protect the business."

In early 1986 when Jim tour-managed Hüsker Dü, I was writing articles for a fanzine based in Dayton, Ohio, called *Hardcore Wrestling,* which covered both punk rock and pro wrestling. It was thick, a hundred-plus pages. We'd write about wrestling and we'd write about punk rock and just throw it all together. Anyone who followed the band knew I was into pro wrestling. I mentioned it in interviews, and often wore wrestling-related T-shirts in press photos.

On that tour Jim invited a longtime friend of his, Gary Juster, to attend our show at the 9:30 Club in DC. Gary was the Northeast promoter for the National Wrestling Alliance. He and I spent a good amount of the evening talking about wrestling, and we then stayed in touch. After I moved to Hoboken in 1989, Kevin and I would drive down to the wrestling shows in Philadelphia and Baltimore and spend time with Gary and his wife, Beverly. Gary had become the arena booker for World Championship Wrestling, an international brand commonly known as WCW, for most of North America. We talked about things our work had in common, like routing tours, booking buildings, and promoting through media outlets. Gary quickly figured out that I was "smart to the business" and started introducing me to some of the creative people at WCW.

One in particular: a gentleman named Jim Barnett. Jim was one of the most successful promoters in the wrestling business; he'd been involved in the Dumont Network stuff in the 1950s and, years later, made millions promoting in Australia. He once lived in a Fifth Avenue penthouse filled with millions of dollars' worth of original art—a first-class lifestyle of the rich and famous. I sat with Jim at arena shows in Baltimore and critiqued the action as an educated fan, and he would listen, saying, "Interesting, interesting, OK."

My friendship with Gary grew through the 1990s, and he introduced me to more key people at WCW. They were interested in the ideas I suggested—not a lot, but at least they listened. I was studying the business through newsletters, watching Japanese wrestling videotapes, and gathering information that was not, at that pre-internet time, easy to get. Even as far back as 1986, I'd been attending wrestling conventions in Kansas City and Las Vegas, and I'd met a lot of the old-time hands who wised me up to a lot of the inner workings. I was carrying around a fairly deep history of the business—more than most people who weren't in it, and maybe as much as a lot of people who were.

So I was pretty excited years later, when in the summer of 1999, Gary Juster, J. J. Dillon, an ex-wrestler who was the head of WCW talent coordination, and then CFO Bill Busch told me big changes in management were about to happen and that I should sit tight and watch. Sure enough, on Friday, September 9, the key person in charge was released from his position. J.J. and Gary included me on a conference call and said, "We want you to come in and sit in on the creative team meetings—which is the writing of the shows, creating characters and story lines, deciding who wins and loses, who gets the most TV time and the championships. Gary says you have great ideas, so we want you to come in and help write the shows. We have a pay-per-view in Cincinnati on Sunday night. Can you come in tomorrow?"

"Of course," I said. I was thrilled that I had a shot at what was always a dream job for me.

"Great. We want you to come in, critique the show, and give some ideas on direction."

I flew to the Raleigh-Durham airport and arrived at the Lawrence Joel Coliseum in Winston-Salem. In the bosses' trailer, Bill Busch and I watched the live feed that was going out on pay-per-view. Bill asked me, "What do you think of the product?"

I had some very definite ideas. "You've got to have all these guys that are really good technical workers in the middle of the show to give you extra minutes," I said, "and the main event guys need to go a little bit quicker because they're looking older, compared to these younger guys in the middle. Hulk Hogan shouldn't always be going thirteen minutes—let the young guys do the heavy lifting."

We watched this one match featuring this guy Sid—Sid Vicious was his previous stage name, but by this time they simply called him Sid. He's six eight, 310 pounds, all gassed up, a good ol' boy from Memphis. He looks like a monster and he's working with this younger guy named Chris Benoit. Back when I was up in Calgary in 1981, I used to watch the Dynamite Kid, a skinhead from England who revolutionized the business through his high-flying, hard-hitting, very believable style. Turns out Chris Benoit grew up watching the Dynamite Kid too—idolized and worshipped him, finally met him, and got into the business and patterned himself completely after this guy. They both worked a state-of-the-art style of wrestling that was huge in Japan in the 1980s. And now I'm watching this match with Benoit and this big galoot from Memphis. I said to Bill Busch, "Chris Benoit is not only the best talent you have, but he is the future of this company and he should be your champ. I don't know how we'd get there (in story line), but he's the guy."

The next night was on live TV, watched by five million households, and the backstage scene was a shit-storm. Nobody had written the show. Everyone was just making shit up on the spot. There were story lines that were evident from the previous night's pay-per-view, the main one being that Sting, who had been a baby face (good guy), had just turned heel (villain) on Hulk Hogan and was going to team up with his old partner, Lex Luger, who was already a heel.

Bill Busch and Gary Juster asked me, "What would you do?"

I quickly responded, "Do what you're *supposed* to do. The first segment is a monologue. Send Sting out to the ring as a newly turned heel with his buddy Lex Luger, who everybody already hates. Have Sting say, 'Here we are in Chapel Hill, North Carolina (cheap heat). We're in the Dean Dome (cheap pop). They should rename this place the Dean Dump (heel heat). This place sucks, to hell with you people, stick it up your ass.' Turn the heel heat up. So Sting's out there as the champ saying, 'I fucked your hero Hogan, and fuck you too.'"

Bill and Gary are listening, looking at each other, and nodding affirmatively. I continued my pitch. "Here's the deal. Hogan's music is gonna hit, he's gonna come down, he's gonna stand, he's gonna look at the ring. Sting and Luger are in there with their baseball bats"—because that was their gimmick at the time—"they're gonna be standing there like they're ready to tee off on Hogan if he dares to come in. Hogan's grabbing at the ropes, walking around the ring, trying to get in on that side, that side, the fourth side. He can't get in. Out comes Bret Hart"—who was one of the other big baby faces at the time—"and Bret comes down to the ring to have this standoff, where they're both outside, not necessarily friends, but united in the face of these two heels with ball bats. The heels chicken shit and powder, and this will set up your main event for the night. Over the course of the three hours, you're gonna tease this thing all night while you have all these other matches going on. Simple formula."

Busch and Juster loved this pitch, and Bill said to an assistant, "Go get Hogan, I want him to hear this." And pretty soon in walks Hulk Hogan, the legend, the guy who has complete creative control, who nobody tells what to do. I betrayed no awe or excitement. I was all business. There's no room for fans in that kind of situation. The last thing the boys want is a mark in the dressing room—that's the best way to get yourself taken out of the equation. Hogan immediately seemed a bit dubious about me. I introduced myself, and in a surprisingly mild and cordial tone, Hogan rumbled, "I hear you got something for me."

"Bill asked me to come up with something, so here's what I

have…" I laid out an eleven-minute opening segment, including how to carry it through to the end of the show. Somewhere within those three hours, the heels would have jumped Hogan in the dressing room, blowing his leg out, then Bret Hart would be sent down by himself for the match. Two heels against one baby face—kill, kill, kill. All of a sudden, two minutes left in the show, coming down the entrance ramp, hobbling on braces is Hogan, with a baseball bat of his own, like the Spirit of '76, the White Knight, stronger than Ajax. He clears the ring, stands over the fallen Bret Hart; crowd cheers, end of show.

It was simple stuff—Pro Wrestling 101. I'd seen it my whole life. The thing was, Hogan and Bret Hart did not get along in real life, and I didn't know the extent of it until I tried to sell this scenario to Hogan. He pretended to listen, nodding, "Uh-huh, yeah, not bad, I'll think about it." Of course, he wasn't really going to think about it. They didn't end up doing anything near that scenario. Still, afterward, I was like, Wow, did that just happen?

I was hired right away and given the title of creative consultant. I made less in one week at WCW than I would have made playing one solo show at the time, but it wasn't about the money. My actual day-to-day duties were undefined until the first writing meeting in Atlanta a few days later. While in the "war room," as the inner sanctum for scripting was called, my aptitude for numbers and time, attention to small details like proper spelling and capitalization, and limited yet accurate understanding of the business put me on a fast track with the booking committee—the small consortium of script writers and ex-wrestlers who decided the fates of all the current wrestlers.

There were two members of the creative team who took an instant liking to me. One was Kevin Nash, who was basically the locker room leader at the time. Kev had been a college basketball star, stood about six ten with long, flowing black hair, and was a very charismatic and charming individual. He quickly picked up on my aptitude for the business, and we immediately started hanging out socially, eating sushi and talking about wrestling.

The second was a wrestler I'd met years before, after a show in Philadelphia one summer evening in 1991. Kevin Sullivan was an Irish guy from Boston. A short, stocky bodybuilder who moved to Florida in the 1970s, Sullivan did a devil gimmick, pretending to be possessed by some otherworldly spirit. He never said "Satan" or "devil," but he had the entire state of Florida thinking it and the territory did unbelievable business. He was married to a stunningly beautiful Italian gal from Jersey named Nancy, who he brought into the business.

Nash, Sullivan, and I got along well, and we began traveling the towns together. Those road trips are a book in themselves. I would be on the road for ten days, then back home in New York for a weekend. Kevin was thrilled for me, he knew this was my dream job. And from the moment I arrived in Winston-Salem, I stopped thinking about music—completely. I could sense this job was going to take all of my attention. It felt very similar to rock touring, in that I was completely consumed by the business at hand. Breathe it, eat it, sleep it. Even after a twelve-hour day of writing at the office, it didn't stop. On the ride to dinner, we talked wrestling. Over meals, we talked about characters, story lines, and angles from thirty years ago. Whether partying or winding down at the hotel, I heard nothing but stories about the business. All wrestling, all the time.

My typical weekly schedule was: A limo picks me up at the loft at 6 PM Sunday evening and goes to Newark Airport for a 7 PM flight to Atlanta, arriving around 9 PM. Then I head to the Hyatt in Marietta, where I meet up with my bosses, and we go out for sushi or get room service. A limo picks us up the next morning at 7 AM and brings us to the Charlie Brown regional airport just outside Atlanta, where we board a Learjet and fly to wherever the show is.

We have to be at the building by noon to read the script for about one hundred production people. That usually takes about two hours. From 2 PM until 8 PM, I'm working with the agents and production team to time out all the segments. In a three-hour show, we usually had about 180 elements across sixteen segments (with fifteen commercial breaks). The typical show opens with pyro and ballyhoo (twenty seconds), throw it to the announcers at ringside (twenty seconds), quick graphics for the main event (ten seconds), quick second set of graphics (ten seconds), then to the arena for a live interview to establish the main story of the night (eight minutes), then a product placement ad (thirty seconds), and finally to a three-minute commercial slot. That's the first segment, which contains at least six elements and lasts nine minutes and thirty seconds.

We have to lay all this out in the six hours between the reading and going live on national TV. A handful of agents (usually ex-wrestlers) work with the wrestlers, helping them figure out how to cooperate with each other to tell these stories. I'd run around with a small laptop, helping to organize how long each match is going to be from start to finish, dealing with wrestlers, agents, and production people to get this thing ready for live TV. Production would print up the final twenty-plus-page format sheets at 7:30 PM to hand out to the hundred people so that everybody would know what they're supposed to do and when. Wrestlers are waiting around, flexing, pumping up, rubbing oil on themselves, primping in mirrors, rehearsing their lines, working out spots with their opponents.

I was at the "go position," also known as the "gorilla position," the area right behind the curtain. It's the last stop before the talent goes live to the arena and television audiences, and it's also where the literal and figurative pyrotechnics go off—the fireworks detonated on just the other side of the curtain, no more than twelve feet away. (My computer bag, which I took to go position, regularly set off explosives detectors at airports. I always had to explain what I did for work.) I sat there with the agents, watching two TV monitors, the bosses yelling at me while I'm trying to tell the production truck what's going on. The boys are coming out with their scripts going, "Bob, what's my cue, what's my cue?" and I'm like, "Kev, your cue is when Sid says 'the ruler of the world' we hit your music and you're out the curtain."

Say we have a match, Disco Inferno versus La Parka. Disco and La Parka each need forty-five seconds for their respective ring intros, then you have thirty seconds of a video recap package to tell the backstory (the incident that caused the match to be made), then there's three minutes of match, so it's roughly five minutes total.

I'm on a microphone right behind the curtain, watching the time code on a screen. Disco and La Parka improvise for two and a half minutes, then I tell the referee, who's wearing a translucent wireless earpiece, to tell them to "go home"—end the match as planned in those clearly scripted final thirty seconds, which is called "the finish." The ref pretends to get distracted, Disco does something like a low blow, La Parka falls into the corner, Disco charges at him, La Parka ducks down, grabs him from behind, rolls him up, and the ref turns around and counts one, two, three. Match over—in three minutes flat.

The show has to stay on schedule—any variance over thirty seconds and I have to start making adjustments on the fly, looking for ways to shave or add time without making noticeable alterations to everything that's been so carefully mapped out. Our best-laid plans often went astray, though, and I spent the better part of those three hours juggling time code and scripting in real time with my production truck counterpart.

I did this for three hours on live television every Monday night. We'd wrap up the show a few minutes after 11 PM, immediately review the show with the bosses for about twenty minutes, and head back to the hotel. If we were lucky, the hotel would have both a bar and a restaurant, and we'd stay up until 3 AM, still buzzing on adrenaline from the live show. We'd get up the next morning at 6 AM, head to the airport, and get on another plane—sometimes the Learjet, sometimes the Atlanta Hawks' commercial jet, sometimes Delta commercial—but we'd fly to another town and do another unique episode, as live-to-tape as possible, for the two-hour Thursday night TBS show.

Early Wednesday morning, with Thursday's show in the can, the creative team would fly to Atlanta and spend twelve hours writing all the story lines for the next week's shows. That night, I'd get to breathe a little bit. We'd go for dinner, some of the guys would drink wine and smoke pot, but the conversation remained pro wrestling. All wrestling, all the time. On top of all the traveling—and little to no sleep—we'd go to the gym every day. Thursday morning, I'd wake up in Atlanta, Sullivan would kick my ass in the gym, then we'd go to the office for a full day and do contract review and medical clearances, recommend hirings and firings, all that stuff. I'd finish by five that evening, head to the airport, and fly back to Newark.

I was home from Thursday night through Sunday night, but I would be dead tired. I'd never had a schedule like this in my life. There was pressure, a heavy workload, and constant travel—I was flying five times a week. In addition, we had a monthly pay-per-view, which added a Sunday night of work every four weeks.

This was also the first time I'd ever had real bosses. But I have nothing other than the utmost respect for the guys in the business, especially two as decorated and successful as Sullivan and J.J. I admired their ideas and their nose-to-the-grindstone work ethic, and it was a pleasure to sit and listen, waiting my turn, until I was asked for my perspective. I enjoyed running at this relentless pace.

I was there for four weeks before I started doing steroids. I was tired from traveling five days a week on no sleep, I was working and thinking so hard every day, and my brain felt as if it were about to explode. I remember riding in the car one day in Florida with my traveling crew and someone saying, "Bobby, you gotta get on the gas."

I was like, "Really?"

"Here, take one of these, it's all right, and tell me how you feel in an hour."

It was a fifty milligram dose of Anadrol, a powerful oral steroid in the form of a small white pill. Anadrol is really hard on the liver, hard on your kidneys, but very effective for muscle and weight gain.

I took that pill, and within a few hours, I was ready to fuck a Coke machine. I thought, all right, this works for me. I went from the quiet, reserved, deferential guy to running right alongside the boys. I was better equipped for the job, the boys approved of my new attitude, and I continued using Anadrol, then Dianabol, for the duration of my time at WCW. I did steroids because I was exhausted and I needed to keep up. This was like war.

Relative to some people around me, I was taking a very light dose, but I felt I had to take them. I had to keep up. We'd get up in the morning and I'd have eight egg whites with salmon, then off to the gym, and then we'd have these sixteen-hour days. The amount of food I consumed was absurd. Whether at lunch in the arena catering halls or at the sushi restaurants, I would eat more food than the boys. It was a running joke: "Bobby, where in the fuck are you putting all that food?" I wasn't putting on much weight, but now I could maintain a much higher intensity level. I might not have been gigantic, but I felt all of my six two around these guys who were typically 220 to 280 pounds. I was getting bigger than I used to be, both physically and mentally; I had more strength and endurance—the steroids helped to build my confidence.

They affected my demeanor too, but not so much as to change my basic personality. I didn't bring any kind of crazy behavior home with me, but by late Thursday night, I was exhausted and Kevin didn't want to hear any more about wrestling. He enjoyed watching but had no interest in hearing me talk about work. For the weekends, Kevin and I tried to have a semblance of a normal life, but most of the time I was either on my ass, completely exhausted, or on the phone talking business.

It was the kind of business where you needed to know

everything that was happening. I was constantly on call. Sullivan would phone me and ask, "So-and-so is hurt, what do you think we should do, where can we go with this story?" You had to keep up, because at any given time, over in a corner of the dressing room, the catering area, or the hotel lobby after the show, some new cabal is forming to stage an uprising that could cost anyone their spot. All wrestling, all the time.

* * *

As head of creative at WCW, Sullivan hired Chris Benoit, who he respected as a performer, and in 1996, Sullivan concocted a story line where Benoit was having an affair with his wife, Nancy, who was now a character called Woman.

There's a term used in the business: "He worked himself into a shoot." Loosely, it means that the story that is written eventually becomes a real-life situation. In an attempt to make the story line seem authentic, Sullivan told Chris and Nancy to get so steamy that even the locker room believed it. All the boys would gossip, "I think Chris is really with Nancy." Write it and it shall be so.

Sullivan—at this time an active wrestler as well as head of creative—was still cooperating with Chris on the job, even now knowing that they all had worked themselves into a shoot. Sullivan and Benoit are having these amazingly stiff, brutal matches. The last match was billed as "loser retires," and Benoit actually broke vertebrae in Kevin's neck. A couple years later, Sullivan was the boss at WCW; Benoit was still there too, and not only was he now married to Nancy in real life, but they were also getting ready to have a child.

Stupid injuries were getting more frequent in pro wrestling. Bret Hart, who was the champ in December 1999, had a match with our top box office draw, Bill Goldberg, that headlined the biggest annual pay-per-view show. Goldberg accidentally kicked Bret in the head and gave him a concussion (that years later may have contributed to a stroke). The next night on television,

Goldberg was supposed to put his fist through the window of a limo; he had gimmicked his glove with a spark plug bit so that it would break the window. But the window wouldn't break, so Goldberg smashed it with his fist, tearing an enormous gash down his entire forearm. He almost bled to death on live TV on top of this white limo, and then spent the evening in an emergency room receiving nearly two hundred stitches. Goldberg, WCW's golden goose, would be out of commission for months.

The following week, head writer Vince Russo arranged a stunt that called for Bret Hart to speed around the large backstage area of the Houston Astrodome in a rental car. Because it was a cool moist night, the already smooth cement flooring had become very slick, almost like black ice. Given Bret's impaired condition, this stunt should have never been allowed to take place.

Earlier that month, in front of all the writers and bosses, I had voiced my concerns about the relative safety of the work environment. Nobody heeded my words and now, in the course of eight days, two medium-risk stunts had gone wrong. I was pissed. After the skidding car stunt, which closed the show, I packed my notes in my work bag, walked up to Bill Busch and J. J. Dillon and said, "I tried to tell you someone would get hurt. I'm going home. I don't want to be around here when something worse happens. Thank you both for the opportunity, but I can't work here any longer."

I went home, still under my week-to-week contract. The following Monday night, minutes before airtime, Gary Juster faxed me the format sheets, and I couldn't believe how crazy the shows were getting. They were even planning to set the ringside area on fire at one of the upcoming TV events. Within the next few weeks, the out-of-retirement Jimmy Snuka dived off a twelve-foot ladder, aggravating Jeff Jarrett's underlying mild concussion. Now WCW had lost their top three guys, including the world champ and the secondary champ.

Soon after, Vince Russo, whose risky stunts were the main

reason I left the job, went home. Soon I got the call saying I could come back to work if I wanted. I showed up in Cincinnati the night before a pay-per-view and quickly realized we were in a sticky situation. Because so many key people had been injured, everything that had been laid out for this, as well as for subsequent story lines, had to be rewritten on the spot.

Twelve of us gathered in the conference room of a suburban Cincinnati hotel and rewrote the scripts. The main concern was how to address the world title, the holy grail of any wrestling promotion, and determine who would walk out of the building that evening as champion. The consensus was to give the title to Chris Benoit. And this was decided with Sullivan present, despite all the real-life heat and animosity between him and Benoit. Sullivan was the head booker, and he agreed that we needed to put the belt on Chris. Finally, this was what every hardcore wrestling fan had been waiting for—for years. It was also the first thing I'd suggested upon arriving at WCW in September of 1999, and now it was about to happen.

But even with this decision, Benoit and some of the younger wrestlers felt the old-timers were holding them down, Sullivan as booker in particular. Many of the company's best technical wrestlers were in that younger faction, and I had been one of their biggest proponents. I was in an awful spot, torn between my belief in those guys and the loyalty I had for my boss, Sullivan.

The championship match took place the following night on a pay-per-view broadcast in Cincinnati. To give the match extra meaning, I suggested to Sullivan that we send the rest of the wrestlers, faces and heels together, out onto the ramp during the match. Then when we award Benoit the belt, they'd all give him a standing ovation. Normally you don't break the illusion by putting faces and heels together, but I said, let's do it so people know this is important. Sullivan agreed.

Sid and Chris did a decent-looking fifteen-minute match, which Chris was booked to win with his finishing move, the

Crippler Crossface, a move where the opponent is facedown on the mat and Benoit gets on his opponent's back and does a choke plus an arm bar. Benoit won the match as planned, strapped on the world title belt, and the postmatch celebration worked like a charm. The crowd loved it.

Chris came back through the curtain with the belt, which meant he was now the face of the company. We'd decided he was the guy. Kevin walked up to Chris, shook his hand, and congratulated him. I was second in line to say, "Congratulations, Chris, you deserve this." We shook hands, and he said thank you.

The next day Benoit showed up at the live TV event with eight of his fellow wrestlers. They went to Bill Busch and threatened to quit unless Sullivan was fired—"Either he goes or we go." It was mutiny. We were trying to do the right thing, and Benoit and his faction didn't believe it was for real.

Bill Busch sent them home. "If they don't want to be here," he said, "I don't want them here." Benoit left the belt with the head of the prop department, and away he and his friends went. We were left to rewrite the entire show just hours before airtime, including having to come up with a way to explain the world title situation.

Sullivan, in his infinite wisdom, had quietly planned for such mutiny. When he laid out the finish, he had told Sid, "Sid, you gotta do the job, you gotta do business for me, but I want you to do one thing. When he puts you in his finishing hold and you tap out and he wins, I want you to have your foot under the bottom rope." By doing so, Sullivan had created a safeguard: if a wrestler's foot is touching (or under) the ropes, the referee is supposed to break up the action. The submission, therefore, would have been null and void. At the time, Sullivan and Sid didn't tell anybody. We went back that day and looked at all the camera angles and found the one where Sid's foot was under the rope. Now we could show that footage to the audience and declare that Benoit didn't actually win the title. Sullivan had clearly suspected he was about to be set up by Benoit and his compadres, so he made sure to protect the title.

Not only were the fans disappointed by this turn in the story line, but I was disappointed in real life. I was so upset that I couldn't sleep for three days, and I wasn't able to rest until J. J. Dillon and Kevin Sullivan sat me down and flatly stated it was business, and things would be OK.

There were even bigger problems though. The WCW show had been the flagship program for TBS since the 1970s, but ratings were sinking. More and more of the writers, producers, and wrestlers were beginning to question the creative direction Sullivan had charted for WCW, which took the long view that things would probably get worse before they got better. But television executives are not wired to look at programming in the long term—shows live and die by ratings. We were doing everything we could, but nothing was working. There was so much turmoil, and we couldn't stop the bleeding. Some wrestlers became uncooperative, while others suddenly became "injured" and didn't show up for work. We were shorthanded in the in-ring talent department, and the dwindling roster didn't help our now suffering story lines.

At the end of March 2000, upper management replaced our creative team with a mishmash of previous writers and offered to reposition us in the company. I soon tendered my resignation. I was sad to leave my dream job and all the incredible people I had worked so closely with for seven months, but if I had stayed, I would have been exiled to corporate Siberia. I was luckier than most of my colleagues though—I had another career to fall back on. (Within a year, WCW was liquidated for micropennies on the dollar to the WWE, World Wrestling Entertainment.)

A little postscript: Remember the wrestler murder-suicide in 2007? That was Chris Benoit. He killed his wife, Nancy, and his son, Daniel, over the course of a weekend and hanged himself a day later. He was on incredibly excessive amounts of painkillers and steroids, his wife was on pills too, and even their seven-year-old son was found with traces of prescription drugs in his system.

Benoit's childhood idol, the Dynamite Kid, used to do this move where he'd stand up on the top rope and just fall forward on the guy—what they call the Diving Headbutt. Benoit took that move and executed it almost every night. After his death, the autopsy revealed he had the brain of an eighty-five-year-old man, filled with protein deposits, much like with full-stage Alzheimer's. The actual medical term is chronic traumatic encephalopathy. The layman's term is punch-drunk.

Pro wrestling is serious business. There's nothing fake about it at all.

CHAPTER 23

For a while after leaving WCW, I still watched the shows with a critical eye. But as the weeks went on, I started to lose interest; I knew the secrets, I had been in the eye of the storm, and the mystery was gone. I was settling back into life at home with Kevin, life in the gay neighborhoods of Manhattan and in my neglected and dusty recording studio on Washington Street.

I wasn't on the road, so I was able to get back to the routines I had started in early 1999, the most enjoyable of which was my daily bike ride around lower Manhattan. I'd start on the West Side Highway at Canal Street, head down through the World Trade Center and Battery Park City, and around the southern tip of the island to the Fulton Fish Market. I would happily ride right through the fish slop, getting it all over my bike.

I had to get on FDR Drive for a bit, which was harrowing, then ride up through the East River Park. Every Wednesday morning at ten thirty, the police cadets were out jogging, which was sort of hot. I'd cut through Stuyvesant Town and westward across the island on Twenty-First Street. At Tenth Avenue I'd ride south to Chelsea Market and shop for the day. I'd put everything in the panniers on my bike and ride home. It was nine miles every day—rain or shine, snowstorms, it didn't matter. I had a very intimate relationship with both rivers and downtown

Manhattan. Stopping to take pictures, sitting on the piers—it was all a big part of my day.

As was electronica. It was a soundtrack that played everywhere I spent time: at the gym, at the Factory Café, and in the clubs. At gay restaurants like Cafeteria and Caffe Torino, the songs were "Believe" by Cher, "Beautiful Stranger" by Madonna, and club music from artists like Paul van Dyk. I was taking it all in, finding it so fresh compared to both alternative rock and hip-hop.

Rebel Rebel, a small Greenwich Village record store that specializes in electronic, independent, and dance music, was the glue that held my old and new lives together. In 1998, the first time I shopped the store, I acted low-key, but David, the owner, looked up at me and asked, "You're Bob Mould, right?" He probably figured it out from the name on the credit card.

I spent a lot of time and money at Rebel Rebel, and in return they gave me a good education about electronica and club music. I even won over an employee named Brian, a likable lug from Milwaukee who'd mastered both stereotypical gay bitchiness and record-store-clerk elitism, rolled them up into one, and could lay it on certain customers. They knew the types of music I might find interesting and would play things for me in the store, not dissimilar to my early days as a wide-eyed music fan at Oar Folkjokeopus in Minneapolis. Once my ear tuned in to the differences and my brain starting responding favorably to certain styles, the hit-to-miss ratio of music they played for me went way up.

There was one song in particular that spoke directly to me and was the true beginning of my fascination with electronic music. The song was Sasha's "Xpander," which was released in July 1999. The song structure reminded me of the second half of *Beaster*'s "JC Auto"—not in the cathartic sense, but in its hypnotic effect, the feeling it gave of simultaneously free-falling through space and time while being called out by a higher voice. It resonated with me and created a gateway to similar artists and music.

This style of music was so contrary to what I had spent my previous life listening to, writing, and performing, and I'm sure longtime fans were (and maybe still are) confounded by my love of dance music. It doesn't emphasize aspects of traditional song-writing like sophisticated chord changes, literate lyrics, and extended melodies—in other words, the high bar my fans set for me. I wish I had some high-art explanation for this whole-sale change in attitude, but after turning away from rock music, I was just excited about working with a new set of tools. The bottom line was, in order to have a new life, I had to have new music.

I went out and bought an expensive sampler, updated my recording software, and began teaching myself how to make electronic music. My new writing and recording process was a continuation of two realizations that had surfaced in 1998: that my home demos were as fully formed as my professional studio recordings, and that an untrained approach often yields unpredictable yet interesting results.

In the first eight months of 1999, I had been writing three different styles of music: purely electronic/ambient music, mechanical pop with more samples and less electric guitar, and traditional acoustic singer-songwriter stuff. After decompressing and recovering from the seven months of nonstop chaos that was WCW, I resumed writing and recording music in April 2000, and I had high ambitions. I had the idea of putting out three distinct albums at once. I had the blueprint for *Modulate,* which was to be a hybrid of guitars and electronics. There was the LoudBomb album, *Long Playing Grooves,* which was almost entirely electronic (LoudBomb is an anagram of Bob Mould). The third album was to be a collection of quiet rock songs called *Body of Song.*

In the summer of 2000, Stephen Trask asked if I would play lead guitar for the soundtrack of the film version of *Hedwig and the Angry Inch.* I'd known Stephen since 1997, originally through his band Cheater. The band began collaborating with actor/

writer John Cameron Mitchell, and the marriage of John's transsexual-themed monologues and Stephen's words and music gave birth to *Hedwig and the Angry Inch,* an amazing and touching musical about a fictional rock band led by a transgender East German singer named Hedwig. The original stage show opened to great acclaim in early 1998; over the course of two years, I spent a fair number of Tuesday nights riding my bike up the river to the Jane Street Theatre to see the show, then going to dinner at Florent with Stephen, John, and various members of the cast and crew.

When the show was adapted for the big screen, I was honored to be included in the recording of the film soundtrack. I spent a week at Bearsville Studios in Woodstock, learning and recording my parts. Under Stephen's direction, I rose to the occasion. Not only was it my first time as a "hired gun" studio player, but through the *Hedwig* experience, I gained a new understanding and appreciation of the transgender community. Before, I hadn't really understood why people would want to change their gender. *Hedwig* is a simple allegory about being transgender, and it shines a light on how complicated it is. A lot of times people aren't that comfortable in their own skin. I could relate to that.

I was feeling good, working again, and in the midst of it all I was turning forty. My fortieth birthday party was a highlight of my year. I organized a three-stage party for forty people— cocktails at the loft, dinner at a wonderful little Argentinean restaurant a block away, then on to Barracuda for more cocktails. The three settings and the guests—musical peers, longtime personal friends, gay neighborhood acquaintances—made for a nice snapshot of my life in 2000. I would have kept it that way if I could, but life doesn't always stay in focus.

In late 2000 Kevin and I started having problems with our upstairs neighbors. They made lots of noise early in the morning, and I couldn't sleep or hear myself think. I was starting to lose my mind. We appealed to the co-op board but got no satisfaction. We felt handcuffed, and the acrimony turned into full-scale anger and resentment. Late one night Kevin was walking Domino around the block, and upon returning to the building entrance, he came face to face with the upstairs tenant. The guy was drunk and had left the keys to both the apartment and his Ferrari in the lock of the building door. He wobbled back toward his car, thinking he had dropped his keys on the ground. When he wasn't looking, Kevin took the key ring out of the door, walked inside the building, and calmly dropped them all down the elevator chute. When the upstairs tenants were being especially noisy, I would blast music as loud as possible, going so far as to face the speakers directly into the ceiling. Our behavior was terrible at times, but all of our buttons had been pushed.

Kevin's parent clock was ticking loudly again, and if we were to have a family, we figured Atlanta might be a better place to do it. The cost of living was much cheaper; also, Kevin's siblings and parents lived in and around Atlanta, and their support would be invaluable. We also had two potential surrogate mothers in mind, both of whom lived in the Atlanta area. Deanna Mann was a lifelong friend of Kevin's, a big-boned gal with a sharp wit, a creative streak, and dozens of tattoos. Lisa Pearl was a friend of mine from my WCW days—petite, demure, and artistic, she had been one of the in-house photographers. The plan was to artificially inseminate the mother—we'd mix our semen and the strongest sperm would win—and keep the birth mothers involved in raising the child, at least as much as everyone felt comfortable with.

But even as we were making these plans, deep down I wasn't so sure Kevin and I should start a family. First, with my family history, I couldn't see myself being a decent parent. Second, the lifestyle Kevin and I were leading at the time wasn't geared toward the stability I felt a child would need. Third, Kevin's marijuana smoking was a real roadblock for me; I just *wasn't sure* that would work as a parent. I share the blame for not bringing that up—once again, by not voicing my concerns I helped to create an even more difficult situation. I was just hoping that Kevin would realize, without any prompting from me, that we needed to make some major changes, both individually and collectively.

In early 2001 we put the Tribeca loft on the market. In the two years since we bought the loft, property values in Manhattan had increased substantially, so we priced it fairly high, hoping to make a healthy profit. But we couldn't find any serious takers. Instead of lowering the price, we took the property off the market in June, after three months. We tabled moving to Atlanta for the time being.

On May 17 I went back to Bearsville Studios in Woodstock to do additional recording for what was to be the *Modulate* album. I worked for a week in a log cabin–type outpost with a large, open recording room, a kitchen area, an outdoor grill, and sleeping quarters. Kevin and I brought Domino, and our friend Micheal Brodbeck, who we knew from the Factory Café, came to visit for a few days. I took the recordings home and spent a few more months refining and detailing the mixes on the computer.

It was especially comforting to have Domino along for those sessions. His health was deteriorating, and I'm certain it meant a lot to him to have access to the woods and nature. It meant a lot to me too—he often spent long stretches of his days in my home studio room, either under the recording console or on a couch in a corner of the room, which was familiar and relaxing as I worked long hours by myself at Bearsville.

I was now using Auto-Tuned vocals and programmed beats and loops, and I was building songs from samples—a relatively synthetic sound that was completely different from anything I had done before. I knew the resulting albums (*Modulate* and *Long Playing Grooves*) might throw my core fans for a loop, but I was fascinated by this new approach and wasn't worried about the commercial or financial consequences. This was a whole new ball game. I was following my muse and not the old road map that I'd tossed out the window of the tour bus in late 1998.

And I felt much more comfortable dealing with homosexual themes. This was clear in the first half of *Modulate,* which dealt with very specific parts of my gay being. The main sample in "Sunset Safety Glass" has a colorful backstory. Early one Sunday morning, I was riding my bike through the Meatpacking District and heard the sounds of South American music emanating from a loft window. That sound was the influence for the signature sample. Later I stopped on a street corner near a meat warehouse that smelled of fresh blood. I then noticed the passenger door of a semitruck swing open, and out came a short, muscled-up Italian-American guy, wiping his lips with a paper towel. That was interesting enough, but more fascinating was the fact that he was perfectly dressed—as a Catholic school-girl.

"Lost Zoloft" touches on same-sex spousal abuse, low self-esteem, and the Chelsea clone culture, phenomena I'd observed many times in my community over the past few years. "Semper Fi" is based on my interest in gay military porn, which set dreamlike scenes where the "grunt" has a convenient out: he was drunk, drugged, and unaware of what was happening.

The charms of military men figured into a nice friendship I struck up later that year with Mark Simpson, a British writer who had gained great notoriety from coining the term *metro-sexual.* We'd communicated via e-mail earlier in the year, and when Mark arrived in New York to celebrate the US release of his book *The Queen Is Dead,* we met at Leshko's in the East Village for lunch. Within ten minutes we found some common ground. We shared an attraction to guys in uniform, Marines in particular, so we hit it off well. At the end of his New York City visit, Mark spent the evening at the loft. As he was turning in for the night, I gave him a Dirk Yates military porn video to view in his room. Mark had heard about these videos but had never seen one. Mark remains a friend, often traveling with me around the UK when he's not busy writing exposés on (and, once, participating in) said military porn industry.

* * *

In June of 2001, Grant Hart and Greg Norton were talking about suing SST for unpaid and delinquent royalties. A lawsuit of this size and scope in the state of California would be very expensive—around $50,000—just to file and set in motion. I offered to pay for the lawsuit, but in return Grant and Greg would have to stay uninvolved so that I could sue SST myself without encumbrances, changes, or midstream indecision. I had Josh Grier draw up an offer for a one-time payment of $15,000 each to Grant and Greg. As ever, they would retain co-ownership of the Hüsker Dü name, but would be silent partners in this lawsuit.

I didn't care about the name Hüsker Dü, nor holding sole ownership of the SST catalog. I had, and still have, no interest in the name Hüsker Dü or in recreating or revisiting that part of my life. But while conducting research for this book, I found and reviewed the document, and it most certainly appeared as if I was trying to buy them out. And yet it meant so little to me that I'd forgotten about it until seeing the document. The suit was never filed.

An incident of much greater consequence to me, however, happened on July 4. Late that night I found Kevin on the roof of our building, having an intimate moment with one of our straight, married neighbors. I had already been through one fracture, and as this second episode was happening—or the second one I knew about, anyway—all I could say to Kevin was, "What the fuck are you doing? What are you thinking?" I felt humiliated.

This was the moment I realized Kevin was never going to be

completely faithful to me. He was never going to change his ways, and I'd begun to resign myself to that fact. This episode wasn't as traumatic as the one in Austin in 1994, but it dragged up all my flight instincts—not flight from Kevin, but flight from the scene of the crime. It was embarrassing to stay there, in that building. I mean, what would I say to the other guy when we're in the elevator? How do I face his wife and kids without saying something about it? So we went back to Atlanta in late July and once again began looking for a place to start a family.

You're probably asking yourself: Bob, why are you staying with this guy? A stupid yet simple answer: I loved him and I didn't know any better.

* * *

Domino was an intense dog. His passions were chasing tennis balls, which he could do for hours, and tug of war, which he never lost at. He was so strong we used to let him latch his jaws onto a broomstick or large branch, and we could grab the broomstick at the far ends, and spin him around so fast that he would levitate, flying like Superman.

In his last summer, I would bring Domino to the living room, lie with him on the carpet, and play tug of war with a soft rubber pull toy. He could barely hold himself steady, but the densely woven carpet offered him the most traction possible. I never let that dog lose a game of tug of war.

Domino's final days were hard to watch. For years he'd suffered from autoimmune disorders and was on several medications. His quality of life had deteriorated to where he could hardly walk, but never once did that dog give up on staying as absolutely active as he was in his prime. Kevin fed him pills, managed his health records, scheduled the veterinary trips, and took the best care of him. Without question, Kevin was Domino's main "parent."

Incontinence set in, and Domino had no choice but to urinate on the wood floors, which were ten-inch-wide slats of barn siding. The urine would seep between the boards, down to the sound batting underneath, and began to foul the apartment. It didn't matter. I tried to train him to urinate in the walk-in shower, but he only managed it one time.

In late August we made the difficult decision to have Domino put to sleep. He still had his incredible focus, but we could see in his eyes that he was failing and that his quality of life was fading to zero. We planned his exit with the vet and tried our best to make Domino's last few days as comfortable as possible.

We put down Domino on September 1, 2001. When his final morning arrived, we cooked a meal of steak and eggs and served it on three dinner plates on the floor. He never wanted to sleep in the bed with us, but for us to get on the floor with him and eat together from the human plates, that was as good as it could get for him. We drove to the veterinary office on the Lower East Side and started the process.

The first shot was a placebo shot of water and sugar, mostly for us humans to process what was about to happen. With tennis ball locked firmly in mouth, Domino lay still on the cool floor, trusting his owners and the vet who had done wonders in extending his life. The first real shot didn't finish him fully so the vet gave him a second shot, and within a few seconds, Domino's eyes went blank. He was gone.

The vet wanted his body up on the steel examination table, so Kevin and I reached underneath him and lifted. Domino weighed fifty-five pounds; when we used to lift him, he had a way of making his body much heavier, as if gravity were holding him close to the ground. Now he was as light as a feather, so much so that we almost tossed him in the air. His spirit had left his body, and he was on to the next destination.

We asked that Domino be cremated and that his remains be mailed to us. Micheal Brodbeck met us at the vet and drove us home. Instead of cutting directly across Soho, Micheal took the long route: from the Lower East Side, down around the tip of Manhattan, up the West Side Highway, past the World Trade Center, to Canal Street.

A few days later, Kevin and I went to Atlanta to visit his family, our friends, and my remaining acquaintances from the WCW days, as well as to go house hunting. We stayed with Andy Mitchell, a mutual friend from the Athens music scene, and his then wife, Anne Hubbell. Kevin and I found a four-bedroom Craftsman-style house near Piedmont Park that was similar to our previous home in Austin. It seemed like we would finally find some peace and quiet after two years enduring the upstairs racket in Manhattan. We made a successful offer on the house on a Monday afternoon; we were set to sign a contract the following morning.

Tuesday morning, Kevin and I were sleeping in the guest room. From years of ringing in my ears after performing, I'd grown accustomed to sleeping with the television on, to provide background noise. Andy had already left for his job at CNN, so only the two of us and Anne were at the house. Anne came running into the room, yelling, "Turn the TV to CNN!" That's when we saw the first tower on fire.

We were transfixed, trying to figure out what was happening. The answer came minutes later when we saw the second plane rip through the center of the other tower. It was clear that not only was this no accident, but that New York City was under attack.

There we were, lying in bed in Atlanta, planning to sign a contract on a house. The thing was, our loft was only about ten blocks from the World Trade Center. We called up the realtor and said we couldn't sign a contract because we didn't know if our home in New York was still standing. The deal was off.

We had to get home but all flights were frozen. We had a rental car, so I called up the agency's main office, explained the situation, and they allowed us to drive the car to New York City with no extra charge.

Kevin, Deanna Mann, and I drove from Georgia to New York. Saturday at sunrise, on the New Jersey Turnpike, we crested the hill where the skyline appears, and we spotted the pillar of smoke on the horizon. The Holland Tunnel was closed so we proceeded to the Lincoln Tunnel and drove down the West Side Highway, which was lined with semi containers, barricaded, and set up for triage.

The loft was inside the restricted area sealed off by police barricades and surrounded by news cameras. We parked a few blocks away, dragged our luggage up to the barricade, and showed our IDs in order to gain entry to our neighborhood. Once we were back in the loft, I went to the roof and filmed the sky for a few minutes. Then I got on my bike, rode down to the site, took one look at the destruction, turned around, and rode home. I never went back down there.

We decided not to leave New York. I'd gotten caught up in the patriotism of the moment. I thought, No way we can leave now, that would be a show of weakness. How dare they do this to our neighborhood?

In October I played a solo show at Brownie's to benefit a firehouse in Greenwich Village that had lost some men. I went out socializing with some of the firemen after the show, and they told me about a maneuver called "turning the pile." At the World Trade Center site, reclaim crews worked around the clock in twelve-hour shifts, from eleven to eleven. Fifteen minutes before the shift was over, the crews would sink their machines deep into the rubble and turn the pile, which released all the toxic dust, fumes, and remains for the incoming crew to deal with. After hearing that, every morning and evening at around ten thirty, we ran around the loft, closing all the windows.

Day after day, for months, we'd look out the window and see a parade of large flatbed trucks, hauling debris and twisted steel up the West Side Highway toward the tunnel and eventually to salvage yards and landfills.

The loft was covered with a layer of pale grey powder. To

this day, when I open boxes that were stored in the Manhattan loft, they let off a distinctive smell—of what can only be a mix of gypsum board, jet fuel, and charred remains.

* * *

After months of enduring both the aftereffects of 9/11 and the continual noise from the neighbors above, we once again put the loft on the market. This time we were going to sell, no matter what—although I knew it wouldn't undo everything that had happened to us, between us, and around us. A change of scenery, perhaps, but if we moved together, it would likely be more of the same. Two moves, from Austin to Midtown Manhattan to Tribeca, and the only change that was certain was the address on the utility bills.

It's the end of 2001, and I have two records finished, the hybrid guitar/electronic *Modulate* and the strictly electronic LoudBomb album, *Long Playing Grooves. Body of Song* went to the back burner. I envisioned that record as a continuation of *Workbook,* a sparser acoustic affair, but over the course of the three years, I didn't write as many songs in that direction as I had hoped. I was wrapped up in the electronica.

I booked a long weekend at Hit Factory in Midtown and sat in the control room by myself for three days, giving *Modulate* the final once-over. The night I finished sequencing the album, I was completely burned out.

One of the interested labels was V2 Records. Kate Hyman was the main A&R person and had worked with Moby, who was still flying high with 1999's *Play.* Kate was very interested, but the business folks at V2 didn't want to do a three-record deal in which all the records come out at once and the potential deal fell apart. It may not have been the wisest business move, but I'd vowed publicly that I was going to release the three albums simultaneously, so that's what I was going to do. I continued searching for a suitable arrangement.

Body of Song wasn't fully realized by then, so I decided to release *Modulate,* the LoudBomb record, and *LiveDog98,* a live album from the 1998 London Forum show, the one show that Michael Cerveris really ripped on. Releasing the live disc would fulfill my stated intent of releasing three albums at once.

After consulting with Josh Grier, I decided to do simultaneous North American and European licensing deals for *Modulate,* similar to the deals with Ryko and Creation in 1992. In the US, *Modulate* (as well as *Long Playing Grooves*) would be released by my own label, Granary Music. The albums would be manufactured by United Musicians, an artist collective run by Aimee Mann and Michael Hausman, and distributed by Sony-owned Red Ink. In Europe, London-based independent label Cooking Vinyl signed on for three albums, the first two being *Modulate* and *Long Playing Grooves.* Neither label was involved with the *LiveDog98* album, which I would sell at upcoming shows.

I put together the packaging for *Modulate* and *Long Playing Grooves* using years of photographs I'd taken in various lower Manhattan locations. The *Modulate* gatefold package features one of the best portraits ever taken of me. Lisa Pearl's photograph captured what I think is my strongest feature—my piercing blue eyes.

Three months before the release of *Modulate,* I came up with the idea of supporting it with a multimedia presentation called Carnival of Light and Sound, which I referred to as COLAS. I would be flanked by two large screens, and would perform by myself in the null space between them, using minimal stage lighting.

I had three months to come up with two hours of video content, as well as recording backing tracks for all but two of the songs. I was playing Sugar and Hüsker Dü songs as well, and I recorded new backing tracks that sounded consistent with the electronica-based *Modulate* material. I was on a self-imposed deadline, and there wasn't a lot of time for me to consider the artistic ramifications of creating blippy backing tracks to songs that so many people seemed to hold sacred. This was all part of the new deal. I worked on those tracks in my studio day and night. When I got burned out on backing tracks, Kevin and I would head out and shoot more video footage. I also reached out to friends, independent filmmakers, and video artists for more content. There wasn't a moment to spare, so I reverted to my DIY ways and taught myself how to make videos on an editing suite we set up in the den.

Unknowingly, I had created a beast of a project for myself. Maybe I was in over my head. Quality control was sneaking out the window. Why did I do this to myself? What was I trying to escape from?

A week before leaving for tour preproduction, we found a buyer for the loft. I hired an attorney to oversee the remainder of the paperwork and finances. We packed the house in a hurry, called a moving company, and had them collect and store our possessions for the foreseeable future.

Then Kevin and I went to Atlanta for two weeks of rehearsal. We stayed in a two-bedroom corporate apartment for the month, trying to keep some semblance of normalcy about our lives. After breakfast we headed to the gym. The Atlanta gym was one step away from a bathhouse, evidenced by both the open displays of arousal in the group shower and by the fellow who casually brought his translucent butt plug into the steam room. It was thoughtful of them to arrange for the hepatitis vaccination truck to come to the gym once a month.

Every day at noon, Daft Punk's "Harder, Better, Faster, Stronger" would sound out across the workout floor. It made me feel like Bill Murray in *Groundhog Day*, when his alarm clock would play "I Got You Babe" every morning at 6 AM. We'd usually follow our workouts with lunch at the gay steak house and a trip to the gay bookstore/coffee shop Outwrite.

The critical response to *Modulate* was mixed when it came out. British magazines like *Q* and *Mojo* were quite generous in their praise, calling it "unfashionable and intensely melodic" and "some of his most effective pop." Other publications such as *Alternative Press* and *Billboard* were much harder on *Modulate,* labeling it "a largely frustrating set of Saturday morning cartoon electronics" and "an unsuccessful attempt at diving into a genre that relies less on the organic than it does on the synthetic." I sensed it was going to be a tough campaign. Little did I know how tough.

We were trying to get "SoundOnSound," a jangly, catchy midtempo song that most closely resembled my previous work, played on the radio, so we hired independent radio promoters, which in plain English translates to payola intermediaries. Tens of thousands of dollars went out the window in a mostly fruitless attempt to gain traction on commercial radio.

In 1998 I had worked with Carla Sacks, a New York–based publicist, on the campaign for *The Last Dog and Pony Show*. I liked Carla, and her staff seemed fine as well, so I hired them to do press (and publicity) for *Modulate*. A few months after the record was out, one of Carla's assistants was at a business dinner and made some unflattering comments about the record. Josh Grier happened to be within earshot and let me know about it weeks later. What a great campaign this was turning out to be.

There were problems with Red Ink as well. They insisted on manufacturing 55,000 copies of Modulate even though I'd suggested we start with 20,000. I knew this record wasn't going to sell 55,000 copies—my previous album had barely cracked 60,000 and this was a less accessible record. There were some good people at Red Ink, Alan Becker in particular, but they had unreasonable expectations for a difficult piece of music. I tried to set more realistic goals, but the machine won out.

Technically, the show ran smoothly thanks to sound and video engineer Colm O'Reilly. But after seven or eight shows performing by myself, with nothing else onstage but the two large screens, I could sense that the presentation was wrong. I would look into the crowd each night and see the faces of indifference and confusion. I couldn't feel too frustrated with them though—for so many years they'd seen me in a certain light and now they were hearing some of their favorite songs performed in this strange new way. I could understand their shock. Actually, I think it was a shock to everyone involved (maybe even myself). I think the audience gave it as fair a shake as they could, but I knew something wasn't clicking.

In hindsight, the biggest mistake I made was not getting somebody to help me make *Modulate* sound like a real electronic record. The genre had become highly sophisticated, and my primitive approach didn't hold up well next to the competition. I knocked myself down on this one. I could tell within weeks of the release that I was going to have a hard time getting up from it. I tried my best to explain to people what I was trying to do, but the more I explained, the more complicated it all sounded and the less people heard what I was saying. It's funny, in a way. Everyone loves *Zen Arcade,* and I barely have an explanation for what precipitated the writing and creating of the record. But with *Modulate,* which most people view as a failure, I feel obliged to show people all the backstory. Commercially speaking, *Modulate* was not one of my finer moments. But I think my songwriting was both innovative and revealing, and someday I'd like to revisit the tracks with my current skill set.

The other mistake was trying to make three distinctly different records at once when I might have been better off taking the twelve best songs, no matter what style they were, and pooling them to make one good record. I got in way over my head, no one stopped me, and I was adrift in the deep blue sea. Sometimes the end result doesn't fly with the masses. That's life.

We toured for four weeks—four very long weeks. Kevin and I were living on the road, the crowds were indifferent, and morale was falling. We were living out of two large roll-aboard duffel bags, our laptop computer bags, and a rental car. Everything was in chaos. Kevin had a car accident in Chicago, admitting afterward that some attractive man had caught his attention and had caused him to slam into the car in front of him. His quip at the time was "I wrecked the house," referring to the fact that we were basically living out of the car.

The intimate incident with Kevin and the neighbor didn't help, Domino dying certainly didn't help, and 9/11 really didn't help. There was a lot of stuff crumbling. There was a lot of stuff falling. There was a lot of shit happening. A lot was collapsing. Everything felt like it was sinking.

An ugly cell phone conversation with my longtime booking agent Frank Riley on the drive from Toronto to New York was indicative of my state of mind. Frank and I have had productive disagreements over the course of our working relationship, but on this day, for some unknown reason, I chose to dump all my frustrations on him, just blind venting about lukewarm reactions and poor advance sales for the New York show. None of this was Frank's fault, which made this one of the more regrettable phone calls I have ever made. I called him back a couple of days later and apologized. Frank knows how tough the road can be on people, and I was grateful that we were able to get our working relationship back on track.

When I finally finished the first leg of the tour in Charlotte, Kevin and I drove overnight to Atlanta and then flew to Las Vegas for some relaxation. After a few days of gambling and eating, we drove to Palm Springs for two days of gay adventure—opening up our physical relationship with strangers. Kevin was clearly comfortable with it, and I went along with it. The fractures in our relationship were all over the place anyway—how much more damage could this do? We had tried this once in New York in 2001, and it was neither an enjoyable nor upsetting experience for me.

I was making a lot of compromises with Kevin. I was sure I wouldn't make a good parent, but I agreed to have children with him. As far as casual sex, I don't want to imply that Kevin dragged me into it—I'm a man, and men think about it all the time—but it wasn't something I would have explored if Kevin hadn't lobbied for it. So I was doing big things I wasn't totally comfortable with. And it wasn't exactly working. Maybe there's a lesson in that.

I'd had such a great long ride with the critics, and now for the first time in my twenty-three-year career they had turned on my work. It was a new thing for me to deal with, and it didn't feel good. That album wasn't just a collection of songs, it was a reflection of some massive changes I'd made in just about every aspect of my life. And now a lot of people were calling it a failure. Sometimes I can easily dismiss negative criticism by saying "They just don't understand" or "They're not musicians, what do they know?" But when they make valid criticisms, and I recognize and agree, it stings. One major criticism was that *Modulate* sounded very rudimentary and didn't play to my strong suits at all (passionate vocals, unique guitar style). The thing is, there was nothing I could do to change what had happened; I could only move forward and learn from the experience.

We resumed the COLAS touring on the West Coast, finishing up on May 7 in Austin. I was relieved to be done with that tour. I was proud of the work I had created, but after weeks of confused faces in the crowd, it was time to move forward—and in a way, back too. I returned to what I knew could work.

I went straight from Austin to David Barbe's studio in Athens to record a dozen guitar-driven songs with David on bass and Matt Hammon on drums for what would become *Body of Song,* the third album of my trilogy. We simply set up a drum kit, a bass amp, a guitar amp, and a vocal mic and started recording.

I'd written this guitar-based material before the *Modulate* backlash, so it's not like I had some kind of career resurrection strategy in mind. I was just trying to get these songs arranged and recorded. It all felt really familiar and natural. When you get together with two other guys in a wooden room with wood instruments, and you're surrounded by the smell of sweat and burning tubes, it's quite different than when you're at home alone with a computer.

Because we had sold the loft before the tour started and put all of our possessions in storage, we were now essentially homeless. It was time to decide where to live. Along the course of the tour, we had narrowed our options down to three cities: Atlanta, Chicago, and DC. By now the family plans were pretty much out, so Atlanta had no real allure. Chicago is a wonderful city, but the hard winters worked against it. DC's positives? It was only four hours down the road from New York and we knew a few people there. Scott Stuckey lived in DC, and he was tight with Kevin. I knew 9:30 Club owner Seth Hurwitz and a fellow musician named Rich Morel.

At the beginning of 2002, David at Rebel Rebel had said, "You've got to hear this record, it's this guy from DC, his name is Morel. The record is called *Queen of the Highway*. We got an advance copy and you're going to love it: it's gay, it's disco, it's guitars, and it's butch." He played it for me and I was instantly sold. It was really great music, an original blend of rock, glam, and disco.

I met Rich a few weeks later, before I started my tour. He was in New York for his record release party, and the guys from Rebel Rebel introduced me to him. Rich and I hit it off right away—we were like two peas in a pod. It reminded me of the first time I met Jim Wilson: talking so easily and enthusiastically about gear, music, and life.

After the May sessions, Kevin and I drove to DC and stayed with Scott Stuckey and his wife, Kristina, until we found and bought a hastily renovated four-story brick townhouse in the gradually gentrifying U Street neighborhood. We were now official residents of the nation's capital.

In June 2002 I flew to Long Beach for an outdoor show with Soul Asylum. I hadn't seen the band since all their success, and a lot had changed in all of our lives. At this point I barely knew the guys, but it was nice to see them again. Actor George Wendt, a big fan of both Soul Asylum and mine, was hanging out in their dressing room/trailer and we exchanged pleasantries. Wendt opened their cooler, which contained nothing but half-melted ice and water, and asked guitarist Dan Murphy if there was more beer. Dan said, "No, George, there's no more beer." Completely deadpan, George proclaimed, "If you're outta beer, I'm outta here," and moved on.

In July 2002 Kevin and I went to England and I played five shows with the Flaming Lips. I brought a VHS tape containing a truncated version of COLAS and played along. These shows went over better than the US dates—Europe in 2002 was much more accepting of various kinds of electronic music. After those dates I played outdoor festivals in New York and Chicago, returned home, and spent the remainder of the summer in DC.

We hadn't realized that DC empties out in the summer, especially in August. Politics goes on vacation and the gays head to the beach. Seventeenth Street, which normally resembled a quieter Christopher Street or Eighth Avenue, looked like a downtown block from a forgotten western town: you could almost see the tumbleweeds rolling down the street. There were very few people in town, and I was having trouble making friends.

Kevin was spending most of his time with Scott Stuckey, and we were heading right back to the same spot we'd gotten ourselves into in Texas in 1995. I was distancing myself from him all over again. I was thinking, I hate this place, why am I here? What did I do to deserve this? I'd wanted out of Austin in 1996, but I now recognized that I'd wanted out of Austin *by myself*. That was the thing—I had really wanted out of the relationship and should have gone back to New York alone. But I didn't do it. Same with the move from New York to DC. I could run but I couldn't hide, and I didn't leave Kevin.

* * *

Perhaps because I was a notable out gay man in DC, I was invited to participate in the Human Rights Campaign National Dinner held October 13, 2002. The Human Rights Campaign (HRC) is the largest LGBT political action committee in the US, and their annual dinner is one of their primary fund-raisers, as well as a hot ticket in the gay scene. HRC also reached out to me to contribute a track to their *Being Out Rocks* compilation CD to coincide with the dinner. I also volunteered to do publicity work, sign pictures, and in return was seated at a dinner table with Judy Shepard, the mother of slain gay teen Matthew Shepard, and Betty DeGeneres, Ellen's mom.

I had helped raise money for God's Love through John Giorno, and at Barracuda for the Anti-Violence Project, but this was a high-visibility fund-raiser, rubbing elbows with the real celebrities of the LGBT world. It was another step in my personal journey as an out gay man, light-years away from the confused homosexual teen who left a gay-intolerant farm town at the age of seventeen. It felt nice, even if my services were paltry compared to the folks who do the heavy lifting for LGBT rights on a daily basis.

After the reaction to the COLAS tour, I wanted to get back out in front of people and start righting the course. So the day after the HRC dinner, I began a three-week solo acoustic tour, playing some of my best-loved songs and reverting to the familiar singer-songwriter format. It was nice to have the pressure of the synchronized show off my back, and people reacted much more favorably this time, which was a relief. The only crisis was that Kevin immediately fell ill with a throat infection. Many nights he would go straight to the hotel to sleep, while I went to the clubs and handled the workload. Along the way he ended up in two emergency rooms. After being discharged a second time, he yelled at me for allowing the hospital staff to administer a light opiate for the pain, knowing that he was a recovering heroin addict. That was more his responsibility than mine, but I took the blame.

In December we went to Australia and did an acoustic tour. I was in Adelaide, singing the chorus of "Hoover Dam," when my lower left molar broke in half. I did the rest of the tour with a superglued molar, eating soft food on one side of my mouth and screaming the rest of the time. When I wasn't on the clock,

I wanted to be alone, to rest, and to have some quiet. Kevin picked up on this and would disappear for hours.

By now I had accepted the fact that Kevin was probably not being sexually faithful or—much more importantly—honest with me. But I simply didn't have the wherewithal to close up the relationship. It was all I had, it was all I knew. And no matter what either one of us did, things got worse.

Personally, things had been rough for well over a year. Professionally, 2002 was the lowest point in my career. No matter which way I turned, no matter what I tried, I couldn't catch a break. There was nowhere to go but down.

Chapter 24

So far DC had been a real letdown. I'd made one or two acquaintances, but I wasn't fitting in anywhere. There was quiet to be had in the house, but not the good kind of quiet. I felt very little enjoyment being with Kevin. We were both miserable.

But late in 2002, Rich Morel and I began building a friendship and started writing music together, strictly for fun. We worked in his comfortable basement studio in Takoma Park, Maryland, sampling sounds, playing guitars, and programming beats. It was the first time since my Minneapolis days I'd truly collaborated with anyone. We built a good amount of trust in a short period of time.

One day I noticed a big square box in Rich's studio. I asked Rich what was in it, and he said, "It's a DJ rig that Deep Dish gave me so I could learn to DJ, but I hate DJs." I think he was being half funny. I was like, "Dude, why don't we DJ? I don't have any friends, and you hardly ever go out and party." Rich replied, "I'm really good friends with the FedEx guy. Seriously." Rich was the kind of guy who did his work, had a longtime partner, and stayed focused on those two things. I said we should throw a gay dance party. Where could we do this? Rich suggested the Velvet Lounge, a small two-story club on U Street between Ninth and Tenth. Rich's band played there sometimes, so he had a connection with the club.

We booked our first party for Sunday, January 26, 2003. When I worked at WCW, we did the monthly pay-per-views on Sunday, and the end of a story line or feud was called the "blow-off." I suggested Blowoff as a name for the party, and Rich was fine with it. We made a business card–size flyer and printed up a box of them. I walked around Dupont, Logan, Seventeenth Street, P Street, and if I saw someone who I thought might be interested in a gay dance party, I would give them a card, which would get them in for free. This hand-to-hand advertising was familiar to me from the old days, as well as being an easy way to introduce myself to cute guys.

We were on the small stage with our laptops and the DJ rig. Although I didn't understand how to beat-match like a proper club DJ, at least I was up there doing something. The crowd of thirty was a mix of friends, rock people, and neighborhood guys. It wasn't a sophisticated presentation, but we played good music, people danced, and everyone was smiling at the end of the night. We made enough to pay for the business cards and the chairs we'd rented so people could sit down. The club was satisfied with the event and asked us to come back. We booked the last Sunday of every month through the summer, and each month we did a little better than the one before.

Sunday was a tough night to throw a party, and DC was a tough town to do it in. DC has always been a type A personality town, but with the Republicans in power, it was exponentially more noticeable. There were lots of big gas-guzzling SUVs with Maryland and Virginia plates tearing through town. You could tell the dark star was in charge. Meanwhile, Blowoff was this sexy gay dance party that was flourishing in the face of all the negative energy. (I have to mention just how many gays there are in the military. I'd talk to guys at Blowoff, and when the conversation turned to occupation, some guys would say, "I work at the Pentagon.")

In June we moved to the last Saturday of the month. People

were paying attention, and attendance was up. After the June event, we managed to get some coverage in the *Washington Post,* and everything was built toward our Saturday in July. But the Friday afternoon before, we received a call informing us that the DC Health Board had closed the Velvet Lange due to a code violation. Apparently they didn't have any hand towels in the men's room. Six months of work, all the building of momentum, and it looked like we were fucked. We called every club in town, but nobody was able to host us.

Late that Friday night, we received a call from Chad, the production manager from the 9:30 Club. He said, "I hear you guys are looking for a place to do your party tonight. We have a show booked upstairs, but we've got the basement space called Backbar. Why don't you come down? We'll put a little PA together, we'll make it work." It was great—not only did I have a long history with Seth Hurwitz, but the 9:30 Club was only one block from Velvet Lounge. We asked one of our friends to stay at Velvet Lounge, so that when people got out of taxis, he could tell them to get back in and go around the corner to Backbar. It was a complete success. Over the course of the night, two hundred people passed through a space that legally holds sixty.

The centerpieces of the Backbar were the drinking bar from the original 9:30 Club, where Hüsker Dü used to play, and the old phone booth that we all used to call home from. They brought us back in September, we started spinning music every week, and all was good in Blowoff land.

That was the good news for 2003. The bad news began one day in late 2002 when I'd said to Kevin, "We both seem so miserable. I really wish that there was something that would make you happy. We are driving each other right down to the bottom." I didn't know it then, but this was yet another "say it and it will be so" moment.

A few months later, Kevin and I were sitting in Dupont Circle and this short, nondescript preppie fellow showed up and basically presented himself to us. This fellow's ex was a Blowoff regular who'd brought the guy one night, and I remembered seeing him and Kevin hanging out while I was working. I could tell Kevin was really fond of this guy right away, and he floated the idea of us spending some intimate time with him.

By this time, March of 2003, I was so miserable that just about anything seemed like a good idea. It was a foolish way to try to save what little of a relationship we had. At first it was fun, a no strings attached booty call, but I could tell Kevin was getting emotionally drawn to the guy. I had told Kevin I wished there was something that would make him happy—and, well, here it was. As time went on, I could feel whatever remaining love Kevin had for me transferring to this other guy. I had no deep feelings for this person, but I went along for the ride. Over the next few months, the three of us tried to negotiate our roles in this relationship, but it seemed like an impractical arrangement, not to mention a mere Band-Aid placed clumsily over a much bigger problem.

In July I had a West Coast acoustic tour, and the three of us were going to go together. At the last minute Kevin proclaimed that he and the other guy were not going. I sensed Kevin was waiting for me to leave so he could make his case to the other guy for the two of them to start a family. It didn't seem like a good idea—at times I felt like the third played the role of the "child" stuck between two fighting parents, as opposed to being a potential parent himself. To Kevin's credit, though, he had finally quit smoking pot a month earlier. I only wish he'd done it sooner, for himself as well as for me.

I guess I wasn't giving Kevin enough hope that we would someday start a family. So for the second time in our relationship, Kevin looked elsewhere for a co-parent. But this time I was completely entwined in the arrangement, and it was happening right in front of me—and without me. I could tell this relationship was going to get interesting.

In August I booked some solo shows in the Northeast to coincide with a vacation the three of us planned in Province-town, Massachusetts. I kept holding on, thinking that maybe something good would come of this. But I was enjoying this three-person relationship less and less. While in Provincetown, the three of us went to a jewelry shop and ordered identical rings, to signify that we were an official "thruple." Friends and acquaintances saw what was happening, scratched their heads, but mostly stayed out of it.

When the HRC did a national print ad campaign focused on gay couples, they contacted Kevin and me and asked if we would agree to be one of the couples featured in this campaign. Kevin was delaying his response, and the reason was obvious. He didn't intend for us to be a couple much longer. I said to Kevin, "I thought you wanted to do this, this is the kind of stuff that you like." He kept hedging, and the opportunity came and went. By now people started coming to me saying, "Do you realize what's happening to you? Just to let you know, Bob, you're about to be odd man out." I said we'd see what happens.

Through it all, Kevin wanted to get more involved with Blowoff, but I was protective of my working relationship with Rich. One day in October, I went out for a business lunch with Rich, his then manager, Richard Reese, and Bug Music publisher Garry Valletri. We were eating outside on Seventeenth Street and Kevin walked by, stopping and motioning as if he wanted to join us. I wasn't having any of it.

A few weeks later we were eating Chinese takeout in the den when Kevin made his proclamation: "We're going to move on without you." This was just after Kevin and I had decided that the three of us were going to live together. I had hired an architect to redo the entire house and design an addition, a $200,000 job. I'd even arranged to rent a place where the three of us could live during the six-month renovation.

I looked at the third guy and said that maybe he should go

back to his own place for a couple days and let me and Kevin sort this out, and that then we'd get back to him. That night, Kevin and I talked about it, and he said, "I really think this is what I want to do." I said, "How about we separate for a couple months, put the renovation on hold, and you can live in the rental place. I prefer that you don't see the other guy while you and I sort it out and talk through this, and if we're going to finish up, let's finish it up properly."

Within days, Kevin and I went into couples therapy. It wasn't very productive—we'd presented a unified front for so many years, it was very easy for us to assume the roles of Bob and Kevin, the couple. But everything Kevin was saying was different from what he'd said to me before. I was bullshitting as well. After these sessions we'd go out to our scooters and, without saying a word, ride away from each other.

I was like, OK, this is nuts. We were six months into this slow and final dissolve of our fourteen-year relationship. And for most nights of those six months, I was in my bed with one eye open, lucky if I got an hour of sleep. My brain wasn't functioning properly—I didn't know who I was, where I was, or what I was doing.

In November and December, I was in the house by myself and Kevin was living at the rental apartment. I presumed he was by himself because he told me he also wanted to be alone while we tried to work through this. He said he would not see the other guy, but other people were telling me different. I didn't care to spy on them, so I had no sure way of knowing. While we were separated, I went on dates with a couple of guys. I wasn't intimate with them, but I was moving away from our relationship as well.

Christmastime arrived and we started to communicate a little bit more than sending a text or two every day, which is what it had degenerated to. In my mind, we were separated but still a couple. We had made no formal closure. Kevin and I decided that we were going to spend the holidays together in an attempt to keep each other from killing ourselves. Killing ourselves, as in being suicidal, as in November when Kevin dropped this line on me: "You make me so miserable, every time I go across the Connecticut Avenue Bridge I want to throw myself off."

What better way to spend the holidays than to go to Las Vegas, Los Angeles, and Palm Springs? We flew into Las Vegas but didn't spend a whole lot of time there together. Both of us were out on the prowl individually, getting together to eat meals and that's about it. I would come back to our hotel room and he'd be on the phone with the third. We spent the three days before Christmas in Las Vegas and the funniest thing happened. Back in Malone I'd dragged home the school Christmas tree that one year, so Kevin and I always loved buying a big tree and doing it up. This year, what did we do for a tree? We went to the drugstore and bought a tabletop light-up tree. We took it back to the room, plugged it in, and of course the lights didn't work. Fucking perfect.

Christmas Day, we drove to Los Angeles, where it was raining and gloomy. We were still not communicating much. It was more nonsense, cruising guys and finding no solace or enjoyment in each other. We did that for a couple days and then off we went to Palm Springs. We were staying at the same clothing-optional resort as before and everything was a complete mess by this point. We were disappearing from each other for hours and then running into each other, and then he'd get angry because he was trying to snag some guy. By this point, I didn't care anymore. I was going to have a good old time, so I dived right into my own mud hole. So what if he walks into the wet area and sees me getting jerked off by some hot guy? After all these years, finally, he would feel how I felt, or so I thought. Turns out he couldn't have cared less.

We went back to Las Vegas for New Year's Eve, where we had a room that overlooked the fireworks on the Strip. We had our fancy New Year's Eve dinner, and I got yelled at because I didn't know you're supposed to order the soufflé at the beginning of the meal. By the time we got back to our room, Kevin was pissed off and noncommunicative. He knocked himself out with either booze or pills or both, and fell asleep at 10 PM. I looked out the window, watching the fireworks go off, thinking this was the worst holiday ever. Spending Christmas Day alone eating turkey dogs in a freezing-cold apartment in Minnesota was way better than this.

We flew home the next day. Kevin was feverish and coming down with the flu. We were at the Vegas airport, and he wouldn't come to the counter to check in. I bumped us up to business class seats, and at least he was grateful for that. We landed in DC, I dropped him off at the rental apartment and continued to the house thinking this whole thing was insane.

If 2001 was brutal, and 2002 was like having my limbs stretched for a year, then 2003 was a total mind-fuck. By December I didn't have a clue as to what was going on in my life, and the final collapse of our relationship was on public display.

In January 2004 I had a solo show booked at the Birchmere in Alexandria, Virginia. My sister, Susan, lives in Roanoke, and she flew my mother up from Florida for the show. They'd met Kevin many times, but I asked Kevin not to go to the show, given the state of things. He understood and suggested that he come over to the house the next day and cook brunch for everyone. I said, "OK, that sounds reasonable."

The '60s folk-pop legend Donovan was in town then for a photo show at Govinda Gallery in DC. Chris Murray is the owner, he knows a lot of famous rock people, and he brought Donovan backstage after my set. Twenty minutes into the aftershow party, my sister comes up and says, "This is the most interesting group of people. I met this guy named Donovan, and it's so weird—I never think of that name except Donovan the singer. He was my favorite singer when I was in college. I loved Donovan." I looked at my sister and said, "Susan, that *is* Donovan. That is 'Wear Your Love Like Heaven,' 'Sunshine Superman' Donovan." She made a beeline toward him and bent his ear for the next half hour.

The next day Kevin came over for brunch, and we put on the Bob and Kevin Show for the last time. My sister and mother left, Kevin and I had sex with each other for the first time in months, and he split quickly after we finished.

A few days later, Brendan Canty, who had played drums in DC band Rites of Spring and the DC post-punk band Fugazi, was filming the first installment of the *Burn to Shine* music DVD series in DC and wanted me to participate. Kevin wanted to tag along, so we rode together in my truck. I filmed my bit, we got twisted around on the way home, and a shouting match started in the car.

The next time I talked to Kevin was a week later. He called from Florida to tell me he was on vacation with the other guy and that he thought we were done and he was going to partner up with the other guy. I said, "Fine, it's probably for the best. Don't worry about me, but if you think that what you've done and what's happened over the last nine months is a solid foundation to build a relationship on, you are fooling yourself. This is like the guy you left me for in Hoboken and the guy you left me for in Texas. You do the same things again and again. Good luck." That was the end.

Kevin soon moved out of the rental apartment and into a house three blocks from mine. For the next six years, I would see him around the neighborhood, but mostly from a distance — across the street, across a bar or restaurant that we happened to be in at the same time — never speaking or even acknowledging each other. The first time we came face to face after that phone call was six months later in June of 2004, at the coffee shop on Seventeenth Street that we used to go to. He was in line waiting to get a coffee. I walked in and was behind him in line. I didn't say anything, but through smell or a sixth sense, he knew I was behind him. He turned around and started to say something to me, and I immediately turned around, turned my back to him, stretched my arms out straight, and tipped my head down as if I were on the cross. I wasn't going to hear a word of what he had to say. I was done with Kevin. We have never spoken again.

*   *   *

I had loved Kevin dearly. I'd often thought of us as the modern-day Verlaine and Rimbaud—but with less nihilism, debauchery, and mutilation. We saw light and hope in each other at the beginning, but time changed our view, with depression, over-protectiveness, and possessiveness corroding our bond. We did the best we could, but we lived and loved in a cycle of darkness. Our relationship wasn't exactly a race to the bottom, but when one of us got too low, the first solution was to get even lower than the other in order to push him out of the hole. We tried to take the best care possible of each other, in our unique way, but over time it became too much for either of us to manage.

Now that it was truly over, I was left with a mixture of feelings. I was kicking myself for holding on to Kevin all those times he clearly wanted to go. But mainly I was relieved that it was over. I wasn't angry or depressed. I felt like I had a clean slate in front of me. Finally, all of these things I'd tried so this relationship could continue—moving here and moving there, going to a therapist, agreeing to have kids, putting up with a third—that was all gone. The worst had already happened. I'd watched the disintegration for nine months and most of the mourning was already done. Now it was time to start over. Oh, and I called the locksmith.

I tried to find the right way to walk away from this relationship. I'd always found running was so much easier, as long as I didn't trip and fall. I'd been searching for the good ending.

Maybe there was no good ending for Kevin and me. Maybe there was only the end.

I don't have any animosity toward Kevin. I wish him the best and hope that he is able to find his own inner peace. I take full responsibility for my share of the problems that ended our relationship. It was an amazing fourteen years.

CHAPTER 25

U nlike in 1989, the last time I went through something like this, I didn't want to move to another city. I decided to make a new life for myself exactly where I was. DC was a big city that brimmed with options, and I didn't hide myself away.

It was a big step for me to open up to people I didn't know so well. I was vulnerable and still somewhat guarded, but I had no choice. And I was also beginning to realize that I had long been putting work above the two things that were even more important: my friends and my health.

When I was younger, work always took precedent. I never took care of myself, I never did enough for my friends, and I never let my friends do enough for me. Because of work, my relationships suffered. Not just my primary relationships, but also the casual ones, the ones I took for granted until they were gone. Those small interactions, the corner-store clerk or the homeless guy selling newspapers or the snooty barista—those are the ones who act as the mortar, holding the bricks of normalcy in place.

Friendships ended up lost, disintegrating, unkempt. They were like the keepsakes that were tossed into boxes in a storage space, blending into the useless information that piled up around me. That's what really haunts me—the friendships I lost.

I had been faithful to Mike, faithful to Kevin, and now I was single. Everything was open and new. I'd been unhitched for one month in the last twenty-one years. Now I was learning the ropes of dating and casual sex in DC. I had my freedom, but I knew I had to be somewhat cautious. I said to Rich, keep an eye on me and tell me if I start acting stupid. I don't think I ever got too crazy.

Other than the six months of no sleep in 2003, I was working out every day, taking out my aggression and frustration in a healthy way. I practically lived at the gym. There was a restaurant that was part of the gym, and I would eat a lot of meals there, courting guys, meeting for a protein shake or a burger. I can remember one night when there was me and three guys in their early 30s sitting around a table as if it were an episode of *The Dating Game*.

Rich and I had a mutual friend named Paul Eley who was a Blowoff regular. Paul would remind me, "You're single, let's go out and have some fun." So he'd get me out of the house to meet new people. Some nights we'd hit the downtown leather bar the Eagle. Playing pool or watching Bill Maher on the big-screen TV with two other people (including the bartender) was not great fun, but at least I was off the couch and out of the house.

The DC nightlife was new to me, and once I was out and about, I was surprised to find how gay the town was. I knew my gym, Seventeenth Street, and Dupont Circle—the old gay neighborhood. Outside of that, there was a thriving gay community made up of many different types of folks in several neighborhoods.

I was still trying to find my place in DC when early one Friday night in April of 2004, Paul and I went to a place called DIK Bar, a cozy little joint above Dupont Italian Kitchen. I walked in and, long story short, I found my crowd: the bears.

Bear culture started in San Francisco in the late 1980s. It was born from an adaptation of the lumberjack image: flannel shirts, beards, and burly bodies. Bears had descended from two other subgroups—bikers and "girth and mirth" men—that didn't fit the urban gay stereotype of the young hairless "twink." Eventually there were magazines like *Bear,* and even bars like the Lone Star, that helped define the bear culture.

The crowd at DIK Bar was made up of regular-looking guys from their mid 20s to their mid 50s, most with facial hair, flannel shirts, and jeans. Some guys were buff, some guys were normal size, some guys were heavy, but everybody was super friendly, drinking beer and giving each other hugs and being normal guys. Nondescript music played in the background at DIK Bar: old disco, 1980s new wave, current pop music. Paul asked, "Do you like this place?" I replied, "Yeah, this crowd is cool, this is a fun place. Let's stay for a while."

It was great to be in a bar where people dressed the same way I did. It reminded me of my punk rock days: guys in flannel shirts, T-shirts, and jeans. There wasn't a lot of pretense, sarcasm, or campy behavior. No offense meant to those who like camp, but at this point in my life, it wasn't my thing. I enjoyed the company of guys who were comfortable with their masculinity. At DIK Bar I didn't feel like I had to do anything to fit in except be myself. I didn't have to try to look or act like a bear because I already was one.

I met guys that night who are still good friends—one special guy in particular. As I was getting ready to leave, I came face to face with this inebriated yet handsome young man. I was wearing a blue flannel shirt, which he grabbed onto and wouldn't let go of. Paul said, "That guy is crazy, we need to get out of here." That crazy guy, Tom Joyce, became one of my best (and most stable) friends. The whole night at DIK Bar was a revelation.

I had a few friends in DC, including Tom, who blogged regularly. And at the beginning of 2004, I also jumped headlong into the online world by starting a blog called Boblog: A Quiet and Uninteresting Life. After my dearth of literary creativity in 2003, it was a great new outlet. Also, now that I had my house to myself, I felt safe enough to write again. I felt compelled to post daily, whether it was something serious, mundane, or comical. By forcing myself to write every day, I started breaking through the writer's block that had started in 2003. And for the first time, I was revealing pieces of myself that I previously wouldn't have felt comfortable sharing in a public forum. I was careful about hitting the "publish" button though—the internet is one big tattoo, and once it's up there, you can't get rid of it.

There was a fairly large community of gay bloggers, and I became acquainted with some of them, hitting it off especially with one fellow from the Midwest. Our online friendship soon became a long-distance phone relationship that turned both comical and sad.

We would arrange these real-life meetings: he'd make a plan to drive to DC, and I would be all excited, telling my friends how thrilled I was that this guy was going to come down and hang out. I really thought the world of him, and I couldn't wait to meet him face to face. But, invariably, something would happen on his end that would nix the visit. One time he got fifty miles into the trip and his brakes went out. One time he had chicken pox. I thought so much of the guy that I called up a Chinese restaurant a mile from his house in Midwest suburbia and had them deliver chicken soup to him. One time his grandmother died so he had to stay behind with his grieving mother.

Finally I said that the only way we would meet is if I went out there to see him. He was in his early 30s and getting his master's degree at an art college, so I chose the weekend of his graduation—"I'm coming for your graduation, I'm going to meet your family, I'm going to bring my suit." I get there, and the guy doesn't resemble the photographs he'd been sending. He's a fair amount heavier than how he portrayed himself online—IRL was a lot different from URL. I'm not a body fascist, but when somebody is claiming to be a muscle boy, and then you get there and he's not, while I've been in the gym busting my ass for months to look good—I was like, Hey, what's going on here?

I spent five days with him. Despite a few hiccups and crossed signals, we had a good time. The last day of my visit, he blew off his graduation ceremony. Instead I went to his house to meet his family. I met his parents and sister, and sure enough, his dead grandmother was also there. My jaw was on the floor. I played along for twenty minutes, then said, "Dude, we have to step outside, I need to have a word with you. That's your grandmother, I thought she was dead." He was saying, "No, no, no, that's my great aunt, that's my grandmother's sister. Don't say anything to my mom because she's still grieving." I was thinking, OK, this whole thing is weird.

Later that night, we were driving around his town and I asked, "What is really going on here?" He broke down and explained that he gained some weight in the last three months. He had been on medication and didn't want to tell me. I believed him, but said he should have brought up some of this stuff earlier. Your car seems fine, your grandmother is alive, and you don't look like your photos.

And, yes, we were intimate, but once the dead grandmother came into the picture, everything was suspect. A few days later, we said our good-byes and I drove back to DC. Along the way I realized that maybe it wasn't just him and that maybe I wasn't ready for a relationship anyway. It was as if I'd had the typical rebound relationship, except this one hadn't been realized. It was pretty weird though.

Later in the summer, another gay blogger was planning a trip to DC, and we made plans to get together for an afternoon. During our walk around town, I asked, "Are you seeing anybody?"

He said, "I've been having this on again/off again online relationship with this guy."

I asked warily, "Does he have a blog?"

"Yes," he said, "he's a hot muscle guy. We've been communicating for over a year, trying to get together, but it never seems to work out."

"By chance does he live in the Midwest?" I asked. He goes yeah. A bell went off in my head. I asked a few more questions just to make sure. It was definitely the same guy. I mentioned his name. My friend was startled.

"I spent five months doing the same thing you've been doing, and I actually went to see him. Those pictures he sent you, that's not the way he looks now."

The guy almost fainted and fell in the middle of P Street. Literally, like with the vapors. I said, "Get yourself together, we're going to go eat, and I'm going to tell you what happened." By the end of the meal, we both felt better and were laughing about it.

*   *   *

I was forty-three and in very good physical shape. In the bear scene, a lot of chest hair, a scruffy beard, and a worked-out body goes a long way. Being in my forties was actually an asset. There's a very specific time-honored dynamic with some gay men, not necessarily the daddy/son dynamic, but more of a bear/cub dynamic. There are guys in their late twenties and thirties who are coming into their own, and are looking for guys in their forties and fifties. These younger guys are usually wiser than their years and are looking to spend their time with older guys. The older guys play the role of mentor, boyfriend, or long-term partner.

As my life as a gay man got fuller and more complicated, sometimes it was all I could do to look at my friends and (half) jokingly say, "Being gay is really hard." It was almost as if "being gay is really hard" was code for "I'm really sorry I slept with your out-of-town trick, but you pushed him at me, and we both know that when he goes back to his town, we'll be left having coffee together."

Being gay *is* really hard—so many parties, so many events, so many exes, so many friends who are now split from their partners, and you have to know how to juggle everybody. It's a difficult life. When is happy hour? Where on Thursday? He slept with *who?*

And if one is to be a bit of a sleep-around, it's just courteous to keep a Costco family pack of toothbrushes on hand. That was me for a moment—always the thoughtful whore.

Kidding aside, I'll share two pieces of advice about being gay: you can't come out soon enough—and it's never too late to come out.

I thought all the way back to when I was a kid, not being able to tell anyone, not even my parents, about who I really was. I never had anyone to talk to, and I never looked to anyone to talk to—because I didn't want to talk about it. If you're young and questioning and not able to voice it in safety, find a gay person in your community who you trust and respect, and get to know him and talk it all through with him. Find the big brother or the parent that you don't have at home and ask him to guide you and help you sort out all the emotions.

I thought about how I'd been so disconnected from the gay community in my teens and twenties that I couldn't find any point at which I could relate to it. I thought about the 1994 *Spin* article and its aftermath. I probably should have come out in 1986, when my homosexuality was an open secret. I knew that everybody knew. I had deep sadness and regret about not coming out sooner—my life would have been so different. But I'd been so worried about how people would perceive my work, not considering the impact I might have had on people for being an out gay rock guy. Still, I eventually came out; there were some rough spots, but overall I was happier for it.

In my two long-term relationships, I had unconsciously built my life upon the traditional construct of marriage. Now that I was single and exploring the full range of the gay community, I was beginning to see all the different options and opportunities in front of me. I was beginning to find my place. It was a very exciting time.

*   *   *

By July I was interested in two different fellows. There was one guy who worked out at my gym during lunchtime, and another guy who I worked out with in the late afternoon. So I was going to the gym twice a day just so I could check out two different people.

The late afternoon guy was a very handsome pediatric radiologist from Birmingham, Alabama, who was in town doing some work at Walter Reed Medical Center. He was ten years younger than me, with a perky personality and a big red goatee. We spent lots of time together. He told me he had a boyfriend, so it was a platonic relationship laced with heavy overtones.

The real tough one, though, was going at noon in hopes of getting a look at this other guy, Will Hiley. He was the most beautiful man I had ever seen, and I was completely head over heels. From moment one, it felt like that love at first sight I had heard about but never experienced. I was petrified around him. He was so gorgeous and radiant and vibrating. The relationship I was hoping for never materialized, but we were as tight as two people who aren't involved could be—and a very intense friendship came out of that.

I also spent a lot of the summer of 2004 in the gay tourist destination of Rehoboth Beach, Delaware. I had money, so I didn't need to work. I would go to Rehoboth two or three days a week, where my dear old friend Steve Fallon and his longtime partner, Arnold, had lived since 1999. I was going to the gym, the beach, the bars, meeting new people, and having a good old time. I was a very different person in Rehoboth. I wasn't going there for dating. I was going there to hook up with guys I didn't know. One thing I figured out early on was that DC was a small town—everybody talks, and it was best to do my tricking elsewhere.

Very few of the guys who came to Rehoboth recognized me as Bob Mould the music guy. Joe from Wilmington, Delaware, didn't know who I was, and I wasn't about to tell him. Bill from Philadelphia, who rolled into town looking to get laid, I'm not about to walk up to and say, "Don't you know who I am?" I wanted him to think, Who's the muscle daddy standing at the end of the bar? I want to get with him for an hour." I didn't want to get recognized—I wanted to get laid.

Back in the 1990s, the Lure was a leather/rubber/fetish bar on Thirteenth Street in Greenwich Village. Two of the owners moved to Rehoboth and opened a leather/biker bar called the Double L. One of the owners was John Meng, who was about my age, a motorcycle collector, a former Massachusetts state cop—and the Double L is his pride and joy. On the wall behind the bar was a framed cover of *Land Speed Record,* and the bathroom was done entirely in flyers from the punk rock days, including some of my earliest shows. John and I yakked about the Germs, Boston hardcore, and gay life at the beach. Once again, I found a place where I felt like I belonged.

* * *

It was no coincidence that I was starting to write music again. In 2003, with the turmoil in my personal life, I didn't feel comfortable making my own music at home. I was collaborating with Rich at his studio, and the only work I did at home was putting on a pair of headphones, firing up my laptop, and making white label remixes of other people's work. I was just reshuffling other people's music instead of creating my own. Now that I had my house to myself, I eased back into writing. There was a handful of good songs from the 2002 Athens sessions with David Barbe and Matt Hammon, but I had to write many more in order to complete what would become *Body of Song.*

I started writing songs about courtship, the false starts and missteps. It was very different from my usual prescient failed relationship perspective. I was trying to write from a more hopeful place. A lot of the newer songs for *Body of Song* were notes to myself about falling for people and how that made me feel. It was really inspiring for me to write about the people I was interested in from a more optimistic emotional view and boiling those feelings down into songs. I didn't have much to lose and plenty to gain.

Ultimately, the album ended up being an interesting hybrid of all the styles I had touched on in the previous six years. There were plenty of electronic elements in the album, particularly the straight-out dance track "(Shine Your) Light Love Hope," the swirling trip-hop track "Always Tomorrow," and the synth/ guitar marriage of "Paralyzed." There were plaintive acoustic ballads like "High Fidelity" (a track I'd written in 1995 but never released), "Days of Rain," and "Gauze of Friendship." The big guitars were back on "Circles" (a song I'd written in New York in 2000), "Underneath Days," and "Beating Heart the Prize."

In the summer of 2004, Brendan Canty and I started playing music together. Brendan is a gifted musician, a great drummer, and a good people person. We got together with veteran engineer Don Zientara at Inner Ear Studio in Arlington, Virginia, and recorded some improvisational pieces, mainly to see if there was any chemistry. It went well, and we made plans to reconvene a few months later to record drum tracks for *Body of Song*.

In October I participated in a number of events that highlighted the changes I was going through. Back in April, I was asked by NYC gay impresario Josh Wood to play a few songs at a same-sex marriage benefit concert called WedRock, so I hastily wrote a gay wedding song specifically for that show. We reprised the event in DC on October 5, using a mix of local and national talent, including our illustrious and magnanimous MC, Henry Rollins (who was the subject of a cover story by local gay pub *Metro Weekly*), Sandra Bernhard, and DC councilperson David Catania, who was spearheading the movement to legalize same-sex marriage in DC. For this show I was accompanied onstage by Brendan Canty and bassist Brandon Butler; we closed the show with electric trio versions of "See a Little

Light" and "Makes No Sense at All." I was on pins and needles the entire day and night, but it wasn't because this was my first time onstage with a power trio since my "retirement" gig in Brussels in 1998; rather, it was because I had invited my gym buddy Will to be my date. He wasn't sure he could make it, and even when he did, I was still pinching myself.

Then I got a call from Soul Asylum's management, requesting my presence at an event titled Rock for Karl, a fund-raiser for bassist Karl Mueller, who was fighting cancer. The show was to be held on October 21 at Quest, a large downtown Minneapolis music venue. Given my long history with Soul Asylum, I quickly said yes, and was confirmed to play a forty-five-minute solo set on a bill with Soul Asylum, Paul Westerberg, Golden Smog, and the Gear Daddies.

The day of the show, my cell phone rang. It was Grant Hart. He had called Josh Grier, who gave him my number. He asked if he could come down to the show, and if it might be OK if we played a song together. I thought for a second...

Here's the core of why I didn't deal with Grant or Greg anymore, here's the core of why I let it go and moved on: After I quit the band, I'd always avoided saying anything derogatory about Hüsker Dü. I was content to "let the music do the talking." I focused on my work and my life. I tried to avoid talking about the past—the good and the bad parts. I hoped the other two would extend that same professional courtesy, but it wasn't to be. I was already on the outs with Grant and Greg when they hired their lawyer Doug Myren in 1993. And once the three of them redid the books, because of the money Grant and I took for producing the last three Hüsker Dü albums, it made sense they would line up against me publicly as well.

According to the other guys, I wasn't in charge of Hüsker Dü, and yet somehow I was solely to blame for the failings of the band. How can it be both ways? And I'd tried to forgive Grant for his continual bitching about me in the press, but I couldn't. It was easier to forget all that nonsense and just move forward with my work and my life. Perhaps Grant's bitterness toward me stemmed from the fact that people felt—wrongly— that his heroin problem was the only reason for the end of Hüsker Dü. Perhaps that led him to paint me with the ugly brush. I simply kept on.

In 1996 Grant had visited me at a First Avenue show, and I had confronted him about the unflattering and often misleading comments he had made about me since 1988. His response was, "Well...you know the press, they always exaggerate the things I say. There's a lot of misquoting going on out there."

...I didn't buy that for one second. But given the reason for the Rock for Karl event, I was able to overlook this bullshit one time, and one time only. I decided to say yes. I put all the nonsense of the past sixteen years behind me and "took one for the team."

I suggested if we were going to play a song, we might as well do two, one from each of our catalogs. We decided on "Hardly Getting Over It" and "Never Talking to You Again," agreed not to tell anyone that we were doing this, and planned to meet at the venue.

During my sound check, I asked the stage manager to prepare another setup onstage: a direct box for plugging an acoustic guitar into the sound board, a vocal mic, and a pair of floor monitors. Grant did not come for sound check, as that would have tipped off the production crew and word would have spread quickly. I didn't want this moment to upstage the reason I came, which was to support the cause, play my set, and see old friends, including Karl. But there was no way it wouldn't cause a total commotion.

When Grant arrived at the venue, we were cool yet cordial with each other. I welcomed him into my modest dressing room, and as a way of breaking the ice, asked him about his experiences playing in Patti Smith's band. Grant immediately started burying people in their camp, claiming he was made a scapegoat of interband politics. Then he started in on Paul Westerberg.

Next was a negative rant about Greg Ginn and SST (who at this point deserved it for not fully paying mechanical royalties). Not fifteen minutes had passed, and he was already in fine form. Despite this jabbering, we had two songs to play. We spent less than five minutes touching on each of the songs, which were both quite simple, then I excused myself and went into catering to say hello to my old Minnesota musician friends.

Most everyone was happy to see me, but also looking at me, as if to say, Why is Grant in your dressing room? In fact, why is he here at all? It did make me wonder for a moment: Why wasn't he invited on his own? I let go of that thought, but even still, I could sense people were a little disconcerted by his presence. Maybe it was simply the fact that people knew we were not the best of friends.

A few minutes before my set started, I told Grant when to come out onstage and that his setup would be ready—all he would have to do is walk out with his guitar and plug in. He told me what he wanted in his monitor mix, and I relayed the last-minute details to the stage manager.

I went out and played a very passionate forty minutes, and then it was time. I let people know there was a special guest coming out to join me for a few songs. At that point I turned and looked to the back, and Grant appeared with his acoustic guitar. A hush fell over the crowd, then murmurs of disbelief, then a huge round of applause. We had managed to surprise the audience.

Then it struck me: Did I just give this guy an open mic on my stage? Sure enough, Grant ambled over to his mic and blurted out something, but no one understood what he said. Then, thankfully, we went straight into "Never Talking to You Again," then an abbreviated version of "Hardly Getting Over It." There was no magic, there wasn't even any nostalgia. But there wasn't any hatred either. I felt nothing special as the songs went by. After the second song, Grant left the stage and I turned to watch him leave, similar to how I turned to watch him arrive.

After my set I packed up my gear, planning to stay the entire evening and socialize. I wandered around the backstage talking with folks, including having my last (brief) conversation with Karl, who appeared to be having a wonderful time, health battle notwithstanding. After a few minutes, I went back to my dressing room to find one wall covered with chunky, reddish puke. I was repulsed and decided I would simply leave for the evening. Grant came running up, offering to carry my bags to my rental car parked a half block away. I politely declined his offer, but he still tagged along, asking if I wanted to go get something to eat with him. I again politely declined. I had had enough for one night, my work was done, and I was planning to stop into a downtown gay bar for a nightcap. I didn't want his company any longer.

When I turned down Grant's dinner invite, I walked away knowing that if there was ever a question as to the remote possibility of Hüsker Dü reuniting, those few hours reminded me that I couldn't go back. It hadn't been a bad experience, but compared to all the new and exciting things happening in my life, socializing and playing music with Grant Hart wasn't on my "to do again" list.

My feelings about Grant were borne out the following year when we both participated in a *Magnet* magazine cover story, an oral history of the Minneapolis music scene—specifically, of Hüsker Dü and the Replacements. My favorite quote in the piece came from Grant: "Sorry about your dead friend David Savoy, Bob, but you're still a fucking prick." I doubt this was a misquote. And people still wonder why there will never be a Hüsker Dü reunion.

Beyond my personal reasons for not looking back, a Hüsker Dü reunion would surely tarnish the history of the band. It's the rare occasion when a reunion tour is close or equal to what a band looked, sounded, and felt like "back in the day." Mission of Burma comes to mind as a rare exception—there was no public acrimony when they first dissolved, and their current enthusiasm is clearly genuine. I've left Hüsker Dü in the past. I'm not interested in diminishing whatever legacy exists just so people can say, "I saw Hüsker Dü." If you have an original ticket stub dated 1979–87, you saw Hüsker Dü. If not, you missed out.

* * *

Plenty of more pleasant experiences were happening all the time, like Andrew Sullivan and up-and-coming NYC blogger Joe Jervis accepting my invitation to read at an event called Blogjam in DC. Another notable blogger buddy of mine, Stephen Cox, closed the show with some outrageous tales from his popular blog GeekSlut. Stephen is a gay man who has been through the wringer and back, and I learned quite a bit about gay life from him.

A month later, while on tour in Pittsburgh, I spent time with the fellow I'd hooked up with in Palm Springs during that horrific 2003 holiday trip with Kevin. The next night, I went for coffee with my Midwest former blog buddy (and his ex), as well as a friend from my Factory Café days, Micheal Brodbeck. After the show that evening, I was sitting on the edge of the stage, selling and signing merch as I normally do. Two younger guys got their CDs signed, and as I was on to the next person, one of them turned to his buddy and made a "I want to give Bob a blow job" motion. As usual, when something like that happens in front of my face, I'm the last one to notice. Then I was off to Ann Arbor, where I spent quality time with a strapping Irish guy. Things were good.

By the end of 2004, I was enjoying being single so much I had no intention of ever going back to a relationship. I was making up for lost time, and having the time of my life.

CHAPTER 26

The previous year sure had been fun on a personal level, but I had a career to attend to. I was excited about the album I had in the works, but the question was, how would I share it with people? I had no label deal, and three years after *Modulate,* my audience (and the industry) were skittish about my recorded work.

Josh Grier knew some folks at Yep Roc, a well-known independent label in North Carolina, and I met with label chief Glenn Dicker in DC in early 2005. I played him the tracks in progress and he was very excited at the prospect of having me at Yep Roc. I didn't have management at the time, but Yep Roc was willing to pay good money for a record and really get behind it and support it.

I soon signed a deal and promised Yep Roc I would tour and do as much press as they could bring to me. With that in mind, I hired Sharon Agnello, who represented Jay Farrar, to run the office. Sharon and I worked well together, and Yep Roc was also pleased with the arrangement.

I finished off *Body of Song* over the next few months. Brendan Canty played along to my home recordings, and the results were great. I took the highlights of the 2002 Athens sessions with David Barbe and Matt Hammon, merged them with the songs I'd recorded with Brendan, and finished up the tracking with engineer Frank Marchand. I mixed the record at home in April 2005 for a July release.

I was productive and having a great time in life. I was single, more sexually active than I'd ever been. I had my work back on track, and there were a lot of things going on. There were a lot of good times, but I still felt a little aimless. One of my go-to friends was music journalist and author Steve Gdula. One day in March, Steve said to me, "Bob, have you ever thought about going to church?"

I said, "No, but why do you ask?"

He said, and I paraphrase, "I go to Catholic Mass at St. Matthew's every week. I really enjoy the quiet time away from everything gay and everything to do with my family and work. It's a nice place. I just go and reflect on things, and it works for me."

I thought a lot of Steve and our friendship, and he'd had some good advice for me in the past. I thought for a moment, then said, "Sure, Steve, I'll go with you this weekend."

It was a late-afternoon Mass on Saturday, and St. Matthew's is one of the biggest Catholic churches in DC—it's where the religious dignitaries come to speak, and also where JFK lay in state. I walked in, went up the stairs, dipped my hand into the water, and motioned the sign of the cross. We went in, found Steve's usual pew, knelt in the aisle before entering, and I again crossed myself. We lowered the altar bench, and for the first time in thirty years, I knelt in front of God. I hadn't been to church since confirmation.

There were maybe 150 people in a cathedral that holds at least 1,200. The cantor, an angelic blonde woman with a very beautiful, soft-spoken voice, makes the opening announcements. "Welcome to St. Matthew's, Father Caulfield will be presiding today, and the opening hymn can be found on page five sixty-three." We all rise and start singing. Down the aisle comes Father Caulfield, thirty-something, handsome, tall, inspirational—the kind of person who believes so hard that, when he looked up to the top of the cathedral, I feared he would shoot right through the roof. He's that close to God, speaking in measured words, and we people begin singing again.

The routine comes back to me, the whole drill; it didn't change one bit. It's not like they start with the sermon and then put a Sun Ra song in the middle—everything stays exactly the same. The set list doesn't change. I'm up, I'm down, I'm kneeling, I'm standing, I'm singing, I'm praying. The service lasted an hour.

Mass was a leveling and humbling experience that gave me a different perspective on life. There was music, there was reading, there was community. There was the moment in the service when you greet your neighbor, someone you've probably never seen before in your life and may never see again outside of the church. Everyone is united around one thing—the religious experience. It brings many different kinds of people together into one room, which is the opposite of living in the gay ghetto.

On the way out, I spotted this frail, white-haired woman in her seventies, dressed in black, very well kempt. She was wandering around the periphery of the service, then stood outside afterward. Turned out she was homeless and slept on the steps of the church. Steve and I continued down the steps to the sidewalk, where we encountered a handful of homeless African-American men begging for money. Steve knew them by first name, gave them money, and asked how they were doing. The whole experience resonated within me.

I didn't walk out of Mass thinking, hallelujah, Jesus, I've seen the light. Over the next few weeks, I mentioned my experience to friends, some of whom were dismissive. But I knew this required a deeper look. I opened myself up and tried to find— through Scripture, song, and community—a different perspective for myself, even if just for that one hour.

The Catholic Church forbids homosexuality, which was a major conflict for me. I was a sexually active single gay man, and returning to services wasn't going to make me a chaste heterosexual. I realized I was going to be a "cafeteria Catholic," picking and choosing the parts that worked for me. Instead of rebelling against or wholesale dismissing the Church, I tried to find the goodness in what the Church had to offer. And I tried to find a point of compassion in the experience that I could build from. I was always a driven person, but I'd not been the most compassionate person on earth.

For the next few years, even while on the road, I went to church every week. One Saturday afternoon in DC, I walked down Seventeenth Street to Mass and found Rhode Island Avenue blocked by a cavalcade of Secret Service vehicles. Several well-dressed men were on the steps of the church, whispering discreetly into the wireless microphones in the lapels of their crisp, dark suits. The reason for the heavy security became clear when the minister's greeting included a formal introduction of our special attendee—George W. Bush. He stayed through Communion, then he and his security detail hustled it out the side door.

I didn't anticipate going back to church, but the rest of it— being comfortable as a single gay man, having a new career with Blowoff, and finding the bears—makes sense when you look at my life. Now I find myself on a new road thanks to all the social, spiritual, and musical changes. It is a new beginning.

This ties around to my notion that the Church and rock music are very similar. There's a ritual in going to Mass and there's the ritual of going to see music or to dance at Blowoff. In reality, the stage was always the pulpit. That's what we do as musicians. We reach out and try to find or build community, and to foster a sense of belonging. When people come together and create a shared experience from a place of goodness, it can be really uplifting. Everyone can elevate together and build something that means a lot to them.

Hüsker Dü, that was preaching—going door to door selling the good word (or seven-inch singles). I was going from stage to stage, telling people, "This is who I am, these are the stories I tell, and this is what I believe in." People can dismiss it and say those stories aren't for them; some people only partly endorse it. Some people believe and spread the word to others. And then there's the people who live and die for all the stories; they believe every word you say, they apply those stories to their lives and build their values and the way they live from them.

We all live and die for the stories and the sounds. Sometimes we find them, other times they just happen upon us. We don't always get a choice.

* * *

Body of Song was released in July 2005. I was relieved that fans and critics liked the album. I was also happy that, unlike in 2002, this record didn't need a lot of explanation. A lot of the success was due to the efforts of the New York PR firm Nasty Little Man. Company head Steve Martin was a longtime fan, and Yep Roc was wise to hire Steve and his staff to supplement the hard work done by their in-house publicist, Angie Carlson. The visibility of the album was high, the music was solid, and there was yet another big hook: I was about to tour once again with a rock band.

Earlier in 2005 Brendan had said to me, "Dude, why don't you just put together a band? I'll go on tour with you. We'll go play the rock." Brendan was pushing for including older material. I trusted his opinion, and besides, I was changing a lot of my hard-and-fast rules. So I loosened up about never playing rock with a band again and said, "Great, let's do it."

I asked Rich Morel if he'd like to play keyboards in the touring band. Blowoff had gotten him out of the house, and now there's an offer of this rock tour with hotels and festivals and all the garnish. He jumped at the opportunity and started learning the songbook. Reenter Jason Narducy, who already knew my music backward and forward. He came in to play bass and help with vocals, so now the four-piece rock band was complete. People were excited that I was playing guitar again and that, for the first time, I was going to finally reopen the Hüsker Dü and Sugar songbooks with a full electric band.

I was feeling really good about things. I was deep into another wild summer, cramming as much beach time into July and August as possible, knowing that once the touring started, there was always that small chance that it could skyrocket and become as unpredictable as the Sugar years. I wasn't planning on it, I wasn't expecting it, but there was always that possibility. And now I was about to hit the road with a rock band for the first time in seven years.

I was surrounded by a bunch of guys I trusted. Besides Brendan, Jason, and Rich, I brought on *Body of Song* engineer Frank Marchand as tour manager/sound engineer and Tim Mech as stage tech, and we rehearsed for two weeks during the dog days of August in DC at Brendan's Blindspot Studios. We fired up the Sugar and Hüsker Dü songs and they sounded great. It sounded like us playing those songs—updated versions, interpretations, not faithful reproductions. Brendan would ask, "Do you want me to play like the record?" And I'd say, "Don't play like Malcolm, don't play like Grant—play like Brendan. Learn the song, play it the way you want, and it will be fine."

The rehearsals lifted this gigantic monkey off my back. Finally, I was relaxed with it. I knew that this time it was about the songs, not about me. After the 2002 COLAS tour, this was the moment to make a nice gesture. I knew people wanted to hear these songs in the loud rock format, so I thought, Why not give the people what they want for once? Let's start the show with the first three songs from *Copper Blue*. It was time to celebrate the work.

The way we played those early songs was music to my ears. Brendan is such an interpretive player, Jason is a wonderful singer, and Rich filled in all the chordal color. I could relax and not try to fill three voices at once. I could concentrate on playing rhythm guitar when I was singing and on playing lead guitar when I stepped back, letting the keyboards reinforce the foundation with dirty Hammond sounds and strings. Playing those songs was like riding a bicycle. But this time I wasn't pedaling away from, or toward, anywhere or anything in particular — I was simply enjoying the moment.

The tour started in September 2005 at an outdoor festival in Ireland called Electric Picnic. We were playing our first show as a band on a big festival stage, and we were using rented gear, which would qualify as trial by fire. There's no better way to figure out if something's going to work than to put it in the most difficult situation. Rich was the least experienced at that level, but he did fine. Brendan and I powered through it, and Jason was right there with us. That was a hell of a way to start things up.

The next day we played the Mean Fiddler in London, and the place came unglued, especially when we played the Sugar material. It felt like 1992 again, except both the crowd and I were thirteen years older, and despite people coming out of their skin over the older songs, the PA didn't fall over.

In years past, by never playing songs like "Makes No Sense at All," "I Apologize," and "Chartered Trips" in the electric band setting, I felt like I'd buried them. I had tried to erase that time. It was liberating to lift the shroud from my older songs and incorporate them into the rock band show. They're beautiful songs that stand the test of time, and I will play them to my grave.

But there was some material I still wouldn't touch: no matter how much people might love to see it, I can't imagine myself playing side two of *Zen Arcade*. I wrote those songs when I was twenty-three years old, angry at the world, feeling misunderstood, persecuted, and disappointed. I can't even get into the head of that person anymore. I can't sing those songs. I'm a different person now.

On we went to Brussels, then through Germany, Denmark, and Holland. Köln was a wild punk rock show — lots of slam dancing and aggressive behavior. Jason had seen a lot of that with his first band, Verboten, at all the hardcore shows in Chicago in the 1980s. Brendan had seen it with Rites of Spring and Fugazi. But when we came offstage, Rich was like, "I've never been in anything like that in my life."

The band dynamics were really good. Onstage, we were well rehearsed and focused, but very relaxed. Offstage, we had fun traveling as a group. Everyone showed up for lobby call on time—one of the little things that mean so much to a smooth tour.

Brendan and Jason are both married with kids, and Rich and I are gay—Rich partnered, me single. We'd get to a town and Brendan and Jason would sightsee, go to the pub, do tourist stuff. Rich and I would do that, and also go to the gay bars. I was still a bad boy at this point, and this was my first real bad boy rock tour. Germany is a hell of a place to be single and gay and on tour with days off. One minute I was in the minibus talking with the tour manager about tomorrow's stage time, and three hours later I was getting freaky with some hot leather motorcycle guy in a bathroom stall in a Hamburg fetish club. It was long overdue. Most guys in bands, and gay guys in general, do that stuff when they're in their twenties. I guess I was a very late bloomer. It's hilarious in hindsight. I told a few of my gay friends about what was happening, and they're saying, "Oh, my god, I'm so jealous." Those things really do happen.

We came back for a four-week tour of the States—and I'm still misbehaving. I'm in the best physical shape of my life, we're playing great rock shows, and there's bears and cubs showing up, wanting to hang out after the show or whatever. You can do the math.

The tour wasn't all fun and games though. After the Atlanta show, we were faced with a 1,000-mile drive to perform at the Austin City Limits outdoor festival. The added challenge was getting through Hurricane Rita. The farther we went into the storm, the less traffic we encountered on the interstate. Eventually there were no other cars, only rented box trucks labeled with Red Cross placards. Through Mississippi and Louisiana we saw billboards ripped from their pillars and long lines for gas.

We finally made it to our layover hotel in north suburban Dallas. Families displaced by the storms wandered around the lobby with ice coolers, their cars filled with their possessions. Nearer the front desk, the refugees were replaced by hundreds of people, in full regalia, who were holding a science fiction convention at the hotel. Displaced families and conventioneers in full fantasy garb singing folk songs—exactly what we needed after twelve hours of driving through a hurricane.

The DC homecoming show was on October 7 at the 9:30 Club, and the show was going to be videotaped for a DVD. We'd been planning it for weeks, hiring a large crew, six cameras, multitrack audio, lighting design, the whole nine yards. It was a big deal to me, as I had never documented a show at this level. I was concerned though—two nights before, the New York show at Irving Plaza had been rough. It wasn't very musical, it was too loud, and I was trying too hard. When I look out at a crowd after the first three songs and I'm not sure if I'm connecting with them, I never think "this is too much, I need to tone it down." Quite the opposite: I always start amplifying—turn up the volume, get more animated, speed things up. Sometimes it works, sometimes it doesn't.

The next night in Philadelphia, we toned everything down and got it back under control. When we took the stage in DC, we opened it back up again, and everything worked out fine. It was one of the best shows I'd played in years, and I'm thrilled we got it on videotape. It was the culmination of a number of good choices: working with Brendan, having Rich on keys instead of a second guitarist, and having the wisdom to tone down the show the night before filming in DC. It was a really special evening, and the footage was eventually released as the *Circle of Friends* DVD.

Later that night we celebrated with yet another successful

Blowoff event in the very same room. There were plenty of folks who attended both events. All my different worlds were coming together, and everything was firing on all cylinders. I had the rock thing and the DJ thing going at once, all under one roof, and it all felt natural and good.

After a few nights off we flew to Seattle to begin a run of West Coast dates, ending with a show in LA on the eve of my forty-fifth birthday. It was probably the most scandalous week of my life to date. I don't know what got into me. I was out of control.

In Seattle I hit on some hot little cub. I got to Portland and, in rounding out my sleeping with someone from every branch of the military, spent time with a former Air Force guy who was about to become an Oregon state trooper. In San Francisco the music bears were out in force, and one of them had his mind made up that he was going to get with me that night—sure enough, he did. For the Los Angeles show, the crew got a cake and did the whole "Happy Birthday" thing on stage. At the show I ran into an old buddy from the East Coast—an ex-Marine, of course—and we ended up spending the night together at my hotel. He woke up at 6 AM for an appointment. What we didn't know the night before was that the AIDS Walk was the next morning in West Hollywood, he had parked on the street, and so his truck got towed.

The tour is over, it's my forty-fifth birthday, and I'm in Los Angeles thinking I just haven't had enough fun this week—I have to get in *more* trouble. But between the four shows and all the mad craziness, I'm pretty worn out. I'm hanging out in West Hollywood, I buy myself some clothes, I'm hitting on guys at Starbucks, but I'm lazy: I don't want to go to the leather bars. I'm tired. I'm going to go to my favorite sushi restaurant in West Hollywood, sit and chill, eat some fish. I get there and order a whole bunch of food. I'm sitting by myself, reading *Frontiers*, a local gay paper. *Frontiers* has all the escort ads, and I think to myself, You know what, I'm not going to go to the bar, I'm going to treat myself for the first time in my life. I'm going to get a massage and a happy ending from an escort. I'm just going to order in tonight.

I'm looking through the ads and there's this and there's that and blah, blah, blah—daddy this, Asian boy that—and I hit this one picture, a totally butch dude, rough trade, a man's man. Nothing but a straight-up worked-out guy. I say to myself, You know what, I'm going to call this guy. I finish dinner and I step out and I call him. I say, "Are you available tonight?"

He goes, "Yeah, what time were you thinking?" I say about ten. "Where do you want to meet?"

I tell him I'm staying at the Ramada on Santa Monica.

"I know the place. I'm there a lot. What's your room number?"

I tell him, and he says, "I'll come to your room at ten o'clock."

I ask, "How much?" A hundred and twenty bucks. "Do you take cash only?" He says yes. So I go to the ATM and get some cash out, and continue walking back to the hotel.

Then all of a sudden something I ate is getting to me and I'm about to fall out. What the fuck do I do now? I've ordered this escort, my stomach is totally rocked, there's no way that I can be in decent shape for getting together with this guy. I'm moving as fast as I can to the hotel so I can relieve myself, but I can't possibly have anybody over in this state. Do I call back and cancel? Fuck it. I go to the drugstore and buy some air freshener and Imodium and batten myself down. Around 9:15 the Imodium kicks in and I've got myself back in shape. It's not like we're going to have mad butt sex all night. We're going to blow and go, and that's going to be about it.

I get myself put together in time for my ten o'clock appointment. The guy shows up and is doting and complimentary and does everything he is supposed to do. Fifty-two minutes into it, we're done and he asks, "Can I go wash up in your sink, and it's one hundred and twenty bucks." I was like, Wow, this guy is a pro. I didn't see a clock or a watch anywhere. He had it totally figured out. He didn't even need a time cue. It was a great massage, and the sex was good too. Happy forty-fifth birthday, I'm officially a middle-aged gay man.

CHAPTER 27

Reenter my old friend Micheal Brodbeck, who used to work behind the counter at Factory Café on Christopher Street—the same Micheal who drove me and Kevin to the vet when we put Domino down in 2001. Micheal had left New York for Cincinnati in early 2002, but we'd stayed in touch. While I was on a solo tour in November 2005, Micheal got hold of me and said, "I see you're coming to Louisville, that's only two hours away. I might come to the show." I said, "Sure, come on down, and if you don't want to drive back and want to crash at my room, that's fine." Sure enough we ended up getting involved. I didn't have that in mind when the day started.

Micheal is five foot nine, average build, a very handsome man with welcoming eyes, a great smile, and a comfortable demeanor. We always enjoyed each other's company, but I wasn't ready to settle down. Still, neither of us dismissed it as just a physical encounter, and we kept in touch. We'd reconnected through our friendship, and now we'd added another layer. We talked about the idea of a relationship for many months. I was hesitant—I was on the road so much and lived in DC, and he lived in Cincinnati. I just didn't see how it could work.

As all this was going on, I kept touring solo, going over to Europe in January, then back for a tour of the United States and

Canada in February and March. I was also beginning to curtail my personal craziness. Micheal and I talked regularly on the phone, and one discovery we made was that both of us were attending church. He'd studied a lot of different religions and somehow ended up back at Catholic church as well. In hindsight, the universe may have been lining up around me. Micheal was the catalyst of, and definitely proactive about, our budding relationship.

We met up in late April in Palm Springs to attend the Coachella music festival, along with my best buddy Will and his then boyfriend. The four of us had a great time together. Daft Punk played their first show in years and unveiled their state-of-the art pyramid stage set. It was the best live show I had seen in fifteen years—I was thoroughly floored. For me, Daft Punk are the Beatles of electronica. That's how huge they are.

Micheal and I were becoming closer, and in June, he decided he was moving to DC to further our relationship. After all I'd been through in past relationships, and given how busy I was with work, I felt it necessary to say, "Don't move here for me, don't move here without a job, and don't move here without your own place." He got a job, a place to live, and we kept building our relationship through 2006. I was happy and excited, but also cautious.

And I was finishing an album without even knowing it. After working together for four years without consciously realizing it, Rich and I had a dozen songs finished, and it was pretty clear that we had made an album. The record had a late-night California drive, a convertible-top-down, sticky marijuana vibe. It was a pretty diverse record though, sexy and dark, sad and joyous. Rich could rock and I knew a fair bit about electronica, and the combination of guitars and beats echoed the music we were playing at Blowoff.

The self-titled *Blowoff* album was released in August 2006. We did a number of events on the West Coast, including Homo

A Go Go in Olympia, Washington, and the Folsom Street Fair in San Francisco, where we played in front of thousands of leather folk. One of our weekend handlers was a fellow from a local leather shop. I thought I had run into him before; as it turned out, he was one of the models I used to see at my first gym in Manhattan. I used to think he was unapproachable, and here we were seven years later in San Francisco, and he was chaperoning me around, telling me how much he loves my music. Go figure. For years I'd been wondering whether guys were attracted to me because they thought I was hot or whether it was just because I was in a band. Maybe the answer is both.

* * *

Momentum was building on all fronts. Two weeks later I began recording my next record with drummer Brendan Canty and engineer Frank Marchand. Frank had torn apart his own recording studio in Maryland, driven it down to Brendan's studio in DC, and built it up all over again. We were all excited to get back to recording. We were one day into recording the drums when I got an unexpected call from my sister, Susan: my mother was suffering from heart failure and was in an intensive-care unit in Florida.

As soon as I finished the call with Susan, I told Brendan and Frank what was happening, postponed the session, and headed straight to the airport. I spent a couple of weeks down in Florida with my family, helping to get my mother back on track. If not for my sister's persistence in riding the hospital staff about giving my mother proper care, she would have certainly died. Three weeks and several specialists later, she was finally fitted with a pacemaker and was able to begin a program that would eventually get her back to health.

But in those few weeks, all the old family dynamics surfaced again, especially the friction between my father and sister. Both of them came to me with the same old refrain: I was the only one who could reason with the other. Just like when I was a child back in Malone, I was placed in the role of peacemaker. There was a big difference though: back then I played the role out of panic and pure survival, and now I was operating from a position of sanity and reason. I was grown up and had long been separated from my family of origin, the hold it had on me, and all the turbulence that it created. At forty-five years of age and with a whole lot of other experiences behind me, I could certainly handle this. That was the first big family health scare I'd ever had to deal with, and all things considered, I think I handled myself and the situation well. I'd come a long way.

Mortality stepped in again when Karin Berg passed away in November of 2006. Julie Panebianco called and said, "We're doing this memorial service at St. Mark's Church in the East Village. People are going to speak and perform, and I would like you to do both." Karin had played a big part in both my career and my life, I was very fond and respectful of her, and without hesitation, I agreed to speak and play.

The service was not only a celebration of Karin's life and a testament to how many people she had touched, but a sobering moment of introspection and reflection for me. I took a hard look at my life, my work, and the people I'd encountered along the way. Seeing some of those folks together in one room, with faces that had grown older in the intervening years, suddenly forced a real retrospective look at my life. I wasn't that eighteen-year-old kid fawning over Patti Smith at a Positively 4th Street in-store in Minneapolis, and I wasn't that twenty-four-year-old drunk refusing to climb through Michael Stipe's living-room window in Athens—now the three of us were sitting side by side at St. Mark's Church in New York at a memorial for our friend.

At one point in the service, Julie came to me and said, "Marshall Crenshaw is going to play a song, and then Robert Christgau is going to talk, and then it's your turn."

Not attending my grade school friend's funeral, not being informed by my parents of my grandfather's death until a month after it happened, and not being able to fully mourn the passing of David Savoy, I had little experience dealing with death, and it was painfully obvious. I felt pretty daunted by the prospect of getting up in front of my friends and peers to deliver my thoughts about Karin. All I could do was solemnly approach the podium, say a few words about Karin being such a good person to me, then play a very somber version of "Makes No Sense at All," which was one of Karin's favorite songs.

I did feel a sense of closure about Karin's passing, but at the same time, the whole incident reminded me of how ill equipped I was to deal with these things. Still, it was a start on understanding the vital process of closure when someone or something, like a relationship, comes to an end.

So one night I was pondering mortality, and the next night I was onstage at a Bob Dylan tribute concert at Avery Fisher Hall in Lincoln Center, as part of a fund-raiser organized by Michael Dorf for the Music for Youth Foundation. Talk about ups and downs. I performed Olivia Newton-John's version of Bob Dylan's "If Not for You." Dylan wasn't a huge influence on my songwriting, to be honest, but that was a really nice, important thing in my career. Still, the emotional whiplash was kind of intense.

* * *

In November 2006 Death Cab for Cutie was playing a show in DC. I knew those guys from running into them at various Seattle shows over the years, so I went backstage to say hello to the band and their manager, Jordan Kurland.

Besides managing Death Cab, Jordan was one of the founders of a successful indie rock festival in San Francisco called Noise Pop. Jordan had booked me at Noise Pop in 2000 and 2005, so we also had some history. I asked Jordan if I could pick his brain about record labels, as my next album was almost finished and I was considering a label change. Jordan said, "Of course, call any time." He was a big fan, and I respected his opinions about the business. I called him a few months later, and we hit it off so well that we started working together in early 2007. It was an unexpected move for me. For most of my professional life, I had been a self-managed artist, and the one time I let someone else take the reins, it ended badly. But over the course of the 2000s, I had seen so many changes in the business and thought it might be wise to have someone else on my team. Jordan's first task as my manager was to find a home for my next album.

I didn't notice it clearly at the time, but there was some sort of congregation gathering around me. It's akin to my "hot potato" theory about music: It's like inspiration is a hot potato you pull out of the oven and then toss to someone else. So we listen, we become fans, we become inspired, we create, and somehow the work we create eventually finds its way back to the ones who inspired us.

Over the years I had crossed paths with Kevin Shields from My Bloody Valentine, Frank Black of the Pixies, and Dave Grohl of Foo Fighters—people who were influenced by me, and influenced my work as well. I also think back to the 1996 solo shows supporting Pete Townshend, the shows he played because he was so impressed that I toured with just a car and a bottle of water. I felt like I lived in a tightly knit little universe of inspirations and connections, and it was only a matter of time before we all met.

The hot potato came around again in April 2007 at the Coachella Festival. I ran into my old friend Adam Shore, who spearheaded Vice Records, a label that worked with many of the top new electronic acts. Adam and I were talking when he stopped for a moment and said, "There's someone I want you to meet." He motioned to a fellow with longish hair and a Night Ranger T-shirt, then said, "Bob, meet Thomas Bangalter. Thomas, meet Bob Mould." Thomas is one half of Daft Punk, one of my very favorite bands, but because they always wear helmets in public, I didn't recognize him. I was momentarily startled, and before I could say anything, Thomas leaned in and said, "I listened to *Copper Blue* every day for six months straight." I was completely floored.

A similar thing happened later that year when I played New Hope, Pennsylvania, and was humbled to meet Steve Garvey of the Buzzcocks, who has a studio in town. It was nice to let him know how important the Buzzcocks were to me—fast, short, catchy songs about sexual confusion made a huge impression on me as a fan and as a musician. I reminded him of their great acid-soaked show in Minneapolis in 1980, when Pete Shelley helpfully shouted out the chord changes to me. I was again reminded that I'm simply part of the lineage, part of the continuum: both listener and storyteller, fan and creator.

*   *   *

I spent the rest of spring 2007 finishing the next album, while playing occasional solo shows. By summer the hunt for a new label was complete, and I eventually signed with Anti-, a small but prestigious label that featured artists like Tom Waits, Merle Haggard, and Mose Allison.

With that squared away, I promptly broke my ankle by falling off the four-foot-high landing in my front yard. I had to cancel a couple of shows—very rare for me, but fortunately, I used the downtime well. Joe Fallon of the Modernista! ad agency was a big fan of mine and had been using "See a Little Light" as place holder music in an ad campaign for TIAA-CREF. The client kept hearing the song go by and soon fell in love with it. Only one hitch: due to the debacle in 1990 with my old management signing away my mechanical royalties, if Joe used the original version from *Workbook,* all the money would go to Virgin Records. I had to rerecord the track.

I spent two days faithfully reproducing one of my most meaningful songs, knowing full well that someone would give me grief about selling it to an ad agency. Quite frankly, it was a very good payday, and it was for a company that I had no problem endorsing—they service the creative community. It wasn't

Halliburton. In fact, thanks to TIAA-CREF, I have my own small retirement fund. It worked out very well.

By this time the new album, now titled *District Line,* was complete and waiting for release. As we had done with *Body of Song,* I recorded everything but drums at home, Brendan drummed along to the tracks at a studio, then I mixed the tracks at home. The songs on *District Line* were a good synthesis of the electronic flourishes that started in 2002 with *Modulate,* when I was building songs from loops, grooves, and samples, and the more fully crafted linear pop-rock songs I'd been writing for over twenty years. The emotional content reflected on the summer of 2005 — my second summer of being single — and that feeling of freedom showed in the music.

"The Silence Between Us" took about as long to write as it did to play. It's a transcription of a long walk with a good friend. "Again and Again" is a painting of the end of my relationship with Kevin. I spent months trying to get the right sound and feel for "Who Needs to Dream?" The musical layers were tough to weave, but the words came easily. It's a common refrain: when looking for a partner, do you look for someone to complement you, to complete you, or a combination of the two?

I thought of the epic "Return to Dust" as the centerpiece of the album. The lyrics filled in as soon as the central line came to me: "Growing old, it's hard to be the angry young man." Looking back on it, I see the song reveals itself to be the outline of my entire life up to that point. Cute little tip of the hat to Leonard Cohen's "Hallelujah" in that song too.

My personal favorite is "Shelter Me." It's a dance song — a little out of place on that album. Despite the dark lyrical tone, the bouncy groove always put me in a good mood, so it was my "getting ready to go out with the guys" song. I would play it at full volume in my truck every Thursday night on the way to the Green Lantern, a funky two-story downtown gay bar where "shirtless men drink free."

"Walls in Time" was a song left over from the 1988 *Work-*

book era, and was the perfect closer for *District Line*. Not only was it an old favorite of mine, but it also foreshadowed the direction I was heading, which was even more rooted in my traditional singer-songwriter style. So even with *District Line* freshly in the can, I'd already started on the next group of songs. Summer 2007 was a productive time; it's amazing how much work you can get done when you're cooped up in the house with a broken ankle for six weeks. Like so many of my best creative periods, I took good advantage of some meditative downtime.

In October, when I was back on my feet, I did a solo tour of intimate rooms in select markets to promote the *Circle of Friends* live DVD. Each evening consisted of a forty-five-minute Q&A, a forty-five-minute acoustic set, and a screening of the DVD. Afterward I'd go to the lobby and sell DVDs directly to the fans. On one level it was a nice, low-key tour; on another it was surprisingly eventful.

One of the highlights of the DVD tour happened on my forty-seventh birthday at Herbst Theatre in San Francisco. Michael Azerrad was the interviewer that night, and our public discussion put me into the frame of mind to write this book. It was an energetic exchange, and it rekindled our relationship, which had started with an earlier interview for his book *Our Band Could Be Your Life*. In the weeks following the San Francisco interview, I reconsidered an offer Michael Pietsch from Little, Brown and Company had made to me in 2001 to write my life story. I called Michael Azerrad and said, "Maybe it's time to write the book now." With age, I was beginning to forget the things I wanted to remember, which is quite different from remembering the things I'd rather forget.

* * *

After months of delays and preparation, *District Line* was released in February 2008, on Anti- in North America and Beggars Banquet in Europe, to solidly positive reviews. Brendan put together an electronic press kit, which featured video clips from throughout my career, a current interview with me, and testimonials from various musical luminaries like Stephen Malkmus and Ben Gibbard. Renowned visual artist Shepard Fairey created a poster of my likeness for his ongoing "icon series" — a limited run of five hundred silk-screen prints that I sold at shows. It was nice to have that happen the same year as the 2008 presidential election, which featured Fairey's iconic blue-and-red image of Barack Obama. The head shots for *District Line* were taken by Peter Ross at the Bunker, with me sitting in one of the same orange chairs that I sat in during my 1985 meeting with William Burroughs.

Once again the rock band was ready to hit the road, but there was a last-minute wrinkle. Brendan couldn't tour because he was about to become a dad for the fourth time. We had to find another drummer. Rich Morel suggested a drummer from DC named Rob Black. Rob was familiar with my songbook and also played with Rich. I had seen Rob play with Rich before and thought he was a pretty good drummer. Rehearsals went well, but the live stage is a different beast.

After only two shows, it was clear that things were not going well. Jason was all banged up from throwing himself around onstage, and I was blowing out my voice. We were overplaying to make up for the energy that was missing behind us. And it was killing us. I was getting more upset as the tour went on, and it finally came to a head after the DC show. I gathered the band in the dressing room, closed the door, and let loose on Rob. Then Jason and Rich joined in. For weeks Rob had been listening, but not hearing, the directions we were giving him. Even something as simple as asking my bandmates to join me in wearing black T-shirts onstage—Rob would ask, "Is dark–navy blue OK?"

The next day Jason came to me with an idea. Superchunk's drummer, Jon Wurster, was about to finish up a tour with the Mountain Goats, and maybe we could get him to join us and replace Rob. Actually, Jon was one of the two drummers I'd originally approached for this tour—the other was Sam Fogarino of Interpol. Jason reached out to Jon Wurster. Good thing.

We had a night off in Denver before the show in Boulder. Rob came to me and said he knew we had European dates coming up but that he really wanted to go see Pet Shop Boys or Depeche Mode or somebody like that when they played DC. He said, "Do you think those Europe dates are going to stay confirmed?" He was testing me. I looked at him and said, "You know what, Rob, I think you should go ahead and get those concert tickets."

A couple hours later Jason told me Wurster could start a few days later in San Diego. The following night, before we went onstage in Boulder, we pulled Rob aside in the dressing room and told him we were letting him go and that he would be paid in full. We also asked if we could rent the drum kit he'd bought for the tour. I felt bad about what was happening, but this was business. Rob went home after the Boulder show. Nice guy, but it didn't work out.

Jon Wurster showed up a few days later in San Diego. I had only met him briefly a few times, so I had no idea what kind of disposition I was getting into or how it was going to change things. At 4 PM we head to the venue, the Belly Up Tavern, meeting each other for the first time as bandmates. We got onstage for sound check/rehearsal with not enough time to run the whole set. I said to Jon and the guys, "How about we run the first three songs, then look through the song list? Jon, if you have any questions about beginnings and endings of certain songs, let me know and we'll do them." Jason said, "Jon, I'll monitor you: I'll give you the sword when we're going to finish." I added, "Watch my right foot, that's the cue to finish if we're improv'ing. If I stomp my right foot three times, that's our out." Jon is nodding, making notes on his song list, saying "OK... got it...got it...got it." We're starting the show with the first three songs from *Copper Blue*: "The Act We Act," "A Good

Idea," and "Changes." We all take a deep breath and prepare to start, and Jon asks, "Do you want me to count it off?" I say, "No, I start it with the guitar riff, and I'll do a 'one, two, three, four' on the microphone, and off we go." I was straddle-legged playing the intro riff, and when I get to the end of the eight bars, I walk up to the microphone and shout "one, two, three, four" to mark the eighth and final bar of the intro.

Out of nowhere, the fireworks start coming off the kit. The drum are three times louder than they've been all year. All this heat is coming off of the cymbals. I get to the guitar solo and look around the stage. Wurster is like a kid in a candy store, swinging his drumsticks around. Jason is grinning ear to ear, and Rich is just mesmerized by the whole thing. We get through the first three songs and I'm like, What the hell was that? Every bit of doubt and uncertainty was instantly lifted from the tour. Jon had walked in, sat down on Rob's kit, and changed the tour completely.

We tore through the show in San Diego like a band that had been playing together for years. It was ridiculous how good we were as a band, after only one night. Our spirits had lifted, my voice came back strong, and Jason healed up instantly. I can't emphasize enough how quickly and strongly Jon's presence elevated the tour. No real rehearsal time, yet he nailed the whole set. The five West Coast shows were effortless.

We began a run of ten European dates on May 23. We played sparsely attended shows in Glasgow, Manchester, and Birmingham. In London we performed at Koko, which was formerly Camden Palace—where Hüsker Dü taped the *Live from London* concert in 1985. It was nice to revisit some of the older songs with a new lineup. Three days later we headlined a secondary stage at Primavera Sound Festival in Barcelona, playing a badass forty-five-minute punk rock show.

After the show we were eating dinner, and as usual at festivals, the mess hall was where one runs into all the other musicians: J. Mascis and Lou Barlow of Dinosaur Jr., Roger Miller from Mission of Burma—it was like old home week. This young guy, walking gingerly with a cane, came up to me and said, "You're Bob Mould. I'm Dean Spunt. I play drums in a band called No Age. I screwed up my leg in Germany, but I hobbled down the hill and saw the last half of your set. It was amazing." I knew their music and let him know I was a fan. I met guitarist Randy Randall, and we got to talking about music.

It was great to find young musicians who were into the music scene I was part of in the 1980s. People had told me about No Age, and when I heard the first minute of their song "Miner," I could hear their influences. When I started to learn more about them, that they have their own community-oriented label, it was so reminiscent of what Hüsker Dü had done in Minneapolis. It made me feel good. I did this thing in the '80s, then in the '90s a bunch of people copied certain pieces of it for all the wrong reasons, and now in 2008 there were people who were influenced by not only the music but the mentality and the aesthetic. I guess this was the second wave of legacy, which made me a grandfather. Ouch. It's both good and bad. Either way, I can neither run nor hide from it.

One of the by-products of becoming even busier as a DJ was once again becoming a voracious fan of new music. Blowoff kept getting bigger, and I had to listen to so much music to stay current and fresh. And not just dance music—my opening sets at Blowoff included lots of indie rock. I was on the front end of a lot of happening music. So I knew about No Age. I knew about the Engineers, I knew about Justice. When I met these younger musicians, I was able to speak in a current musical language.

At many music festivals, there's usually a legacy act that shows up and plays the hits but doesn't know anything about current music. Had it not been for Blowoff, I might have become that guy. Again, this is the irony of people being so dismissive in 2002 around *Modulate,* saying things like, "Why is he into dance music?" Well, if it wasn't for that transgression, none of this might have happened: Blowoff, discovering new bands well into my forties, collaborating with great new musicians like No Age.

I couldn't have planned that. In fact, I couldn't have planned any of the great things that happened in the last few years: a wonderful new partner, a killer new band, three albums, a DVD, a book deal. The thing is, I stayed curious and active, something a lot of people don't do later in life, or don't have the luxury of doing because of life obligations—family, health, work. It's led me to some brilliant people, unexpected places, and unbelievable situations. It's been an amazing journey so far.

CHAPTER 28

Micheal and I were now a couple living under one roof, but he was having a tough time with DC. Micheal is a peaceful, spiritual, unconditionally kind, and giving person. But in a type A town like DC, that's not always the best way to be. He had occasional but dramatic bursts of frustration with living in the nation's capital.

In some ways I was right there with him. For one thing, I was starting to get tired of the roasting, unbearably humid Washington summers. Also, I'd recorded three albums in three different parts of the house, and the magic was wearing off. The last straw was when a local developer bought one of the adjacent row houses and turned it into condominiums, throwing my once-sunny back deck into shade. I had cooked 90 percent of our meals and entertained many friends on that back deck. The meals stopped shortly after the building was complete. So even though I'd renovated the entire house, I felt like I needed another big change of scenery. It was time to move on. But where to go?

In September 2008 Rich Morel and I held our first Blowoff at Slim's in San Francisco. During that week-long trip, I was calling Micheal and raving about how great a town it was, all the things to do and see, and all these guys I was meeting from back in the punk rock days. I could tell Micheal was a little upset that he wasn't with me on that trip, but he was happy for me. When I got home, we started talking about a possible move to San Francisco. Both Jordan Kurland and Frank Riley were based in the Bay Area, so my professional network was there. And now, through Blowoff, I was building a personal network. In my mind I gave myself eighteen months to make the move. This was also five weeks before the 2008 presidential election. Part of me was afraid that the Republicans were going to win again, and of how unbearable the town would be if they did.

Election night, I was sitting in my den with Micheal and a couple of friends. We were watching CNN, and at 10 PM Eastern time, the California polls closed. The projection came in that Obama was going to win California and would therefore win the entire election. We heard this dull roar outside. We looked out and people were coming out of their houses, gathering in the streets, and carrying on. I hit the record button on the DVR and joined the massive celebration. U Street is the middle of everything in DC—the African-American community, the gay community, the liberal community. The street shut down for the whole night as people just went nuts. It seemed like change was upon us.

When the new people arrived by January, all of a sudden there were fewer SUVs and more fixed-gear bikes, younger people wearing fashionable clothes, and professional guys with beards. The race and class tensions that were always bubbling under DC began to recede. But it wasn't something I'd be sticking around to witness. I'd already made up my mind to leave.

* * *

In August 2008 I finished writing and recording my most recent album, which I titled *Life and Times,* just before I announced I'd be writing this book. I'd written the title track in July 2007, months before I decided to write my autobiography—yet another case of "write it and it shall be so." Besides, it was one of my strongest, most emotional album openers ever, right up there with "Circles" and "New #1."

The title track came about when I was sorting through boxes, mostly of work-related memorabilia, that had sat unopened in the corner of my Tribeca studio space since 1998. After I opened the first box, a haunting and familiar smell rose from the press clippings. I called Micheal into the room and had him take a whiff. We looked at each other in sadness—he had been witness to the collapse of the towers on 9/11.

What the fuck, what kicked up all this dust?
You're taking me back to the places I left behind
The old—the old life and times.

Sad and delicate, "The Breach" chronicles the end of a relationship. The early voice in the song speaks very quietly and simply about the reason: there was a leak, it got worse, and nobody fixed it. That was a familiar refrain in my life. The song builds, and when it gets to the bridge—when the electric guitar comes in and the second voice comes in—that's the other person yelling. That person is angry and upset, and then it tempers back down to the very end where there are two voices side by side, both very quiet, as if they've come together in peace to say good-bye. It came from a familiar place, where the details are cloudy during the event but the hindsight is 20/20.

"City Lights" and "MM 17" are transitory songs—songs about journeys and moving somewhere new, songs of moving forward, songs of motion and farewell. "Argos" is named after the oldest leather bar in Amsterdam, and the song is about anonymous dark-room sex. "Bad Blood Better" is a lyrical reprise of "Lost Zoloft" from *Modulate,* another look at same-sex spousal abuse. "Wasted World" is about spending way too much time on the computer obsessing over the darker parts of life. "Spiraling Down" takes it even lower, and then the last two songs try to find some sort of beauty and redemption, try to lift the listener out of the emotional hole.

"I'm Sorry, Baby, But You Can't Stand in My Light Any

More" was all-out '70s AM gold. The song begins with the signature chorus—sparse acoustic guitar and voice. The verses sound more like bridges: leaning forward with a couple of minor chord elevations as I'm telling and advancing the story. Then, forty-four seconds into the song, the last line of the second verse has this very subtle chord substitution where it barely glances across a major chord, so you're reminded of where it started. It's a magical little touch that makes the hair on my backside go up—every time. To me, that song is up there with "If I Can't Change Your Mind" and "See a Little Light."

"Lifetime" is built upon warbled synthesizers that evoke *Beaster* and *Copper Blue*. The reference to the smell of overheated vacuum tubes ("the scent of burning dust") and the outright mention of religion are very personal references, going back to my earliest childhood memories. It's the last song, and it wraps around to the top of the album—dust to dust. *Life and Times* is very poetic, a complete story, a long journey. I think it's the strongest record I've written in many years.

* * *

That March I played a couple of momentous shows. The first was during Noise Pop in San Francisco, when I sat in for two songs with No Age at the Bottom of the Hill club, joining them for an encore of "New Day Rising" and their song "Miner." The crowd response was great, and the three of us left the door open for future collaborations. On one level, I was just sitting in on a punk rock gig. But on another, something really important had happened: it was clear that my music was going to last. Dean and Randy from No Age were still in diapers when *Zen Arcade* came out. They were two musical generations removed, but they loved my work. To me, that's a big deal.

Ten days later I was standing center stage at Carnegie Hall for the first time, as part of another benefit for Music for Youth. All those years of practice paid off, I guess. This time the songbook was REM, and I played "Sitting Still" with the cracker-jack house band. Much like Karin Berg's memorial service, this was an emotional gathering of peers and friends from the past three decades of my life. When Kevin and I split, I conceded my friendships with esteemed singer-songwriters Kristin Hersh and Vic Chesnutt, but backstage before the show, the three of us talked for fifteen minutes and caught up a little bit. My performance was quite good; somehow, in my mind, I made up for my spotty performance at the Royal Albert Hall in 1994. The night belonged to Vic though; his version of "Everybody Hurts" was stunningly raw and beautiful, and it is the memory I keep of Vic.

Life and Times, my second album for Anti-, came out on April 7, 2009, which roughly coincided with my thirtieth anniversary of performing onstage—the first Hüsker Dü show was at Ron's Randolph Inn in St. Paul on March 30, 1979. It was a significant moment, but also mundane in the sense that I was just on the road: As a way to get the album up and running, I was doing a series of acoustic dates. The next three days were filled with collisions, intersections, and reminders.

I had a bit of a health scare, and it fortunately didn't amount to much. And yet everything around it said so much about my life thus far, the way things and people keep recurring, giving shape, substance, and serendipity to my life. Monday, March 30, I'm in Chicago, which is where I've done my best business ever since I started performing. Having played a sold-out show the night before at Old Town School of Folk Music, I showered, ate breakfast, and took a taxi to WXRT, a radio station that has supported me for twenty years. I spoke with station head Norm Winer, then interviewed and played two songs on air. I headed to O'Hare, flew to Minneapolis, my city of musical birth, and picked up my rental car; the radio was tuned to a station playing a progressive house remix of "Tainted Love"—something I never would have listened to in the old days. I had a bad case of cellulitis on my chest, so I called my DC doctor to make an appointment for April 1. I checked into my hotel, then headed to sound check with bassist Jason Narducy, who'd been playing with me since 2005; I'd known Jason since 1990.

It was my thirtieth anniversary show, and the crowd at the Varsity Theater in Minneapolis was very appreciative. The stage manager said he was at the very first Hüsker Dü show at Randolph Inn. There were moments, especially during "Brasilia Crossed with Trenton," when I could almost feel myself back on the farm in Pine City. At one point I was staring at the large disco ball on the ceiling, thinking, This would be a great room for Blowoff. Everything was coming together. During the encore, I said something to the effect of "If I made it this far, they can't get rid of me now." After the show, I signed lots of CDs, posed for pictures with fans, and went to dinner with friends.

Here's the glamorous part: at 3 AM, I went to Hennepin County Medical ER and spent three hours getting pus drained from the infection in my chest. It was funny; after all these years, they still had my old Minneapolis address on file. A brutish yet sexy male assistant was rubbing a sonogram wand over my nipples, which aroused me. The residing doctor had tickets for my show, but wasn't able to attend. Had I waited any longer, the infection would have made it to my lymphatic system, and I could have died. Then they stuffed a wick in the wound, drew a purple circle fifteen centimeters in diameter around the infection site, and gave me Vicodin and antibiotics.

On three hours' rest, I made that familiar drive across the bridge to St. Paul to perform on the radio for my friend Mary Lucia at KCMP the Current, then teach a master's class at McNally Smith College of Music, which is my former mentor Chris Osgood's music academy. Then an acquaintance invited me to dinner at a sushi restaurant that happened to be right across the street from the former Hüsker Dü office/recording studio at Twenty-Sixth and Nicollet.

I flew home to DC the next morning and went to see my

regular doctor. He thought there might still be some gauze stuck in my chest, so he sent me to Sibley Hospital to get cut open once again. They found nothing.

These events back in the Midwest—some were intentional, some accidental, and many were ironic—I realized were all part of a vast constellation of connections I'd built over the course of thirty years. As life goes on, I'm much more aware of how all my experiences have contributed to who I am and what I do, and how those connections lead me from one place to the next.

*   *   *

Emotionally, I had begun to leave DC, but I hadn't yet moved to San Francisco so I was floating in a netherworld. I was winding down my DC life, dealing with the sadness that comes with moving on, and yet trying not to put off my DC friends with my enthusiasm about San Francisco. On top of these feelings of dislocation and transition, I was traveling all over the country for Blowoff gigs.

Much like the old connections I'd made in all the cities I'd lived in and toured through for so many years, Blowoff events helped me continue to build a network of new friends around the country. The difference was, instead of sleeping on floors and stealing food, we were the toast of many towns. The Blowoff shows were a total blast. We were the main event of several major gatherings: International Mr. Leather/Bear Pride weekend in Chicago, Capital Pride in DC, Heritage of Pride in New York, and a phenomenal July evening in Provincetown as part of Bear Week. These are the gay community's equivalent of the biggest rock festivals—and even more fun.

Then it was time. I put the DC house on the market in July and soon began renting a bedroom in Noe Valley, a quiet neighborhood just south of the Castro in San Francisco. And in September I once again hit the road with Blowoff, with a rock tour just around the corner.

* * *

In September 2009 I played a full set with No Age at the All Tomorrow's Parties festival in Monticello, New York. We alternated between Hüsker Dü songs and their punkier material; Bradford Cox from Deerhunter came up and sang the Heartbreakers' "Chinese Rocks" with us for the encore. Revisiting my old songs with these guys was a great time, and the set was very well received. Later that evening I found myself DJing a crazy five-hour house party for music website Pitchfork, complete with drunk gals on chairs behind me waving their bras in the air as indie rock musicians wandered into the spectacle with looks of disbelief at seeing me DJ this throw-down. Not only was it great fun, but when Pitchfork kingpin Ryan Schreiber gave my playlist an enthusiastic two thumbs-up, it once again validated the point that, way back in 2001, I'd been on to something with the melding of electronica and indie rock.

A few days after ATP, an anxious buyer for the DC house appeared, wanting to close in three weeks, which was way sooner than I anticipated. So in the last three weeks of September, I did four Blowoff parties across the states, a press tour, and Micheal and I packed a four-story house into storage. The sale was final on October 2, but the madness wasn't over. Two days later I flew to Toronto, and after one day of rehearsal, the band and I started a North American tour.

Rich Morel wasn't available, so Jason Narducy, Jon Wurster, and I toured as a three-piece. The shows went great. Attendance was a bit down, but I think that was indicative of all touring business in the fall of 2009. I'd turned in a great record and had a great band, so I'd done my part of the job.

The tour was a whirlwind, covering most of North America in fifteen days. Because of the quick sale of the house, I barely had time to say good-bye to all my friends in DC, the town where I'd learned so much about myself, and also where I'd found my new gang.

The 9:30 Club show on October 10 was my impromptu farewell. During the set I conjured up a few minutes' worth of words to the audience. Later that night, while hosting a packed edition of Blowoff in the same room, I was able to personalize those words to my closest friends while on the dance floor.

After a few more days of good-byes, Micheal and I flew to Seattle to meet up with Jason and Jon. Now that we were on the West Coast—the home stretch—I thought I could relax and let my hair down a little, but real life caused yet another wrinkle in my best-laid plans. October 16, my forty-ninth birthday, we were driving southbound on I-5 just outside Olympia, Washington, when Jason's cell phone rang. It was his wife, Emily: her water had broken and she was about to give birth two weeks early. That night, in Portland, Oregon, we opened for our support act Spiral Stairs so Jason could go right from the stage to an overnight nonstop flight to Chicago. He made it home one hour before his wife gave birth to a beautiful bouncing girl named Eva. One crisis averted.

Next crisis: I still had three more shows in California. Former Posies guitarist Jon Auer was playing bass for Spiral Stairs. Jon was very familiar with my songbook, and he rehearsed for two days with his laptop and bass, then stepped in for the final two shows in Los Angeles and San Diego. Given the circumstances, he did a great job.

But before those two gigs, there was my first "hometown show" as a San Franciscan. I reached out to Sugar bassist David Barbe, and he flew into town the morning of the show. I picked David and Jon up at their hotel, and the second David put his bass in the car before we drove across the bridge to Treasure Island, it was like old times. I always knew David was accountable. He's always on it. David is a worker like me.

We ran through the set on unplugged electric guitars in our windy outdoor dressing room tent, then hit the stage and tore through half a set of Sugar songs followed by half a set of Hüsker Dü songs. It was nice to look over and see David having a good time, and it was also great to look back at Jon with that big grin on his face. It seemed natural. It sounded great. It felt right.

*   *   *

I'd had all this anger and inner conflict when I was younger. I used music to express it, but the irony was that touring the world in a rock band, cooped up with three other guys in a van, was also keeping me from both growing up and coming out. Now, with Blowoff as a featured attraction at several premier gay events and three albums that put my solo career back in the spotlight, music was helping me heal the wounds and grow as a human being.

Back when I was watching fistfights around the pool table at the Calgarian Hotel in 1981, there is no way I would have believed you if you had said that thirty years later, I would be DJing house music to a room full of dancing leathermen and bears at Chicago's Cabaret Metro—a room I'd played dozens of times since 1984, thanks to the unrelenting support of the club's mastermind, Joe Shanahan.

As Blowoff got bigger, more guys were coming up to me saying, "You're *the* Bob Mould." They were sharing their stories about being gay, being in their forties, and having seen Hüsker Dü at the old 9:30 Club. Turns out there were more gay people in the underground scene in the 1980s than I ever realized— that "don't advertise, don't worry" thing worked a little too well, I guess. It's been great to reconnect with some of the guys who used to slam dance in the mosh pit while I was up there onstage, feeling lost and alone in my self-hatred, agitating them with my music. Now, years later at Blowoff, I'm up there playing music for the guys, music that makes us all dance and feel happy and together. And they come up to me and say, "I was there then, and I'm here now."

Not all the guys in the crowd are leathermen or bears or ex-punkers—there's disco heads and industrial fans and regular folks as well. But as lost as I felt for so many years, it's interesting that so many of us followed the same path: being part of the indie music community and years later finding ourselves reconnected through a very different type of music, as well as through our shared gay identities. Maybe the other guys were always connected, and it just took me way too long to wake up and find my place.

I'm sure some of the guys faded away from punk rock and then embraced the gay community as they grew older. I'm sure some of the guys went through crystal meth problems—it was certainly around in the punk rock days. And I'm sure some of the guys became HIV-positive and maybe didn't make it to middle age. So for those of us who are still here, going out to see live music, going to the bear bar on Sunday afternoon for happy hour, congregating and having a community experience at this stage of our lives—it's unbelievable. People think Blowoff is funny—ha-ha, Bob is DJing with his shirt off, how silly. They have no idea how much it means to me. We give them a place to belong, and in return, they've given me a place too.

My old tribe is not only reunited, but we're out and integrated. We survived the catastrophe of the first wave of AIDS, the Reagan years, the Moral Majority, Anita Bryant, and everything else we had to deal with—alone, together, or in whatever variation. It's a great joy to be playing music for the guys, looking out and seeing everybody grinning and dancing and having a good time. And again, thirty years later, there's not one fucking thing anyone can do to stop us. We are back together and we are having the time of our lives.

* * *

I was born into a house of chaos and loss. My parents grieved the death of their first child and acted out through alcoholism, domestic violence, passive-aggression, and psychological abuse. And yet I was overprotected as a child, sexual abuse by a babysitter notwithstanding. I found music as the way to drown out the chaos. I realized I was gay, planned my escape from my small-town life, and went to the big city for college.

I was a young self-hating alcoholic at seventeen, miserable

and agitated at the world. I sobered up at twenty-five, fearful of both becoming my father and of dying young. I came out publicly and professionally at thirty-three, yet remained awkward and unable to fully erase the self-hatred. I felt insecure in my relationships.

In my musical life as well as my personal life, I had locked myself into very limited worlds. For so long I was the rock guy, never venturing far from my formula. Throughout two long-term relationships, I never explored the outside world. I was unhappy and blocked, and I didn't know why. I endured my lowest professional point in 2002, then watched a fourteen-year relationship fall apart in 2003. I had to break free and find myself.

I shook my career, then my partner. It was only when I'd cleared everything away and was left with just myself and what I had to offer that my true transformation happened. That was when I began to find out who I was and where I was supposed to be.

I spent two years rebuilding and reinventing myself. I gradually got out of my handcuffs and learned how to celebrate my freedom. I fell into the bear community, a wonderful group of gay men who embrace their masculinity, where I feel totally at ease. I began making rock music again, while holding on to the club music that was the soundtrack of my transformation.

Now that I've integrated who I am and what I do, I finally feel whole. Now I'm much better at both music and relationships. Most importantly, I'm finally able to enjoy life.

After years with little money for food and no permanent address, I am blessed to be living in a home that looks out across the city of my dreams. After years filled with unpredictable experiences, I'm happy and grateful to have lasted thirty years at the job I love. And after two failed relationships, I've been with Micheal for five years, building a healthy and happy bond. I'm trying as best I can to carry the good lessons along with me.

If you had asked me at twenty-one if I would make it to fifty,

I would have scoffed at you, made some painfully existential comment, and headed off to my next self-destructive adventure. But as I write this, I look at myself and am pretty content with what I see. Restless, always. Happy, mostly. Satisfied, occasionally. But the cathartic thing? Those days have come and gone.

Finally, I am able to enjoy life as it happens.

My first fifty years were pretty incredible. From here on out, life might get even better.

Acknowledgments

There's a number of people I'd like to thank — for many different reasons. First, to my partner of five years, Micheal Brodbeck. You'll recognize Micheal by his oddly spelled name, the result of a birth certificate mishap. Micheal has always been a saint in my life, but never more vigilant than over the past three years. He gave me comfort when I was troubled, he showed me the ladder when I was low, and he saw through my foolish mind games and kept me in check. I am amazed that our relationship survived this book. I am eternally grateful to have him in my life.

Michael Azerrad has had an enormous influence on this book. He helped me sort through all the different phases of my life, the contradictions and uncertain memories, and forced me to examine and distill it all into a readable manuscript. In essence, he taught me how to write this book. We battled at times, but I'm pleased with the end result, and really proud of the work we did together.

I would have done a terrible job of chronicling the events without the resources of Paul Hilcoff. Paul has been a longtime archivist of my work, and his meticulous attention to history gave me an invaluable database, which I used to corroborate, organize, and collate my professional life. (Paul's work can be found at www.thirdav.com.)

Michael Pietsch approached me in 2001 about writing this book. At that time, I wasn't anywhere near ready to confront my past. Fortunately, when late 2007 rolled around and I found the maturity and resolve to give voice to my experiences, Michael was still very interested in publishing this book. I am thrilled to be a writer at such a prestigious publishing house as Little, Brown.

As my literary agent, David Dunton has done an admirable job both of helping me navigate through the logistics and mechanics of assembling this book and of keeping me centered and motivated through those moments when the weight of reconciling my story caused me great personal sway. John Parsley's light yet focused editorial touch defied and shattered the frightening expectations I (and other authors) had concocted and congealed in my mind, and Ben Allen's fine eye for detail worked wonders in the copyedit stage.

I'd like to thank three professional colleagues who have stood by me for decades: attorney Josh Grier and booking agents Frank Riley and Paul Boswell. Their steady efforts kept me working, which in turn made many of these stories possible.

Beyond the musicians mentioned throughout the book, I've been fortunate to be surrounded and supported by many fine crew guys who ran the roads with me, did the heavy lifting for me, and kept the show in professional form: Terry Katzman, Robin Davies, Lou Giordano, Bill Batson, Zop, Mick Brown, Josiah McIlheny, John Henderson, Casey MacPherson, Mitchell Drosin, Andrew Burns, Bill Rahmy, Barry Duryea, Dewitt Burton, Randy Hawkins, Charles Scott, Colm O'Reilly, Gary Andrews, Dave Domizi, Menko Leeuw, Erik Drost, Frank Marchand, and Tim Mech.

There were periods during the writing process when I needed to get away from my normal surroundings. Three of those times, Andy Mitchell, Dan McBride, and Andy Samwick were gracious in allowing me to set up writing camp in their respective homes.

Thanks to my family of origin: my father, Willis; my mother, Sheila; and my siblings, Susan and Brian. My parents have always been supportive of me and my work, and I love them dearly.

Thanks to my family of choice, many of whom currently reside in, and make me feel abundantly welcome in, my new hometown of San Francisco. Through them, around them, and with them, I continue to learn how to recognize, accept, and embrace my flaws without the worry of judgment.

Finally, thanks to those of you who've stayed with me for thirty-plus years of music—through all the twists and turns, the experimentation and repetition, the successes and failures. The nights you spend with me, the stories you share of your first exposure to my work, the meaning it holds for you in troubled times—I am always humbled and honored to be a small part of your lives.

INDEX

A&A Records (Montreal), 23
A&M Records, 102, 160
Abbo (of Big Cat Records), 186
"ABC-Easytime Music," 8
About to Choke (Chesnutt album), 250
Academy Theater (New York), 235, 247
Ackerman Ballroom (UCLA), 102, 109
"Act We Act, The" (song), 369
Aerosmith (band), 17, 19, 21, 76
"Again and Again" (song), 366
Agnello, Sharon, 347
Ahl, Dave, 23, 118
AIDS, 56–57, 78, 107, 200, 273, 383; AIDS
    Treatment Project benefit, 147; AIDS Walk
    (Los Angeles), 356
Albini, Steve, 72, 83
Album of the Year (*NME*), 203, 208
Allison, Mose, 365
All-Star Wrestling (TV program), 280
All Tomorrow's Parties festival (Monticello,
    NY), 380
Almaas, Steve, 23
Altamont concert, 33
Alternative Press magazine, 313
Alternative Tentacles label, 61
"Always Tomorrow" (song), 341
American Express, 253
American Wrestling Association, 281
amplifiers. *See* sound equipment
"Amusement" (song), 44
"Anarchy in the UK" (song), 20
Anderson, Laurie, 147
Angel Orensanz Center (New York), 264–65
Anti- label, 365, 367, 377
Anti-Violence Project, 275, 319
Apollo Theater (Harlem), 128
"Argos" (song), 375
Arias, Joey, 273
"Armenia City in the Sky" (song), 191
Arnold, Tom, 74
Around the World in 80 Days (movie), 6

Articles of Faith (band), 72, 105
Athens sessions (2002), 316, 340, 347
Atkins, Chet, 162
Atlantic Records, 159
Auer, Jon, 381
Austin City Limits outdoor festival, 354
Avalanches (band), 272
Aycroff, Jeff, 160
Ayers, Dave, 158, 250
Azerrad, Michael, 367

B-52s (band), 109, 170
Babes in Toyland (band), 123
Backbar, 323. *See also* 9:30 Club
BAD (band), 128
"Bad Blood Better" (song), 375
Bad Brains (band), 48–49, 56
Baker, Ginger, 159
Baker, Steven, 116
Bakker, Jim and Tammy, 198
Bale, Jeff, 113
Bangaltar, Thomas, 364–65
Bangor, Larry, 153
Barbe, Amy, 229, 230
Barbe, David, 188, 190–92, 196–97, 204–5,
    215–18, 228–31, 381; foreign tour, 210–11,
    213; studio sessions, 316, 340, 347
Barbero, Lori, 123
Bar d'O lounge (Manhattan), 273
Barefoot & Pregnant (compilation album), 105
Barlow, Lou, 370
Barnett, Jim, 282–83
Barracuda (New York bar), 274–75, 301, 319
Bates, Rick, 142, 163
Batman (TV series), 194
Bators, Stiv, 17
Batson, Bill, 133, 145, 148, 160, 169
Battalion of Saints (band), 63, 65
Bay City Rollers (band), 16
BBC radio, 198
Beach Boys, the (band), 7, 200

bear culture, 333–34, 337, 356, 383, 384; Bear Week event (Provincetown), 379
Bear magazine, 334
Bearsville Studios (Woodstock), 301, 303
Beaster (Mould album), 203–5, 212–16, 219, 226, 299, 376
"Beating Heart the Prize" (song), 341
Beatles, the (band), 7, 8, 33, 103, 188, 360; *Sgt. Pepper* album, 83, 241
Beat movement, 106, 140
"Beautiful Stranger" (song), 299
Beck, Jeff, 76
Becker, Alan, 313
Becker, Howard, 45
"Bed of Nails" (song), 127
Bee Gees, the (band), 87
Beggars Banquet label (Europe), 367
Being Out Rocks (compilation CD), 319
"Believe" (song), 299
"Believe What You're Saying" (song), 219, 227
Belly Up Tavern (San Diego), 369
Belushi, John, 25
Benatar, Pat, 68, 275
Benny's (Virginia rock joint), 75
Benoit, Chris, 284, 292, 294–97
Benoit, Nancy and Daniel, 292, 296
Benson, George, 136
Berg, Karin, 102, 109–12, 116, 118, 126–30, 133, 140, 157; memorial concert, 362–63, 377
Bernhard, Sandra, 270, 341
Berry, Chuck, 120–21
Bessette, Steve and Chris, 16
Biafra, Jello, 51–53, 61, 63, 140
Big Audio Dynamite (band), 128
Big Blue (Chicago punk house), 72
Big Boys (band), 65
Big Cat Records (UK), 186
"Biggest Lie, The" (song), 90
Billboard magazine, 313
Binion's Horseshoe (Vegas club), 201
Birchmere Music Hall (Alexandria, VA), 328
Biscuit (singer with Big Boys), 65
Black, Frank, *see* Black Francis
Black, Rob, 368–69, 370
Blackberry Way Studios, 44, 61
Black Crowes, the (band), 211
Black Flag (band), 45–46, 51–52, 58, 60, 63–66, 95, 105–6
Black Francis (Charles Thompson IV, aka Frank Black), 172, 364
Black Party (Fire Island), 277
Black Sheets of Rain (Mould album), 173–77, 182, 185, 193, 200
Bley, Carla, 160–61
Blindspot Studios, 352
"Blitzkrieg Bop" (song), 20
Blogjam (DC event), 346
Blondie (band), 32
Blowoff (dance parties), 322–25, 333, 350–51, 356, 371–74, 378–83
Blowoff (Mould album), 360

Blue Jay Studio (Carlisle, MA), 161
Blue Note (Columbia, MO, club), 200
Blue Öyster Cult (band), 76
Blue Velvet (film), 165
"Blue Wind" (song), 76
Boblog: A Quiet and Uninteresting Life (blog), 334–35
Bob Mould (Mould "Hubcap"album), 247, 253, 259–60
Bob Mould Band, version one, 177
Body of Song (Mould album), 300, 310, 316, 340–41, 347, 351–52, 366
Bondi, Vic, 72
Bongos, the (band), 74
Bonham, John, 159
Bono (performer), 211
Boon, D., 64, 101
Boo Radleys, the (band), 200
"Born to Run" (song), 124
Boston (band), 19
Boswell, Paul, 106, 182, 184
Bottom of the Hill club (San Francisco), 376
Boutis, Kle, 199
Bowie, David, 40, 187, 253
Boyce, Tommy, 7
Boyer, Steve, 174–75
Boy George (performer), 173
"Brasilia Crossed with Trenton" (song), 155, 159, 161, 200, 378
"Breach, The" (song), 375
Brian (Rebel Rebel employee), 299
"Bricklayer" (song), 59
Britpop, 22, 204
Brodbeck, Micheal, viii–ix, 303, 307, 346, 359–60, 373–75, 380–81, 384
"Broken Home, Broken Heart" (song), 89
Bronan's Music (Potsdam, NY), 22
Brown, Bobby, 214
Brown, Dennis, 51
Brown, Mick, 138
Browne, David, 163
Brownie's (Village rock club), 264–65, 309
Browning, Tom, 16
Bruce, John, 170, 189, 197–98, 219–20
Buck, Peter, 170, 171, 198
Buckley, Jeff, 186
Buddha (San Francisco nightclub), 54
Buddy and the Returnables (band), 30–31
Bug Music (publishers), 325
Burnham, Hugo, 39
Burnstein, Cliff, 130
Burn to Shine (DVD series), 329
Burroughs, William, 36, 106–8, 140, 147, 159, 201, 262; at the Bunker, 107, 368
Burton, David, 201
Burton, Dewitt, 201, 210, 212
Busch, Bill, 283, 284–85, 293, 295
Bush, George W., 350
Butcher, Belinda, 187
Butler, Brandon, 341
Butler, Richard, 247

Butthole Surfers (band), 207
Buzzcocks, the (band), 39, 57, 365
Byrds, the (band), 82, 87, 200

Cabaret Metro (Chicago rock club), 382
Cabaret Voltaire (band), 33, 107
Cafeteria and Caffe Torino (Village restaurants), 299
Cale, John, 59–60
Camden Palace (London venue), 106, 370
Cameron, Keith, 198, 199
Camper Van Beethoven (band), 122
Canadian bands. See punk rock
Canadian tours, 49–51, 62, 360, 382
Candy Apple Grey (Hüsker Dü album), 116–17, 118, 121, 226
Cannibal Club (Austin, TX), 182
Canty, Brendan, 329, 341, 347, 351–55, 361, 366–68
Capital Pride event (DC), 379
Capitol Records, 7, 250
Carducci, Joe, 63–64
Carlos, Bun E., 188
Carlson, Angie, 351
Carlton, Bob, 227
Carnegie Hall concert, 376
Carnival of Light and Sound (COLAS), 311, 316, 318–19, 352
Carr, Tim, 33
Carriage House recording studio, 196, 238, 263
Carroll, Jim, 140
Carter, Jimmy, 38
Cash, Rosanne, 165
Catania, David, 341
Catholic Church, 3, 11, 193, 254, 348–50, 360
Catholic Youth Organization, 14
Caulfield, Father, 348–49
Cavanaugh, Dave, 199
Cayne, Candis, 275
CBGB (New York club), 73
C C Club (Minneapolis), 123, 124
Cedar Creek Recording studio, 214, 217–18, 238, 261
"Celebrated Summer" (song), 97, 141, 236
Cerveris, Michael, 236, 255, 264–66, 311
Cesstone Music label, 95
Chad (club manager), 323
"Changes" (song), 198, 203, 370
"Charity, Chastity, Prudence, and Hope" (song), 125
Charlie Rose show, 268
"Chartered Trips" (song), 89, 353
Cheapo Records (St. Paul), 26
Cheap Trick (band), 22–23, 188, 200
Cheater (band), 300
Cher (performer), 275, 299
Chesley, Alison, 246, 263
Chesnutt, Vic, 182–83, 238, 250, 264, 377
Children's Crusade '81, 47, 56
Chilton, Alex, 165
"Chinese Rocks" (song), 380

Christgau, Robert, 102, 362
Christmas (band), 135
Christmas Money Tour, 143
CH3 (band), 65
Church, the (East St. Paul club), 82, 120
Cincinnati Reds, 16
Circle Jerks (band), 52, 65
Circle of Friends (DVD), 355, 367
"Circles" (song), 341, 374
City Gardens (Trenton, NJ, club), 74
"City Lights" (song), 375
City Pages (Minneapolis–St. Paul weekly), 82
Clark, Linda, 141–42, 151, 153–54, 159, 163, 180–81, 185, 209
Clark, Petula, 153
Clash, the (band), 26, 39, 128
"Classifieds" (song), 262
Club COD (Chicago), 45
CMJ (College Music Journal), 109
CNN (Cable News Network), 216, 308, 374
Coachella music festival, vii–viii, x, 360, 364
Cobain, Kurt, 158, 216, 240
Coffey, King, 65, 67, 207–8
Cohen, Leonard, viii, 366
Coleman, Ornette, 28
college rock, 74–75, 104, 109
Columbia House record club, 22
Comedy Central network, 252
"Company Book" (song), 218
"Compositions for the Young and Old" (song), 153
Conflict (fanzine), 74
Conley, Clint, 42
Cook, Richard, 106
Cooking Vinyl label, 311
Cooper, Dennis, 221–23, 247
Copper Blue (Mould album), 199, 208, 215–16, 219, 365, 376; songs, 200, 352, 369–70
Corbin, Steve "Mugger," 63
Cornell, Joseph, 162
Corrigan, Daniel, 128
Corrosion of Conformity (band), 182
Cortese, Rich, 154
Cosloy, Gerard, 74
Costello, Elvis, 138
"Could You Be the One?" (song), 127, 131, 135–36
Covington, Michael Allen "Mike," 76–78, 81–82, 88, 96, 101, 118, 124–26, 131, 157, 171, 332; at farm, 143–44, 152, 153–54; split with, 138–39, 141, 146, 166–68, 173, 206, 233–35; on travels abroad, 176, 229; and Workbook cover, 162, 193
Cox, Bradford, 380
Cox, Stephen, 346
Crash, Darby, 52
Cray, Robert, 139
Creation Records, 185–87, 199–201, 215, 219, 228, 230, 240, 264, 266; 10th anniversary, 226
Crenshaw, Marshall, 362

Crocus Behemoth (performer), 17
Crosby, Bing, 253
Crow, Sheryl, 161
"Crush on You" (song), 119
"Crystal" (song), 116
Crystal Pistol (Tulsa club), 67
Cubby Bear Lounge (Chicago), 72
Cudahy, Michael, 135
Cumbre, La (San Francisco taqueria), 52–53
Cure, the (band), 32, 210
Curtis, Ian, 42
Curtiss A (performer), 32, 44

Dachau concentration camp, 176, 229
Daft Punk (band), 213, 312, 360, 364
Daily Show, The (TV program), 74, 252–53
Daniel, Ivan, 125, 138, 146, 148
David (owner of Rebel Rebel), 299, 317
Davies, Robin, 62–63, 65
Day, Morris, 105
"Days of Rain" (song), 341
dB's, the (band), 74, 164
DC3 (band), 111
Dead Kennedys (band), 48, 51, 55, 59
Deal, Kim, 172, 200
Death Cab for Cutie (band), 363
"Debaser" (song), 200
Decline of Western Civilization, The (punk
    documentary), 52
Deep Dish (band), 321
Deerhunter (band), 380
Def Jam label, 75
DeGeneres, Betty and Ellen, 319
"Demonstration Tape" (Mould demo), 153
Denesha, Jim, 21
De Palma, Brian, 212
Depeche Mode (band), 122, 369
Descendents, the (band), 65–66
Destroyer (Kiss album), 16
Devo (band), 33
Diamanda Galás (performer), 107
Diamond, A, Hidden in the Mouth of a Corpse
    (compilation album), 107
"Diane" (song), 80
Dicker, Glenn, 347
Dickies, the (band), 57
Dicks, the (band), 64
Dictators, the (band), 26
DIK Bar (DC), 333–34
Dillon, J. J., 283, 290, 293, 296
Dinosaur Jr. (band), 183–84, 370
Diodes (Canadian band), 23
Dirksen, Dirk "Pope of Punk," 53
Discharge (band), 42, 60
District Line (Mould album), 366–68
"Divide and Conquer" (song), 100, 103
DNA (band), 42
D.O.A. (Vancouver band), 48, 51, 55, 65–66
"Dog on Fire" (song), 253
Dolphin Records, 182
Domino (Australian cattle dog), 215, 240, 252,
    302–3, 306–7, 315, 359

Donovan (folk-pop performer), 328–29
"Don't Fear the Reaper" (song), 76
"Don't Try to Call" (song), 31
"Don't Want to Know If You Are Lonely"
    (song), 116
"Door into Summer, The" (song), 191
Dorf, Michael, 363
"Do the Bee" (song), 31, 59
Double L (Rehoboth bar), 340
Double Nickels on the Dime (Minutemen
    album), 94, 100
Dreamboat Annie (Heart album), 17
Dream Syndicate (band), 98
Dryden, Darren, 275
Duffy's (rock club), 42
Dukowski, Chuck, 63, 64, 72
Dumont Network, 282
Duplantis, Andrew, 249–52, 262
Duryea, Barry, 197
"Dying from the Inside Out" (song), 212
Dylan, Bob, 76, 363
Dynamite Kid (wrestler), 284, 297

"Egøverride" (song, video for), 248
"Eight Miles High" (song), 87, 91, 93
Electric Ballroom (London venue), 111
Electric Banana (Pittsburgh club), 94
Electric Picnic (Ireland festival), 353
electronic music, 314, 318; three different
    styles of, 300
Eley, Paul, 333, 334
Emerick, Geoff, 140
EMF (band), 186
Empty Glass (Townshend album), 163
Engineers, the (band), 371
Escovedo, Alejandro, 237, 239
"Everybody Hurts" (song), 377
"Every Everything" (song), 103
Everything Falls Apart (Hüsker Dü album), 64,
    66, 68, 103
"Explode and Make Up" (song), 218

Factory Café, 261, 271–73, 299, 303, 346, 359
Fairey, Shepard, 368
Faith No More (band), 122
Fallon, Joe, 365
Fallon, Steve, 94, 158–59, 164, 168, 169–71,
    181, 234, 339
Farrar, Jay, 346
Farrell, Ray, 104, 110
Fartz, the (band), 51
Fastbacks (band), 62
"Fast Cars" (song), 30
Feelies, the (band), 140, 159
"Feeling Better" (song), 194, 196
Ferlinghetti, Lawrence, 108
Fields, Danny, 17
Fier, Anton, 140, 159–60, 164–65, 168, 170,
    172, 174, 176–78; band of, 212
Fifty Foot Hose (band), 82
File Under: Easy Listening (FU:EL) (Mould
    album), 215, 219–20, 227–28, 237

Fingerprintz (band), 44
Fire Island, 78, 276–77
First Avenue (Minneapolis nightclub), 72, 102, 173, 205–6, 235, 343
"First Drag of the Day" (song), 262
"First of the Last Calls" (song), 80
"500 Songs that Shaped Rock and Roll," 90
Fjelstad, Steve, 44, 57, 96, 102, 118, 152, 267
Flaming Lips (band), 318
Fleetwood Mac (band), 17
Fleming, Pete, 131
Fleshtones, the (band), 33
Flip Your Wig (Hüsker Dü album), 102, 104, 109–11, 119, 196
Flowers, Phil, 65
Floyd, Gary, 64
Fogarino, Sam, 369
Foghat (band), 12
Folsom Street Fair (San Francisco), 361
Foo Fighters (band), 364
40 Watt Club (Athens, GA), 191
45 Grave (band), 65–66
Fox TV network, 135
Frank, Hartley, 31–32
Frith, Heather, 186
Frontiers (paper), 356–57
"Frustration" (song), 218
Fugazi (band), 329, 354
Fugs, the (band), 140

Gadi (homeless Israeli), 254–55
Gallagher, Liam, 226
"Games" (song), 103
Gang of Four (band), 39
Gang War (band), 41
Gartner, Fred, 60
Garvey, Steve, 365
Gates, (Ann) Spencer, 74
"Gauze of Friendship" (song), 341
Gdula, Steve, 348, 349
Gear Daddies (band), 342
"Gee Angel" (Sugar video), 229
GeekSlut (blog), 346
Geffen, David, 276
Geffen Records, 159, 180, 185
Gerde's Folk City (New York), 76–77
Germs, the (band), 52, 340
Gersh, Gary, 185
(GI) (Germs album), 52
Gibbard, Ben, 368
"Gift" (song), 227
Gilbert, Rich, 153–54
"Gilligan's Island" (song), 59
Ginn, Greg, 46, 63, 64, 66, 95, 111–12, 344
Ginsberg, Allen, 108, 140
Giordano, Lou, 74, 111, 121, 133, 148, 217, 267; joins band, 92–93, (as house engineer) 138, 145, 160, 188, 191–93, 196
Giorno, John, 106–7, 140, 147, 319
Giorno Poetry Systems label, 106
Glass, Philip, 147
Glastonbury Festival, 138

Global Booking, 64
God's Love We Deliver (organization), 107, 319
Goffin, Gerry, 7
Goldberg, Bill, 292–93
Golden Palominos (band), 159, 212
Golden Smog (band), 342
"Good Idea, A" (song), 183, 200, 369–70
Goodier, Mark, 198
"Good Vibrations" (song), 7
Goofy's Upper Deck (Minneapolis club), 60
Gorilla Room (Seattle club), 51, 280
Govinda Gallery (DC), 328
Graham, Superstar Billy, 280
Granary Music label, 311
Grateful Dead, the (band), 122
Grauerholz, James, 107–8, 201
Great Gildersleeves (New York club), 73, 76, 164, 213
Green, Barrie, 191
Green (REM album), 161
Green Day (band), 210
"Green Eyes" (song), 100, 103
Green Lantern (DC bar), 366
Gregg, Dave, 48
Grier, Josh, 181–82, 249, 253, 342; and record deals, 187, 209, 264, 305, 311, 313, 347
Grog Kill Studio (Willow, NY), 161
Grohl, Dave, 364
Groundhog Day (movie), 312
Ground Zero (band), 105
Gruen, Bob, 17
Grundy, Bill, 20
Guided by Voices (band), 237
Guidry, Ann, 240
guitars: Fender Stratocaster, 155; Gibson SG copy, 16, 22; Ibanez Artist, 139; Ibanez Rocket Roll Flying V, 22, 28, 54, 79, 131, 139; Yamaha APX acoustic twelve-string, 155–56, 237
Gumbel, Bryant, 136–37
"Guns at My School" (song), 58
Guns N' Roses (band), 62

Hacienda (Manchester club), 111
Haggard, Merle, 365
Haigler, Steve, 161
Halberstam, David, 162
"Hallelujah" (song), 366
Hallman, Charlie, 44
Hammon, Matt, 252, 263–67, 316, 340, 347
Hammond, John, 187, 227, 232
Hammond, Stefan, 36
Hancock, Herbie, 164
"Hanging Tree" (song), 176
"Happy Jack" (song), 7, 58
Hardcore Wrestling (fanzine), 282
"Harder, Better, Faster, Stronger" (song), 312
"Hardly Getting Over It" (song), 117, 119, 176, 343–44, 353
Haring, Keith, 140
Harris, Jordan, 160
Harry, Jim, 170, 173, 177

Hart, Bobby, 7
Hart, Bret, 285–86, 292–93
Hart, Grant, 27–28, 34, 51–52; with Hüsker
    Dü, 30–31, 43–46, 54, 88, (artwork)
    127–28, 137, (management) 98–99,
    137–38, 140, 142, 148–50, 208, 342,
    (replaces Greg's bass) 125, (style) 352,
    (tours) 47–49, 56, 76, 85–86, 92–93, 111;
    lawsuit against SST, 305; Nova Mob, 208;
    relationships, 29–30, 82, 114–15, 125,
    130–34, 136–39, 342–45, (addiction and)
    144–50, (returns to Twin Cities) 205–6;
    son born, 120; songs by, 80, 84, 87,
    89–90, 98, 102–5, 116–18, 126
Hart, Tom, 29, 46
Harvard Field House, 93
"Hate Paper Doll" (song), 100, 103
Hausman, Michael, 311
Havens, Richie, 184
Hawkins, Randy, 265
Hazelden (substance-abuse facility), 148
"Hear Me Calling" (song), 174, 175
Heart (band), 17
Heartbreakers, the (band), 40, 42, 380
Heath, Kevin, 21
Hedwig and the Angry Itch (movie
    soundtrack), 300–301
Heighton, Stephen, 275
Hell's Angels, 111
"Helpless" (song), 198, 200, 203
Henderson, John, 133
Herbert, Jim, 170
Herbst Theatre (San Francisco), 367
Heritage of Pride event (New York), 379
Herman's Hermits (band), 7
Hersh, Kristin, 377
"Hey Jude" (song), 126, 262
"High Fidelity" (song), 341
Hiley, Will, 339, 342, 360
Hill, Michael, 76
Hill, Nick, 158, 170
Hit Factory (Manhattan), 310
Hoeger, Mike, 82
Hogan, Hulk, 284–86
Hole (band), 215
Hollies, the (band), 76
Homo A Go Go (film/music festival), 360–61
homosexuality, 13–15, 346; anti-gay bands, 49,
    56; Cooper interview and Spin piece,
    221–25; dangers and difficulties, 34,
    337–38, (Catholic Church forbids) 349,
    (struggle over outing) 202–3, 256, 384;
    and disease, 52, (AIDS crisis) 56–57;
    father's and mother's attitudes toward, 89,
    224, 268–69; gay publications, 270;
    "hanky code," 53; and "metrosexual,"
    304; in the military, 56, 304, 322; relation-
    ships, 29–30, 36–37, 67, 94, (blog) 335–37,
    (first partnership) 75–79 (see also Brodbeck,
    Micheal; Covington, Mike; O'Neill,
    Kevin); same-sex marriage benefit concert,
    341–42; self-acceptance, 261, 319; self-
    hatred, 36–37, 88, 268, 271, 384; song

about, 90; therapy, 243–45, 251–52, 254,
    256; in West Village, 274–75
"Hoover Dam" (song), 188, 200, 226, 319
Hopper, Dennis, 165
Hose (band), 75
Houston, Whitney, 174, 192
H. P. Lovecraft (band), 82
Hubbell, Anne, 308
"Hubcap" album. See Bob Mould
Hudson, Jeff, 243–45, 251, 257
Hudson, Rock, 56
Hugh Beaumont Experience, the (band),
    65, 67
Hultquist, Linda, 24
Human Rights Campaign (HRC), 318–19, 325
Human Sexual Response (band), 154
Hurley, George, 64
Hurricane Rita, 354–55
Hurwitz, Seth, 75, 122, 317, 323
Hüsker Dü (band), 39–46, 48–57, 59–71,
    73–75, 137, 281, 323; bad show, shows
    canceled, 145–47; created, named, 31,
    (developed) 82, 99, 101, 105, 225, (first
    live shows) 32, 45–47, 377–78, (first
    prime-time network shows) 135–36;
    disagreement within, 98, 104, 137–38,
    206, (at crossroads) 147–48; fans of, 104,
    186, 221; influence of, 172, 184, 371; last
    meeting, 148–50, (Bob leaves, band breaks
    up) 150–52, 162, 230, 234, 261, 342–43,
    (final performance) 200, (finances) 208–9,
    212–13, 305, 342, (reunion not considered)
    345–46; outside management, 141–42; as
    preaching, 49, 350; recordings by: (albums)
    61, 66, 77, 79, 102–4, 125, (first and last)
    44, 66, 126, (invests in recording studio)
    118, (rift with SST) 95, 109–13, 127, (sales
    doubled) 203, (tape of live album) 211–12
    (see also individual album titles; Warner
    Brothers label); songs, 311, 352, 380, 381;
    sound and tempo, 61, 79, 177; tours
    abroad, 106, 110–11, 121, 138, 370; Wig
    Out East tour, 119, 281
Hüsker Dü (board game), 31, 135
HX magazine, 270
Hyde, Mary, 116, 133
Hyman, Kate, 310

"I Apologize" (song), 97, 353
Idiot, The (Iggy Pop album), 22
"I Don't Know for Sure" (song), 116–17
"If I Can't Change Your Mind" (song), 183,
    201–3, 376
"If Not for You" (song), 363
"If You're True" (song), 159, 163
"I Got You Babe" (song), 312
"I Hate Alternative Rock" (song), 260
IMP Productions, 122
"I'm Sorry, Baby, But You Can't Stand in My
    Light Any More" (song), 375–76
"In a Free Land" (song), 61
In Color (Cheap Trick album), 188
"I Need a Beat" (song), 75

Inner Ear Studio (Arlington, VA), 341
Inside/Out performance, 170
International Mr. Leather / Bear Pride weekend (Chicago), 379
Interpol (band), 369
"In the Eyes of My Friends" (song), 218, 227
Irving Plaza shows (New York), 121, 353
"It's Too Late" (video), 202
I Wanna See the Bright Lights Tonight (Thompson album), 158

Jack (West Village friend), 272
James, Cole, 275
Jarrett, Jeff, 293
Jay's Longhorn (restaurant), 24, 31–32, 39–40
"JC Auto" (song), 194, 213, 299
Jervis, Joe, 346
Jesperson, Peter, 24, 44, 70, 123, 129
Jesus and Mary Chain (Scottish band), 186
Jets, the (band), 119
Jimmy Jam (performer), 105
Jockey Club (Kentucky), 73
John, Elton, 16
Johnson, Chris, 123
Jones, Hugh, 140
Jones, Mick, 40, 128
Joyce, Tom, 334
Joy Division (band), 32, 42
Julius (Greenwich Village tavern), 274
"Jump" (song), 194
Juster, Beverly, 282
Juster, Gary, 282–85, 293
Justice (band), 371

Kane, Abbie, 148
Kaplan, Ira, 76
Karbo, Wally, 281–82
Katzman, Terry, 24, 61, 123
KCMP the Current (Minneapolis–St. Paul), 378
Keene, Tommy, 182
KEEY-FM (Minneapolis–St. Paul), 36
Kennedy, Ted, 38–39
Kerouac-Parker, Edie, 140
Kerr, Tim, 65
Kerslake, Kevin, 202
"Kids Don't Follow" (song), 80
Kilborn, Craig, 253
King, Carole, 7
Kiss (band), 16, 17–18, 19, 20, 22, 264
Kitten (compilation album), 105
Klaverkamp, Geoff, 24–25, 40
Koko (London venue), 370
Kramer, Wayne, 41
Kravitz, Lenny, 211
Kregel, Lou, 220
Kristen (Grant Hart's girlfriend), 120
KROQ (Los Angeles), 203
Kurilla, Jody, 39
Kurland, Jordan, 363–64, 374

Lamacq, Steve, 100
Lame (band), 264

Land Speed Record (Hüsker Dü album), 61, 340
lang, k.d., 224
Largent, Lewis, 203
Last Dog and Pony Show, The (Mould album), 260–61, 264–65, 313
"Last Night, The" (song), 174, 175–76
Late Show Starring Joan Rivers, The (TV program), 135–36
Laughner, Peter, 17
Leary, Timothy, 140
Leave Home (Ramones album), 21
Led Zeppelin (band), 122, 154
Left Banke (band), 200
Leibowitz, Jon (Stewart), 74
Lenardi, Jo, 116
Lennon, John, 174
Lester, Ken, 48, 51
Let It Be (Replacements album), 100
"Let Me Live Today" (song), 8
Let's Active (band), 182
"Let's Go Die" (song), 44
Levene, Keith, 33
Lewis, Terry, 105
LGBT, 318–19; Community Center, 273, 275
Liberty Lunch (live music venue), 122, 252
Life and Times (Mould album), 374–77
"Lifetime" (song), 376
Lincoln, Cathy, 116
Linehan, Kelly, 43, 45, 101
Liquor Lyle's (Minneapolis club), 124
Litter (band), 82
Little (Chesnutt album), 183
Little, Brown and Company, 367
"Little Drummer Boy" (skit), 253
LiveDog98 (London Forum show), 311
Live from London TV series, 106, 370
Live magazine, 30
Live Through This (Hole album), 215–16
Living End, The (Mould album), 209
LL Cool J (performer), 75
Lockett, Glen "Spot," 64, 66, 86–87, 90, 95–96, 102–3, 267
London Forum show (1998), 311
"Lonely Afternoon" (song), 157
Lone Star Bar (San Francisco), 334
Longhorn Bar. *See* Jay's Longhorn
Long Playing Grooves (LoudBomb album), 300, 303, 310–11
"Look Through Any Window" (song), 76
Los Lobos (band), 141
"Lost Zoloft" (song), 304, 375
LoudBomb recordings, 272, 300, 310–11
Loud Fast Rules (band), 71
Lounge Lizards (band), 159
Love, Courtney, 216
Love Hall (Philadelphia), 92
Loveless (My Bloody Valentine album), 186–87, 188, 194
Love Undetectable (Sullivan), 268
LSD, 39, 82, 120

Lucas, Andrei (Michael), 273, 275–76
Lucia, Mary, 378
Luger, Lex, 284–85
Lure (Greenwich Village bar), 340
Luscious Jackson (band), 270

M-80 Festival (Minneapolis), 33
Mabuhay Gardens "Fab Mab" nightclub (San Francisco), 53–55
Macalester College, 23–24, 27, 38, 44–45, 124, 280; flag-burning at, 61
Macpherson, Casey, 133, 147–48
Madden, Dick, 43, 60, 70
Madden, Mike, 43
Made to Be Broken (Soul Asylum album), 105, 119
Madison Square Garden (Phoenix, AZ), 92
Madonna (performer), 275, 299
Magnapop (band), 214, 219
Magnet magazine, 345
Maimone, Tony, 159–60, 164, 168, 170, 174, 176–78
Make a Record (Suicide Commandos album), 23
"Makes No Sense at All" (song), 103, 110, 130, 227, 342, 353, 363
Malkmus, Stephen, 368
Mann, Aimee, 311
Mann, Deanna, 302, 309
Manny's Music store (New York), 20
Mansfield, Colin, 44
Man Sized Action (band), 43, 71, 105
Many Loves of Dobie Gillis, The (TV sitcom), 10
Marchand, Frank, 348, 352, 361
March 4th clothing store (Minneapolis), 40
Mark (flight attendant), 272
Marks, Craig, 223
Marquee (London venue), 110
Mars, Chris, 70–71
Martin, George, 140
Martin, Steve, 351
Mary Tyler Moore Show, The (TV sitcom), 110
Mascis, J., 370
Massive Leasing (recording studio), 118, 152
Masterdisk label, 116
Matter (fanzine), 74, 83
Maximumrocknroll (*MRR*) fanzine, 49, 113, 136
Maxwell's (Hoboken club), 94, 164–65, 169–70, 189
McCabe's Guitar Shop (Santa Monica), 165–66
McCall, Professor (at Macalester), 45
McCartney, Linda, 262
McCartney, Paul, viii
McClellan, Steve, 60, 99
McGee, Alan, 185–86, 203, 227, 240
McGrew, Ken, 24–25
McIlheny, Josiah, 133, 134, 148
McKagan, Duff, 62
McKellen, Ian, 136
McLaren, Malcolm, 26
McLuhan, Marshall, 103

McNally Smith College of Music (St. Paul), 378
MDC (band), 63
Mean Fiddler (London club), 353
Meat Puppets, the (band), 60, 92, 100, 102, 111
Meat Puppets II (Meat Puppets album), 100
Mech, Tim, 352
Mecht Mensch (band), 105
"Megamanic" (song), 262
Mel Bay instruction books, 16, 22
Melby, "Diamond" Jim, 120, 281–82
Melody Maker (UK magazine), 26
Meloni, Chris, 270
Melvins, the (band), 102
Meng, John, 340
"Men Seeking Men" (song), 263
Mercyland (band), 188
Meridian studio (Boerne, TX), 218
Metal Circus EP (Hüsker Dü album), 66, 77, 79, 103, 107, 113, 280–81
Metallica (band), 130, 211, 230
Metro Records (Chicago), 246
Metro Weekly (publication), 341
MGM Records, 7
"MIC" (song), 61
Michelangelo (band), 82
Mikutowski, Balls, 30
Miller, Roger, 370
"Mind Is an Island" (song), 227
"Miner" (song), 371, 376
Minnesota Daily, 36
Minor Threat (band), 55–56, 65
Mintz, Alan, 163, 181
Minutemen (punk trio), 46, 60, 64, 94, 100–102
Mission of Burma (band), 42, 345–46, 370
Mississippi Nights (St. Louis club), 120, 144–45
Mitchell, Andy, 308
Mitchell, John Cameron, 301
Mitchell, Joni, 109
"MM 17" (song), 375
Moby (performer), 158, 310
Modern English (band), 140
Modernista! ad agency, 365
Mods (UK band), 25
Modulate (Mould album), 300, 303–4, 310–16, 347, 366, 371, 375
Mojo (British magazine), 312
Monkees, the (band), 8, 103, 191
Monlux, Chris, 122
Monochrome Set, the (band), 33
Monqui Productions, 122
Montreal Forum, 21, 280
Moore, R. Stevie, 158
Moore, Thurston, 180
Moral Majority, 383
Morel, Rich, 317, 333, 380; collaboration with, 321, 340, 351–55, 360, 368–70, (in Blow-off) 322, 325, 373
Morris, Ray, 59
Morrissey, Steven Patrick, viii

Motown Records, 7, 38
Mould, Brian (brother), 4, 5–6, 11, 19, 238, 244
Mould, Susan (sister), 4–6, 19, 244, 328–29, 361
Mould, Willis F. III "Bill" (father), 3–12, 123, 257; family relationships, 24, 34, 225, 243–44, 259, 361; son's homosexuality, 89, 224, 268; son's musical ambitions, 7–8, 18, 22–23, 40, 47, 62, 88, 112, 245
Mould, Mrs. Willis F. (Sheila Murphy, mother), 3–11, 24, 34, 89, 112, 243–45, 259, 328–29; son's homosexuality, 224, 268–69
Mountain Goats (band), 368
"Moving Trucks" (song), 262
"MTC" (song), 58
MTV (Music Television), 109, 110, 203
Mueller, Karl, 342, 343, 345
Mugger (Steve Corbin), 63
Munch, Edvard, 73
Muppet Show, 43
Murphy, Dan, 318
Murphy, Sheila. See Mould, Mrs. Willis F.
Murray, Bill, 312
Murray, Chris, 328
Music for Dozens series, 76
Music for 18 Musicians (Reich), 38
Music for Youth foundation concerts, 363, 376
My Bloody Valentine (band), 186, 227, 266, 364
Myren, Doug, 208–9, 342
"Mystery Girls, The" (radio show), 74

Naked Lunch (Burroughs), 36, 38, 107
Naked Raygun (band), 45, 56
Narducy, Emily and Eva, 381
Narducy, Jason, 246–47, 351–54, 368–70, 378, 380–81
Nash, Kevin "Kev," 286–87, 289
Nasty Little Man (PR firm), 351
National Wrestling Alliance, 282
NBC (National Broadcasting Company), 20, 136
Necros (band), 55–56
Nelson, Willie, 214
Nevermind (Nirvana album), 184, 185, 216
"Never Talking to You Again" (song), 89, 343, 344
New Alliance Records, 46, 58, 61, 66
New Day Rising (Hüsker Dü album), 96–97, 100–103, 106, 119, 121
"New Day Rising" (song), 130, 376
"Newest Industry" (song), 87
"New Music Awards" show (Harlem), 128
"New #1" (song), 262, 374
New Order (band), 138
Newton-John, Olivia, 363
new wave acts, 26, 42
New York Dolls (band), 17, 20, 22, 42
New York Rocker magazine, 76
Next magazine, 270
Nicks, Stevie, 144

Nico (singer), 42
Nicollet Studios (Minneapolis), 96, 102, 104, 109, 112, 116, 118, 133
Nig-Heist (band), 63
9:30 Club (DC), 75, 246, 282, 323, 327, 355, 380–82
Nippon Columbia (Japanese record company), 201
Nirvana (band), 161, 184–85, 199, 216
NME (UK music magazine), 26, 106; Album of the Year, 203, 208
NNB (band), 32, 40
No Age (band), 371–72, 376, 380
Noise Pop (San Francisco rock festival), 363, 376
"Non-Alignment Pact" (song), 30
"No Promise Have I Made" (song), 117
"No Reservations" (song), 127
Northern Lights record store (St. Paul), 27, 31, 120
Norton, Gil, 161
Norton, Greg, 27–28, 29–31, 43, 47, 82, 88–90, 131; and Hüsker Dü management, 98–99, 102, 104, 115–16, 118, 130, 139, 145, 148–51, (finances) 137, 208–9, 212–13, 342, (lawsuit against SST) 305; performance, 43, 125; personal relationships, 132–33, 136, 342, (wedding) 123, 124; on tours, 45, 49, 51–56, 76, 85–86, 93, 138
Norton, Mrs. Greg (Jeri), 118, 125, 138
NOTA (None of the Above, band), 67
Nova Mob (band), 208
Nugent, Ted, 16, 17
Nylon, Judy, 33

Oar Folkjokeopus (Oar Folk) record store (Minneapolis), 25–26, 44, 123, 199, 299
Oasis (band), 226
Obama, Barack, 368, 374
O'Banion's (Chicago rock club), 55, 59, 65
"Obnoxious" (song), 68
Oi (punk style), 26, 38
Old Town School of Folk Music (Chicago), 377
Olympic Auditorium (Los Angeles), 65–66, 121–22
O'Neal, Alexander, 105
120 Minutes (rock show), 203, 248
O'Neill, Kevin, 170–77, 179–80, 197, 202, 207, 212, 234, 267, 278, 282, 332; assists in business, 188, 213, 232–33, 312; Cooper interview, 221–23; difficulties and first split with, 193–95, 236–40, 246, 248, (back together) 241–42, 245–46, 249–55, 258, 262–64, 270–77, 291, 298, 301–2, 308–9, 321, 346, (illness) 319, 328, (and parenting) 241, 302–3, 315–16, 324, 330, (unfaithful) 305–6, 314–15, 317–18, 320; and Domino, 214–15, 302, 306–7, 359; final split, 323–31, 366, 377, 384; on travels abroad, 183, 186, 201, 210, 226, 230–31, 318
"One Step at a Time" (song), 87

Only Ones (band), 123
"Only Shallow" (song), 186
O'Reilly, Colm, 313
Orlovsky, Peter, 140
Osgood, Chris, 23, 24, 28, 105, 378
Otto's Chemical Lounge (band), 105
Our Band Could Be Your Life (Azerrad), 367
"Out of Your Life" (song), 174
"Out on a Limb" (song), 80
Outpost studio (Stoughton, MA), 191
Oz (Chicago club), 45

"Paint It Black" (song), 76
Paisley Park recording studio, 160, 174
"Panama City Motel" (song), 227
Panebianco, Julie, 74, 116, 133, 185, 362
"Paralyzed" (song), 341
PBS (Public Broadcasting Service), 268
Pearl, Lisa, 302, 311
Pedernales Studio (Texas), 214
Pere Ubu (band), 26, 30, 33, 159
"Perfect Example" (song), 97
Peter, Paul and Mary (band), 172
Peterson, Jim, 123
Pet Shop Boys (band), 369
Pettibon, Raymond, 64
Pezzati, Jeff and Patty, 56
Phantom of the Paradise (movie), 212
Phelps, Rick, 170
Phipps, Sandra-Lee, 176
Phoenix, River, 220
Pietsch, Michael, 367
Pine, Charlie, 30–31
Pinfield, Matt, 248
"Pink Turns to Blue" (song), 87, 130
Pitchfork (music website), 380
Pixies, the (band), 154, 161, 172, 200, 364
Plant, Robert, 266
Play (Moby album), 310
"Poison Years" (song), 159, 161, 194
Police, the (band), 32
Pop, Iggy, 21–22, 211
Posies (band), 381
"Positively 4th Street" (song), 362
Power Station studio (Manhattan), 174–75, 192
Pratz, Mark, 122
Primavera Sound Festival (Barcelona), 370
Prince (performer), 105, 160
Pro Tools recording studio, 192
Psychedelic Furs (band), 247
Public Image Ltd (PiL, band), 33, 44
Pucci, Tony, 43
"Punch Drunk" (song), 68
punk rock, 20, 25–26, 32, 85, 190; Canadian, 23, 48–51, 55, 65–66; punk rock acts, 42, 46, 52–53; rebellion against, 83, 227
"Purple Haze" (song), 210
"Push the Button" (song), 59

Q (British magazine), 312
Q Prime Management (agency), 130

Quadrophenia (the Who album and film), 25, 83
Quality Park Products, Bob works for, 35
Queen Is Dead, The (Simpson), 304
Queen of the Highway (Morel record), 317
Quinn, Mike, 122

Radiobeat (recording studio), 74
Rahmy, Bill and Vanessa, 197, 210
Ramone, Dee Dee, 21
Ramone, Joey, 21, 247–48
Ramone, Johnny, 20, 31
Ramones, the (band), 17–18, 19–22, 26, 42, 44, 57, 71, 143
Randall, Randy, 371, 376
Rat, the (Boston punk club), 93–94
Ray (Hoboken friend), 170
Reagan, Ronald, 38, 56–57, 59, 78, 383
"Real World" (song), 79
Rebel Rebel (record store), 299, 317
Record Town (Plattsburgh, NY), 18, 23
Red Ink recording studios, 311, 313
Reed, Lou, 30
Reese, Richard, 325
Reflex Records/Reflex Music label, 44, 95, 105
Regis, George, 127, 147, 150
Rehoboth Beach, Delaware, 339–40
Reich, Steve, 38
REM (band), 74, 93, 101, 161, 176, 377
Remmert, Fred and Travy, 217
"Reoccurring Dreams" (song), 90–91, 93
Replacements, the (band), 73, 96, 105, 110, 129, 345; as rivals, 57, 70–71, 80, 100–101, 114
Reprise Records (Warner label), 121
Republican party, 38, 322, 374
"Return to Dust" (song), 366
Reyes, Ron, 51
Richard (Navy friend), 56–57, 59
Rifle Sport (band), 71, 105, 123
Riley, Frank, 128–29, 182, 315, 374
Risk (game), 113
Rites of Spring (band), 329, 354
River City Reunion (Lawrence, Kansas), 140
Rivers, Joan, 135–36
Robinson, Richard and Lisa, 17
Robinson brothers, 211
Rock and Roll Hall of Fame, 90
Rockers (UK band), 25
Rocket from the Tombs (band), 17
Rock for Karl (fundraising event), 342–43
Rockpool media, 109
Rock Scene magazine, 17, 23, 24, 40, 73
Rolling Stone magazine, 163
Rolling Stones, the (band), 76
Rollins, Henry, 63 64, 72, 96, 341
Ron's Randolph Inn, 30, 377, 378
Rose, Charlie, 268
Ross, Peter, 368
Roth, Tippy, 43, 60
Rougvie, Jeff, 187, 205

Roulette Records, 7
Roxy show (West Hollywood), 121–22
Royal Albert Hall (London), 226, 377
Rubin, Rick, 75
Rumours (Fleetwood Mac album), 17
"Run It" (song), 71
Run Westy Run ("Westies," band) 125, 133, 146, 148
Rush (band), 21
Russo, Vince, 293–94
Rykodisc label, 187, 201–5, 215–17, 219, 227, 240, 246, 264; and Cooper interview, 221–23

Sacks, Carla, 313
"Sacrifice/Let There Be Peace" (song), 193
Sandbloom, Gene, 203
Sasha (songwriter), 299
Saunders, Andy, 199
Savoy, David, 104–5, 125, 126, 129, 130, 345; suicide of, 131–33, 134, 146, 176, 363
Scarpantoni, Jane, 161
Schellenbach, Kate, 270
Schreiber, Ryan, 380
Schwartz, Ruth, 113
Scream, The (Munch), 73
"Sea Cruise" (song), 30
Sebadoh (band), 237
"See a Little Light" (song), 164, 341–42, 365, 376
"Semper Fi" (song), 304
7th Street Entry (Minneapolis music club), 42–43, 57, 58, 60, 72, 74, 183
Sex Pistols (band), 20
Sgt. Pepper (Beatles album), 83, 241
Shanahan, Joe, 382
Sheena (Lisa Buchholz) of "Mystery Girls," 74
Sheila E. (percussionist), 160
Shelley, Pete, 39, 365
"Shelter Me" (song), 366
Shepard, Judy and Matthew, 319
"She's a Woman" (song), 136
Shields, Kevin, 187, 194, 227, 364
"(Shine Your) Light Love Hope" (song), 341
Shithead, Joey, 48
Shoot Out the Lights (Thompson album), 158
Shore, Adam, 364
Showbox (Seattle), 51
Siamese Dream (Smashing Pumpkins album), 215
Sice (singer), 201
"Signals from Above" (song), 68
"Sign of the Times, A" (song), 153
"Silence Between Us, The" (song), 366
Simmons, Gene, 16
Simpson, Mark, 304–5
Since I Left You (Avalanches album), 272
Singles Only label, 158
"Sinners and Their Repentances" (song), 155, 159
Sioux, Siouxie (performer), 26
Sire Records (Warner subsidiary), 114, 129

"Sitting Still" (song), 377
Six Feet Under (band), 59
ska, 26
"Skintrade" (song), 262
Skull and Bones record store, 69
Slacker (movie), 214
Slash Records, 102, 122, 141, 153
"Slim, The" (song), 200
Slim's (San Francisco club), 373
Smashing Pumpkins (band), 215
Smilin' Buddha Cabaret (Vancouver), 51
Smith, Patti, 17, 343, 362
Smith, Robert, 210
Smith, Winston, 52
Smithberg, Madeleine, 252
Snuka, Jimmy, 293
"Something I Learned Today" (song), 89
"Somewhere" (song), 87
Sondheim, Stephen, 249
Sonic Youth (band), 100, 107, 180, 184, 201
Sony 550 Music, 246
"Soon" (song), 187
"Sorry Somehow" (song), 117, 119
Soul Asylum (band), 71, 105, 119–20, 158, 317, 342
sound equipment, 22, 79, 139, 152, 153, 174, 194–96, 216, 238, 262–63, 303
Sound Garden (Soundgarden, band), 102
"SoundonSound" (song), 313
Sounds (UK music magazine), 26
South by Southwest (SXSW, film and music festival), 182, 214, 215
Spin magazine, 191, 221–26, 228, 230
"Spiraling Down" (song), 375
Spiral Stairs (band), 381
Spot (recording engineer). *See* Lockett, Glen
Springfield, Rick, 114
Springsteen, Bruce, 154, 161
Spunt, Dean, 371, 376
Squirrel Bait (band), 73
SST label, 46, 88; Hüsker Dü with, 58, 63–64, 66, 92–95, 99–100, 102–4, 106, 180, 186, (rift) 95, 109–13, 127, 344; lawsuit against, 305
Stamey, Chris, 164–65
"Stand Guard" (song), 175
Stark, Paul, 44
Statman, Anna, 102, 122
"Statues" (song), 44, 49
Stewart, Duncan, 38
Stewart, Jon (Leibowitz), 74
Stiff Little Fingers (Irish band), 26, 38
Stiles, Brad, 65, 67
Sting (wrestler), 284–85
Stipe, Michael, 171, 183, 362
Stonewall riots, 273
"Strawberry Fields Forever" (song), 7
Strike Under (band), 45
Strummer, Joe, 39–40, 128
Stuckey, Scott and Kristina, 317–318
Stuto, Mike, 264
Suburbs, the (band), 32, 40–41, 44

Sudo, Phil, 24, 81
Sugar (band), 190–93, 198–200, 208–11, 214,
    216, 219, 247, 352; breaks up, 228, 230–31,
    235–36, 266; songs of, 311, 353, 381
suicide, 214, 216; of business manager David
    Savoy, 131–33, 134, 146, 176, 363;
    thoughts of, 36–37, 195
Suicide (band), 17
Suicide Commandos, the (band), 17, 23–24,
    28, 32, 41, 118
Sullivan, Andrew, 268, 346
Sullivan, Kevin, 287, 290, 292, 294–96
Sullivan, Nancy (later Nancy Benoit), 287, 292
Sun Ra Arkestra (band), 28, 39, 349
"Sunset Safety Glass" (song), 304
"Sunshine Superman" (song), 329
"Sunspots" (song), 156
Superchunk (band), 73, 368
Supper Club (New York), 246–47
"Surrender" (song), 200
Svingen, Carrie, 223
Sweet Potato (arts weekly), 61
Sylvain, Syl, 22

"Tainted Love" (song), 377
Talking Heads (band), 26, 31
Tanzer, Mark, 162
Tar Babies (band), 62, 105
"Target" (song), 68
Tate Center (University of Georgia), 120
TBS (Turner Broadcasting Station), 296
Television (band), 17, 26, 40, 109
Theresa (Biafra's girlfriend), 52, 63
"There's a Kind of Hush" (song), 7
Thompson, Richard and Linda, 158
"Thoughts and Words" (song), 200
Thrasher (skateboarding magazine), 68
Throbbing Gristle (UK band), 35–36, 68–69
Throwing Muses (band), 154
"Thumbtack" (song), 237
Thunders, Johnny, 27, 31, 41–42, 50, 71
TIAA-CREF ad campaign, 365–66
Today Show, The (TV program), 20, 136
Tommy (the Who album and later rock opera),
    83, 236
Tonight Show, The (TV program), 135
"Too Far Down" (song), 117, 226
Total Access Studios (Redondo Beach, CA), 64,
    86, 174
"Tour, The" (SST package), 102
tours abroad: Australia, 183, 319; Europe and
    UK, 173, 180, 183–87, 198–200, 209–13,
    215, 226, 228, 265–67, 318, 353–54, 359,
    370–71; Japan, 201–2, 215, 229–31 (see
    also Hüsker Dü [band]). See also Canadian
    tours
Townshend, Pete, 140, 163, 235–36, 246–48,
    255, 264, 364
"Trade" (song), 153
"Train Kept A-Rollin'" (song), 76
Tramps (New York club), 250–51
Trash and Vaudeville (clothing stores), 40
Trask, Stephen, 300–301

Travis, Malcolm, 247, 352; with Sugar, 190–92,
    197, 204, 215, 218–19, 230–31; with
    Zulus, 153–54, 187–88
Trees club (Dallas), 184–85
Trehus, Mark, 123
Triclops Studio (Atlanta), 215–16
Trouser Press magazine, 44
True, Everett, 199
TSOL (band), 66
"Turn On the News" (song), 90
20 Jazz Funk Greats (Throbbing Gristle
    album), 68–69
Twin/Tone Records, 44, 46, 58, 70, 105, 112,
    133, 148
"2541" (song), 98, 102, 126

"Ultracore" (song), 59
"Uncle Ron" (song), 31
"Underneath Days" (song), 341
Undertones, the (Irish band), 26, 38
Undrugged (Creation 10th anniversary event),
    226
Unicorn bookstore (New York), 275
United Musicians (artist collective), 311
Unknown Pleasures (Joy Division album), 32
USA Network, 128, 281
U2 (band), 101

Valletri, Garry, 325
van Dyk, Paul, 299
Van Halen (band), 194
Varsity Theater (Minneapolis), 378
Vasquez, Junior, 277
Veggies, the (band), 43, 47, 60
Velvet Lounge (DC club), 321–23
Ventura, Jesse "The Body," 74, 280–81
Venture Booking, 128
Verboten (band), 354
Verbow (band), 246, 263
Verfaillie, Laurence, 199
Vice Records, 364
Vicious, Sid, 284, 289, 294, 295
Vietnam War, 61
Vig, Butch, 185
Viletones (Canadian band), 23
Village Voice (weekly), 102, 263
Violent Femmes (band), 74, 141
Virgin Records, 159–60, 163–64, 178,
    181, 187, 209, 365; Virgin Megastore, 198
V2 Records, 310

Wainwright, Rufus, 273
Waits, Tom, 365
Waldman, Anne, 140
Walker Art Center (St. Paul), 33, 159
"Walking Away" (song), 194, 226
"Walls in Time" (song), 159, 366–67
Warehouse: Songs and Stories (Hüsker Dü
    album), 125–28,130–31, 135, 137, 141,
    159, 261
Warhol, Andy, 42
Warner Brothers label, 102, 109, 121; Bob
    leaves, 157–58, 160; Hüsker Dü with, 110,

112–16, 122, 131, 133–35; (finances) 127, 208–9, (management) 129, 130, 140–141, 150–51

Washington Post, 323

"Wasted World" (song), 375

Waterfront Studios (Hoboken), 250

Waters, John, 147

Watt, Mike, 46, 58, 64

Wax Trax records, 45

"Wear Your Love Like Heaven" (song), 329

Webb, Jimmy, 7

WedRock (benefit concert), 341

Weinberg, Howie, 116, 196, 241

Wendt, George, 317–18

Westerberg, Paul, 70–71, 123, 342, 343

West of Rome (Chesnutt album), 183

West Side Club (Philadelphia), 73

Westword (music publication), 135

WFMU (Jersey City), 158

"Whatcha Drinkin'" (song), 97

"What Do I Want" (song), 61

"Whatever" (song), 87, 90

"Whichever Way the Wind Blows" (song), 172

White Party (Fire Island), 277

White Trash (band), 62

Who, the (band), 7, 25, 122, 163, 191, 236, 246–47, 264

"Who Needs to Dream?" (song), 366

"Who Was Around?" (song), 265

Wig Out East tour, 119, 281

Williams, Mark, 102, 160

Williams, Paul, 212

Wilson, Gary, 28

Wilson, Jim, 182, 252–53, 317; collaboration with, 214, 217–19, 237–38, 246, 259, 261–67

Winer, Norm, 377

Winger, Richard, 273, 275–76

Winstead, Lizz, 74, 252

"Wipe Out" (song), 30

"Wishing Well" (song), 155, 159, 246, 300

WMBR (Cambridge, MA), 74

WMCN-FM (Macalester), Bob as DJ at, 37–38

"Won't Change" (song), 107

Wood, Josh, 341

Woods, Pat, 43

Woodstock festival, 33, 184

Workbook (Mould album), 160–63, 168, 177, 193, 200, 219, 310, 365–67; artbox for, 233

Workshop (Atkins album), 162

World Championship Wrestling (WCW), 279, 282–83, 286, 291–96, 302, 308, 322; Bob leaves, 298, 300

World Wrestling Entertainment (WWE), 296

World Trade Center, 308–10

wrestling, 279–97

WREX (Seattle), 51

"Writer's Cramp" (song), 44

Wurster, Jon, 73, 368–70, 380–81

Wuxtry Records, 170

WWF (World Wrestling Federation), 281

WXRT (Chicago), 377

X (band), 552

"Xpander" (song), 299

X-Ray Spex (band), 26

Yates, Dirk, 305

Year Punk Broke, The (documentary film), 183

Yep Roc label, 347, 351

Yoakam, Dwight, 121

Yohannan, Tim, 113

Yo La Tengo (band), 76

"You Can Live at Home" (song), 126

"You Made Me Realize" (song), 227

Young, Neil, 174

Young and the Useless, the (band), 73

"Young Republicans," 38

"Your Favorite Thing" (song), 219, 227

You Think You Really Know Me (Wilson album), 28

Zappa, Frank, 187

Zen Arcade (Hüsker Dü album), 77, 82, 86–91, 93–103, 203, 314, 353, 376

Zientara, Don, 341

Zoltak, Mark, 169

Zop (British tour manager), 138

Zulus, the (band), 153–54, 187–88, 190

Bob Mould is an American musician, singer-songwriter, producer, and DJ. An original member of the influential 1980s punk band Hüsker Dü, he released several albums after the band separated, including *Workbook, Body of Song,* and *Life and Times,* as well as Sugar's legendary album *Copper Blue.* He lives in San Francisco.

Michael Azerrad is the author of the books *Our Band Could Be Your Life: Scenes from the American Indie Underground, 1981–1991,* and *Come As You Are: The Story of Nirvana.* His writings on music and musicians have appeared in numerous magazines, including *Rolling Stone, The New Yorker, Spin,* and the *New York Times.* He lives in New York City.

Visit www.bobmould.com for more information.